PROPAGANDA

PROPAGANDA

The Formation of
Men's Attitudes

BY

JACQUES ELLUL

TRANSLATED FROM THE FRENCH BY
KONRAD KELLEN AND JEAN LERNER

WITH AN INTRODUCTION BY
KONRAD KELLEN

VINTAGE BOOKS
A DIVISION OF RANDOM HOUSE
NEW YORK

VINTAGE BOOKS EDITION, FEBRUARY 1973

Copyright © 1965 by Alfred A. Knopf, Inc.

Library of Congress Cataloging in Publication Data

Ellul, Jacques.

Propaganda.

Reprint of the 1965 ed.
Bibliography: p.
1. Propaganda.
[HM263.E413 1973]   301.15′4   72–8053
ISBN 0–394–71874–7

Introduction

Jacques Ellul's view of propaganda and his approach to the study of propaganda are new. The principal difference between his thought edifice and most other literature on propaganda is that Ellul regards propaganda as a sociological phenomenon rather than as something *made* by certain people for certain purposes. Propaganda exists and thrives; it is the Siamese twin of our technological society. Only in the technological society can there be anything of the type and order of magnitude of modern propaganda, which is with us forever; and only with the all-pervading effects that flow from propaganda can the technological society hold itself together and further expand.

Most people are easy prey for propaganda, Ellul says, because of their firm but entirely erroneous conviction that it is composed only of lies and "tall stories" and that, conversely, what is true cannot be propaganda. But modern propaganda has long disdained the ridiculous lies of past and outmoded forms of propaganda. It operates instead with many different kinds of truth—half truth, limited truth, truth out of context. Even Goebbels always insisted that Wehrmacht communiqués be as accurate as possible.

A second basic misconception that makes people vulnerable to propaganda is the notion that it serves only to change opinions.

That is one of its aims, but a limited, subordinate one. Much more importantly, it aims to intensify existing trends, to sharpen and focus them, and, above all, to lead men to *action* (or, when it is directed at immovable opponents, to non-action through terror or discouragement, to prevent them from interfering). Therefore Ellul distinguishes various forms of propaganda and calls his book *Propagandes*—that plural is one of the keys to his concept. The most trenchant distinction made by Ellul is between *agitation propaganda* and *integration propaganda.* The former leads men from mere resentment to rebellion; the latter aims at making them adjust themselves to desired patterns. The two types rely on entirely different means. Both exist all over the world. Integration propaganda is needed especially for the technological society to flourish, and its technological means—mass media among them —in turn make such integration propaganda possible.

A related point, central in Ellul's thesis, is that modern propaganda cannot work without "education"; he thus reverses the widespread notion that education is the best prophylactic against propaganda. On the contrary, he says, education, or what usually goes by that word in the modern world, is the absolute prerequisite for propaganda. In fact, education is largely identical with what Ellul calls "pre-propaganda"—the conditioning of minds with vast amounts of incoherent information, already dispensed for ulterior purposes and posing as "facts" and as "education." Ellul follows through by designating intellectuals as virtually the most vulnerable of all to modern propaganda, for three reasons: (1) they absorb the largest amount of secondhand, unverifiable information; (2) they feel a compelling need to have an opinion on every important question of our time, and thus easily succumb to opinions offered to them by propaganda on all such indigestible pieces of information; (3) they consider themselves capable of "judging for themselves." They literally need propaganda.

In fact, the *need* for propaganda on the part of the "propagandee" is one of the most powerful elements of Ellul's thesis. Cast out of the disintegrating microgroups of the past, such as family, church, or village, the individual is plunged into mass society and thrown back upon his own inadequate resources, his isolation, his loneliness, his ineffectuality. Propaganda then hands him in veritable abundance what he needs: a *raison d'être,* personal involvement and participation in important events, an outlet and excuse for some of his more doubtful impulses, righteousness —all factitious, to be sure, all more or less spurious; but he drinks it all in and asks for more. Without this intense collaboration by the propagandee the propagandist would be helpless.

Thus propaganda, by first creating pseudo-needs through "pre-propaganda" and then providing pseudo-satisfactions for them, is pernicious. Can wholesome propaganda be made for a wholesome cause? Can Democracy, Christianity, Humanism be propagated by modern propaganda techniques? Ellul traces the similarities among all propaganda efforts—Communist, Nazi, Democratic. He thinks that no one can use this intrinsically un-democratic weapon—or, rather, abandon himself to it—unscathed or without undergoing deep transformations in the process. He shows the inevitable, unwilled propaganda effects of which the "good" propagandist is unaware, the "fallout" from any major propaganda activity and all its pernicious consequences. Most pernicious of all: the process, once fully launched, tends to become irreversible.

Ellul critically reviews what most American authors have writ-ten on the subject of propaganda and mass media, having studied the literature from Lasswell to Riesman with great thoroughness. Accepting some of their findings, he rejects others, particularly the efforts to gauge the effects of propaganda. Ellul believes that, on the whole, propaganda is much more effective, and effective in many more ways, than most American analysis shows. Particu-larly, he rejects as unrealistic and meaningless all experiments that have been conducted with small groups; propaganda is a unique phenomenon that results from the totality of forces pressing in upon an individual in his society, and therefore cannot be dupli-cated in a test tube.

To make his many original points, Ellul never relies on statistics or quantification, which he heartily disdains, but on observation and logic. His treatise is a fully integrated structure of thought in which every piece fits in with all the others—be they a hundred pages apart. In this respect his work resembles Schopenhauer's *The World as Will and Idea,* of which the philosopher said that the reader, really to understand the book, must read it twice because no page in the book could be fully understood without knowledge of the whole. This procedure can hardly be suggested to the reader in our busy days. But he ought to be warned that to leaf through this book will not suffice. Paul Pickrel, in *Harper's Magazine*, said of Ellul's *The Technological Society* that Ellul—"a great man"—had written with "monumental calm and maddening thoroughness . . . a magnificent book." Ellul's *Propaganda* is no less maddening, monumental, and thorough.

What, in Ellul's view, can mankind do? At the end of this book, Ellul reaches neither a pessimistic nor an optimistic conclusion with regard to the future. He merely states that, in his view, propaganda is today a greater *danger* to mankind than any of the other more grandly advertised threats hanging over the human race. His super-analysis ends with a warning, not a prophecy.

KONRAD KELLEN

February 1965

Preface

———————————————————

———————————————————

Propaganda, by whatever name we may call it, has become a very
general phenomenon in the modern world. Differences in political
regimes matter little; differences in social levels are more important; and most important is national self-awareness. In the world
today there are three great propaganda blocs: the U.S.S.R., China,
and the United States. These are the most important propaganda
systems in terms of scope, depth, and coherence. Incidentally,
they represent three entirely different types and methods of propaganda.

Next are the propaganda systems—in various stages of development and effectiveness, but less advanced than in the "Three"—
of a whole group of countries. These are the socialist republics of
Europe and Asia: Poland, Czechoslovakia, Hungary, Yugoslavia,
East Germany, North Vietnam; they model their propaganda on
that of the U.S.S.R., albeit with some gaps, some lack of understanding, and without adequate resources. Then there are West
Germany, France, Spain, Egypt, South Vietnam, and Korea, with
less elaborate and rather diffuse forms of propaganda. Countries
such as Italy and Argentina, which once had powerful propaganda
systems, no longer use this weapon.

Whatever the diversity of countries and methods, they have one characteristic in common: concern with effectiveness.[1] Propaganda is made, first of all, because of a will to action, for the purpose of effectively arming policy and giving irresistible power to its decisions.[2] Whoever handles this instrument can be concerned solely with effectiveness. This is the supreme law, which must never be forgotten when the phenomenon of propaganda is analyzed. Ineffective propaganda is no propaganda. This instrument belongs to the technological universe, shares its characteristics, and is indissolubly linked to it.

Not only is propaganda itself a technique, it is also an indispensable condition for the development of technical progress and the establishment of a technological civilization. And, as with all techniques, propaganda is subject to the law of efficiency. But whereas it is relatively easy to study a precise technique, whose scope can be defined, a study of propaganda runs into some extraordinary obstacles.

From the outset it is obvious that there is great uncertainty about the phenomenon itself, arising first of all from a priori moral or political concepts. Propaganda is usually regarded as an *evil*; this in itself makes a study difficult. To study anything properly, one must put aside ethical judgments. Perhaps an objective study will lead us back to them, but only later, and with full cognizance of the facts.

A second source of confusion is the general conviction, derived from past experience, that *propaganda consists mainly of "tall stories,"* disseminated by means of lies. To adopt this view is to prevent oneself from understanding anything about the actual phenomenon, which is very different from what it was in the past.

Even when these obstacles have been removed, it is still very difficult to determine what constitutes propaganda in our world and what the nature of propaganda is. This is because it is a *secret* action. The temptation is then twofold: to agree with Jacques

---

[1] Goebbels said: "We do not talk to say something, but to obtain a certain effect." And F. C. Bartlett accurately states that the goal of propaganda is not to increase political understanding of events, but to obtain results through action.
[2] Harold D. Lasswell's definition of the goal of propaganda is accurate: "To maximize the power at home by subordinating groups and individuals, while reducing the material cost of power." Similarly, in war, propaganda is an attempt to win victory with a minimum of physical expense. Before the war, propaganda is a substitute for physical violence; during the war, it is a supplement to it.

Driencourt that "everything is propaganda" because everything in the political or economic spheres seems to be penetrated and molded by this force; or, as certain modern American social scientists have done, to abandon the term *propaganda* altogether because it cannot be defined with any degree of precision. Either course is inadmissible intellectual surrender. To adopt either attitude would lead us to abandon the study of a phenomenon that exists and needs to be defined.

We then came up against the extreme difficulty of definition.

We can immediately discard such simplistic definitions as Marbury B. Ogle's: "Propaganda is any effort to change opinions or attitudes. . . . The propagandist is anyone who communicates his ideas with the intent of influencing his listener." Such a definition would include the teacher, the priest, indeed any person conversing with another on any topic. Such a broad definition clearly does not help us to understand the specific character of propaganda.

As far as definitions are concerned, there has been a characteristic evolution in the United States. From 1920 to about 1933 the main emphasis was on the psychological: Propaganda is a manipulation of psychological symbols having goals of which the listener is not conscious.[3]

Since the appearance of Lasswell's studies, propaganda by other means and with stated objectives has been considered possible. Attention then became focused on the *intention* of the propagandist. In more recent books, the *aim to indoctrinate*— particularly in regard to political, economic, and social matters —has been regarded as the hallmark of propaganda. Within this frame of reference one could determine what constitutes propaganda by looking at the propagandist—such and such a person is a propagandist, therefore his words and deeds are propaganda.

But it appears that American authors eventually accepted the definition given by the Institute for Propaganda Analysis and inspired by Lasswell:

"Propaganda is the expression of opinions or actions carried out deliberately by individuals or groups with a view to influencing

---

[3] John Albig has named these elements of definition: the secret character of the sources and goals of propaganda; the intention to modify opinions; the dissemination of conclusions of doubtful validity; the notion of inculcating ideas rather than explaining them. This is partially correct, but outdated.

the opinions or actions of other individuals or groups for predetermined ends and through psychological manipulations."[4]

We could quote definitions for pages on end. An Italian author, Antonio Miotto, says that propaganda is a "technique of social pressure which tends to create psychological or social groups with a unified structure across the homogeneity of the affective and mental states of the individuals under consideration." For Leonard W. Doob, the well-known American specialist, it is "an attempt to modify personalities and control the behavior of individuals in relation to goals considered non-scientific or of doubtful value in a specific society and time period."

And we would find even more remote definitions, if we examined the German or Russian literature on the subject.

I will not give a definition of my own here. I only wanted to show the uncertainty among specialists on the question. I consider it more useful to proceed with the analysis of the characteristics of propaganda as an existing sociological phenomenon. It is perhaps proper to underline this term. We shall examine propaganda in both its past and present forms; for obviously we cannot eliminate from our study the highly developed propaganda systems of Hitler's Germany, Stalin's Russia, and Fascist Italy. This seems obvious, but is not: many writers do not agree with this approach. They establish a certain image or definition of propaganda, and proceed to the study of whatever corresponds to their definition; or, yielding to the attraction of a scientific study, they try to experiment with some particular method of propaganda on small groups and in small doses—at which moment it ceases to be propaganda.

To study propaganda we must turn not to the psychologist, but to the propagandist; we must examine not a test group, but a whole nation subjected to real and effective propaganda. Of course this excludes all so-called scientific (that is, statistical) types of study, but at least we shall have respected the object of our study—unlike many present-day specialists who establish a rigorous method of observation, but, in order to apply it, lose the

---

[4] The idea is often added that propaganda deals with "controversial questions in a group." More profound is Daniel Lerner's idea that propaganda is a means of altering power ratios in a group by modifying attitudes through manipulation of symbols. However, I am not entirely in agreement with the exclusively psychological character of this definition.

object to be studied. Rather, we shall consider what the nature of propaganda is wherever it is applied and wherever it is dominated by a concern for effectiveness.

Finally, we take the term *propaganda* in its broadest sense, so that it embraces the following areas:

Psychological action: The propagandist seeks to modify opinions by purely psychological means; most often he pursues a semi-educative objective and addresses himself to his fellow citizens.
Psychological warfare: Here the propagandist is dealing with a foreign adversary whose morale he seeks to destroy by psychological means so that the opponent begins to doubt the validity of his beliefs and actions.[5]
Re-education and brainwashing: Complex methods of transforming an adversary into an ally which can be used only on prisoners.
Public and human relations: These must necessarily be included in propaganda. This statement may shock some readers, but we shall show that these activities are propaganda because they seek to adapt the individual to a society, to a living standard, to an activity. They serve to make him conform, which is the aim of all propaganda.

Propaganda in its *broad sense* includes all of these. In the *narrow sense* it is characterized by an institutional quality. In propaganda we find techniques of psychological influence combined with techniques of organization and the envelopment of people with the intention of sparking action. This, then, will be the broad field of our inquiry.

From this complete universe of propaganda I have deliberately excluded the following subjects found in most propaganda studies:

Historical accounts of propaganda, particularly of the recent past: propaganda in 1914 or 1940, and so forth.

Propaganda and public opinion as an entity, considering public opinion, its formation, and so forth, as the major problem, and propaganda as a simple instrument for forming or changing opinion as the minor problem.

Psychological foundations of propaganda: On what prejudices, drives, motivations, passions, complexes, does the propagandist play? What psychic force does he utilize to obtain his results?

The techniques of propaganda: How does the propagandist

[5] Maurice Mégret's analysis distinguishes three parts: a propaganda agency (support of military operations); a politico-military action (to insure the submission of the population by technical, non-violent means); a coherent thought system.

put the psychic force into action, how can he reach people, how can he induce them to act?

The media of propaganda: the mass media of communication.

Such are the five chapter headings found everywhere. Somewhat less common are studies on the characteristics of the great examples of propaganda: Hitlerite, Stalinist, American, and so on. These are omitted here precisely because they have been frequently analyzed. The reader will find in the bibliography all that is useful to know on each of these questions. I have instead tried to examine aspects of propaganda very rarely treated—to adopt a point of view, a perspective, an unorthodox view. I have sought to use a method that is neither abstract nor statistical, but occasionally relies on existing studies. The reader should know that he is not dealing with an Encyclopedia of Propaganda, but with a work that assumes his familiarity with its psychological foundations, techniques, and methods, and that endeavors to bring contemporary man a step closer to an awareness of propaganda—the very phenomenon that conditions and regulates him.

On the other hand, I have considered propaganda as a whole. It is usual to pass ethical judgments on its ends, judgments that then redound on propaganda considered as a means, such as: Because democracy is good and dictatorship bad, propaganda serving a democracy is good even if as a technique it is identical with propaganda serving a dictatorship. Or, because Socialism is good and Fascism bad, propaganda is not altogether evil in the hands of Socialists, but is totally evil in Fascist hands.[6] I repudiate this attitude. Propaganda as a phenomenon is essentially the same in China or the Soviet Union or the United States or Algeria. Techniques tend to align themselves with one another. The media of dissemination may be more or less perfected, more or less directly used, just as organizations may be more or less effective, but that does not change the heart of the problem: those who accept the principle of propaganda and decide to utilize it will inevitably employ the most effective organization and methods.[7] Moreover, the premise of this book is that propaganda, no matter who makes it—be he the most upright and best-intentioned of

---

[6] This is what Serge Tchakhotin claims.

[7] As Mégret has said, the officers in Indochina who came in contact with North Vietnamese propaganda had an "over-all political view" that substituted itself for the "fragmented use of the technical means" of propaganda; all this is part of the progression from old ideas to new phenomena.

men—has certain identical results in Communism or Hitlerism or Western democracy, inevitable results on the individual or groups, and different from the doctrine promulgated, or the regime supported, by that propaganda. In other words, Hitlerism as a regime had certain effects, and the propaganda used by the Nazis undeniably had certain specific characteristics. But whereas most analysts stop at this specificity, I have tried to eliminate it in order to look only at the most general characteristics, the effects common to all cases, to all methods of propaganda. Therefore I have adopted the same perspective and the same method in studying propaganda as in studying any other technique.

I shall devote much space to the fact that propaganda has become an inescapable necessity for everyone. In this connection I have come upon a source of much misunderstanding. Modern man worships "facts"—that is, he accepts "facts" as the ultimate reality. He is convinced that what is, is good. He believes that facts in themselves provide evidence and proof, and he willingly subordinates values to them; he obeys what he believes to be necessity, which he somehow connects with the idea of progress. This stereotyped ideological attitude inevitably results in a confusion between judgments of probability and judgments of value. Because fact is the sole criterion, it must be good. Consequently it is assumed that anyone who states a fact (even without passing judgment on it) is, therefore, in favor of it. Anyone who asserts (simply stating a judgment of *probability*) that the Communists will win some elections is immediately considered pro-Communist; anyone who says that all human activity is increasingly dominated by technology is viewed as a "technocrat"; and so on.

As we proceed to analyze the development of propaganda, to consider its inescapable influence in the modern world and its connection with all structures of our society, the reader will be tempted to see an approval of propaganda. Because propaganda is presented as a necessity, such a work would *therefore* force the author to make propaganda, to foster it, to intensify it. I want to emphasize that nothing is further from my mind; such an assumption is possible only by those who worship facts and power. In my opinion, necessity never establishes legitimacy; the world of necessity is a world of weakness, a world that denies man. To say that a phenomenon is *necessary* means, for me, that it denies man: its necessity is proof of its power, not proof of its excellence.

However, confronted by a necessity, man must become *aware* of it, if he is to master it. As long as man denies the inevitability of a phenomenon, as long as he avoids facing up to it, he will go astray. He will delude himself, by submitting in fact to "necessity" while pretending that he is free "in spite of it," and simply because he claims to be free. Only when he realizes his delusion will he experience the beginning of genuine freedom—in the act of realization itself—be it only from the effort to stand back and look squarely at the phenomenon and reduce it to raw fact.

The force of propaganda is a direct attack against man. The question is to determine how great is the danger. Most replies are based on unconscious a priori dogmas. Thus the Communists, who do not believe in human nature but only in the human condition, believe that propaganda is all-powerful, legitimate (whenever they employ it), and instrumental in creating a new type of man. American sociologists scientifically try to play down the effectiveness of propaganda because they cannot accept the idea that the individual—that cornerstone of democracy—can be so fragile; and because they retain their ultimate trust in man. Personally, I, too, tend to believe in the pre-eminence of man and, consequently, in his invincibility. Nevertheless, as I observe the facts, I realize man is terribly malleable, uncertain of himself, ready to accept and to follow many suggestions, and is tossed about by all the winds of doctrine. But when, in the course of these pages, I shall reveal the full power of propaganda against man, when I advance to the very threshold of showing the most profound changes in his personality, it does not mean I am anti-democratic.

The strength of propaganda reveals, of course, one of the most dangerous flaws of democracy. But that has nothing to do with my own opinions. If I am in favor of democracy, I can only regret that propaganda renders the true exercise of it almost impossible. But I think it would be even worse to entertain any illusions about a co-existence of true democracy and propaganda. Nothing is worse in times of danger than to live in a dream world. To warn a political system of the menace hanging over it does not imply an attack against it, but is the greatest service one can render the system. The same goes for man: to warn him of his weakness is not to attempt to destroy him, but rather to encourage him to strengthen himself. I have no sympathy with the haughty aristocratic intellectual who judges from on high, believing himself invulnerable to the destructive forces of his time, and disdainfully considers the common people as cattle to be manipulated, to be molded by the action of propaganda in the most intimate aspects of their being. I insist that to give such warning is an act in the defense of man, that I am not judging propaganda with Olympian detachment, and that having suffered, felt, and analyzed the impact of the power of propaganda on myself, having been time and again, and still being, the object of propaganda, I want to speak of it as a menace which threatens the total personality.

In order to delineate the real dimensions of propaganda we must always consider it within the context of civilization. Perhaps the most fundamental defect of most studies made on the subject is their attempt to analyze propaganda as an isolated phenomenon. This corresponds to the rather prevalent attitude that separates socio-political phenomena from each other and of not establishing any correlation between parts, an attitude that in turn reassures the student of the validity of the various systems. Democracy, for example, is studied as if the citizen were an entity separate from the State, as if public opinion were a "thing in itself"; meanwhile, the scientific study of public opinion and propaganda is left to other specialists, and the specialist in public opinion in turn relies on the jurist to define a suitable legal framework for democracy. The problems of the technological society are studied without reference to their possible influence on mental and emotional life; the labor movement is examined without attention to the changes brought about by psychological means, and so on.

Again I want to emphasize that the study of propaganda must be conducted within the context of the technological society. Propaganda is called upon to solve problems created by technology, to play on maladjustments, and to integrate the individual into a technological world. Propaganda is a good deal less the political weapon of a regime (it is that also) than the effect of a technological society that embraces the entire man and tends to be a completely integrated society. At the present time, propaganda is the innermost, and most elusive, manifestation of this trend. Propaganda must be seen as situated at the center of the growing powers of the State and governmental and administrative techniques. People keep saying: "Everything depends on what *kind* of a State makes use of propaganda." But if we really have understood the technological State, such a statement becomes meaningless. In the midst of increasing mechanization and technological organization, propaganda is simply the means used to prevent these things from being felt as too oppressive and to persuade man to submit with good grace. When man will be fully adapted to this technological society, when he will end by obeying with enthusiasm, convinced of the excellence of what he is forced to do, the constraint of the organization will no longer be felt by him; the truth is, it will no longer be a constraint, and the police will have nothing to do. The civic and technological good will and the enthusiasm for the right social myths—both created by propaganda—will finally have solved the problem of man.

JACQUES ELLUL

1962

Contents

_____

CHAPTER I—*The Characteristics of Propaganda*

1. EXTERNAL CHARACTERISTICS   6

     The Individual and the Masses   6
     Total Propaganda   9
     Continuity and Duration of Propaganda   17
     Organization of Propaganda   20
     Orthopraxy   25

2. INTERNAL CHARACTERISTICS   33

     Knowledge of the Psychological Terrain   33
     Fundamental Currents in Society   38
     Timeliness   43
     Propaganda and the Undecided   48
     Propaganda and Truth   52
         The Problem of Factuality   53
         Intentions and Interpretations   57

3. CATEGORIES OF PROPAGANDA   61

     Political Propaganda and Sociological Propaganda   62
     Propaganda of Agitation and Propaganda of Integration   70

Vertical and Horizontal Propaganda 79
Rational and Irrational Propaganda 84

**CHAPTER II—*The Conditions for the Existence
of Propaganda***

1. THE SOCIOLOGICAL CONDITIONS 90

Individualist Society and Mass Society 90
Opinion 99
The Mass Media of Communication 102

2. OBJECTIVE CONDITIONS OF TOTAL
PROPAGANDA 105

The Need of an Average Standard of Living 105
An Average Culture 108
Information 112
The Ideologies 116

CHAPTER III—*The Necessity for Propaganda*

1. THE STATE'S NECESSITY 121

The Dilemma of the Modern State 121
The State and Its Function 133

2. THE INDIVIDUAL'S NECESSITY 138

The Objective Situation 139
The Subjective Situation 147

CHAPTER IV—*Psychological Effects of Propaganda*

Psychological Crystallization 163
Alienation through Propaganda 169
The Psychic Dissociation Effect of Propaganda 178
Creation of the Need for Propaganda 182
Mithridatization 183
Sensibilization 184
The Ambiguity of Psychological Effects 187

CHAPTER V—*The Socio-Political Effects*

1. PROPAGANDA AND IDEOLOGY   193

   The Traditional Relationship   193
   The New Relationship   196

2. EFFECTS ON THE STRUCTURE OF PUBLIC
   OPINION   202

   *Modification of the Constituent Elements of Public
      Opinion*   203
   From Opinion to Action   207

3. PROPAGANDA AND GROUPING   212

   The Partitioning of Groups   212
   Effects on Political Parties   216
   Effects on the World of Labor   222
   Effects on the Churches   228

4. PROPAGANDA AND DEMOCRACY   232

   Democracy's Need of Propaganda   232
   Democratic Propaganda   235
   Effects of International Propaganda   242
   Effects of Internal Propaganda   250

APPENDIX I—*Effectiveness of Propaganda*

1. DIFFICULTIES OF MEASURING
   EFFECTIVENESS   259

   Difficulty of the Subject   260
   Inadequacy of Methods   265

2. INEFFECTIVENESS OF PROPAGANDA   277

3. EFFECTIVENESS OF PROPAGANDA   287

4. THE LIMITS OF PROPAGANDA   294

APPENDIX II—*Mao Tse-tung's Propaganda*

1. THE WAR: FROM 1926 TO 1949   304

    Education   304
    Organization   305

2. SINCE 1949   307

    Education   308
    Encirclement   310

3. BRAINWASHING   311

BIBLIOGRAPHY   315

INDEX   *follows page* 320

PROPAGANDA

[1]

THE
CHARACTERISTICS
OF PROPAGANDA

———————————

———————————

True modern propaganda can only function within the context of the modern scientific system. But what is it? Many observers look upon propaganda as a collection of "gimmicks" and of more or less serious practices.[1] And psychologists and sociologists very often reject the scientific character of these practices. For our part, we completely agree that propaganda is a technique rather than a science.[2] But it is a *modern* technique—that is, it is based on one or more branches of science. Propaganda is the expression of these branches of science; it moves with them, shares in their suc-

---

[1] Most French psychologists and psycho-sociologists do not regard propaganda as a serious practice or as having much influence.

[2] In this connection Albig is right to stress that propaganda cannot be a science because in the field in which it applies there can be neither valid generalizations nor constant factors.

cesses, and bears witness to their failures. The time is past when propaganda was a matter of individual inspiration, personal subtlety, or the use of unsophisticated tricks. Now science has entered propaganda, as we shall reveal from four different points of view.

First of all, modern propaganda is based on scientific analyses of psychology and sociology. Step by step, the propagandist builds his techniques on the basis of his knowledge of man, his tendencies, his desires, his needs, his psychic mechanisms, his conditioning—and as much on social psychology as on depth psychology. He shapes his procedures on the basis of our knowledge of groups and their laws of formation and dissolution, of mass influences, and of environmental limitations. Without the scientific research of modern psychology and sociology there would be no propaganda, or rather we still would be in the primitive stages of propaganda that existed in the time of Pericles or Augustus. Of course, propagandists may be insufficiently versed in these branches of science; they may misunderstand them, go beyond the cautious conclusions of the psychologists, or claim to apply certain psychological discoveries that, in fact, do not apply at all. But all this only shows efforts to find new ways: only for the past fifty years have men sought to apply the psychological and sociological sciences. The important thing is that propaganda has decided to submit itself to science and to make use of it. Of course, psychologists may be scandalized and say that this is a misuse of their science. But this argument carries no weight; the same applies to our physicists and the atomic bomb. The scientist should know that he lives in a world in which his discoveries will be utilized. Propagandists inevitably will have a better understanding of sociology and psychology, use them with increasing precision, and as a result become more effective.

Second, propaganda is scientific in that it tends to establish a set of rules, rigorous, precise, and tested, that are not merely recipes but impose themselves on every propagandist, who is less and less free to follow his own impulses. He must apply, increasingly and exactly, certain precise formulas that can be applied by anybody with the proper training—clearly a characteristic of a technique based on science.

Third, what is needed nowadays is an exact analysis of both the environment and the individual to be subjected to propaganda. No longer does the man of talent determine the method, the approach, or the subject; all that is now being calculated (or must be calculated). Therefore, one type of propaganda will be found suitable in one situation and completely useless in another. To undertake an active propaganda operation, it is necessary to make a scientific, sociological, and psychological analysis first, and then utilize those branches of science, which are becoming increasingly well known. But, here again, proper training is necessary for those who want to use them with their full effectiveness.

Finally, one last trait reveals the scientific character of modern propaganda: the increasing attempt to control its use, measure its results, define its effects. This is very difficult, but the propagandist is no longer content to have obtained, or to believe he has obtained, a certain result; he seeks precise evidence. Even successful political results do not completely satisfy him. He wants to understand the how and why of them and measure their exact effect. He is prompted by a certain spirit of experimentation and a desire to ponder the results. From this point on, one can see the beginning of scientific method. Admittedly, it is not yet very widespread, and those who analyze results are not active propagandists but philosophers. Granted, that reveals a certain division of labor, nothing more. It indicates that propaganda is no longer a self-contained action, covering up for evil deeds. It is an object of serious thought, and proceeds along scientific channels.

Some people object to this. One frequently hears psychologists ridicule the claim to a scientific basis advanced by the propagandist and reject the latter's claims of having employed scientific techniques. "The psychology he uses is not scientific psychology; the sociology he uses is not scientific sociology." But after a careful look at the controversy one comes to this conclusion: Stalinist propaganda was in great measure founded on Pavlov's theory of the conditioned reflex. Hitlerian propaganda was in great measure founded on Freud's theory of repression and libido. American propaganda is founded in great measure on Dewey's theory of teaching. Now, if a psychologist does not accept the idea of the conditioned reflex and doubts that it can be created in man, he then rejects Pavlov's interpretation of psychological phenomena and concludes that all propaganda based on it is pseudo-scientific. It is obviously the same for those who question the findings of Freud, Dewey, or anybody else.

What does this mean, then? That propaganda does *not* rest on a scientific base? Certainly not. Rather, that scientists are not agreed among themselves on the domains, methods, or conclusions of psychology and sociology. A psychologist who rejects the theory of one of his colleagues rejects a scientific theory and not merely the inferences that a technician may draw from it. One cannot blame the propagandist if he has confidence in a particular sociologist or psychologist whose theory is generally accepted and who is, at a given time and in a given country, considered a scientist. Moreover, let us not forget that if this theory, put to use by the propagandist, brings results and proves to be effective, it thereby receives additional confirmation and that simple doctrinal criticism can then no longer demonstrate its inaccuracy.

1. External Characteristics

The Individual and the Masses

Any modern propaganda will, first of all, address itself at one and the same time to the individual and to the masses. It cannot separate the two elements. For propaganda to address itself to the individual, in his isolation, apart from the crowd, is impossible. The individual is of no interest to the propagandist; as an isolated unit he presents much too much resistance to external action. To be effective, propaganda cannot be concerned with detail, not only because to win men over one by one takes much too long, but also because to create certain convictions in an isolated individual is much too difficult. Propaganda ceases where simple dialogue begins. And that is why, in particular, experiments undertaken in the United States to gauge the effectiveness of certain propaganda methods or arguments on isolated individuals are not conclusive: they do not reproduce the real propaganda situation. Conversely, propaganda does not aim simply at the mass, the crowd. A propaganda that functioned only where individuals are gathered together would be incomplete and insufficient. Also, any propaganda aimed only at groups as such—as if a mass were a specific body having a soul and reactions and feelings entirely different from individuals' souls, reactions, and feelings—would be an abstract propaganda that likewise would have no effectiveness. Modern propaganda reaches individuals enclosed in the mass and as participants in that mass, yet it also aims at a crowd, but only as a body composed of individuals.

What does this mean? First of all, that the individual never is considered as an individual, but always in terms of what he has in common with others, such as his motivations, his feelings, or his myths. He is reduced to an average; and, except for a small percentage, action based on averages will be effectual. Moreover, the individual is considered part of the mass and included in it (and so far as possible systematically integrated into it), because in that way his psychic defenses are weakened, his reactions are easier to provoke, and the propagandist profits from the process of diffusion of emotions through the mass, and, at the same time, from the pressures felt by an individual when in a group. Emotionalism, impulsiveness, excess, etc.—all these characteristics of the individual caught up in a mass are well known and very helpful to propaganda. Therefore, the individual must never be considered as being alone; the listener to a radio broadcast, though actually alone, is nevertheless part of a large group, and he is aware of it. Radio listeners have been found to exhibit a mass mentality. All are tied together and constitute a sort of society in which all individuals are accomplices and influence each other without knowing it. The same holds true for propaganda that is carried on by door-to-door visits (direct contacts, petitions for signatures); although apparently one deals here with a single individual, one deals in reality with a unit submerged into an invisible crowd composed of all those who have been interviewed, who are being interviewed, and who will be interviewed, because they hold similar ideas and live by the same myths, and especially because they are targets of the same organism. Being the target of a party or an administration is enough to immerse the individual in that sector of the population which the propagandist has in his sights; this simple fact makes the individual part of the mass. He is no longer Mr. X, but part of a current flowing in a particular direction. The current flows through the canvasser (who is not a person speaking in his own name with his own arguments, but one segment of an administration, an organization, a collective movement); when he enters a room to canvass a person, the mass, and moreover the organized, leveled mass, enters with him. No relationship exists here between man and man; the organization is what exerts its attraction on an individual already part of a mass because he is in the same sights as all the others being canvassed.

Conversely, when propaganda is addressed to a crowd, it must touch each individual in that crowd, in that whole group. To be effective, it must give the impression of being personal, for we must never forget that the mass is composed of individuals, and is in fact nothing but assembled individuals. Actually, just because men are in a group, and therefore weakened, receptive, and in a state of psychological regression, they pretend all the more to be "strong individuals." The mass man is clearly sub-human, but pretends to be superman. He is more suggestible, but insists he is more forceful; he is more unstable, but thinks he is firm in his convictions. If one openly treats the mass as a mass, the individuals who form it will feel themselves belittled and will refuse to participate. If one treats these individuals as children (and they are children because they are in a group), they will not accept their leader's projections or identify with him. They will withdraw and we will not be able to get anything out of them. On the contrary, each one must feel individualized, each must have the impression that *he* is being looked at, that *he* is being addressed personally. Only then will he respond and cease to be anonymous (although in reality remaining anonymous).

Thus all modern propaganda profits from the structure of the mass, but exploits the individual's need for self-affirmation; and the two actions must be conducted jointly, simultaneously. Of course this operation is greatly facilitated by the existence of the modern mass media of communication, which have precisely this remarkable effect of reaching the whole crowd all at once, and yet reaching each one in that crowd. Readers of the evening paper, radio listeners, movie or TV viewers certainly constitute a mass that has an organic existence, although it is diffused and not assembled at one point. These individuals are moved by the same motives, receive the same impulses and impressions, find themselves focused on the same centers of interest, experience the same feelings, have generally the same order of reactions and ideas, participate in the same myths—and all this at the same time: what we have here is really a psychological, if not a biological mass. And the individuals in it are modified by this existence, even if they do not know it. Yet each one is alone—the newspaper reader, the radio listener. He therefore feels himself individually concerned as a person, as a participant. The movie spectator also is alone; though elbow to elbow with his neighbors, he still is, because of the darkness and the hypnotic attraction of the screen, perfectly alone. This is the situation of the "lonely crowd," or of isolation in the mass, which is a natural product of present-day society and which is both used and deepened by the mass media. The most favorable moment to seize a man and influence him is when he is alone in the mass: it is at this point that propaganda can be most effective.

We must emphasize this circle which we shall meet again and again: the structure of present-day society places the individual where he is most easily reached by propaganda. The media of mass communication, which are part of the technical evolution of this society, deepen this situation while making it possible to reach the individual man, integrated in the mass; and what these media do is exactly what propaganda must do in order to attain its objectives. In reality propaganda cannot exist without using these mass media. If, by chance, propaganda is addressed to an organized group, it can have practically no effect on individuals before that group has been fragmented.[3] Such fragmentation can be achieved through action, but it is equally possible to fragment a group by psychological means. The transformation of very small groups by purely psychological means is one of the most important techniques of propaganda. Only when very small groups are thus annihilated, when the individual finds no more defenses, no equilibrium, no resistance exercised by the group to which he belongs, does total action by propaganda become possible.[4]

Total Propaganda

Propaganda must be total. The propagandist must utilize all of the technical means at his disposal—the press, radio, TV, movies, posters, meetings, door-to-door canvassing. Modern propaganda must utilize *all* of these media. There is no propaganda as long as one makes use, in sporadic fashion and at random, of a newspaper article here, a poster or a radio program there, organizes a few meetings and lectures, writes a few slogans on walls; that is not propaganda. Each usable medium has its own particular way of penetration—specific, but at the same time localized

---

[3] Edward A. Shils and Morris Janowitz have demonstrated the importance of the group in the face of propaganda; the Germans, they claim, did not yield earlier in World War II because the various groups of their military structure held fast. Propaganda cannot do much when the social group has not disintegrated: the play of opinions has relatively little importance. See below, Appendix I.
[4] See below, Appendix II.

and limited; by itself it cannot attack the individual, break down his resistance, make his decisions for him. A movie does not play on the same motives, does not produce the same feelings, does not provoke the same reactions as a newspaper. The very fact that the effectiveness of each medium is limited to one particular area clearly shows the necessity of complementing it with other media. A word spoken on the radio is not the same, does not produce the same effect, does not have the same impact as the identical word spoken in private conversation or in a public speech before a large crowd. To draw the individual into the net of propaganda, each technique must be utilized in its own specific way, directed toward producing the effect it can best produce, and fused with all the other media, each of them reaching the individual in a specific fashion and making him react anew to the same theme—in the same direction, but *differently*.

Thus one leaves no part of the intellectual or emotional life alone; man is surrounded on all sides—man and men, for we must also bear in mind that these media do not all reach the same public in the same way. Those who go to the movies three times a week are not the same people who read the newspapers with care. The tools of propaganda are thus oriented in terms of their public and must be used in a concerted fashion to reach the greatest possible number of individuals. For example, the poster is a popular medium for reaching those without automobiles. Radio newscasts are listened to in the better circles. We must note, finally, that each medium includes a third aspect of specialization—saving for later our analysis of the fact that there are quite diverse forms of propaganda.

Each medium is particularly suited to a certain type of propaganda. The movies and human contacts are the best media for sociological propaganda in terms of social climate, slow infiltration, progressive inroads, and over-all integration. Public meetings and posters are more suitable tools for providing shock propaganda, intense but temporary, leading to immediate action. The press tends more to shape general views; radio is likely to be an instrument of international action and psychological warfare, whereas the press is used domestically. In any case, it is understood that because of this specialization not one of these instruments may be left out: they must *all* be used in combination. The propagandist uses a keyboard and composes a symphony.

It is a matter of reaching and encircling the whole man and all men. Propaganda tries to surround man by all possible routes, in the realm of feelings as well as ideas, by playing on his will or on his needs, through his conscious and his unconscious, assailing him in both his private and his public life. It furnishes him with a complete system for explaining the world, and provides immediate incentives to action. We are here in the presence of an organized myth that tries to take hold of the entire person. Through the myth it creates, propaganda imposes a complete range of intuitive knowledge, susceptible of only one interpretation, unique and one-sided, and precluding any divergence. This myth becomes so powerful that it invades every area of consciousness, leaving no faculty or motivation intact. It stimulates in the individual a feeling of exclusiveness, and produces a biased attitude. The myth has such motive force that, once accepted, it controls the whole of the individual, who becomes immune to any other influence. This explains the totalitarian attitude that the individual adopts—wherever a myth has been successfully created —and that simply reflects the totalitarian action of propaganda on him.

Not only does propaganda seek to invade the whole man, to lead him to adopt a mystical attitude and reach him through all possible psychological channels, but, more, it speaks to all men. Propaganda cannot be satisfied with partial successes, for it does not tolerate discussion; by its very nature, it excludes contradiction and discussion. As long as a noticeable or expressed tension or a conflict of action remains, propaganda cannot be said to have accomplished its aim. It must produce quasi-unanimity, and the opposing faction must become negligible, or in any case cease to be vocal. Extreme propaganda must win over the adversary and at least use him by integrating him into its own frame of reference. That is why it was so important to have an Englishman speak on the Nazi radio or a General Paulus on the Soviet radio; why it was so important for the propaganda of the *fellagha* to make use of articles in *L'Observateur* and *L'Express* and for French propaganda to obtain statements from repentant *fellagha*.

Clearly, the ultimate was achieved by Soviet propaganda in the self-criticism of its opponents. That the enemy of a regime (or of the faction in power) can be made to declare, *while he is still the enemy,* that this regime was right, that his opposition was criminal, and that his condemnation is just—that is the ultimate result of totalitarian propaganda. The enemy (while still remaining the enemy, and because he is the enemy) is converted into a supporter of the regime. This is not simply a very useful and effective means of propaganda. Let us also note that, under the Khrushchev regime, the propaganda of self-criticism continued to function just as before (Marshal Bulganin's self-criticism was the most characteristic example). Here we are seeing the total, all-devouring propaganda mechanism in action: it cannot leave *any* segment of opinion outside its sphere; it cannot tolerate any sort of independence. Everything must be brought back into this unique sphere of action, which is an end in itself and can be justified only if virtually every man ends up by participating in it.

This brings us to another aspect of total propaganda. The propagandist must combine the elements of propaganda as in a real orchestration. On the one hand he must keep in mind the stimuli that can be utilized at a given moment, and must organize them. This results in a propaganda "campaign."[5] On the other hand, the propagandist must use various instruments, each in relation to all the others. Alongside the mass media of communication propaganda employs censorship, legal texts, proposed legislation, international conferences, and so forth—thus introducing elements seemingly alien to propaganda. We should not only consider the mass media: personal contacts are considered increasingly ef-

[5] Many analyses of various possible topics, of "gimmicks," have been made often. The most elementary was made in 1942 by the Institute for Propaganda Analysis (see Eugene L. Hartley: *Fundamentals of Social Psychology.* New York: Alfred A. Knopf; 1952). A more profound analysis is that of Lenin's strategy of propaganda: first stage—the creation in each organization of solid cores of well-indoctrinated men; second stage—cooperation with allies in political tasks that can compromise them; third stage—when the maximum advantage is reached—propaganda to demoralize the adversaries (inevitability of the Communist victory, injustice of the adversary's cause, failure of his means, etc.). The analysis of the type of campaign conducted by Hitler has been well done (Curt Riess: *Joseph Goebbels: A Biography* [New York: Doubleday & Company; 1948]), demonstrating the precise timing of the moment when a campaign should start and when it should stop, the silences and the verbal assaults; a schedule of the use of rumors, neutral information, commentaries, monumental mass meetings. Crowning all, and aiming at "concentrating the fire" of all media on one particular point—a single theme, a single enemy, a single idea—the campaign uses this concentration of all media, but progressively, for the public will take better to gradual attacks. (A good analysis of a Hitlerian campaign has been made by Jerome S. Bruner, in Katz *et al.*: *Public Opinion and Propaganda* [New York: Dryden Press; 1954], and on propaganda campaigns in general by Leonard W. Doob: *Propaganda: Its Psychology and Technique* [New York: Henry Holt & Company; 1935].)

fective. Educational methods play an immense role in political indoctrination (Lenin, Mao). A conference on Lenin's Doctrine of the State *is* propaganda. Information is extremely helpful to propaganda, as we shall demonstrate. "To explain correctly the present state of affairs is the great task of the agitator." Mao emphasizes that in 1928 an effective form of propaganda was the release of prisoners *after* they had been indoctrinated. The same was true of the care given to the enemy wounded; all this was to show the good will of the Communists. Everything can serve as a means of propaganda and everything must be utilized.

In this way diplomacy becomes inseparable from propaganda. We shall study this fact in Chapter IV. Education and training are inevitably taken over, as the Napoleonic Empire demonstrated for the first time. No contrast can be tolerated between teaching and propaganda, between the critical spirit formed by higher education and the exclusion of independent thought. One must utilize the education of the young to condition them to what comes later. The schools and all methods of instruction are transformed under such conditions, with the child integrated into the conformist group in such a way that the individualist is tolerated not by the authorities but by his peers. Religion and the churches are constrained to hold on to their own places in the orchestra if they want to survive.[6] Napoleon expressly formulated the doctrine of propaganda by the Church. The judicial apparatus is also utilized.[7] Of course, a trial can be an admirable springboard of propaganda for the accused, who can spread his ideas in his defense and exert an influence by the way he suffers his punishment. This holds true in the democracies. But the situation is reversed where a totalitarian state makes propaganda. During

---

[6] This was the case in the Orthodox Church in the U.S.S.R. during the war.

[7] In France, an example is the trial of the Jeanson network (September 1960), which aided the propaganda against insubordination and aid to the F.L.N. It is interesting to find this same idea of "educational" trials in Goebbels and Soviet jurists. The law itself in the U.S.S.R. is an instrument of propaganda intended to make people *like* the Soviet order. The tribunal is a means of preaching to the public. Finally, Mao has shown how the army can become a most effective propaganda instrument for those who are in it *and* for the occupied peoples. The French army tried to do the same in Algeria, but with less success. It is evident that information itself becomes propaganda, or rather, wherever propaganda appears, there follows an inextricable confusion between propaganda and information. Amusements, distractions, or games can be instruments of propaganda, as well as films for children (in the U.S.S.R.) and the games used in American social group work.

a trial there, the judge is forced to demonstrate a lesson for the
education of the public: verdicts are educational. And, we know
the importance of confessions in the great show trials (*e.g.*, the
Reichstag fire, the Moscow trials of 1936, the Nuremberg trials,
and innumerable trials in the People's Democracies after 1945).

Finally, propaganda will take over literature (present *and* past)
and history, which must be rewritten according to propaganda's
needs. We must not say: this is done by tyrannical, autocratic,
totalitarian governments. In fact, it is the result of propaganda
itself. Propaganda carries within itself, of intrinsic necessity, the
power to take over everything that can serve it. Let us remember
the innocent example of democratic, liberal, republican propaganda, which without hesitation took over many things in the
nineteenth century (perhaps without realizing it and in good
faith, but that is not an excuse). Let us remember the Athenian
democracy, the Roman Republic, the movement of the medieval
Communes, the Renaissance, and the Reformation. History was
hardly less modified then than Russian history was by the Bol-
sheviks. We know, on the other hand, how propaganda takes
over the literature of the past, furnishing it with contexts and
explanations designed to re-integrate it into the present. From a
thousand examples, we will choose just one:

In an article in *Pravda* in May 1957, the Chinese writer Mao
Dun wrote that the ancient poets of China used the following
words to express the striving of the people toward a better life:
"The flowers perfume the air, the moon shines, man has a long
life." And he added: "Allow me to give a new explanation of these
poetic terms. The flowers perfume the air—this means that the
flowers of the art of socialist realism are incomparably beautiful.
The moon shines—this means that the sputnik has opened a new
era in the conquest of space. Man has a long life—this means
that the great Soviet Union will live tens and tens of thousands
of years."

When one reads this once, one smiles. If one reads it a thousand
times, and no longer reads anything else, one must undergo a
change. And we must reflect on the transformation of perspective
already suffered by a whole society in which texts like this (published by the thousands) can be distributed and taken seriously not
only by the authorities but by the intellectuals. This complete
change of perspective of the *Weltanschauung* is the primary totalitarian element of propaganda.

Finally, the propagandist must use not only all of the instruments, but also different forms of propaganda. There are many types of propaganda, though there is a present tendency to combine them. Direct propaganda, aimed at modifying opinions and attitudes, must be preceded by propaganda that is sociological in character, slow, general, seeking to create a climate, an atmosphere of favorable preliminary attitudes. No direct propaganda can be effective without pre-propaganda, which, without direct or noticeable aggression, is limited to creating ambiguities, reducing prejudices, and spreading images, apparently without purpose. The spectator will be much more disposed to believe in the grandeur of France when he has seen a dozen films on French petroleum, railroads, or jetliners. The ground must be sociologically prepared before one can proceed to direct prompting. Sociological propaganda can be compared to plowing, direct propaganda to sowing; you cannot do the one without doing the other first. Both techniques must be used. For sociological propaganda alone will never induce an individual to change his actions. It leaves him at the level of his everyday life, and will not lead him to make decisions. Propaganda of the word and propaganda of the deed are complementary. Talk must correspond to something visible; the visible, active element must be explained by talk. Oral or written propaganda, which plays on opinions or sentiments, must be reinforced by propaganda of action, which produces new attitudes and thus joins the individual firmly to a certain movement. Here again, you cannot have one without the other.

We must also distinguish between covert propaganda and overt propaganda. The former tends to hide its aims, identity, significance, and source. The people are not aware that someone is trying to influence them, and do not feel that they are being pushed in a certain direction. This is often called "black propaganda." It also make use of mystery and silence. The other kind, "white propaganda," is open and aboveboard. There is a Ministry of Propaganda; one admits that propaganda is being made; its source is known; its aims and intentions are identified. The public knows that an attempt is being made to influence it.

The propagandist is forced to use both kinds, to combine them, for they pursue different objectives. Overt propaganda is necessary for attacking enemies; it alone is capable of reassuring one's own forces, it is a manifestation of strength and good organiza-

tion, a token of victory. But covert propaganda is more effective
if the aim is to push one's supporters in a certain direction without
their being aware of it. Also, it is necessary to use sometimes one,
sometimes the other on the same group; the Nazis knew very
well how to alternate long silences, mystery, the secret revealed,
the waiting period that raises anxiety levels, and then, suddenly,
the explosive decision, the tempest, the *Sturm* that seems all the
more violent because it breaks into the silence. Finally, we well
know that the combination of covert propaganda and overt propaganda is increasingly conducted so that white propaganda actually
becomes a cover and mask for black propaganda—that is, one
openly admits the existence of one kind of propaganda and of its
organization, means, and objectives, but all this is only a façade
to capture the attention of individuals and neutralize their instinct to resist, while other individuals, behind the scenes, work
on public opinion in a totally different direction, seeking to arouse
very different reactions, utilizing even existing resistance to overt
propaganda.[8]

Let us give one last example of this combination of differing
types of propaganda. Lasswell divides propaganda into two main
streams according to whether it produces direct incitement
or indirect incitement. Direct incitement is that by which
the propagandist himself acts, becomes involved, demonstrates
his conviction, his belief, his good faith. He commits himself
to the course of action that he proposes and supports, and in order
to obtain a similar action, he solicits a corresponding response
from the propagandee. Democratic propaganda—in which the
politician extends a hand to the citizen—is of this type. Indirect
incitement is that which rests on a difference between the states-
man, who takes action, and the public, which is limited to passive
acceptance and compliance. There is a coercive influence and

_____

[8] The secret element can be a theoretically independent "faction," a network of
rumors, and so on. The same effect is obtained by contrasting the real methods
of action, which are never acknowledged, with totally different overt propaganda
proclamations. This is the most frequently used system in the Soviet Union. In
this case it is necessary to have an overt propaganda, in accordance with Goebbels:
"We openly admit that we wish to influence our people. To admit this is the best
method of attaining it." Hence the creation of an official Ministry of Propaganda.
In any case, as Goebbels also said, when the news to be disseminated is unbelievable it must be disseminated by secret, black propaganda. As for censorship, it
should be as hidden and secret as possible. Moreover, all serious propagandists
know that censorship should be used as little as possible.

there is obedience; this is one of the characteristics of authoritarian propaganda.

Although this distinction is not altogether useless, we must again point out that every modern propagandist combines the two types of propaganda because each responds to different sectors of action. These two types no longer belong to different political regimes, but are differing needs of the same propaganda and of the various levels on which propaganda is organized. Propaganda of action presupposes positive incitement; propaganda through mass media will generally be contrasted incitement. Similarly, on the level of the performer in direct contact with the crowd, there must be positive incitement (it is better if the radio speaker *believes* in his cause); on the level of the organizer, that of propaganda strategy, there must be separation from the public. (We shall return to this point below.) These examples suffice to show that propaganda must be total.

Continuity and Duration of Propaganda

Propaganda must be continuous and lasting—continuous in that it must not leave any gaps, but must fill the citizen's whole day and all his days; lasting in that it must function over a very long period of time.[9] Propaganda tends to make the individual live in a separate world; he must not have outside points of reference. He must not be allowed a moment of meditation or reflection in which to see himself vis-à-vis the propagandist, as happens when the propaganda is not continuous. At that moment the individual emerges from the grip of propaganda. Instead, successful propaganda will occupy every moment of the individual's life: through posters and loudspeakers when he is out walking, through radio and newspapers at home, through meetings and movies in the evening. The individual must not be allowed to recover, to collect himself, to remain untouched by propaganda during any relatively long period, for propaganda is not the touch of the magic wand. It is based on slow, constant impregnation. It creates

---

[9] The famous principle of repetition, which is not in itself significant, plays a part only in this situation. Hitler was undoubtedly right when he said that the masses take a long time to understand and remember, thus it is necessary to repeat; but the emphasis must be placed on "a long time": the public must be conditioned to accept the claims that are made. In any case, repetition must be discontinued when the public has been conditioned, for at that point repetition will begin to irritate and provoke fresh doubts with respect to former certainties.

18)   THE CHARACTERISTICS OF PROPAGANDA

convictions and compliance through imperceptible influences
that are effective only by continuous repetition. It must create a
complete environment for the individual, one from which he never
emerges. And to prevent him from finding external points of
reference, it protects him by censoring everything that might
come in from the outside. The slow building up of reflexes and
myths, of psychological environment and prejudices, requires
propaganda of very long duration. Propaganda is not a stimulus
that disappears quickly; it consists of successive impulses and
shocks aimed at various feelings or thoughts by means of the many
instruments previously mentioned. A relay system is thus established. Propaganda is a continuous action, without failure or in-
terruption: as soon as the effect of one impulse is weakened, it is
renewed by another. At no point does it fail to subject its recipi-
ent to its influence. As soon as one effect wears off, it is followed
by a new shock.

Continuous propaganda exceeds the individual's capacities for
attention or adaptation and thus his capabilities of resistance.
This trait of continuity explains why propaganda can indulge in
sudden twists and turns.[1] It is always surprising that the content
of propaganda can be so inconsistent that it can approve today
what it condemned yesterday. Antonio Miotto considers this
changeability of propaganda an indication of its nature. Actually
it is only an indication of the grip it exerts, of the reality of its
effects. We must not think that a man ceases to follow the line
when there is a sharp turn. He continues to follow it because he is
caught up in the system. Of course, he notices the change that
has taken place, and he is surprised. He may even be tempted
to resist—as the Communists were at the time of the German-
Soviet pact. But will he then engage in a sustained effort to resist propaganda? Will he disavow his past actions? Will he break
with the environment in which his propaganda is active? Will he
stop reading a particular newspaper? Such breaks are too painful;
faced with them, the individual, feeling that the change in line
is not an attack on his real self, prefers to retain his habits.

---

[1] The propagandist does not necessarily have to worry about coherence and unity
in his claims. Claims can be varied and even contradictory, depending on the
setting (for example, Goebbels promised an increase in the price of grain in
the country and, at the same time, a decrease in the price of bread in the city);
and the occasion (for example, Hitler's propaganda *against* democracy in 1936
and *for* democracy in 1943).

Immediately thereafter he will hear the new truth reassessed a hundred times, he will find it explained and proved, and he does not have the strength to fight against it each day on the basis of yesterday's truth. He does not even become fully involved in this battle. *Propaganda* continues its assault without an instant's respite; *his* resistance is fragmentary and sporadic. He is caught up in professional tasks and personal preoccupations, and each time he emerges from them he hears and sees the new truth proclaimed. The steadiness of the propaganda prevails over his sporadic attention and makes him follow all the turns from the time he has begun to eat of this bread.

That is why one cannot really speak of propaganda in connection with an election campaign that lasts only two weeks. At such a time, some intellectual always will show that election propaganda is ineffectual; that its gross methods, its inscriptions on walls, can convince nobody; that opposing arguments neutralize each other. And it is true that the population is often indifferent to election propaganda. But it is not surprising that such propaganda has little effect: none of the great techniques of propaganda can be effective in two weeks.

Having no more relation to real propaganda are the experiments often undertaken to discover whether some propaganda method is effective on a group of individuals being used as guinea pigs. Such experiments are basically vitiated by the fact that they are of short duration. Moreover, the individual can clearly discern any propaganda when it suddenly appears in a social environment normally not subject to this type of influence; if one isolated item of propaganda or one campaign appears without a massive effort, the contrast is so strong that the individual can recognize it clearly as propaganda and begin to be wary. That is precisely what happens in an election campaign; the individual can defend himself when left to himself in his everyday situation. This is why it is fatal to the effectiveness of propaganda to proceed in spurts, with big noisy campaigns separated by long gaps. In such circumstances the individual will always find his bearings again; he will know how to distinguish propaganda from the rest of what the press carries in normal times. Moreover, the more intense the propaganda campaign, the more alert he will become —comparing this sudden intensity with the great calm that reigned before.

What is needed, then, is continuous agitation produced artificially even when nothing in the events of the day justifies or arouses excitement. Therefore, continuing propaganda must slowly create a climate first, and then prevent the individual from noticing a particular propaganda operation in contrast to ordinary daily events.

Organization of Propaganda

To begin with, propaganda must be organized in several ways. To give it the above-mentioned characteristics (continuity, duration, combination of different media), an organization is required that controls the mass media, is capable of using them correctly, of calculating the effect of one or another slogan or of replacing one campaign with another. There must be an *administrative* organization; every modern state is expected to have a Ministry of Propaganda, whatever its actual name may be. Just as technicians are needed to make films and radio broadcasts, so one needs "technicians of influence"—sociologists and psychologists. But this indispensable administrative organization is not what we are speaking of here. What we mean is that propaganda is always institutionalized to the extent of the existence of an *"Apparat"* in the German sense of the term—a machine. It is tied to realities. A great error, which interferes with propaganda analysis, is to believe that propaganda is solely a psychological affair, a manipulation of symbols, an abstract influence on opinions. A large number of American studies on propaganda are not valid for that reason. These studies are concerned only with means of psychological influence and regard only such means as propaganda, whereas all great modern practitioners of propaganda have rigorously tied together psychological and physical action as inseparable elements. No propaganda is possible unless psychological influence rests on reality,[2] and the recruiting of individuals into cadres or movements goes hand in hand with psychological manipulation.

As long as no physical influence is exerted by an organization on the individual, there is no propaganda. This is decidedly not

---

[2] Obviously propaganda directed at the enemy succeeds when it is coupled with victories. German propaganda in France during the Occupation failed because of the presence in France of German soldiers. (Thus the more victories, the more necessary propaganda becomes, said Goebbels.)

an invention of Mao Tse-tung, or merely an accessory of propaganda, or the expression of a particular type of propaganda. Separation of the psychological and physical elements is an arbitrary simplification that prevents all understanding of exactly what propaganda is. Of course, the physical organization can be of various types. It can be a party organization (Nazi, Fascist, Communist) in which those who are won over are absorbed and made to participate in action; such an organization, moreover, uses force and fear in the form of *Macht Propaganda*. Or such physical organization can be the integration of an entire population into cells by agents in each block of residences; in that case, it operates inside a society by integrating the whole social body. (Of course, this is accompanied by all the psychological work needed to press people into cells.) Or an effective transformation can be made in the economic, political, or social domain. We know that the propagandist is also a psychological consultant to governments; he indicates what measures should or should not be taken to facilitate certain psychological manipulations. It is too often believed that propaganda serves the purpose of sugar-coating bitter pills, of making people accept policies they would not accept spontaneously. But in most cases propaganda seeks to point out courses of action desirable in themselves, such as helpful reforms. Propaganda then becomes this mixture of the actual satisfaction given to the people by the reforms and subsequent exploitation of that satisfaction.

Propaganda cannot operate in a vacuum. It must be rooted in action, in a reality that is part of it. Some positive and welcome measure may be only a means of propaganda; conversely, coercive propaganda must be tied to physical coercion. For example, a big blow to the propaganda of the *Forces de Libération Nationale* (F.L.N.) in France in 1958 was the noisy threat of the referendum that the roads leading to the polls would be mined and booby-trapped; that voters would be massacred and their corpses displayed; that there would be a check in each *douar* of those who had dared to go to the polls. But none of these threats was carried out. Failure to take action is in itself counter-propaganda.

Because propaganda enterprises are limited by the necessity for physical organization and action—without which propaganda is practically non-existent—effective propaganda can work only inside a group, principally inside a nation. Propaganda outside the group—toward other nations for example, or toward an enemy —is necessarily weak.[3] The principal reason for this is undoubtedly the absence of physical organization and of encirclement of the individual. One cannot reach another nation except by way of symbols, through press or radio, and even then only in sporadic fashion. Such an effort may at best raise some doubts, plant some sense of ambiguity, make people ask themselves questions, influence them by suggestion. In case of war, the enemy will not be demoralized by such abstract propaganda unless he is at the same time beaten by armies and pounded by bombers. We can hardly expect great results from a simple dissemination of words unless we prepare for it by education (pre-propaganda) and sustain it by organization and action.

This points up a major difference between Communist and Western countries. Western countries conduct their propaganda against Soviet nations solely by psychological means, with the propaganda clearly emanating from a base situated in the democratic countries themselves.[4] By contrast, the Soviet Union makes very little propaganda itself; it does not seek to reach Western peoples by its radio. It confines its propaganda to organizations in the form of national Communist parties inside the national boundaries of the people to be propagandized. Because such parties are external propaganda structures of the Soviet Union, their propaganda is effective precisely because it is attached to a concrete organization capable of encirclement and continuity. One should note here the tremendous counter-propagandistic effect that ensued when the United States, after all the promises by the Voice of America, failed to come to the aid of Hungary during the 1956 rebellion. To be sure, it was hardly possible for the Americans to come to the aid of the Hungarians. Nevertheless, all propaganda that makes false promises turns against the propagandist.

The fact that the presence of an internal organization is indispensable to propaganda explains in large measure why the same statements advanced by a democracy and by an authoritarian government do not have the same credibility. When France and England proclaimed that the elections held in Syria and

---

[3] See below, Appendix I.
[4] Nevertheless, the Soviet Union's concern with this form of purely psychological propaganda confirms its effectiveness.

Egypt in connection with the formation of the United Arab Republic had been a fraud and evidence of a dictatorial government, they aroused no repercussions. It was a simple affirmation from the outside which was not repeated often enough, and not heard by the people. Yet when Nasser launched a propaganda campaign a year later on the same theme, claiming that the election results in Iraq had been "falsified by the imperialists" and that the Iraqi parliament was mockery, he set off reverberations. The Egyptian people reacted,[5] the Iraqi people followed suit, and international opinion was troubled. Thus the propaganda apparatus moves the people to action and the popular movement adds weight to the argument abroad. Propaganda, then, is no longer mere words; it incites an enormous demonstration by the masses and thus becomes a fact—which gives strength to the words outside the frontiers.

We must not, however, conclude from the decisive importance of organization that psychological action is futile. It is one—but not the only one—indispensable piece of the propaganda mechanism. The manipulation of symbols is necessary for three reasons. First of all, it persuades the individual to enter the framework of an organization. Second, it furnishes him with reasons, justifications, motivations for action. Third, it obtains his total allegiance. More and more we are learning that genuine compliance is essential if action is to be effective. The worker, the soldier, and the partisan must believe in what they are doing, must put all their heart and their good will into it; they must also find their equilibrium, their satisfactions, in their actions. All this is the result of psychological influence, which cannot attain great results alone, but which can attempt anything when combined with organization.

Finally, the presence of organization creates one more phenomenon: the propagandist is always separated from the propagandee, he remains a stranger to him.[6] Even in the actual contact

---

[5] The Egyptian campaign, launched in May 1958, was to get a hearing before the United Nations and to lead to the decision of August 22, whereas the Anglo-French protestations on the annexation of Syria in 1957 led to no action.

[6] A note that appeared in *Le Monde* (August 2, 1961) criticizing the psychological campaign in Algeria shows clearly that its ineffectiveness was due in part to the "self-intoxication" of the propagandists, who came to believe so much in their system that they were no longer capable of considering reality; they were caught in their own trap.

of human relations, at meetings, in door-to-door visits, the propagandist is of a different order; he is nothing else and nothing more than the representative of the organization—or, rather, a delegated fraction of it. He remains a manipulator, in the shadow of the machine. He knows why he speaks certain words and what effect they should have. His words are no longer human words but technically calculated words; they no longer express a feeling or a spontaneous idea, but reflect an organization even when they seem entirely spontaneous. Thus the propagandist is never asked to be involved in what he is saying, for, if it becomes necessary, he may be asked to say the exact opposite with similar conviction. He must, of course, believe in the *cause* he serves, but not in his particular argument. On the other hand, the propagandee hears the word spoken to him here and now and the argument presented to him in which he is asked to believe. He must take them to be human words, spontaneous and carried by conviction. Obviously, if the propagandist were left to himself, if it were only a matter of psychological action, he would end up by being taken in by his own trick, by believing it. He would then be the prisoner of his own formulas and would lose all effectiveness as a propagandist. What protects him from this is precisely the organization to which he belongs, which rigidly maintains a line. The propagandist thus becomes more and more the technician who treats his patients in various ways but keeps himself cold and aloof, selecting his words and actions for purely technical reasons. The patient is an object to be saved or sacrificed according to the necessities of the cause.

But then, the reader may ask, why the system of human contacts, why the importance of door-to-door visits? Only a technical necessity dictates them. We know how important human relations can be to the individual and how essential personal contact is in making decisions. We know that the distant word of the radio must be complemented by the warmth of a personal presence. This is exactly what puts the human-relations technique of propaganda into play. But this human contact is false and merely simulated; the presence is not that of the individual who has come forward, but that of the organization behind him. In the very act of pretending to speak as man to man, the propagandist is reaching the summit of his mendacity and falsifications, even when he is not conscious of it.

Orthopraxy

We now come to an absolutely decisive fact. Propaganda is very frequently described as a manipulation for the purpose of changing ideas or opinions, of making individuals "believe" some idea or fact, and finally of making them adhere to some doctrine— all matters of mind. Or, to put it differently, propaganda is described as dealing with beliefs or ideas. If the individual is a Marxist, it tries to destroy his conviction and turn him into an anti-Marxist, and so on. It calls on all the psychological mechanisms, but appeals to reason as well. It tries to convince, to bring about a decision, to create a firm adherence to some truth. Then, obviously, if the conviction is sufficiently strong, after some soul searching, the individual is ready for action.

This line of reasoning is completely wrong. To view propaganda as still being what it was in 1850 is to cling to an obsolete concept of man and of the means to influence him; it is to condemn oneself to understand nothing about modern propaganda. The aim of modern propaganda is no longer to modify ideas, but to provoke action. It is no longer to change adherence to a doctrine, but to make the individual cling irrationally to a process of action. It is no longer to lead to a choice, but to loosen the reflexes. It is no longer to transform an opinion, but to arouse an active and mythical belief.

Let us note here in passing how badly equipped opinion surveys are to gauge propaganda. We will have to come back to this point in the study of propaganda effects. Simply to ask an individual if he believes this or that, or if he has this or that idea, gives absolutely no indication of what behavior he will adopt or what action he will take; only *action* is of concern to modern propaganda, for its aim is to precipitate an individual's action, with maximum effectiveness and economy.[7] The propagandist

---

[7] When one analyzes the great modern systems of propaganda one always finds this primary aim of producing action, of mobilizing the individual. Occasionally it is expressly stated, as when Goebbels distinguished between *Haltung* (behavior) and *Stimmung* (morale). But the former is of greater importance. After a bloody raid Goebbels could state: "The *Stimmung* is quite low but that means little; the *Haltung* holds well." The *Stimmung* is volatile and varies readily; therefore, above all, the right action must be obtained, the right behavior maintained. In the analysis of propaganda, specialists have especially noted this desire to obtain immediate action rather than a change of opinion. The same idea is held by Mao Tse-tung: propaganda aims at mobilizing the masses, thus it is not necessary

therefore does not normally address himself to the individual's intelligence, for the process of intellectual persuasion is long and uncertain, and the road from such intellectual conviction to action even more so. The individual rarely acts purely on the basis of an idea. Moreover, to place propaganda efforts on the intellectual level would require that the propagandist engage in individual debate with each person—an unthinkable method. It is necessary to obtain at least a minimum of participation from everybody.[8] It can be active or passive, but in any case it is not simply a matter of public opinion. To see propaganda only as something related to public opinion implies a great intellectual independence on the part of the propagandee, who is, after all, only a third party in any political action, and who is asked only one opinion. This obviously coincides with a conception of liberal democracy, which assumes that the most one can do with a citizen is to change his opinion in such fashion as to win his vote at election time. The concept of a close relationship between public opinion and propaganda rests on the presumption of an independent popular will. If this concept were right, the role of propaganda would be to modify that popular will which, of course, expresses itself in votes. But what this concept does not take into consideration is that the injection of propaganda into the mechanism of popular action actually *suppresses* liberal democracy, after which we are no longer dealing with votes or the people's sovereignty; propaganda therefore aims solely at *participation*. The participation may be active or passive: active, if propaganda has been able to mobilize the individual for action; passive, if the individual does not act directly but psychologically supports that action.

But, one may ask, does this not bring us right back to public opinion? Certainly not, for opinion leaves the individual a mere spectator who may eventually, but not necessarily, resort to action. Therefore, the idea of participation is much stronger. The

---

to change their opinions but to make all individuals jointly attack a task. Even political education, so important with Mao, aims essentially at mobilization. And in the Soviet Union political education has occasionally been criticized for taking some intellectual and purely domestic turn to secure action, and then failing in its aim; the task of agitation is not to educate but to mobilize people. And there is always the matter of actual involvement in precise tasks defined by the party, for example to obtain increased productivity.

[8] This passive participation is what Goebbels meant when he said: "I conceive of a radio program that will make each listener participate in the events of the nation." But at the same time the listener is forced into passivity by the dictator.

supporter of a football team, though not physically in the game, makes his presence felt psychologically by rooting for the players, exciting them, and pushing them to outdo themselves. Similarly the faithful who attend Mass do not interfere physically, but their communicant participation is positive and changes the nature of the phenomenon. These two examples illustrate what we mean by passive participation obtained through propaganda.

Such an action cannot be obtained by the process of choice and deliberation. To be effective, propaganda must constantly short-circuit all thought and decision.[9] It must operate on the individual at the level of the unconscious. He must not know that he is being shaped by outside forces (this is one of the conditions for the success of propaganda), but some central core in him must be reached in order to release the mechanism in the unconscious which will provide the appropriate—and expected —action.

We have just said that action exactly suited to its ends must be obtained. This leads us to state that if the classic but outmoded view of propaganda consists in defining it as an adherence of man to an *orthodoxy,* true modern propaganda seeks, on the contrary, to obtain an *orthopraxy*—an action that in itself, and not because of the value judgments of the person who is acting, leads directly to a goal, which for the individual is not a conscious and intentional objective to be attained, but which is considered such by the propagandist. The propagandist knows what objective should be sought and what action should be accomplished, and he maneuvers the instrument that will secure precisely this action.

This is a particular example of a more general problem: the separation of thought and action in our society. We are living in a time when systematically—though without our wanting it so— action and thought are being separated. In our society, he who thinks can no longer act for himself; he must act through the agency of others, and in many cases he cannot act at all. He who acts cannot first think out his action, either because of lack of time and the burden of his personal problems, or because society's plan demands that he translate others' thoughts into action. And we see the same division within the individual himself. For he can use his mind only outside the area of his job—in order to find

[9] The application of "motivational research studies" to advertising also leads to this.

himself, to use his leisure to better himself, to discover what best suits him, and thus to individualize himself; whereas in the context of his work he yields to the common necessity, the common method, the need to incorporate his own work into the overall plan. Escape into dreams is suggested to him while he performs wholly mechanized actions.

Propaganda creates the same division. Of course it does not cancel out personality; it leaves man complete freedom of thought, except in his political or social action where we find him channeled and engaged in actions that do not necessarily conform to his private beliefs. He even can have political convictions, and still be led to act in a manner apparently contradictory to them. Thus the twists and turns of skillful propaganda do not present insurmountable difficulties. The propagandist can mobilize man for action that is not in accord with his previous convictions. Modern psychologists are well aware that there is not necessarily any continuity between conviction and action[1] and no intrinsic rationality in opinions or acts. Into these gaps in continuity propaganda inserts its lever. It does not seek to create wise or reasonable men, but proselytes and militants.

This brings us back to the question of organization. For the proselyte incited to action by propaganda cannot be left alone, cannot be entrusted to himself. If the action obtained by propaganda is to be appropriate, it cannot be individual; it must be collective. Propaganda has meaning only when it obtains convergence, coexistence of a multiplicity of individual action-reflexes whose coordination can be achieved only through the intermediary of an organization.

Moreover, the action-reflex obtained by propaganda is only a beginning, a point of departure; it will develop harmoniously

---

[1] There is a certain distance and divergence between opinion and action, between morale and behavior. A man may have a favorable opinion of Jews and still exhibit hostile behavior; the morale of a military unit may be very low and yet it may still fight well. Similarly we observe that people rarely know in advance what they want, and even less what they want to do. Once they have taken action, they are capable of declaring in good faith that they acted in a way other than the way they actually did act. Man does not obey his clear opinions or what he believes to be his deliberate will. To control opinion one must be aware that there is an abyss between what a man says and what he does. His actions often do not correspond to any clear motive, or to what one would have expected from a previous impression he made. Because of this difference between opinion and action, the propagandist who seeks to obtain action by changing opinions cannot be at all certain of success; he must, therefore, find other ways to secure action.

only if there is an organization in which (and thanks to which) the proselyte becomes militant.[2] Without organization, psychological incitement leads to excesses and deviation of action in the very course of its development. Through organization, the proselyte receives an overwhelming impulse that makes him act with the whole of his being. He is actually transformed into a religious man in the psycho-sociological sense of the term; justice enters into the action he performs because of the organization of which he is a part. Thus his action is integrated into a group of conforming actions. Not only does such integration seem to be the principal aim of all propaganda today; it is also what makes the effect of propaganda endure.

For action makes propaganda's effect irreversible.[3] He who acts in obedience to propaganda can never go back. He is now obliged to *believe* in that propaganda because of his past action. He is obliged to receive from it his justification and authority, without which his action will seem to him absurd or unjust, which would be intolerable. He is obliged to continue to advance in the direction indicated by propaganda, for action demands more action. He is what one calls committed—which is certainly what the Communist party anticipates, for example, and what the Nazis accomplished. The man who has acted in accordance with the existing propaganda has taken his place in society. From then on he has enemies. Often he has broken with his milieu or his family; he may be compromised. He is forced to accept the new milieu and the new friends that propaganda makes for him. Often he has committed an act reprehensible by traditional moral standards

---

[2] We must insist again that organization is an intrinsic part of propaganda. It is illusory to think one can separate them. Since 1928, an agitator in the Soviet Union must be an organizer of the masses; before that, Lenin said that a newspaper is propaganda, collective agitation, and collective organization. Similarly Mao Tse-tung insists on the difference between Communist and Capitalist armies, reminding us that the former is responsible for mobilizing the masses through propaganda and organization. He always ties these two elements together; propaganda among the masses goes hand in hand with organization of the masses. And Maurice Mégret, recalls the relationship between the two elements in connection with the May 13 demonstrations in Algiers. These examples demonstrate the error made by writers who want to separate propaganda and organization.

[3] This recourse to action permits the propagandist to compensate for a particular weakness of propaganda at the psychological level and to engage the individual in action, either because he is included in a small group, which as a whole is action-oriented, or because the role of the propagandist—located on the level of human relations—is to give an example of action and to bring others into this action. Thus the Soviet agitator's first duty is to "set a shining example of effort, discipline, and sacrifice."

and has disturbed a certain order; he needs a justification for this
—and he gets more deeply involved by repeating the act in order
to prove that it was just. Thus he is caught up in a movement
that develops until it totally occupies the breadth of his conscience.
Propaganda now masters him completely—and we must bear in
mind that any propaganda that does not lead to this kind of participation is mere child's play.

But we may properly ask how propaganda can achieve such
a result, a type of reflex action, by short-circuiting the intellectual
process. The claim that such results are indeed obtained by
propaganda will beget skepticism from the average observer,
strenuous denial from the psychologist, and the accusation that
this is mere fantasy contradicted by experience. Later, we shall
examine the validity of experiments made by psychologists in
these fields, and their adequacy in regard to the subject. For the
moment we shall confine ourselves to stating that observation
of men who were subjected to a real propaganda, Nazi or Communist, confirms the accuracy of the schema we have just drawn.

We must, however, qualify our statement. We do not say that
any man can be made to obey *any* incitement to action in *any*
way whatever from one day to the next. We do not say that in
each individual prior elementary mechanisms exist on which it
is easy to play and which will unfailingly produce a certain effect.
We do not hold with a mechanistic view of man. But we must
divide propaganda into two phases. There is pre-propaganda
(or sub-propaganda) and there is active propaganda. This follows
from what we have said earlier about the continuous and permanent nature of propaganda. Obviously, what must be continuous is not the active, intense propaganda of crisis but the
sub-propaganda that aims at mobilizing individuals, or, in the
etymological sense, to make them mobile[4] and mobilizable in
order to thrust them into action at the appropriate moment. It is
obvious that we cannot simply throw a man into action without
any preparation, without having mobilized him psychologically
and made him responsive, not to mention physically ready.

The essential objective of pre-propaganda is to prepare man for
a particular action, to make him sensitive to some influence, to
get him into condition for the time when he will effectively, and

---

[4] The term "to mobilize" is constantly applied by Lenin, Stalin, Mao, Goebbels,
and others to the work that precedes propaganda itself.

without delay or hesitation, participate in an action. Seen from this angle, pre-propaganda does not have a precise ideological objective; it has nothing to do with an opinion, an idea, a doctrine. It proceeds by psychological manipulations, by character modifications, by the creation of feelings or stereotypes useful when the time comes. It must be continuous, slow, imperceptible. Man must be penetrated in order to shape such tendencies. He must be made to live in a certain psychological climate.

The two great routes that this sub-propaganda takes are the conditioned reflex and the myth. Propaganda tries first of all to create conditioned reflexes in the individual by training him so that certain words, signs, or symbols, even certain persons or facts, provoke unfailing reactions. Despite many protests from psychologists, creating such conditioned reflexes, collectively as well as individually, is definitely possible. But of course in order for such a procedure to succeed, a certain amount of time must elapse, a period of training and repetition. One cannot hope to obtain automatic reactions after only a few weeks' repetition of the same formulas. A real psychic re-formation must be undertaken, so that after months of patient work a crowd will react automatically in the hoped-for direction to some image. But this preparatory work is not yet propaganda, for it is not yet immediately applicable to a concrete case. What is visible in propaganda, what is spectacular and seems to us often incomprehensible or unbelievable, is possible only because of such slow and not very explicit preparation; without it nothing would be possible.

On the other hand, the propagandist tries to create myths by which man will live, which respond to his sense of the sacred. By "myth" we mean an all-encompassing, activating image: a sort of vision of desirable objectives that have lost their material, practical character and have become strongly colored, overwhelming, all-encompassing, and which displace from the conscious all that is not related to it. Such an image pushes man to action precisely because it includes all that he feels is good, just, and true. Without giving a metaphysical analysis of the myth, we will mention the great myths that have been created by various propagandas: the myth of race, of the proletariat, of the Führer, of Communist society, of productivity. Eventually the myth takes possession of a man's mind so completely that his life is consecrated to it. But that effect can be created only by slow,

patient work by all the methods of propaganda, not by any immediate propaganda operation. Only when conditioned reflexes
have been created in a man and he lives in a collective myth can
he be readily mobilized.

Although the two methods of myth and conditioned reflex can
be used in combination, each has separate advantages. The United
States prefers to utilize the myth; the Soviet Union has for a long
time preferred the reflex. The important thing is that when the
time is ripe, the individual can be thrown into action by active
propaganda, by the utilization of the psychological levers that
have been set up, and by the evocation of the myth. No connection necessarily exists between his action and the reflex or the content of the myth. The action is not necessarily psychologically
conditioned by some aspect of the myth. For the most surprising
thing is that the preparatory work leads only to man's *readiness*.
Once he is ready, he can be mobilized effectively in very different
directions—but of course the myth and the reflex must be continually rejuvenated and revived or they will atrophy. That is
why pre-propaganda must be constant, whereas active propaganda
can be sporadic when the goal is a particular action or involvement.[5]

---

[5] Political education, in Lenin and Mao's sense, corresponds exactly to our idea of
sub-propaganda, or basic propaganda, as Goebbels would say. For this education
is in no way objective or disinterested. Its only goal is to create in the individual a
new *Weltanschauung*, inside which each of the propositions of propaganda will
become logical; each of its demands will be indisputable. It is a matter of forming
new presuppositions, new stereotypes that are prior justifications for the reasons
and objectives which propaganda will give to the individual. But while the prejudices and stereotypes in our societies are created in a somewhat incoherent fashion
—singly and haphazardly—in political education we have the systematic and deliberate creation of a coherent set of presuppositions that are above challenge.
Probably, at the beginning of the Soviet revolution such political education did not
have precise objectives or practical aims; indoctrination was an end in itself. But
since 1930 this concept has changed, and political education has become the
foundation of propaganda. Mao has done this even earlier. In the Soviet Union
ideological indoctrination is now the means of achieving an end; it is the foundation on which propaganda can convince the individual *hic et nunc* of whatever it
wants to convince him.
   To make this clear we will use the classic terms of propaganda and agitation,
taken in a new sense. Propaganda is the elucidation of the Marxist-Leninist doctrine
(and corresponds to pre-propaganda); agitation's goal is to make individuals act
hic et nunc, as a function of their political education and also in terms of this
"education" (which corresponds to what we call propaganda). Active experience,
in effect, makes further education easier. The different elements are easily mixed:
the radio network is given the task to increase "political knowledge" and "political
awareness" (pre-propaganda) and to rally the population to support the policy of
the party and the government (propaganda). The film industry is given orders that

2. *Internal Characteristics*

Knowledge of the Psychological Terrain

The power of propaganda to incite action has often been challenged by the alleged fact that propaganda cannot really modify or create anything in man. We frequently find that psychological manipulations do not appreciably change an individual's firmly established opinion. A Communist or a Christian with strong beliefs is very little, if at all, shaken by adverse propaganda. Similarly, a prejudice or a stereotype is hardly ever changed by propaganda; for example it is almost impossible to break down racial prejudice by propaganda. What people think of Negroes, Jews, bourgeois, or colonialists will be only slightly altered by propaganda attempts. Similarly, a reflex or myth cannot be created out of nothing, as if the individual were neutral and empty ground on which anything could be built. Furthermore, even when the reflex has been created, it cannot be utilized to make an individual act in just any direction; the individual cannot be manipulated as if he were an object, an automaton—the automatic nature of created reflexes does not transform him into a robot.

We can conclude from a large body of experience that the propagandist cannot go contrary to what is in an individual; he cannot create just any new psychological mechanism or obtain just any decision or action. But psychologists who make these observations draw a very hasty conclusion from them: that propaganda has very little effect, that it has so limited a field of action that it hardly seems useful. We shall show later why we consider this conclusion incorrect. But the observations themselves give us some very good indications as to what is effective propaganda. The propagandist must first of all know as precisely as possible

---

even comedies "must organize the thoughts and feelings of the audience in the required proletarian direction." The effects of such political education are often described by Mao: it creates class-consciousness; it destroys the individualist and petit-bourgeois spirit while assimilating the individual in a collectivity of thought; it creates ideological conformity in a new framework; it leads to understanding the necessity for the sharing of property, obedience to the state, creation of authority and hierarchy; it leads the comrade to vote for suitable representatives, and to withstand the weariness and the difficulties of the battle for increased production. This describes perfectly the role of infrastructure assigned to political education in the process of propaganda.

the terrain on which he is operating. He must know the sentiments and opinions, the current tendencies and the stereotypes
among the public he is trying to reach.[6] An obvious point of departure is the analysis of the characteristics of the group and its
current myths, opinions, and sociological structure. One cannot
make just any propaganda any place for anybody. Methods and
arguments must be tailored to the type of man to be reached.
Propaganda is definitely not an arsenal of ready-made, valid techniques and arguments, suitable for use anywhere.[7] Obvious errors
in this direction have been made in the recent course of propaganda's history.[8] The technique of propaganda consists in precisely
calculating the desired action in terms of the individual who is
to be made to act.

The second conclusion seems to us embodied in the following rule: never make a direct attack on an established, reasoned,
durable opinion or an accepted cliché, a fixed pattern. The propagandist wears himself out to no avail in such a contest. A propagandist who tries to change mass opinion on a precise and
well-established point is a bad propagandist. But that does not
mean that he must then leave things as they are and conclude

---

[6] The propagandist must know the principal symbols of the culture he wishes to
attack and the symbols which express each attitude if he is to be effective. The
Communists always make a thorough study of the content of opinion before
launching their propaganda. A person is not sufficient unto himself; he belongs to
that whole called culture by the Americans. Each person's psychology is shaped
by that culture. He is conditioned by the symbols of that culture, and is also a
transmitter of that culture; each time its symbols are changed he is deeply affected.
Thus, one can change him by changing these symbols. The propagandist will act
on this, keeping in mind that the most important man to be reached is the so-
called marginal man: that is, the man who does not believe what the propagandist
says, but who is interested because he does not believe the opposition either; the
man who in battle has good reason to lay down his arms.
[7] Beyond this, propaganda must vary according to circumstances. The propagandist
must constantly readjust it according to changes in the situation and also according
to changes made by his opponent; the content of propaganda has special reference
to the opponent and must therefore change if he changes.
[8] Here one can see the famous boomerang: When he is wrong in his analysis of a
milieu, the propagandist may create the reverse effect of what he expected, and
his propaganda can turn against him. There are innumerable examples of this. For
instance, during the Korean War the Americans, who wanted to show that prisoners
were well treated, distributed in China and Korea pictures of war prisoners at play,
engaging in sports, and so forth. So that the prisoners should not be recognized and
persecuted by the Communists after the war, their eyes were blacked out in the
pictures. These photos were interpreted by the Chinese to mean "the Americans
gouge out the eyes of their prisoners," an interpretation which stemmed from their
prior belief that it is impossible to treat prisoners well, and normal to gouge out
their eyes.

that nothing can be done. He need only understand two subtle aspects of this problem.

First of all, we recall that there is not necessarily any continuity between opinion or fixed patterns and action. There is neither consistency nor logic, and a man can perfectly well hold on to his property, his business, and his factory, and still vote Communist—or he can be enthusiastic about social justice and peace as described by the Communists, and still vote for a conservative party. Attacking an established opinion or stereotype head on would make the propagandee aware of basic inconsistencies and would produce unexpected results.[9] The skillful propagandist will seek to obtain action without demanding consistency, without fighting prejudices and images, by taking his stance deliberately on inconsistencies.

Second, the propagandist can alter opinions by diverting them from their accepted course, by changing them, or by placing them in an ambiguous context.[1] Starting from apparently fixed and immovable positions, we can lead a man where he does not want to go, without his being aware of it, over paths that he will not notice. In this way propaganda against German rearmament, organized by the "partisans of peace" and ultimately favorable to the Soviet Union, utilized the anti-German sentiment of the French Right.

Thus, existing opinion is not to be contradicted, but utilized. Each individual harbors a large number of stereotypes and established tendencies; from this arsenal the propagandist must select those easiest to mobilize, those which will give the greatest strength to the action he wants to precipitate. Writers who insist that propaganda against established opinion is ineffective would be right if man were a simple being, having only one opinion with fixed limits. This is rarely the case among those who have not yet been propagandized, although it is frequently the case among individuals who have been subjected to propaganda for a long time. But the ordinary man in our democracies has a wide range

---

[9] The most frequent response is that of flight. In the face of direct propaganda against a prejudice the propagandee flees: he rejects (often unconsciously) what he is told; he wants no part of it; he justifies himself by dissociating himself from what is attacked, projecting the attack onto another person, and so on—but he does not change.

[1] Other methods of altering opinion are to offer forms of action, or to provoke rifts in a group, or to turn a feeling of aggression toward some specified object.

of feelings and ideas.[2] Propaganda need only determine which opinions must not be attacked head on, and be content to undermine them gradually and to weaken them by cloaking them in ambiguity.[3]

The third important conclusion, drawn from experiments made chiefly in the United States, is that propaganda cannot create something out of nothing. It must attach itself to a feeling, an idea; it must build on a foundation already present in the individual. The conditioned reflex can be established only on an innate reflex or a prior conditioned reflex. The myth does not expand helter-skelter; it must respond to a group of spontaneous beliefs. Action cannot be obtained unless it responds to a group of already established tendencies or attitudes stemming from the schools, the environment, the regime, the churches, and so on. Propaganda is confined to utilizing existing material; it does not create it.

This material falls into four categories. First there are the psychological "mechanisms" that permit the propagandist to know more or less precisely that the individual will respond in a certain way to a certain stimulus. Here the psychologists are far from agreement; behaviorism, depth psychology, and the psychology of instincts postulate very different psychic mechanisms and see essentially different connections and motivations. Here the propagandist is at the mercy of these interpretations. Second, opinions, conventional patterns and stereotypes exist concretely in a particular milieu or individual. Third, ideologies exist which are more or less consciously shared, accepted, and disseminated, and which form the only intellectual, or rather para-intellectual, element that must be reckoned with in propaganda.

Fourth and finally, the propagandist must concern himself above all with the needs of those whom he wishes to reach.[4] All propa-

---

[2] This is true of individuals and groups. It has been said quite accurately, for example, that if public opinion were really unanimous there would be no way for propaganda to work. It is only because in any body of public opinion there are groups of private opinions that propaganda can use these as seeds with which to reverse the trend of opinion.

[3] It goes without saying that propaganda must also change *its* character according to the results it wishes to attain in given circumstances. For example, propaganda must be strongly personalized when it seeks to create a feeling of guilt in the adversary (e.g., "the French are colonialists"). On the other hand it must be impersonal when it seeks to create confidence and exaltation (e.g., "France is great").

[4] At the most elementary level, propaganda will play on the need for physical survival (in time of war). This can be further utilized, either to weaken resistance or to stiffen it. For example, Goebbels used this theme in 1945 to prolong resistance: "By fighting you have a chance for survival."

ganda must respond to a need, whether it be a concrete need (bread, peace, security, work) or a psychological need.[5] (We shall discuss this last point at length later on.) Propaganda cannot be gratuitous. The propagandist cannot simply decide to make propaganda in such and such a direction on this or that group. The group must need something, and the propaganda must respond to that need. (One weakness of tests made in the United States is that far too often the experimental propaganda used did not correspond to a single need of the persons tested.) A frequent error on the part of propagandists "pushing" something is the failure to take into account whether or not the propagandee needs it.

Of course, when we say that the propagandist has to use existing elements, we do not mean that he must use them in direct or unequivocal fashion. We have already indicated that he often must use them in indirect and equivocal fashion. When he does so, he can indeed create something new. The propagandist's need to base himself on what already exists does not prevent him from going further. If committed to a particular opinion, would he be obligated simply to repeat it indefinitely? Because he must pay lip service to a certain stereotype, is he limited to do nothing but reproduce that stereotype? Obviously not. What exists is only the raw material from which the propagandist can create something strictly new, which in all probability would not have sprung up spontaneously. Take, for example, unhappy workers, threatened by unemployment, exploited, poorly paid, and without hope of improving their situation: Karl Marx has clearly demonstrated that they might have a certain spontaneous reaction of revolt, and that some sporadic outbursts might occur, but that this will not develop into anything else and will lead nowhere. With propaganda, however, this same situation and the existing sentiments might be used to create a class-consciousness and a lasting and organized revolutionary trend.

Similarly, if we take a population, not necessarily of the same race or language or history, but inhabiting the same territory, oppressed by the same conqueror, feeling a common resentment or hatred toward the occupying force (a sentiment generally found at a purely individual level), and in the grip of the enemy

---

[5] Propaganda must also consider the image that the propagandee has of the ways in which his needs can be satisfied (*structure of expectation*). Propaganda also aims at modifying this image of what people expect.

administration, only a few individual acts of violence will occur spontaneously—and more often nothing at all. But propaganda can "take it from there" and arouse a nationalism, the *foundations* of which are perfectly natural but which as an integrated force is entirely fabricated. This is true for Algerian, Yugoslavian, or African nationalism.

In this way propaganda can be creative. And it is in complete control of its creations; the passions or prejudices that it instills in a man serve to strengthen its hold on him and thus make him do what he would never have done otherwise. It is not true that propaganda is powerless simply because at the start it is limited to what already exists. It can attack from the rear, wear down slowly, provide new centers of interest, which cause the neglect of previously acquired positions; it can divert a prejudice; or it can elicit an action contrary to an opinion held by the individual, without his being clearly aware of it.

Finally, it is obvious that propaganda must not concern itself with what is best in man—the highest goals humanity sets for itself, its noblest and most precious feelings. Propaganda does not aim to elevate man, but to make him *serve*. It must therefore utilize the most common feelings, the most widespread ideas, the crudest patterns, and in so doing place itself on a very low level with regard to what it wants man to do and to what end.[6] Hate, hunger, and pride make better levers of propaganda than do love or impartiality.

Fundamental Currents in Society

Propaganda must not only attach itself to what already exists in the individual, but also express the fundamental currents of the society it seeks to influence. Propaganda must be familiar with collective sociological presuppositions, spontaneous myths, and broad ideologies. By this we do not mean political currents or temporary opinions that will change in a few months, but the fundamental psycho-sociological bases on which a whole society

------

[6] Propaganda must stay at the human level. It must not propose aims so lofty that they will seem inaccessible; this creates the risk of a boomerang effect. Propaganda must confine itself to simple, elementary messages (Have confidence in our leader, our party. . . . Hate our enemies, etc.) without fear of being ridiculous. It must speak the most simple, everyday language, familiar, individualized—the language of the group that is being addressed, and the language with which a person is familiar.

rests, the presuppositions and myths not just of individuals or of particular groups but those shared by all individuals in a society, including men of opposite political inclinations and class loyalties.

A propaganda pitting itself against this fundamental and accepted structure would have no chance of success. Rather, all effective propaganda is based on these fundamental currents and expresses them.[7] Only if it rests on the proper collective beliefs will it be understood and accepted. It is part of a complex of civilization, consisting of material elements, beliefs, ideas, and institutions, and it cannot be separated from them. No propaganda could succeed by going against these structural elements of society. But propaganda's main task clearly is the psychological reflection of these structures.

It seems to us that this reflection is found in two essential forms: the collective sociological presuppositions and the social myths. By presuppositions we mean a collection of feelings, beliefs, and images by which one unconsciously judges events and things without questioning them, or even noticing them. This collection is shared by all who belong to the same society or group. It draws its strength from the fact that it rests on general tacit agreement. Whatever the differences of opinion are among people, one can discover beneath the differences the same beliefs —in Americans and in Russians, in Communists and in Christians. These presuppositions are sociological in that they are provided for us by the surrounding milieu and carry us along in the sociological current. They are what keeps us in harmony with our environment.

It seems to us that there are four great collective sociological presuppositions in the modern world. By this we mean not only the Western world, but all the world that shares a modern technology and is structured into nations, including the Communist world, though not yet the African or Asian worlds. These common presuppositions of bourgeois and proletarian are that man's aim in life is happiness, that man is naturally good, that history develops in endless progress, and that everything is matter.[8]

The other great psychological reflection of social reality is the

---

[7] It must be associated with the dominant cultural values of the entire society.
[8] Formulated in this way, they seem to be philosophical notions but are not. We certainly do not see here any of the philosophical schools, hedonism or materialism, but only the instinctive popular belief marking our epoch and shared by all, expressing itself in very concrete forms.

myth. The myth expresses the deep inclinations of a society. Without it, the masses would not cling to a certain civilization or its
process of development and crisis. It is a vigorous impulse, strongly
colored, irrational, and charged with all of man's power to believe.
It contains a religious element. In our society the two great fundamental myths on which all other myths rest are Science and History. And based on them are the collective myths that are man's
principal orientations: the myth of Work, the myth of Happiness
(which is not the same thing as the presupposition of happiness), the myth of the Nation, the myth of Youth, the myth of
the Hero.

Propaganda is forced to build on these presuppositions and to
express these myths, for without them nobody would listen to
it. And in so building it must always go in the same direction as
society; it can only reinforce society. A propaganda that stresses
virtue over happiness and presents man's future as one dominated by austerity and contemplation would have no audience
at all. A propaganda that questions progress or work would arouse
disdain and reach nobody; it would immediately be branded as
an ideology of the intellectuals, since most people feel that the
serious things are material things because they are related to
labor, and so on.

It is remarkable how the various presuppositions and aspects
of myths complement each other, support each other, mutually
defend each other: If the propagandist attacks the network at
one point, all myths react to the attack. Propaganda must be
based on current beliefs and symbols to reach man and win him
over. On the other hand, propaganda must also follow the general
direction of evolution, which includes the belief in progress. A
normal, spontaneous evolution is more or less expected, even if
man is completely unaware of it, and in order to succeed, propaganda must move in the direction of that evolution.

The progress of technology is continuous; propaganda must
voice this reality, which is one of man's convictions. All propaganda must play on the fact that the nation will be industrialized,
more will be produced, greater progress is imminent, and so on.
No propaganda can succeed if it defends outdated production
methods or obsolete social or administrative institutions. Though
occasionally advertising may profitably evoke the good old days,
political propaganda may not. Rather, it must evoke the future,

the tomorrows that beckon, precisely because such visions impel the individual to act.[9] Propaganda is carried along on this current and cannot oppose it; it must confirm it and reinforce it. Thus, propaganda will turn a normal feeling of patriotism into a raging nationalism. It not only reflects myths and presuppositions, it hardens them, sharpens them, invests them with the power of shock and action.

It is virtually impossible to reverse this trend. In a country in which administrative centralization does not yet exist, one can propagandize for centralization because modern man firmly believes in the strength of a centrally administered State. But where centralization *does* exist, no propaganda can be made against it. Federalist propaganda (true federalism, which is opposed to national centralism; not such supernationalism as the so-called Soviet or European federalism) can never succeed because it is a challenge to both the national myth and the myth of progress; every reduction, whether to a work unit or an administrative unit, is seen as regression.

Of course, when we analyze this necessary subordination of propaganda to presuppositions and myths, we do not mean that propaganda must express them clearly all the time; it need not speak constantly of progress and happiness (although these are always profitable themes), but in its general line and its infrastructure it must allow for the same presuppositions and follow the same myths as those prevalent in its audience. There is some tacit agreement: for example, a speaker does not have to say that he believes "man is good": this is clear from his behavior, language, and attitudes, and each man unconsciously feels that the others share the same presuppositions and myths. It is the same with propaganda: a person listens to a particular propaganda because it reflects his deepest unconscious convictions without expressing them directly. Similarly, because of the myth of progress, it is much easier to sell a man an electric razor than a straight-edged one.

---

[9] But in this straining toward the future the propagandist must always beware of making precise promises, assurances, commitments. Goebbels constantly protested the affirmations of victory emanating from the Führer's headquarters. The pull toward the future should refer to general currents of society rather than to precise events. Nevertheless, the promise made by Khrushchev that Communism would be achieved by 1980 leaves enough margin; for though the desired effect is obtained in 1961, the promise will be forgotten in 1980 if it has not been fulfilled.

Finally, alongside the fundamental currents reflected in pre-suppositions and myths, we must consider two other elements. Obviously the material character of a society and its evolution, its fundamental sociological currents, are linked to its very structure. Propaganda must operate in line with those material currents and at the level of material progress. It must be associated with all economic, administrative, political, and educational development, otherwise it is nothing. It must also reflect local and national idiosyncrasies. Thus, in France, the general trend toward socialization can be neither overridden nor questioned. The political Left is respectable; the Right has to justify itself before the ideology of the Left (in which even Rightists participate). All propaganda in France must contain—and evoke—the principal elements of the ideology of the Left in order to be accepted.

But a conflict is possible between a local milieu and the national society. The tendencies of the group may be contrary to those of the broader society; in that case one cannot lay down general rules. Sometimes the tendencies of the local group win out because of the group's solidarity; sometimes the general society wins out because it represents the mass and, therefore, unanimity. In any case, propaganda must always choose the trend that normally will triumph because it agrees with the great myths of the time, common to all men. The Negro problem in the American South is typical of this sort of conflict. The *local* Southern milieu is hostile to Negroes and favorable to discrimination, whereas American society *as a whole* is hostile to racism. It is almost certain, therefore, despite the deep-rooted prejudices and the local solidarities, that racism will be overcome. The Southerners are on the defensive; they have no springboard for external propaganda—for example, toward the European nations. Propaganda can go only in the direction of world opinion—that of Asia, Africa, almost all of Europe. Above all, when it is anti-racist, it is helped along by the myth of progress.

It follows that propaganda cannot be applied everywhere alike, and that—at least up to now—propaganda in both Africa and Asia must be essentially different from propaganda in the rest of the world. We stress "at least up to now" because those countries are being progressively won over by Western myths and are developing national and technological forms of society. But for the moment these myths are not yet everyday reality, flesh and blood, spiritual bread, sacred inheritance, as they are with us. To sum up, propaganda must express the fundamental currents of society.[1]

Timeliness

Propaganda in its explicit form must relate solely to what is timely.[2] Man can be captured and mobilized only if there is consonance between his own deep social beliefs and those underlying the propaganda directed at him, and he will be aroused and moved to action only if the propaganda pushes him toward a *timely* action. These two elements are not contradictory but complementary, for the only interesting and enticing news is that which presents a timely, spectacular aspect of society's profound reality. A man will become excited over a new automobile because it is immediate evidence of his deep belief in progress and technology. Between *news* that can be utilized by propaganda and *fundamental currents* of society the same relationship exists as between waves and the sea. The waves exist only because the underlying mass supports them; without it there would be nothing. But man sees only the waves; they are what attracts, entices, and fascinates him. Through them he grasps the grandeur and majesty of the sea, though this grandeur exists only in the immense mass of water. Similarly, propaganda can have solid *reality* and *power* over man only because of its rapport with fundamental currents, but it has seductive excitement and a capacity to move him only by its ties to the most volatile immediacy.[3] And the timely event that man considers worth retaining, preserving, and disseminating is always an event related to the expression of the myths and presuppositions of a given time and place.

Besides, the public is sensitive only to contemporary events.

---

[1] In this respect, a high-ranking officer made a completely valid criticism of the psychological campaign in Algeria (*Le Monde*, August 2, 1961) when he pointed out that the weakness of the Lacheroy system was to stress the material environment of the Algerian population without taking into account its instincts and myths, its nationalism, and its adherence to Western ideologies.

[2] The history of Soviet propaganda is full of such reminders of the necessity for a propaganda of timeliness, relating to practical problems, and it rejects vague and dogmatic propaganda. For example, public acceptance must be obtained for new work norms, salary reforms, and so on.

[3] Propaganda must remember: "Goebbels said that the face of politics changes each day, but the lines of propaganda must change only imperceptibly."

They alone concern and challenge it. Obviously, propaganda can succeed only when man feels challenged. It can have no influence when the individual is stabilized, relaxing in his slippers in the midst of total security. Neither past events nor great metaphysical problems challenge the average individual, the ordinary man of our times. He is not sensitive to what is tragic in life; he is not anguished by a question that God might put to him; he does not feel challenged except by current events, political or economic. Therefore, propaganda must start with current events; it would not reach anybody if it tried to base itself on historical facts. We have seen Vichy propaganda fail when it tried to evoke the images of Napoleon and Joan of Arc in hopes of arousing the French to turn against England. Even facts so basic and deeply rooted in the French consciousness are not a good springboard for propaganda; they pass quickly into the realm of history, and consequently into neutrality and indifference: A survey made in May 1959 showed that among French boys of fourteen and fifteen, 70 percent had no idea who Hitler and Mussolini were, 80 percent had forgotten the Russians in the list of victors of 1945, and not a single one recognized the words *Danzig* or *Munich* as having figured in relatively recent events.

We must also bear in mind that the individual is at the mercy of events. Hardly has an event taken place before it is outdated; even if its significance is still considerable, it is no longer of interest, and if man experiences the feeling of having escaped it, he is no longer concerned. In addition, he obviously has a very limited capacity for attention and awareness; one event pushes the preceding one into oblivion. And as man's memory is short, the event that has been supplanted by another is forgotten; it no longer exists; nobody is interested in it any more.[4] In November 1957, a Bordeaux association organized a lecture on the atomic bomb by a well-known specialist; the lecture would surely have been of great interest (and not for propaganda purposes). A wide

---

[4] Man remembers no specific news. He retains only a general impression (which propaganda furnishes him) inserted in the collective current of society. This obviously facilitates the work of the propagandist and permits extraordinary contradictions. What the listener retains, in the long run determines his loyalties. A remarkable study by Carl I. Hovland and Walter Weiss has shown that the individual who questions an item of information because he distrusts the informant, ultimately forgets the suspicious nature of the source and retains only the impression of the information. In the long run, belief in a reliable source of information decreases and belief in information from the suspicious source increases.

distribution of leaflets had announced it to the student public, but not a single student came. Why? Because this happened at exactly the same time as Sputnik's success, and the public was concerned only with this single piece of news; its sole interest was in Sputnik, and the permanent problem was "forgotten."

Actually, the public is prodigiously sensitive to current news. Its attention is focused immediately on any spectacular event that fits in with its myths. At the same time, the public will fix its interest and its passion on one point, to the exclusion of all the rest. Besides, people have already become accustomed to, and have accommodated themselves to "the rest" (yesterday's news or that of the day before yesterday). We are dealing here not just with forgetfulness, but also with plain loss of interest.

A good example is Khrushchev's ultimatum at the beginning of 1959, when he set a time limit of three months to solve the Berlin problem. Two weeks passed; no war broke out. Even though the same problem remained, public opinion grew accustomed to it and lost interest—so much so, that on the expiration date of Khrushchev's ultimatum (27 May 1959), people were surprised when they were reminded of it. Khrushchev himself said nothing on May 27; not having obtained anything, he simply counted on the fact that everyone had "forgotten" his ultimatum[5]—which shows what a subtle propagandist he is. It is impossible to base a propaganda campaign on an event that no longer worries the public; it is forgotten and the public has grown accustomed to it. On November 30, 1957, the Communist states met and signed an agreement concerning several political problems and the problem of peace; its text was truly remarkable, one of the best that has been drawn up. But nobody discussed this important matter. The progressives were not troubled by it; the partisans of peace did not say one word—though in itself, objectively, the text was excellent. But everything it contained was "old hat" to the public; and the public could not get interested all over again in an outdated theme when it was not uneasy over a specific threat of war.

It would appear that propaganda for peace can bear fruit only

---

[5] Exactly the same thing happened in 1961 with the second ultimatum on Berlin: on June 15 Khrushchev issued an ultimatum to be met by the end of the year, and on August 2 he announced that he would use force to secure compliance. By the end of the year everyone had forgotten.

when there is fear of war. The particular skill of Communist propaganda in this area is that it creates a threat of war while conducting peace propaganda. The constant threat of war, arising from Stalin's posture, made the propaganda of the partisans for peace effective and led non-Communists to attach themselves to the fringe of the party via that propaganda. But in 1957, when the threat of war seemed much less real, because Khrushchev had succeeded Stalin, such propaganda had no hold at all on the public. The news about Hungary seemed far more important to the Western world than the general problem of world peace. These various elements explain why the well-written text on the problem of peace fell flat, though it would have aroused considerable attention at some other time. Once again we note that propaganda should be continuous, should never relax, and must vary its themes with the tide of events.

The terms, the words, the subjects that propaganda utilizes must have in themselves the power to break the barrier of the individual's indifference. They must penetrate like bullets; they must spontaneously evoke a set of images and have a certain grandeur of their own. To circulate outdated words or pick new one that can penetrate only by force is unavailing, for timeliness furnishes the "operational words" with their explosive and affective power. Part of the power of propaganda is due to its use of the mass media, but this power will be dissipated if propaganda relies on operational words that have lost their force. In Western Europe, the word *Bolshevik* in 1925, the word *Fascist* in 1936, the word *Collaborator* in 1944, the word *Peace* in 1948, the word *Integration* in 1958, were all strong operational terms; they lost their shock value when their immediacy passed.

To the extent that propaganda is based on current news, it cannot permit time for thought or reflection. A man caught up in the news must remain on the surface of the event; he is carried along in the current, and can at no time take a respite to judge and appreciate; he can never stop to reflect. There is never any awareness—of himself, of his condition, of his society—for the man who lives by current events. Such a man never stops to investigate any one point, any more than he will tie together a series of news events. We already have mentioned man's inability to consider several facts or events simultaneously and to make a synthesis of them in order to face or to oppose them. One thought drives away another; old facts are chased by new ones. Under these conditions there can be no thought. And, in fact, modern man does not think about current problems; he feels them. He reacts, but he does not understand them any more than he takes responsibility for them. He is even less capable of spotting any inconsistency between successive facts; man's capacity to forget is unlimited. This is one of the most important and useful points for the propagandist, who can always be sure that a particular propaganda theme, statement, or event will be forgotten within a few weeks. Moreover, there is a spontaneous defensive reaction in the individual against an excess of information and—to the extent that he clings (unconsciously) to the unity of his own person—against inconsistencies. The best defense here is to forget the preceding event. In so doing, man denies his own continuity; to the same extent that he lives on the surface of events and makes today's events his life by obliterating yesterday's news, he refuses to see the contradictions in his own life and condemns himself to a life of successive moments, discontinuous and fragmented.[6]

This situation makes the "current-events man" a ready target for propaganda. Indeed, such a man is highly sensitive to the influence of present-day currents; lacking landmarks, he follows all currents. He is unstable because he runs after what happened today; he relates to the event, and therefore cannot resist any impulse coming from that event. Because he is immersed in current affairs, this man has a psychological weakness that puts him at the mercy of the propagandist. No confrontation ever occurs between the event and the truth; no relationship ever exists between the event and the person. Real information never concerns such a person. What could be more striking, more distressing, more decisive than the splitting of the atom, apart from the bomb itself? And yet this great development is kept in the background, behind the fleeting and spectacular result of some catastrophe or sports event because that is the superficial news the average man wants. Propaganda addresses itself to that man; like him, it can relate only to the most superficial aspect of a spectacular event, which alone can interest man and lead him to make a certain decision or adopt a certain attitude.

But here we must make an important qualification. The news

[6] All this is also true of those who claim to be "informed" because they read some weekly periodical filled with political revelations.

event may be a real fact, existing objectively, or it may be only an item of information, the dissemination of a supposed fact. What makes it news is its dissemination, not its objective reality. The problem of Berlin is a constant one, and for that reason it does not interest the public; it is not news. But when Khrushchev decrees that the problem is dramatic, that it merits the risk of war, that it must be solved immediately, and when he demands that the West yield, then (though there is objectively nothing new in Berlin), the question becomes news—only to disappear as soon as Khrushchev stops waving the threat. Remember that when this happened in 1961, it was for the fourth time.

The same thing occurred with Soviet agitation about supposed Turkish aggression plans in November 1957. An editorial in *Le Monde* on this subject contained a remark essentially as follows: "If the events of recent days can teach us a lesson, it is that we must not attach too much importance to the anxieties created by the proclamations of the Soviets. The supposed bacteriological warfare, among other examples, has shown that they are capable of carrying on a full campaign of agitation, of accusing others of the worst intentions and crimes, and of decreeing one fine day that the danger has passed, only to revive it several days or months later."

We shall examine elsewhere the problem of "fact" in the context of propaganda. But here we must emphasize that the current news to which a man is sensitive, in which he places himself, need have no objective or effective origins; in one way this greatly facilitates the work of propaganda. For propaganda can suggest, in the context of news, a group of "facts" which becomes actuality for a man who feels personally concerned. Propaganda can then exploit his concern for its own purposes.

Propaganda and the Undecided

All of the foregoing can be clarified by a brief examination of a question familiar to political scientists, that of the Undecided— those people whose opinions are vague, who form the great mass of citizens, and who constitute the most fertile public for the propagandist. The Undecided are not the Indifferent—those who say they are apolitical, or without opinion and who constitute no more than 10 percent of the population. The Undecided, far from being outside the group, are participants in the life of the group, but do not know what decision to make on problems that seem urgent to them. They are susceptible to the control of public opinion or attitudes, and the role of propaganda is to bring them under this control, transforming their potential into real effect. But that is possible only if an undecided man is "concerned" about the group he lives in. How is this revealed? What is the true situation of the Undecided?

One strong factor here is the individual's degree of integration in the collective life. Propaganda can play only on individuals more or less intensely involved in social currents. The isolated mountaineer or forester, having only occasional contact with society at the village market, is hardly sensitive to propaganda. For him it does not even exist. He will begin to notice it only when a strict regulation imposed on his activities changes his way of life, or when economic problems prevent him from selling his products in the usual way. This clash with society may open the doors to propaganda, but it will soon lose its effect again in the silence of the mountain or the forest.

Conversely, propaganda acts on the person embroiled in the conflicts of his time, who shares the "foci of interest" of his society. If I read a good newspaper advertisement for a particular automobile, I will not have the slightest interest in it if I am indifferent to automobiles. This advertisement can affect me only to the extent that I share, with my contemporaries, the mania for automobiles. A prior general interest must exist for propaganda to be effective. Propaganda is effective not when based on an *individual* prejudice, but when based on a *collective* center of interest, shared by the crowds.

That is why religious propaganda, for example, is not very successful; society as a whole is no longer interested in religious problems. At Byzantium, crowds fought in the streets over theological questions, so that in those days religious propaganda made sense. At present, only isolated individuals are interested in religion. It is part of their private opinions, and no real public opinion exists on this subject. On the other hand, propaganda related to technology is sure to arouse response, for everybody is as passionately interested in technology as in politics. Only within the limits of collective foci of interest can propaganda be effective.

We are not dealing here with prejudices or stereotypes, which imply minds that are already made up; we are dealing with foci of interest, where minds are not necessarily made up as yet. For example, politics is presently a focus of interest; it was not so in the twelfth century. The prejudices of the Right or the Left come later; that is already more individual, whereas the focus of interest on politics as such is truly collective. (Not individual prejudices, but the collective shared foci of interest are the best fields of action for propaganda.) Prejudices and stereotypes can be the result of a person's background, stemming from his education, work, environment, and so on; but the foci of interest are truly produced by the whole of society. Why is modern man obsessed with technology? One can answer that question only by an analysis of present-day society as a whole. This goes for all the centers of interest of contemporary man. It should be noted, incidentally, that these centers of interest are becoming more alike in all parts of the world. Thus a focus of political interest is developing among the Asian peoples, the Moslems, and the Africans. This expansion of interest inevitably entails a simultaneous expansion of propaganda, which may not be identical in all countries, but which will be able to operate in the same basic patterns and be related to the same centers of interest everywhere.

We now take up another basic trait of the social psychology of propaganda: the more intense the life of a group to which an individual belongs, the more active and effective propaganda is. A group in which feelings of belonging are weak, in which common objectives are imprecise or the structure is in the process of changing, in which conflicts are rare, and which is not tied to a collective focus of interest, cannot make valid propaganda either to its members or to those outside. But where the vitality of a group finds expression in the forms mentioned, it not only can make effective propaganda but also can make its members increasingly sensitive to propaganda in general. The more active and alive a group, the more its members will listen to propaganda and believe it.[7]

But this holds true only for propaganda by the group itself toward its members. If we go a bit further, we meet the connected

---

[7] The more the individual is integrated into a group, the more he is receptive to propaganda, and the more he is apt to participate in the political life of his group. The group does not even have to be solidly structured; thus, in a group of friends, when almost all vote the same way, there is little chance of any of them going astray. The friendly group involuntarily exerts pressure.

but more general problem of the intensity of collective life. Vigorous groups can definitely have a collective life of little intensity; conversely, weak groups can have an intense collective life. Historically we can observe that an intense collective life develops even while a society is disintegrating—as in the Roman Empire about the fourth century, in Germany at the time of the Weimar Republic, or in France today. Whether or not this collective life is wholesome matters little. What counts for propaganda is the intensity of that life, whatever its sources. In a trend toward social disintegration, this intensity predisposes individuals to accept propaganda without determining its meaning in advance. Such individuals are not prepared to accept this or that orientation, but they are more easily subjected to psychological pressure.

Furthermore, it matters little whether the intensity of such collective life is spontaneous or artificial. It can result from a striving, a restlessness, or a conviction deriving directly from social or political conditions, as in France in 1848, or in the medieval city-states. It can result from manipulation of the group, as in Fascist Italy or Nazi Germany. In all such cases the result is the same: the individual who is part of an intense collective life is prone to submit to the influence of propaganda. And anyone who succeeds in keeping aloof from the intense collective life is generally outside the influence of propaganda, because of his ability to escape that intensity.

Of course, the intensity is connected with the centers of interest; it is not an unformed or indeterminate current without direction. It is not just a haphazard explosion. Rather, it is a force for which the focus of interest is the compass needle. Social relations in the group are often very active because of its focus of interest: for example, the interest in politics invigorated social relations in all Europe during the nineteenth century. In any case, intensity will be greatest around such an interest. For example, an important center of interest today is one's profession; an individual who cares little for the social life of his group, his family life, or books reacts vigorously on the subject of his profession. And his reaction is not individual; it is the result of his participation in the group.

Thus we can present the following three principles:

(1) The propagandist must place his propaganda inside the limits of the foci of interest.

(2) The propagandist must understand that his propaganda

has the greatest chance for success where the collective life of the individuals he seeks to influence is most intense.

(3) The propagandist must remember that collective life is most intense where it revolves around a focus of interest.

On the basis of these principles the propagandist can reach the Undecided and act on the majority of 93 percent;[8] and only in connection with this mass of Undecided can one truly speak of ambiguity, majority effect, tension, frustration, and so on.

Propaganda and Truth

We have not yet considered a problem, familiar but too often ignored: the relationship between propaganda and truth or, rather, between propaganda and accuracy of facts. We shall speak henceforth of accuracy or reality, and not of "truth," which is an inappropriate term here.

The most generally held concept of propaganda is that it is a series of *tall stories*, a tissue of lies, and that lies are necessary for effective propaganda. Hitler himself apparently confirmed this point of view when he said that the bigger the lie, the more its chance of being believed. This concept leads to two attitudes among the public. The first is: "Of course we shall not be victims of propaganda because we are capable of distinguishing truth from falsehood." Anyone holding that conviction is extremely susceptible to propaganda, because when propaganda does tell the "truth," he is then convinced that it is no longer propaganda; moreover, his self-confidence makes him all the more vulnerable to attacks of which he is unaware.

The second attitude is: "We believe *nothing* that the enemy says because *everything* he says is necessarily untrue." But if the enemy can demonstrate that he has told the truth, a sudden turn in his favor will result. Much of the success of Communist propaganda in 1945–48 stemmed from the fact that as long as Communism was presented as the enemy, both in the Balkans and in the West, everything the Soviet Union said about its economic progress or its military strength was declared false. But after 1943,

---

[8] On the subject of this 93 percent, it is often stated—and opinion surveys tend to confirm this—that between 7 and 10 percent of all individuals consciously and voluntarily adhere to a trend, to a grouping, whereas about 90 percent fluctuate according to the circumstances. The first correct estimate of this apparently was made by Napoleon. It was revived by Hitler.

the visible military and economic strength of the Soviet Union led to a complete turnabout: "What the Soviet Union said in 1937 was true; therefore it always speaks the truth."

The idea that propaganda consists of lies (which makes it harmless and even a little ridiculous in the eyes of the public) is still maintained by some specialists; for example, Frederick C. Irion gives it as the basic trait in his definition of propaganda.[9] But it is certainly not so. For a long time propagandists have recognized that lying must be avoided.[1] "In propaganda, truth pays off"— this formula has been increasingly accepted. Lenin proclaimed it. And alongside Hitler's statement on lying one must place Goebbels's insistence that facts to be disseminated must be accurate.[2] How can we explain this contradiction? It seems that in propaganda we must make a radical distinction between a fact on the one hand and intentions or interpretations on the other; in brief, between the material and the moral elements. The truth that pays off is in the realm of *facts*. The necessary falsehoods, which also pay off, are in the realm of *intentions* and *interpretations*. This is a fundamental rule for propaganda analysis.

The Problem of Factuality. It is well known that veracity and exactness are important elements in advertising. The customer

[9] It is true that for a long time propaganda was made up of lies. In *Falsehood in Wartime,* Ponsonby said: "When war is declared truth is the first victim. . . . Falsehood is the most useful weapon in case of war." He revealed innumerable lies, deliberate or not, used during the war of 1914–18. Today, too, the propagandist may be a liar, he may invent stories about his adversaries, falsify statistics, create news, and so on. The public, however, is firmly convinced that such is *always* the case in propaganda; that propaganda is never true.

[1] Certain authors have strongly stressed this danger of falsehood: Alfred Sauvy shows that the "creative lie" can be justified only by success, and he recalls the famous words: "We shall win because we are the stronger." The public, when it recognizes a lie, will turn completely against its authors. Goebbels's great method for ruining English propaganda in 1940 was to recall England's 1916 propaganda lies, which had since been admitted. This cast doubt on English propaganda as a whole.

[2] This idea is now generally accepted. In the United States it is the Number One rule in propaganda manuals, except for unbelievable and harmful truths, about which it is better to be silent. SHAEF said in its manual: "When there is no compelling reason to suppress a fact, tell it. . . . Aside from considerations of military security, the only reason to suppress a piece of news is if it is unbelievable. . . . When the listener catches you in a lie, your power diminishes. . . . For this reason, never tell a lie which can be discovered." As far back as 1940 the American psychological services already had orders to tell the truth; in carrying them out, for example, they distributed the same newspapers to American and German soldiers. In the Communist bloc we find exactly the same attitude: Mao has always been very careful to state the facts exactly, including bad news. On the basis of Lenin's general theory of information, it is incorrect that the dissemination of false news

must be able to have confidence in the advertisement. When he has been deceived several times, the result is obviously unfavorable. That is why advertisers make it a rule to be accurate and organize a bureau of standards to denounce false claims. But here we refer to an essential factor: *experience*. The customer has good or bad experiences with a product. In political matters, however, personal experience is very rare, difficult to come by, and inconclusive. Thus one must distinguish between local facts, which can be checked, and others. Obviously, propaganda must respect local facts, otherwise it would destroy itself. It cannot hold out for long against local evidence unless the population is so securely in the palm of the propagandist's hand that he could say absolutely anything and still be believed; but that is a rare condition.

With regard to larger or more remote facts that cannot be the object of direct experience, one can say that accuracy is now generally respected in propaganda. One may concede, for example, that statistics given out by the Soviets or the Americans are accurate. There is little reason to falsify statistics. Similarly, there is no good reason to launch a propaganda campaign based on unbelievable or false facts. The best example of the latter was the Communist campaign on bacteriological warfare. Of course it was useful from certain points of view, and the true believers still believe what was said at the time. But among the Undecided it had a rather negative effect because of its extreme improbability and its contradictions. However, although many, especially in Western Europe, considered it a blunder, the campaign produced considerable credence in North Africa and India. Consequently, falsehood bearing on fact is neither entirely useless

---

does not create problems. French propagandists also have discovered that truthfulness is effective, and that it is better to spread a piece of bad news oneself than to wait until it is revealed by others.

There remains the problem of Goebbels's reputation. He wore the title of Big Liar (bestowed by Anglo-Saxon propaganda) and yet he never stopped battling for propaganda to be as accurate as possible. He preferred being cynical and brutal to being caught in a lie. He used to say: "Everybody must know what the situation is." He was always the first to announce disastrous events or difficult situations, without hiding anything. The result was a general belief, between 1939 and 1942, that German communiqués not only were more concise, clearer, and less cluttered, but were more truthful than Allied communiqués (American and neutral opinion)—and, furthermore, that the Germans published all the news two or three days before the Allies. All this is so true that pinning the title of Big Liar on Goebbels must be considered quite a propaganda success.

nor to be strictly avoided. Nevertheless, bear in mind that it is increasingly rare.[3]

Three qualifications of this statement must be made. First of all, propaganda can effectively rest on a claim that some fact is *untrue* which may actually *be true* but is difficult to prove. Khrushchev made a specialty of this kind of operation; he denounced lies on the part of his predecessors in order to give a ring of truth to his own pronouncements. Thus, when he called Malenkov an "inveterate liar" before the Central Committee of the Communist Party in December 1958 and declared that Malenkov's statistics were false, there was no reason to believe Khrushchev more than Malenkov. But the foray made sense. First of all, as Khrushchev was denouncing a lie, it seemed that he must, therefore, be telling the truth. Secondly, by lowering the figures given by Malenkov, Khrushchev could show a much higher rise in production since 1952. If it is true that in 1958, 9.2 billion pounds of grain were produced, and if Malenkov's figure of 8 billion in 1952 was accurate, that meant a 15 percent increase in six years. If, however, the 1952 figure was only 5.6 billion, as Khrushchev claimed, that meant an increase of 75 percent—a triumph. It seems more reasonable to consider Malenkov's figures accurate, rather than Khrushchev's—until proved otherwise.[4]

A second qualification obviously concerns the *presentation* of facts; when these are used by propaganda, one is asked to swallow the bald fact as accurate. Also, most of the time the fact is presented in such a fashion that the listener or reader cannot really understand it or draw any conclusions from it. For example, a figure may be given without reference to anything, without a correlation or a percentage or a ratio. One states that production has risen by 30 percent, without indicating the base year, or that the standard of living has risen by 15 percent, without indicating how it is calculated, or that such and such a movement has grown by so many people, without giving figures for previous years. The lack

---

[3] As we have emphasized, such lies must not be told except about completely unverifiable facts. For example, Goebbels's lies could be on the successes achieved by German U-boats, because only the captain of the U-boat knew if he had sunk a ship or not. It was easy to spread detailed news on such a subject without fear of contradiction.

[4] This evaluation, written in 1959, has been proved true since we learned (in 1961) of the disaster of Soviet agriculture.

of coherence and cohesion of such data is entirely deliberate.[5] Of course, starting with such data, it is not impossible to reconstruct the whole; with much patience, work, and research, one can bring order into such facts and relate them to each other. But that is a job for a specialist, and the results would not appear until long after the propaganda action had obtained its effect. Besides, they would be published as a technical study and be seen by only a handful of readers. Therefore, the publication of a true fact in its raw state is not dangerous. When it would be dangerous to let a fact be known, the modern propagandist prefers to hide it, to say nothing rather than to lie. About one fifth of all press directives given by Goebbels between 1939 and 1944 were orders to keep silent on one subject or another. Soviet propaganda acts the same way. Well-known facts are simply made to disappear; occasionally they are discovered after much delay. The famous Khrushchev report to the Twentieth Congress is an example: the Communist press in France, Italy, and elsewhere simply did not speak of it for weeks. Similarly, the Egyptian people did not learn of the events in Hungary until May 1960; up to that time the Egyptian press had not said one word about them. Another example is Khrushchev's silence on the Chinese communes in his report to the Central Committee of the Communist Party in December 1958.

Silence is also one way to pervert known facts by modifying their context. There were admirable examples of this in the propaganda against Mendès-France. Propaganda said: Mendès-France has abandoned Indochina, Mendès-France has abandoned Tunisia, Mendès-France has liquidated the French banks in India, and so on. Those were the plain facts. But there was complete silence on past policies in Indochina, past events in Morocco that had led to events in Tunisia, and agreements on Indian banks signed by the preceding government.[6]

Finally, there is the use of accurate facts by propaganda. Based on them, the mechanism of suggestion can work best. Americans call this technique innuendo. Facts are treated in such a fashion that they draw their listener into an irresistible sociological current. The public is left to draw obvious conclusions

---

[5] Sauvy states that this type of propaganda consists in "respecting detail in order to eventually compose a static whole which gives misleading information on the movement. Thus . . . truth becomes the principal form of Falsehood."

[6] This technique, called *selection* by American authors, leads to an effective distortion of reality. The propagandist automatically chooses the array of facts which will be favorable to him and distorts them by using them out of context.

from a cleverly presented truth,[7] and the great majority comes to the same conclusions. To obtain this result, propaganda must be based on some truth that can be said in few words and is able to linger in the collective consciousness. In such cases the enemy cannot go against the tide, which he might do if the basis of the propaganda were a lie or the sort of truth requiring a proof to make it stick. On the contrary, the enemy now must provide proof, but it no longer changes the conclusions that the propagandee already has drawn from the suggestions.

Intentions and Interpretations. This is the real realm of the lie; but it is exactly here that it cannot be detected. If one falsifies a fact, one may be confronted with unquestionable proof to the contrary. (To deny that torture was used in Algeria became increasingly difficult.) But no proof can be furnished where motivations or intentions are concerned or interpretation of a fact is involved. A fact has different significance, depending on whether it is analyzed by a bourgeois economist or a Soviet economist, a liberal historian, a Christian historian, or a Marxist historian. The difference is even greater when a phenomenon created deliberately by propaganda is involved. How can one suspect a man who talks peace of having the opposite intent—without incurring the wrath of public opinion? And if the same man starts a war, he can always say that the others forced it on him, that events proved stronger than his intentions. We forget that between 1936 and 1939 Hitler made many speeches about his desire for peace, for the peaceful settlement of all problems, for conferences. He never expressed an explicit desire for war. Naturally, he was arming because of "encirclement." And, in fact, he did manage to get a declaration of war from France and England; so *he* was not the one who started the war.[8]

---

[7] The only element in the publication of a fact which one must scrupulously take into account is its probability or credibility. Much news was suppressed during the war because it would not have been believed by the public; it would have been branded as pure propaganda. A 1942 incident is an excellent example of this. At the moment of Montgomery's decisive victory in North Africa, Rommel was absent. The Nazis had not expected an attack at that time and had called Rommel back to Germany. But Goebbels gave the order not to reveal this fact because everybody would have considered it a lie to explain the defeat and prove that Rommel had not really been beaten. Truth was not probable enough to be told.

[8] The confusion between judgment of fact and judgment of value occurs at the level of these qualifications of fact and interpretation. For example: All bombings by the enemy are acts of savagery aimed only at civilian objectives, whereas all bombings by one's own planes are proof of one's superiority, and they never destroy anything but military objectives. Similarly, when another government shows good will, it is a sign of weakness; when it shows authority, it wants war or dictatorship.

Propaganda by its very nature is an enterprise for perverting the significance of events and of insinuating false intentions. There are two salient aspects of this fact. First of all, the propagandist must insist on the purity of his own intentions and, at the same time, hurl accusations at his enemy. But the accusation is never made haphazardly or groundlessly.[9] The propagandist will not accuse the enemy of just any misdeed; he will accuse him of the very intention that he himself has and of trying to commit the very crime that he himself is about to commit. He who wants to provoke a war not only proclaims his own peaceful intentions but also accuses the other party of provocation. He who uses concentration camps accuses his neighbor of doing so. He who intends to establish a dictatorship always insists that his adversaries are bent on dictatorship. The accusation aimed at the other's intention clearly reveals the intention of the accuser. But the public cannot see this because the revelation is interwoven with facts.

The mechanism used here is to slip from the facts, which would demand factual judgment, to moral terrain and to ethical judgment. At the time of Suez the confusion of the two levels in Egyptian and progressivist propaganda was particularly successful: Nasser's intentions were hidden behind the fully revealed intentions of the French and English governments. Such an example, among many others, permits the conclusion that even intelligent people can be made to swallow professed intentions by well-executed propaganda. The breadth of the Suez propaganda operation can be compared only with that which succeeded at the time of Munich, when there was the same inversion of the interpretation of facts. We also find exactly the same process in the propaganda of the F.L.N. in France and in that of Fidel Castro.

The second element of falsehood is that the propagandist naturally cannot reveal the true intentions of the principal for whom he acts: government, party chief, general, company director. Propaganda never can reveal its true projects and plans or

---

[9] Because political problems are difficult and often confusing, and their significance and their import not obvious, the propagandist can easily present them in *moral* language—and here we leave the realm of fact, to enter into that of passion. Facts, then, come to be discussed in the language of *indignation*, a tone which is almost always the mark of propaganda.

divulge government secrets. That would be to submit the projects to public discussion, to the scrutiny of public opinion, and thus to prevent their success. More serious, it would make the projects vulnerable to enemy action by forewarning him so that he could take all the proper precautions to make them fail. Propaganda must serve instead as a veil for such projects, masking true intentions.[1] It must be in effect a smokescreen. Maneuvers take place behind protective screens of words on which public attention is fixed. Propaganda is necessarily a declaration of one's intentions. It is a declaration of purity that will never be realized, a declaration of peace, of truth, of social justice. Of course, one must not be too precise at the top level, or promise short-term reforms, for it would be risky to invite a comparison between what was promised and what was done. Such comparison would be possible if propaganda operated in the realm of future fact. Therefore, it should be confined to intentions, to the moral realm, to values, to generalities. And if some angry man were to point out the contradictions, in the end his argument would carry no weight with the public.

Propaganda is necessarily false when it speaks of values, of *truth*, of *good*, of *justice*, of *happiness*—and when it interprets and colors facts and imputes meaning to them. It is true when it serves up the plain fact, but does so only for the sake of establishing a pretense and only as an example of the interpretation that it supports with that fact. When Khrushchev made his great claims in 1957, proving that the Soviet Union was catching up with the United States in the production of consumer goods, he cited several figures to prove that the growth of agricultural production over ten years showed such a trend. On the basis of these figures he concluded that in 1958 the Soviets would have as much butter as the United States (which even in 1959 was still not true); and that in 1960 they would have as much meat (in 1959 they

---

[1] Many authors have stressed this role of covert propaganda. Speier says that the role of the propagandist is to hide political reality by talking about it. Sauvy says that the propagandist administers the anesthetic so the surgeon can operate without public interference. This is why, in many cases, according to Mégret, complete secrecy is a handicap to the propagandist; he must be free to speak, for only then can he sufficiently confuse things, reveal elements too disconnected to be put together, and so on. He must keep the public from understanding reality, while giving the public the opposite impression, that it understands everything clearly. Riess says he must give the public distorted news and intentions, knowing clearly beforehand what conclusions the public will draw from them.

were very far from it). And he provoked his audience to laughter by ridiculing his economists, who estimated that such levels would not be reached until 1975. At that moment he drew a veil over reality in the very act of interpreting it.

Lies about intentions and interpretations permit the integration of the diverse methods of propaganda. In fact Hitler's propaganda was able to make the lie a precise and systematic instrument, designed to transform certain values, to modify certain current concepts, to provoke psychological twists in the individual. The lie was the essential instrument for that, but this was not just a falsification of some figure or fact. As Hermann Rauschning shows, it was falsehood in depth.[2] Stalinist propaganda was the same. On the other hand, American and Leninist propaganda[3] seek the truth, but they resemble the preceding types of propaganda in that they provoke a general system of false claims. When the United States poses as the defender of liberty —of all, everywhere and always—it uses a system of false representation. When the Soviet Union poses as the defender of true democracy, it is also employing a system of false representation. But the lies are not always deliberately set up; they may be an expression of a belief, of good faith—which leads to a lie regarding intentions because the belief is only a rationalization, a veil drawn deliberately over a reality one wishes not to see. Thus it is possible that when the United States makes its propaganda for freedom, it really *thinks* it is defending freedom; and that the Soviet Union, when presenting itself as the champion of democracy, really *imagines* itself to be a champion of democracy. But these beliefs lead definitely to false claims, due in part to propaganda itself. Certainly a part of the success of Communist propaganda against capitalism comes from the effective denunciation of capitalism's claims; the false "truth" of Communist propaganda consists in exposing the contradiction between the values stressed by the bourgeois society (the virtue of work, the family, liberty, political democracy) and the reality of that society

---

[2] Except that Goebbels used falsehood very subtly to discredit the enemy; he secretly disseminated false news about Germany to enemy intelligence agents; then he proved publicly that their news was false, thus that the enemy lied.

[3] Alex Inkeles has emphasized that Lenin did not have the same cynical attitude towards the masses as did Hitler, and that he was less concerned with technique than with the "truth of the message."

(poverty, unemployment, and so on). These values are false because they are only claims of self-justification. But the Communist system expresses false claims of the same kind.

Propaganda feeds, develops, and spreads the system of false claims—lies aimed at the complete transformation of minds, judgments, values, and actions (and constituting a frame of reference for systematic falsification). When the eyeglasses are out of focus, everything one sees through them is distorted. This was not always so in the past. The difference today lies in the voluntary and deliberate character of inaccurate representation circulated by propaganda. While we credit the United States and the Soviet Union with some good faith in their beliefs, as soon as a system of propaganda is organized around false claims, all good faith disappears, the entire operation becomes self-conscious, and the falsified values are recognized for what they are. The lie reveals itself to the liar. One cannot make propaganda in pretended good faith. Propaganda reveals our hoaxes even as it encloses and hardens us into this system of hoaxes from which we can no longer escape.

Having analyzed these traits, we can now advance a definition of propaganda—not an exhaustive definition, unique and exclusive of all others, but at least a partial one: *Propaganda is a set of methods employed by an organized group that wants to bring about the active or passive participation in its actions of a mass of individuals, psychologically unified through psychological manipulations and incorporated in an organization.*

3. *Categories of Propaganda*

Despite a general belief, propaganda is not a simple phenomenon, and one cannot lump together all of its forms. Types of propaganda can be distinguished by the regimes that employ them. Soviet propaganda and American propaganda do not resemble each other either in method or in psychological technique. Hitler's propaganda was very different from present-day Chinese propaganda, but it substantially resembled Stalinist propaganda. The propaganda of the F.L.N. in Algeria cannot be compared to French propaganda. Even within the same regime completely different conceptions can co-exist; the Soviet Union is the most striking example of this. The propagandas of Lenin, Stalin, and Khrushchev offer three types which differ in their techniques, in their themes, and in their symbolism; so much so that when we set up too narrow a frame for the definition of propaganda, part of the phenomenon eludes us. Those who think of Soviet propaganda only as it was under Stalin are inclined to say that Khrushchev does not make propaganda. But Khrushchev's propaganda was as extensive as Stalin's and perhaps more so; he carried certain propaganda techiques to their very limits. But aside from these political and external categories of propaganda, one must define other differences that rest on certain internal traits of propaganda.

Political Propaganda and Sociological Propaganda

First we must distinguish between political propaganda and sociological propaganda. We shall not dwell long on the former because it is the type called immediately to mind by the word propaganda itself. It involves techniques of influence employed by a government, a party, an administration, a pressure group, with a view to changing the behavior of the public. The choice of methods used is deliberate and calculated; the desired goals are clearly distinguished and quite precise, though generally limited. Most often the themes and the objectives are political, as for example with Hitler's or Stalin's propaganda. This is the type of propaganda that can be most clearly distinguished from advertising: the latter has economic ends, the former political ends. Political propaganda can be either strategic or tactical. The former establishes the general line, the array of arguments, the staggering of the campaigns; the latter seeks to obtain immediate results within that framework (such as wartime pamphlets and loudspeakers to obtain the immediate surrender of the enemy).

But this does not cover all propaganda, which also encompasses phenomena much more vast and less certain: the group of manifestations by which any society seeks to integrate the maximum number of individuals into itself, to unify its members' behavior according to a pattern, to spread its style of life abroad, and thus to impose itself on other groups. We call this phenomenon "sociological" propaganda, to show, first of all, that the entire group, consciously or not, expresses itself in this fashion; and to indicate, secondly, that its influence aims much more at an entire style of life than at opinions or even one particular course of behavior.[4]

Of course, within the compass of sociological propaganda itself one or more political propagandas can be expressed. The propaganda of Christianity in the middle ages is an example of this type of sociological propaganda; Benjamin Constant meant just this when he said of France, in 1793: "The entire nation was a vast propaganda operation." And in present times certainly the most accomplished models of this type are American and Chinese propaganda. Although we do not include here the more or less effective campaigns and methods employed by governments, but rather the over-all phenomenon, we find that sociological propaganda combines extremely diverse forms within itself. At this level, advertising as the spreading of a certain style of life can be said to be included in such propaganda, and in the United States this is also true of public relations, human relations, human engineering, the motion pictures, and so on. It is characteristic of a nation living by sociological propaganda that all these influences converge toward the same point, whereas in a society such as France in 1960, they are divergent in their objectives and their intentions.

Sociological propaganda is a phenomenon much more difficult to grasp than political propaganda, and is rarely discussed. *Basically it is the penetration of an ideology by means of its sociological context.* This phenomenon is the reverse of what we have been studying up to now. Propaganda as it is traditionally known implies an attempt to spread an ideology through the mass media of communication in order to lead the public to accept some political or economic structure or to participate in some action. That is the one element common to all the propaganda we have studied. Ideology is disseminated for the purpose of making various political acts acceptable to the people.

But in sociological propaganda the movement is reversed. The existing economic, political, and sociological factors progressively allow an ideology to penetrate individuals or masses. Through the

---

[4] This notion is a little broader than that of Doob on unintentional propaganda. Doob includes in the term the involuntary effects obtained by the propagandist. He is the first to have stressed the possibility of this unintentional character of propaganda, contrary to all American thought on the subject, except for David Krech and Richard S. Crutchfield, who go even further in gauging the range of unintentional propaganda, which they even find in books on mathematics.

medium of economic and political structures a certain ideology is established, which leads to the active participation of the masses and the adaptation of individuals. The important thing is to make the individual participate actively and to adapt him as much as possible to a specific sociological context.

Such propaganda is essentially diffuse. It is rarely conveyed by catchwords or expressed intentions. Instead it is based on a general climate, an atmosphere that influences people imperceptibly without having the appearance of propaganda; it gets to man through his customs, through his most unconscious habits. It creates new habits in him; it is a sort of persuasion from within. As a result, man adopts new criteria of judgment and choice, adopts them spontaneously, as if he had chosen them himself. But all these criteria are in conformity with the environment and are essentially of a collective nature. Sociological propaganda produces a progressive adaptation to a certain order of things, a certain concept of human relations, which unconsciously molds individuals and makes them conform to society.

Sociological propaganda springs up spontaneously; it is not the result of deliberate propaganda action. No propagandists deliberately use this method, though many practice it unwittingly, and tend in this direction without realizing it. For example, when an American producer makes a film, he has certain definite ideas he wants to express, which are not intended to be propaganda. Rather, the propaganda element is in the American way of life with which he is permeated and which he expresses in his film without realizing it. We see here the force of expansion of a vigorous society, which is totalitarian in the sense of the integration of the individual, and which leads to involuntary behavior.

Sociological propaganda expresses itself in many different ways —in advertising, in the movies (commercial and non-political films), in technology in general, in education, in the *Reader's Digest;* and in social service, case work, and settlement houses. All these influences are in basic accord with each other and lead spontaneously in the same direction; one hesitates to call all this propaganda. Such influences, which mold behavior, seem a far cry from Hitler's great propaganda setup. Unintentional (at least in the first stage), non-political, organized along spontaneous patterns and rhythms, the activities we have lumped together (from a concept that might be judged arbitrary or artificial) are not considered propaganda by either sociologists or the average public.

And yet with deeper and more objective analysis, what does one find? These influences are expressed through the same media as propaganda. They are *really directed* by those who make propaganda. To me this fact seems essential. A government, for example, will have its own public relations, and will also make propaganda. Most of the activities described in this chapter have identical purposes. Besides, these influences follow the same stereotypes and prejudices as propaganda; they stir the same feelings and act on the individual in the same fashion. These are the similarities, which bring these two aspects of propaganda closer together, more than the differences, noted earlier, separate them.

But there is more. Such activities are propaganda to the extent that the combination of advertising, public relations, social welfare, and so on produces a certain general conception of society, a particular way of life. We have not grouped these activities together arbitrarily—they express the same basic notions and interact to make man adopt this particular way of life. From then on, the individual in the clutches of such sociological propaganda believes that those who live this way are on the side of the angels, and those who don't are bad; those who have this conception of society are right, and those who have another conception are in error. Consequently, just as with ordinary propaganda, it is a matter of propagating behavior and myths both good and bad. Furthermore, such propaganda becomes increasingly effective when those subjected to it accept its doctrines on what is *good or bad* (for example, the American Way of Life). There, a whole society actually expresses itself through this propaganda by advertising its kind of life.

By doing that, a society engages in propaganda on the deepest level. Sociologists have recognized that, above all, propaganda must change a person's environment. Krech and Crutchfield insist on this fact, and show that a simple modification of the psychological context can bring about changes of attitude without ever directly attacking particular attitudes or opinions. Similarly, MacDougall says: "One must avoid attacking any trend frontally. It is better to concentrate one's efforts on the creation of psychological conditions so that the desired result seems to come from them naturally." The modification of the psychological climate brings about still other consequences that one cannot obtain directly. This is what Ogle calls "suggestibility"; the degree of suggestibility depends on a man's environment and psychological climate. And that is precisely what modifies the activities mentioned above. It is what makes them propaganda, for their aim is simply to instill in the public an attitude that will prepare the ground for the main propaganda to follow.

Sociological propaganda must act gently. It conditions; it introduces a truth, an ethic in various benign forms, which, although sporadic, end by creating a fully established personality structure. It acts slowly, by penetration, and is most effective in a relatively stable and active society, or in the tensions between an expanding society and one that is disintegrating (or in an expanding group within a disintegrating society). Under these conditions it is sufficient in itself; it is not merely a preliminary sub-propaganda. But sociological propaganda is inadequate in a moment of crisis. Nor is it able to move the masses to action in exceptional circumstances. Therefore, it must sometimes be strengthened by the classic kind of propaganda, which leads to action.

At such times sociological propaganda will appear to be the medium that has prepared the ground for direct propaganda; it becomes identified with sub-propaganda. Nothing is easier than to graft a direct propaganda onto a setting prepared by sociological propaganda; besides, sociological propaganda may itself be transformed into direct propaganda. Then, by a series of intermediate stages, we not only see one turn into the other, but also a smooth transition from what was merely a spontaneous affirmation of a way of life to the deliberate affirmation of a truth. This process has been described in an article by Edward L. Bernays: this so-called "engineering approach" is tied to a combination of professional research methods through which one gets people to adopt and actively support certain ideas or programs as soon as they become aware of them. This applies also to political matters; and since 1936 the National Association of Manufacturers has attempted to fight the development of leftist trends with such methods. In 1938 the N.A.M. spent a half-million dollars to support the type of capitalism it represents. This sum was increased to three million in 1945 and to five million in 1946; this propaganda paved the way for the Taft-Hartley Law. It was a matter of "selling" the American economic system. Here we are truly in the domain of propaganda; and we see the multiple methods employed to influence opinion, as well as the strong tie between sociological and direct propaganda.

Sociological propaganda, involuntary at first, becomes more and more deliberate, and ends up by exercising influence. One example is the code drawn up by the Motion Picture Association, which requires films to promote "the highest types of social life," "the proper conception of society," "the proper standards of life," and to avoid "any ridicule of the law (natural or human) or sympathy for those who violate the law." Another is J. Arthur Rank's explanation of the purpose of his films: "When does an export article become more than an export article? When it is a British film. When the magnificent productions of Ealing Studios appear in the world, they represent something better than just a step forward toward a higher level of export. . . ." Such films are then propaganda for the British way of life.

The first element of awareness in the context of sociological propaganda is extremely simple, and from it everything else derives. What starts out as a simple situation gradually turns into a definite ideology, because the way of life in which man thinks he is so indisputably well off becomes a criterion of value for him. This does not mean that objectively he *is* well off, but that, regardless of the merits of his actual condition, he *thinks* he is. He is perfectly adapted to his environment, like "a fish in water." From that moment on, everything that expresses this particular way of life, that reinforces and improves it, is *good*; everything that tends to disturb, criticize, or destroy it is *bad*.

This leads people to believe that the civilization representing their way of life is best. This belief then commits the French to the same course as the Americans, who are by far the most advanced in this direction. Obviously, one tries to imitate and catch up to those who are furthest advanced; the first one becomes the model. And such imitation makes the French adopt the same criteria of judgment, the same sociological structures, the same spontaneous ideologies, and, in the end, the same type of man. Sociological propaganda is then a precise form of propaganda; it is comparatively simple because it uses all social currents, but is slower than other types of propaganda because it aims at long-term penetration and progressive adaptation.

But from the instant a man uses that way of life as his criterion of good and evil, he is led to make judgments: for example, anything un-American is evil. From then on, genuine propaganda limits itself to the use of this tendency and to leading man into actions of either compliance with or defense of the established order.

This sociological propaganda in the United States is a natural result of the fundamental elements of American life. In the beginning, the United States had to unify a disparate population that came from all the countries of Europe and had diverse traditions and tendencies. A way of rapid assimilation had to be found; that was the great political problem of the United States at the end of the nineteenth century. The solution was psychological standardization—that is, simply to use a way of life as the basis of unification and as an instrument of propaganda. In addition, this uniformity plays another decisive role—an economic role— in the life of the United States; it determines the extent of the American market. Mass production requires mass consumption, but there cannot be mass consumption without widespread identical views as to what the necessities of life are. One must be sure that the market will react rapidly and massively to a given proposal or suggestion. One therefore needs fundamental psychological unity on which advertising can play with certainty when manipulating public opinion. And in order for public opinion to respond, it must be convinced of the excellence of all that is "American." Thus conformity of life and conformity of thought are indissolubly linked.

But such conformity can lead to unexpected extremes. Given American liberalism and the confidence of Americans in their economic strength and their political system, it is difficult to understand the "wave of collective hysteria" which occurred after 1948 and culminated in McCarthyism. That hysteria probably sprang from a vague feeling of ideological weakness, a certain inability to define the foundations of American society. That is why Americans seek to define the American way of life, to make it conscious, explicit, theoretical, worthy. Therefore the soul-searching and inflexibility, with excessive affirmations designed to mask the weakness of the ideological position. All this obviously constitutes an ideal framework for organized propaganda.

We encounter such organized propaganda on many levels: on the government level, for one. Then there are the different pressure groups: the Political Action Committee, the American Medical Association, the American Bar Association, the National Small Business Men's Association—all have as their aim the defense of the private interests of the Big Three: Big Business, Big Labor, and Big Agriculture. Other groups aim at social and political reforms: the American Legion, the League of Women Voters, and the like. These groups employ lobbying to influence the government and the classic forms of propaganda to influence the public; through films, meetings, and radio, they try to make the public aware of their ideological aims.

Another very curious and recent phenomenon (confirmed by several American sociologists) is the appearance of "agitators" alongside politicians and political propagandists. The pure agitator, who stirs public opinion in a "disinterested" fashion, functions as a nationalist. He does not appeal to a doctrine or principle, nor does he propose specific reforms. He is the "true" prophet of the American Way of Life. Usually he is against the New Deal and for laissez-faire liberalism; against plutocrats, internationalists, and socialists—bankers and Communists alike are the "hateful other party in spite of which well-informed 'I' survives." The agitator is especially active in the most unorganized groups of the United States. He uses the anxiety psychoses of the lower middle class, the neo-proletarian, the immigrant, the demobilized soldier —people who are not yet integrated into American society or who have not yet adopted ready-made habits and ideas. The agitator uses the American Way of Life to provoke anti-Semitic, anti-Communist, anti-Negro, and xenophobic currents of opinion. He makes groups act in the illogical yet coherent, Manichaean universe of propaganda, of which we will have more to say. The most remarkable thing about this phenomenon is that these agitators do not work for a political party; it is not clear which interests they serve. They are neither Capitalists nor Communists, but they deeply influence American public opinion, and their influence may crystalize suddenly in unexpected forms.

The more conscious such sociological propaganda is, the more it tends to express itself externally, and hence to expand its influence abroad, as for example in Europe. It frequently retains its sociological character, and thus does not appear to be pure and simple propaganda. There is no doubt, for example, that the Marshall Plan—which was above all a real form of aid to underdeveloped countries—also had propaganda elements, such as the spreading of American products and films coupled with publicity about what the United States was doing to aid underprivileged nations. These two aspects of indirect propaganda are altogether sociological. But they may be accompanied by specific propaganda, as when, in 1948, subsidies of fifteen million dollars were poured into American publications appearing in Europe. The French edition of the New York *Herald Tribune* stated that it received important sums in Marshall credits for the purpose of making American propaganda. Along with reviews specializing in propaganda, such as *France-Amérique,* and with film centers and libraries sponsored by the Americans in Europe, we should include the *Reader's Digest,* whose circulation has reached millions of copies per issue in Europe and is so successful that it no longer needs a subsidy.

However, the success of such American propaganda is very uneven. Technical publications have an assured audience, but bulletins and brochures have little effect because the Americans have a "superiority complex," which expresses itself in such publications and displeases foreigners. The presentation of the American Way of Life as the only way to salvation exasperates French opinion and makes such propaganda largely ineffective in France. At the same time, French opinion has been won over by the obvious superiority of American technical methods.

All forms of sociological propaganda are obviously very diffuse, and aimed much more at the promulgation of ideas and prejudices, of a style of life, than of a doctrine, or at inciting action or calling for formal adherence. They represent a penetration in depth until a precise point is struck at which action will occur. It should be noted, for example, that in all the French *départements* in which there were Americans and propaganda bureaus, the number of Communist voters decreased between 1951 and 1953.

Propaganda of Agitation and Propaganda of Integration

The second great distinction within the general phenomenon of propaganda is the distinction between propaganda of agitation and propaganda of integration. Here we find such a *summa divisio* that we may ask ourselves: if the methods, themes, characteristics, publics, and objectives are so different, are we not really dealing with two separate entities rather than two aspects of the same phenomenon?

This distinction corresponds in part to the well-known distinction of Lenin between "agitation" and "propaganda"—but here the meaning of these terms is reversed. It is also somewhat similar to the distinction between propaganda of subversion (with regard to an enemy) and propaganda of collaboration (with the same enemy).

Propaganda of agitation, being the most visible and widespread, generally attracts all the attention. It is most often subversive propaganda and has the stamp of opposition. It is led by a party seeking to destroy the government or the established order. It seeks rebellion or war. It has always had a place in the course of history. All revolutionary movements, all popular wars have been nourished by such propaganda of agitation. Spartacus relied on this kind of propaganda, as did the communes, the Crusades, the French movement of 1793, and so on. But it reached its height with Lenin, which leads us to note that, though it is most often an opposition's propaganda, the propaganda of agitation can also be made by government. For example, when a government wants to galvanize energies to mobilize the entire nation for war, it will use a propaganda of agitation. At that moment the subversion is aimed at the enemy, whose strength must be destroyed by psychological as well as physical means, and whose force must be overcome by the vigor of one's own nation.

Governments also employ this propaganda of agitation when, after having been installed in power, they want to pursue a revolutionary course of action. Thus Lenin, having installed the Soviets, organized the agitprops and developed the long campaign of agitation in Russia to conquer resistance and crush the kulaks. In such a case, subversion aims at the resistance of a segment or a class, and an internal enemy is chosen for attack. Similarly, most of Hitler's propaganda was propaganda of agitation. Hitler could work his sweeping social and economic transformations only by constant agitation, by overexcitement, by straining energies to the utmost. Nazism grew by successive waves of feverish enthusiasm and thus attained its revolutionary objectives. Finally, the great campaigns in Communist China were precisely propaganda of agitation. Only such propaganda could produce those "great leaps forward." The system of the communes was accepted only because of propaganda of agitation which unleashed simultaneously physical action by the population and a change in their behavior, by subverting habits, customs, and beliefs that were obstacles to the "great leap forward." This was internal propaganda. And Mao was perfectly right in saying that the enemy is found within each person.[5] Propaganda of agitation addresses itself, then, to internal elements in each of us, but it is always translated into reality by physical involvement in a tense and overexcited activity. By making the individual participate in this activity, the propagandist releases the internal brakes, the psychological barriers of habit, belief, and judgment.

The *Piatiletka* campaign in the Soviet Union must also be classified as propaganda of agitation. Like the Chinese campaign, its aim was to stretch energies to the maximum in order to obtain the highest possible work output. Thus for a while propaganda of agitation can serve productivity, and the principal examples of propaganda of agitation conducted by governments are of that type. But agitation propaganda most often is revolutionary propaganda in the ordinary sense of the term. Thus Communist propaganda in the West, which provokes strikes or riots, is of this type. The propaganda of Fidel Castro, that of Ho Chi Minh before he seized power, and that of the F.L.N. are the most typical recent examples.

In all cases, propaganda of agitation tries to stretch energies to the utmost, obtain substantial sacrifices, and induce the individual to bear heavy ordeals. It takes him out of his everyday life, his normal framework, and plunges him into enthusiasm and adventure; it opens to him hitherto unsuspected possibilities, and suggests extraordinary goals that nevertheless seem to him completely within reach. Propaganda of agitation thus unleashes an explosive movement; it operates inside a crisis or actually provokes the crisis itself. On the other hand, such propaganda can obtain only effects of relatively short duration. If the proposed objective is not achieved fast enough, enthusiasm will give way to discouragement and despair. Therefore, specialists in agitation propaganda break up the desired goals into a series of stages to be reached one by one. There is a period of pressure to obtain some result, then a period of relaxation and rest; this is how Hitler, Lenin, and Mao operated. A people or a party cannot be kept too long at the highest level of sacrifice, conviction, and devotion.

---

[5] Mao's theory of the "mold." See below, Appendix II.

The individual cannot be made to live in a state of perpetual enthusiasm and insecurity. After a certain amount of combat he needs a respite and a familiar universe to which he is accustomed.

This subversive propaganda of agitation is obviously the flashiest: it attracts attention because of its explosive and revolutionary character. It is also the easiest to make; in order to succeed, it need only be addressed to the most simple and violent sentiments through the most elementary means. Hate is generally its most profitable resource. It is extremely easy to launch a revolutionary movement based on hatred of a particular enemy. Hatred is probably the most spontaneous and common sentiment; it consists of attributing one's misfortunes and sins to "another," who must be killed in order to assure the disappearance of those misfortunes and sins. Whether the object of hatred is the bourgeois, the Communist, the Jew, the colonialist, or the saboteur makes no difference. Propaganda of agitation succeeds each time it designates someone as the source of all misery, provided that he is not too powerful.

Of course, one cannot draw basic conclusions from a movement launched in this way. It is extraordinary to see intellectuals, for example, take anti-white sentiments of Algerians or Negroes seriously and believe that these express fundamental feelings. To label the white man (who is the invader and the exploiter, it is true) as the source of all ills, and to provoke revolts against him, is an extremely easy job; but it proves neither that the white man *is* the source of all evil nor that the Negro automatically hates him. However, hatred once provoked continues to reproduce itself.

Along with this universal sentiment, found in all propaganda of agitation (even when provoked by the government, and even in the movement of the Chinese communes), are secondary motives more or less adapted to the circumstances. A sure expedient is the call to liberty among an oppressed, conquered, invaded, or colonized people: calls summoning the Cuban or Algerian people to liberty, for example, are assured of sympathy and support. The same is true for the promise of bread to the hungry, the promise of land to the plundered, and the call to truth among the religious.

As a whole these are appeals to simple, elementary sentiments requiring no refinement, and thanks to which the propagandist can

gain acceptance for the biggest lies, the worst delusions—sentiments that act immediately, provoke violent reactions, and awaken
such passions that they justify all sacrifices. Such sentiments
correspond to the primary needs of all men: the need to eat, to
be one's own master, to hate. Given the ease of releasing such
sentiments, the material and psychological means employed can
be simple: the pamphlet, the speech, the poster, the rumor. In
order to make propaganda of agitation, it is not necessary to have
the mass media of communication at one's disposal, for such
propaganda feeds on itself, and each person seized by it becomes
in turn a propagandist. Just because it does not need a large
technical apparatus, it is extremely useful as subversive propaganda. Nor is it necessary to be concerned with probability or
veracity. Any statement whatever, no matter how stupid, any
"tall tale" will be believed once it enters into the passionate current of hatred. A characteristic example occurred in July 1960,
when Patrice Lumumba claimed that the Belgians had provoked
the revolt of the Congolese soldiers in the camp at Thysville.

Finally, the less educated and informed the people to whom
propaganda of agitation is addressed, the easier it is to make
such propaganda. That is why it is particularly suited for use
among the so-called lower classes (the proletariat) and among
African peoples. There it can rely on some key words of magical
import, which are believed without question even though the
hearers cannot attribute any real content to them and do not
fully understand them. Among colonized peoples, one of these
words is *Independence,* an extremely profitable word from the
point of view of effective subversion. It is useless to try to explain
to people that national independence is not at all the same as
individual liberty; that the black peoples generally have not
developed to the point at which they can live in political independence in the Western manner; that the economy of their
countries permits them merely to change masters. But no reason
can prevail against the magic of the word. And it is the least
intelligent people who are most likely to be thrown into a revolutionary movement by such summary appeals.

In contrast to this propaganda of agitation is the propaganda
of integration—the propaganda of developed nations and characteristic of our civilization; in fact it did not exist before the
twentieth century. It is a propaganda of conformity. It is related

to the fact, analyzed earlier, that in Western society it is no longer sufficient to obtain a transitory political act (such as a vote); one needs total adherence to a society's truths and behavioral patterns. As the more perfectly uniform the society, the stronger its power and effectiveness, each member should be only an organic and functional fragment of it, perfectly adapted and integrated. He must share the stereotypes, beliefs, and reactions of the group; he must be an active participant in its economic, ethical, esthetic, and political doings. All his activities, all his sentiments are dependent on this collectivity. And, as he is often reminded, he can fulfill himself only through this collectivity, as a member of the group.[6] Propaganda of integration thus aims at making the individual participate in his society in every way. It is a long-term propaganda, a self-reproducing propaganda that seeks to obtain stable behavior, to adapt the individual to his everyday life, to reshape his thoughts and behavior in terms of the permanent social setting. We can see that this propaganda is more extensive and complex than propaganda of agitation. It must be permanent, for the individual can no longer be left to himself.

In many cases such propaganda is confined to rationalizing an existing situation, to transforming unconscious actions of members of a society into consciously desired activity that is visible, laudable, and justified—Pearlin and Rosenberg call this "the elaboration of latent consequences." In such cases it must be proved that the listeners, the citizens in general, are the beneficiaries of the resultant socio-political developments.

Integration propaganda aims at stabilizing the social body, at unifying and reinforcing it. It is thus the preferred instrument of government, though properly speaking it is not exclusively political propaganda. Since 1930 the propaganda of the Soviet Union, as well as that, since the war, of all the People's Republics, has been a propaganda of integration.[7] But this type of propaganda can also be made by a group of organizations other than those of government, going in the same direction, more or less spontaneously, more or less planned by the state. The most important example of the use of such propaganda is the United

---

[6] This is one of the points common to all American works on micro-sociology.
[7] At the conference on ideological problems held in Moscow at the end of December 1961, the need to "shape the Communist man" was reaffirmed, and the propagandists were blamed for the twenty-year delay in achieving this goal.

States. Obviously, integration propaganda is much more subtle and complex than agitation propaganda. It seeks not a temporary excitement but a total molding of the person in depth. Here all psychological and opinion analyses must be utilized, as well as the mass media of communication. It is primarily this integration propaganda that we shall discuss in our study, for it is the most important of our time despite the success and the spectacular character of subversive propaganda.

Let us note right away a final aspect of integration propaganda: the more comfortable, cultivated, and informed the milieu to which it is addressed, the better it works. Intellectuals are more sensitive than peasants to integration propaganda. In fact, they share the stereotypes of a society even when they are political opponents of the society. Take a recent example: French intellectuals opposed to war in Algeria seemed hostile to integration propaganda. Nevertheless, they shared all the stereotypes and myths of French society—Technology, Nation, Progress; all their actions were based on those myths. They were thoroughly ripe for an integration propaganda, for they were already adapted to its demands. Their temporary opposition was not of the slightest importance; just changing the color of the flag was enough to find them again among the most conformist groups.

One essential problem remains. When a revolutionary movement is launched, it operates, as we have said, with agitation propaganda; but once the revolutionary party has taken power, it must begin immediately to operate with integration propaganda (save for the exceptions mentioned). That is the way to balance its power and stabilize the situation. But the transition from one type of propaganda to the other is extremely delicate and difficult. After one has, over the years, excited the masses, flung them into adventures, fed their hopes and their hatreds, opened the gates of action to them, and assured them that all their actions were justified, it is difficult to make them re-enter the ranks, to integrate them into the normal framework of politics and economics. What has been unleashed cannot be brought under control so easily, particularly habits of violence or of taking the law into one's own hands—these disappear very slowly. This is all the more true because the results achieved by revolution are usually deceptive; just to seize power is not enough. The people want to give full vent to the hatred developed by agitation propaganda, and to have the promised bread or land immediately. And the troops that helped in the seizure of power rapidly become the opposition and continue to act as they did under the influence of subversion propaganda. The newly established government must then use propaganda to eliminate these difficulties and to prevent the continuation of the battle. But this must be propaganda designed to incorporate individuals into the "New Order," to transform their opponents into collaborators of the State, to make them accept delays in the fulfillment of promises—in other words, it must be integration propaganda.

Generally, only one element—hatred—can be immediately satisfied; everything else must be changed. Obviously, this conversion of propaganda is very difficult: the techniques and methods of agitation propaganda cannot be used; the same feelings cannot be aroused. Other propagandists must be employed, as totally different qualities are required for integration propaganda. The greatest difficulty is that agitation propaganda produces very rapid and spectacular effects, whereas integration propaganda acts slowly, gradually, and imperceptibly. After the masses have been subjected to agitation propaganda, to neutralize their aroused impulses with integration propaganda without being swept away by the masses is a delicate problem. In some cases it is actually impossible to regain control of the masses. The Belgian Congo is a good example: the black people, very excited since 1959 by Lumumba's propaganda, first released their excitement by battling among themselves; then, once the black government was installed, they ran wild and it was impossible to get them under control. That was the direct effect of Lumumba's unrestrained propaganda against the Belgians. It seems that only a dictatorship can help this situation.[8]

Another good example is given by Sauvy: during the war, broadcasts from London and Algiers aroused the French people on the subject of food shortages and accused the Germans of artificially creating scarcity through requisitioning (which was not true). After Liberation, the government was unable to overcome the effects of this propaganda; abundance was expected to return immediately. It was impossible to control inflation and maintain rationing; integration failed because of prior agitation.

In some cases, agitation propaganda leads to a partial failure.

---

[8] Written in September 1960.

Sometimes there is a very long period of trouble and unhappiness, during which it is impossible to restore order, and only after a dozen years of integration propaganda can the situation be controlled again. Obviously, the best example is the Soviet Union. As early as 1920, integration propaganda as conceived by Lenin was employed, but it dampened the revolutionary mentality only very slowly. Only after 1929 did the effects of agitation propaganda finally disappear. The Kronstadt Rebellion was a striking example.

In other cases the government must follow the crowds, which cannot be held back once they are set off; the government is forced, step by step, to satisfy appetites aroused by agitation propaganda. This was partly the case with Hitler. After taking power, he continued to control the people by agitation propaganda; he thus had to hold out something new all the time on the road to war—rearmament, the Rhineland, Spain, Austria, Czechoslovakia. The propaganda aimed at the S.A. and S.S. was agitation propaganda, as was the propaganda pushing the German people into war in 1937-9. At the same time, the population as a whole was subjected to a propaganda of assimilation. Thus Hitler used two kinds of propaganda simultaneously. Similarly, in the Soviet Union, agitation propaganda against imperialists and saboteurs, or for the fulfillment of the Plan, is employed simultaneously with propaganda of integration into the system (using different arguments and media) through political education, youth movements, and so on. This is exactly the situation today of Castro in Cuba; he is incapable of integrating and can only pursue his agitation propaganda. This will lead him inevitably to dictatorship, and probably to war.

Other regimes, however, have managed perfectly well to pass from one propaganda to the other, and to make integration propaganda take the lead rapidly. This was the case of North Vietnam and China, and was owing to the remarkable conception of propaganda which they have had since the time of the revolution. In fact, since 1927 Mao's propaganda has been subversive; it appeals to the most basic feelings in order to arouse revolt, it leads to combat, it conditions people, and it relies on slogans. But, at the same time, as soon as the individual is pressed into the army he is subjected to an integration propaganda that Mao calls *political education*. Long-winded explanations tell him why it is necessary to act in a particular way; a biased but seemingly objective news system is set up as part of that propaganda; behavior is regimented and disciplined. The integration of the revolutionary rebel into a prodigiously disciplined, organized, and regimented army, which goes hand in hand with his intellectual and moral indoctrination, prepares him to be taken into custody by integration propaganda after victory, and to be inserted into the new society without resistance or anarchical excursions. This patient and meticulous shaping of the whole man, this "putting into the mold," as Mao calls it, is certainly his principal success. Of course, he began with a situation in which man was already well integrated into the group, and he substituted one complete framework for another. Also, he needed only to shape the minds of people who had had very little education (in the Western sense of the term), so that they learned to understand everything through images, stereotypes, slogans, and interpretations that he knew how to inculcate. Under such conditions, integration is easy and practically irreversible.

Lastly, the distinction between the two types of propaganda partly explains the defeat of French propaganda in Algeria since 1955. On one side, the propaganda of the F.L.N. was an act of agitation designed to arouse feelings of subversion and combat; against this the French army pitted a propaganda of integration, of assimilation into a French framework and into the French administration, French political concepts, education, professional training, and ideology. But a world of difference lay between the two as to speed, ease, and effectiveness; which explains why, in this competition between propagandas, the F.L.N. won out at almost every stage. This does not mean that F.L.N. propaganda reflected the real feeling of the Algerians. But if some say: "You are unhappy, so rise and slay your master and tomorrow you will be free," and others say: "We will help you, work with you, and in the end all your problems will be solved," there is little question as to who will command allegiance. In spite of everything, however, integration propaganda, as we have said above, is by far the most important new fact of our day.

Vertical and Horizontal Propaganda

Classic propaganda, as one usually thinks of it, is a vertical propaganda—in the sense that it is made by a leader, a technician, a political or religious head who acts from the superior position of his authority and seeks to influence the crowd below. Such propaganda comes from above. It is conceived in the secret recesses of political enclaves; it uses all technical methods of centralized mass communication; it envelops a mass of individuals; but those who practice it are on the outside. Let us recall here the distinction, cited above, made by Lasswell between direct propaganda and effect propaganda, though both are forms of vertical propaganda.

One trait of vertical propaganda is that the propagandee remains alone even though he is part of a crowd. His shouts of enthusiasm or hatred, though part of the shouts of the crowd, do not put him in communication with others; his shouts are only a response to the leader. Finally, this kind of propaganda requires a passive attitude from those subjected to it. They are seized, they are manipulated, they are committed; they experience what they are asked to experience; they are really transformed into objects. Consider, for instance, the quasi-hypnotic condition of those propagandized at a meeting. There, the individual is depersonalized; his decisions are no longer his own but those suggested by the leader, imposed by a conditioned reflex. When we say that this is a passive attitude, we do not mean that the propagandee does not act; on the contrary, he acts with vigor and passion. But, as we shall see, his action is not his own, though he believes it is. Throughout, it is conceived and willed outside of him; the propagandist is acting through him, reducing him to the condition of a passive instrument. He is mechanized, dominated, hence passive. This is all the more so because he often is plunged into a mass of propagandees in which he loses his individuality and becomes one element among others, inseparable from the crowd and inconceivable without it.

In any case, vertical propaganda is by far the most widespread —whether Hitler's or Stalin's, that of the French government since 1950, or that of the United States. It is in one sense the easiest to make, but its direct effects are extremely perishable, and it must be renewed constantly. It is primarily useful for agitation propaganda.

Horizontal propaganda is a much more recent development. We know it in two forms: Chinese propaganda and group dynamics in human relations. The first is political propaganda; the second is sociological propaganda; both are integration propaganda. Their characteristics are identical, surprising as that may seem when we consider their totally different origins—in context, research methods, and perspective.

This propaganda can be called horizontal because it is made *inside* the group (not from the top), where, in principle, all individuals are equal and there is no leader. The individual makes contact with others at his own level rather than with a leader; such propaganda therefore always seeks "conscious adherence." Its content is presented in didactic fashion and addressed to the intelligence. The leader, the propagandist, is there only as a sort of *animator* or discussion leader; sometimes his presence and his identity are not even known—for example, the "ghost writer" in certain American groups, or the "police spy" in Chinese groups. The individual's adherence to his group is "conscious" because he is aware of it and recognizes it, but it is ultimately involuntary because he is trapped in a dialectic and in a group that leads him unfailingly to this adherence. His adherence is also "intellectual" because he can express his conviction clearly and logically, but it is not *genuine* because the information, the data, the reasoning that have led him to adhere to the group were themselves deliberately falsified in order to lead him there.

But the most remarkable characteristic of horizontal propaganda is the small group. The individual participates actively in the life of this group, in a genuine and lively dialogue. In China the group is watched carefully to see that each member speaks, expresses himself, gives his opinions. Only in speaking will the individual gradually discover his own convictions (which also will be those of the group), become irrevocably involved, and help others to form their opinions (which are identical). Each individual helps to form the opinion of the group, but the group helps each individual to discover the correct line. For, miraculously, it is always the correct line, the anticipated solution, the "proper" convictions, which are eventually discovered. All the participants are placed on an equal footing, meetings are intimate, discussion is informal, and no leader presides. Progress is slow; there must be many meetings, each recalling events of the preceding one, so that a common experience can be shared. To produce "voluntary" rather than mechanical adherence, and to create a solution that is "found" by the individual rather than imposed from above, is indeed a very advanced method, much more effective and binding than the mechanical action of vertical propaganda. When the individual is mechanized, he can be manipulated easily. But to put the individual in a position where he apparently has a freedom of choice and still obtain from him what one expects, is much more subtle and risky.

Vertical propaganda needs the huge apparatus of the mass media of communication; horizontal propaganda needs a huge organization of people. Each individual must be inserted into a group, if possible into several groups with convergent actions. The groups must be homogeneous, specialized, and small: fifteen to twenty is the optimum figure to permit active participation by each person. The group must comprise individuals of the same sex, class, age, and environment. Most friction between individuals can then be ironed out and all factors eliminated which might distract attention, splinter motivations, and prevent the establishment of the proper line.

Therefore, a great many groups are needed (there are millions in China), as well as a great many group leaders. That is the principal problem. For if, according to Mao's formula, "each must be a propagandist for all," it is equally true that there must be liaison men between the authorities and each group. Such men must be unswerving, integrated into the group themselves, and must exert a stabilizing and lasting influence. They must be members of an integrated political body, in this case the Communist Party.

This form of propaganda needs two conditions: first of all, a lack of contact between groups. A member of a small group must not belong to other groups in which he would be subjected to other influences; that would give him a chance to find himself again and, with it, the strength to resist. This is why the Chinese Communists insisted on breaking up traditional groups, such as the family. A private and heterogeneous group (with different ages, sexes, and occupations), the family is a tremendous obstacle to such propaganda. In China, where the family was still very powerful, it had to be broken up. The problem is very different in the United States and in the Western societies; there the social structures are sufficiently flexible and disintegrated to be no obstacle. It is not necessary to break up the family in order to make the group dynamic and fully effective: the family already is broken up. It no longer has the power to envelop the individual; it is no longer the place where the individual is formed and has his roots. The field is clear for the influence of small groups.

The other condition for horizontal propaganda is identity between propaganda and education. The small group is a center of total moral, intellectual, psychological, and civic education (information, documentation, catechization), but it is primarily a political group, and everything it does is related to politics. Education has no meaning there except in relation to politics. This is equally true for American groups, despite appearances to the contrary. But the term *politics* must be taken here in its broadest sense. The political education given by Mao is on the level of a catechism, which is most effective in small groups. Individuals are taught what it is to be a member of a Communist society; and though the verbal factor (formulas to learn, which are the basic tenets of Marxist Communism) is important, the propagandist seeks above all to habituate the group members to a particular new behavior, to instill belief in a human type that the propagandist wishes to create, to put its members in touch with reality through group experience. In this sense the education is very complete, with complete coordination between what is learned "intellectually" and what is "lived" in practice.

Obviously, no political "instruction" is possible in American groups. All Americans already know the great principles and institutions of democracy. Yet these groups *are* political: their education is specifically democratic—that is to say, individuals are taught how to take action and how to behave as members of a democracy. It is indeed a civic education, a thorough education addressed to the entire man.

These groups are a means of education, but such education is only one of the elements of propaganda aimed at obtaining adherence to a society, its priciples, its ideology, and its myths—and to the behavior required by the authorities. The small groups are the chosen place for this active education, and the regime employing horizontal propaganda can permit no other style or form of instruction and education than these. We have already seen that the importance of these small groups requires the breaking up of other groups, such as the family. Now we must understand that the education given in the political small groups requires either the disappearance of academic education, or its integration into the system. In *The Organization Man*, William H. Whyte clearly shows the way in which the American school is becoming more and more a simple mechanism to adapt youngsters to American society. As for the Chinese school, it is only a system of propaganda charged with catechizing children while teaching them to read.

Horizontal propaganda thus is very hard to make (particularly because it needs so many instructors), but it is exceptionally efficient through its meticulous encirclement of everybody, through the effective participation of all present, and through their public declarations of adherence. It is peculiarly a system that seems to coincide perfectly with egalitarian societies claiming to be based on the will of the people and calling themselves democratic: each group is composed of persons who are alike, and one actually can formulate the will of such a group. But all this is ultimately much more stringent and totalitarian than explosive propaganda. Thanks to this system, Mao has succeeded in passing from subversive propaganda to integration propaganda.

Rational and Irrational Propaganda

That propaganda has an irrational character is still a well-established and well-recognized truth. The distinction between propaganda and information is often made: information is addressed to reason and experience—it furnishes facts; propaganda is addressed to feelings and passions—it is irrational. There is, of course, some truth in this, but the reality is not so simple. For there is such a thing as rational propaganda, just as there is rational advertising. Advertisements for automobiles or electrical appliances are generally based on technical descriptions or proved performance—rational elements used for advertising purposes. Similarly there is a propaganda based exclusively on facts, statistics, economic ideas. Soviet propaganda, especially since 1950, has been based on the undeniable scientific progress and economic development of the Soviet Union; but it is still propaganda, for it uses these *facts* to *demonstrate, rationally,* the superiority of its system and to demand everybody's support.

It has often been noted that in wartime the successful propaganda is that based directly on obvious facts: when an enemy army has just suffered a defeat, an appeal to enemy soldiers to surrender will seem rational. When the superiority of one of the combatants becomes apparent, his appeal for surrender is an appeal to reason.

Similarly, the propaganda of French grandeur since 1958 is a rational and factual propaganda; French films in particular are almost all centered around French technological successes. The film *Algérie française* is an economic film, overloaded with economic geography and statistics. But it is still propaganda. Such rational propaganda is practiced by various regimes. The education provided by Mao in China is based on pseudo-rational proofs, but they are effective for those who pay attention to them and accept them. American propaganda, out of concern for honesty and democratic conviction, also attempts to be rational and factual. The news bulletins of the American services are a typical example of rational propaganda based on "knowledge" and information. And nothing resembles these American publications more than the *Review of the German Democratic Republic,* which has taken over exactly the same propaganda style. We can say that the more progress we make, the more propaganda becomes rational and the more it is based on serious arguments, on dissemination of knowledge, on factual information, figures, and statistics.[9]

Purely impassioned and emotional propaganda is disappearing. Even such propaganda contained elements of fact: Hitler's most inflammatory speeches always contained some facts which served as base or pretext. It is unusual nowadays to find a frenzied propaganda composed solely of claims without relation to reality. It is still found in Egyptian propaganda, and it appeared in July 1960 in Lumumba's propaganda in the Belgian Congo. Such propaganda is now discredited, but it still convinces and always excites.

Modern man needs a relation to facts, a self-justification to convince himself that by acting in a certain way he is obeying reason and proved experience. We must therefore study the close relationship between information and propaganda. Propaganda's content increasingly resembles information. It has even clearly been proved that a violent, excessive, shock-provoking propaganda text leads ultimately to less conviction and participation

---

[9] Ernst Kris and Nathan Leites have correctly noted the differences, in this connection, between the propaganda of 1914 and that of 1940: the latter is more sober and informative, less emotional and moralistic. As we say in fashionable parlance, it is addressed less to the superego and more to the ego.

than does a more "informative" and reasonable text on the same subject. A large dose of fear precipitates immediate action; a reasonably small dose produces lasting support. The listener's critical powers decrease if the propaganda message is more rational and less violent.

Propaganda's content therefore tends to be rational and factual. But is this enough to show that propaganda is rational? Besides content, there is the receiver of the content, the individual who undergoes the barrage of propaganda or information. When an individual has read a technical and factual advertisement of a television set or a new automobile engine, and if he is not an electrician or a mechanic, what does he remember? Can he describe a transistor or a new type of wheel-suspension? Of course not. All those technical descriptions and exact details will form a general picture in his head, rather vague but highly colored—and when he speaks of the engine, he will say: "It's terrific!"

It is exactly the same with all rational, logical, factual propaganda. After having read an article on wheat in the United States or on steel in the Soviet Union, does the reader remember the figures and statistics, has he understood the economic mechanisms, has he absorbed the line of reasoning? If he is not an economist by profession, he will retain an over-all impression, a general conviction that "these Americans (or Russians) are amazing. . . . They have methods. . . . Progress is important after all," and so on. Similarly, emerging from the showing of a film such as *Algérie française,* he forgets all the figures and logical proofs and retains only a feeling of rightful pride in the accomplishments of France in Algeria. Thereafter, what remains with the individual affected by this propaganda is a perfectly irrational picture, a purely emotional feeling, a myth. The facts, the data, the reasoning—all are forgotten, and only the impression remains. And this is indeed what the propagandist ultimately seeks, for the individual will never begin to act on the basis of facts, or engage in purely rational behavior. What makes him act is the emotional pressure, the vision of a future, the myth. The problem is to create an irrational response on the basis of rational and factual elements. That response must be fed with facts, those frenzies must be provoked by rigorously logical proofs. Thus propaganda in itself becomes honest, strict, exact, but its effect remains irrational because of the spontaneous transformation of all its contents by the individual.

We emphasize that this is true not just for propaganda but also for information. Except for the specialist, information, even when it is very well presented, gives people only a broad image of the world. And much of the information disseminated nowadays—research findings, facts, statistics, explanations, analyses—*eliminate* personal judgment and the capacity to form one's own opinion even more surely than the most extravagant propaganda. This claim may seem shocking; but it is a fact that excessive data do not enlighten the reader or the listener; they drown him. He cannot remember them all, or coordinate them, or understand them; if he does not want to risk losing his mind, he will merely draw a general picture from them. And the more facts supplied, the more simplistic the image. If a man is given *one* item of information, he will retain it; if he is given a hundred data in *one* field, on *one* question, he will have only a general idea of that question. But if he is given a hundred items of information on all the political and economic aspects of a nation, he will arrive at a summary judgment—"The Russians are terrific!" and so on.

A surfeit of data, far from permitting people to make judgments and form opinions, prevents them from doing so and actually paralyzes them. They are caught in a web of facts and must remain at the level of the facts they have been given. They cannot even form a choice or a judgment in other areas or on other subjects. Thus the mechanisms of modern information induce a sort of hypnosis in the individual, who cannot get out of the field that has been laid out for him by the information. His opinion will ultimately be formed solely on the basis of the facts transmitted to him, and not on the basis of his choice and his personal experience. The more the techniques of distributing information develop, the more the individual is shaped by such information. It is not true that he can choose freely with regard to what is presented to him as the truth. And because rational propaganda thus creates an irrational situation, it remains, above all, propaganda—that is, an inner control over the individual by a social force, which means that it deprives him of himself.

CHAPTER

[II]

THE CONDITIONS
FOR THE
EXISTENCE OF
PROPAGANDA

Why and how does propaganda exist?

We have already noted that propaganda was not the same in the past as it is today, that its nature has changed. We have also said that one cannot simply make any propaganda just anywhere, at anytime, or in any fashion. Without a certain milieu propaganda cannot exist. Only under certain conditions can the phenomenon of propaganda appear and grow. The most obvious of these are accidental or purely historical conditions. Beyond that, it is clear, for example, that the emergence of propaganda is connected with a number of scientific discoveries.

Modern propaganda could not exist without the mass media—the inventions that produced press, radio, television, and motion pictures, or those that produced the means of modern transportation and which permit crowds of diverse individuals from all over to assemble easily and frequently. Present-day propaganda meetings no longer bear any relation to past assemblies, to the meetings of the Athenians in the Agora or of the Romans in the Forum. Then there is the scientific research in all the other fields—sociology and psychology, for example. Without the discoveries made in the past half-century by scientists who "never wanted this," there would be no propaganda. The findings of social psychology, depth psychology, behaviorism, group sociology, sociology of public opinion are the very foundations of the propagandist's work.

In a different sense, political circumstances have also been effective and immediate causes of the development of massive propaganda. The first World War; the Russian revolution of 1917; Hitler's revolution of 1933; the second World War; the further development of revolutionary wars since 1944 in China, Indochina, and Algeria, as well as the Cold War—each was a step in the development of modern propaganda. With each of these events propaganda developed further, increased in depth, discovered new methods. At the same time it conquered new nations and new territories: To reach the enemy, one must use his weapons; this undeniable argument is the key to the systematic development of propaganda. And in this way propaganda has become a permanent feature in nations that actually despise it, such as the United States and France.

Let us also note the influence of doctrines and men. It is clear that a particular doctrine can make propaganda the very center of political life, the essence of political action, rather than merely an accessory or an incidental and rather suspect instrument. Leninism as developed by Mao is really a doctrine of propaganda plus action, indissolubly linked to Marxism, of which it is an expression. As Leninism spreads, propaganda develops with it —by necessity and not by choice. In addition, certain men have greatly helped the development of propaganda: Hitler and Goebbels, for example, had a genius for it. But the role of such men is never decisive. They do not invent propaganda; it does not exist just because they want it to. They are only the producers and directors, the catalysts, who profit from the confluence of favorable circumstances. All this is too well known and too obvious to dwell on.

But the sum of certain conditions is still not enough to explain the development of propaganda. The over-all sociological conditions in a society must provide a favorable environment for propaganda to succeed.[1]

1. The Sociological Conditions

Individualist Society and Mass Society

For propaganda to succeed, a society must first have two complementary qualities: it must be both an individualist and a mass society. These two qualities are often considered contradictory. It is believed that an individualist society, in which the individual is thought to have a higher value than the group, tends to destroy groups that limit the individual's range of action, whereas a mass society negates the individual and reduces him to a cipher. But this contradiction is purely theoretical and a delusion. In actual fact, an individualist society *must* be a mass society, because the first move toward liberation of the individual is to break up the small groups that are an organic fact of the entire society. In this process the individual frees himself completely from family, village, parish, or brotherhood bonds—only to find himself directly vis-à-vis the entire society. When individuals are not held together by local structures, the only form in which they can live together is in an unstructured mass society. Similarly, a mass society can only be based on individuals—that is, on men in their isolation, whose identities are determined by their relationships with one another. Precisely because the individual claims to be equal to all other individuals, he becomes an abstraction and is in effect reduced to a cipher.

---

[1] The same factors of influence will have different weight and effectiveness in different contexts. The media employed by the propagandists can work only in a particular sociological structure. This reciprocal influence of propaganda and social structure is precisely one of the problems that need to be studied.

Ernst Kris and Nathan Leites have properly noted that public responses to the impact of propaganda have changed considerably in the past few decades and that this change is the result of trends in the psycho-sociological conditions of twentieth-century life.

As soon as local organic groupings are reformed, society tends to cease being individualistic, and thereby to lose its mass character as well. What then occurs is the formation of organic groups of *elite* in what remains a mass society, but which rests on the framework of strongly structured and centralized political parties, unions, and so on. These organizations reach only an active minority, and the members of this minority cease to be individualistic by being integrated into such organic associations. From this perspective, individualist society and mass society are two corollary aspects of the same reality. This corresponds to what we have said about the mass media: to perform a propagandistic function they must capture the individual and the mass at the same time.

Propaganda can be effective only in an individualist society, by which we do not mean the theoretical individualism of the nineteenth century, but the genuine individualism of our society. Of course, the two are not diametrically opposed. Where the greatest value is attributed to the individual, the end result is a society composed in essence only of individuals, and therefore one that is not integrated. But although theory and reality are not in total opposition, a great difference nevertheless exists between them. In individualist *theory* the individual has eminent value, man himself is the master of his life; in individualist *reality* each human being is subject to innumerable forces and influences, and is not at all master of his own life. As long as solidly constituted groups exist, those who are integrated into them are subject to them. But at the same time they are protected by them against such external influences as propaganda.

An individual can be influenced by forces such as propaganda only when he is cut off from membership in local groups. Because such groups are organic and have a well-structured material, spiritual, and emotional life, they are not easily penetrated by propaganda. For example, it is much more difficult today for outside propaganda to influence a soldier integrated into a military group, or a militant member of a monolithic party, than to influence the same man when he is a mere citizen. Nor is the organic group sensitive to psychological *contagion,* which is so important to the success of mass propaganda.

One can say, generally, that nineteenth-century individualist society came about through the disintegration of such small groups as the family or the church. Once these groups lost their importance, the individual was left substantially isolated. He was plunged into a new environment, generally urban, and thereby "uprooted." He no longer had a traditional place in which to live; he was no longer geographically attached to a fixed place, or historically to his ancestry. An individual thus uprooted can only be part of a mass. He is on his own, and individualist thinking asks of him something he has never been required to do before: that he, the individual, become the measure of all things. Thus he begins to judge everything for himself. In fact he *must* make his own judgments. He is thrown entirely on his own resources; he can find criteria only in himself. He is clearly responsible for his own decisions, both personal and social. He becomes the beginning and the end of everything. Before him there was nothing; after him there will be nothing. His own life becomes the only criterion of justice and injustice, of Good and Evil.

In theory this is admirable. But in practice what actually happens? The individual is placed in a minority position and burdened at the same time with a total, crushing responsibility. Such conditions make an individualist society fertile ground for modern propaganda. The permanent uncertainty, the social mobility, the absence of sociological protection and of traditional frames of reference—all these inevitably provide propaganda with a malleable environment that can be fed information from the outside and conditioned at will.

The individual left to himself is defenseless, the more so because he may be caught up in a social current, thus becoming easy prey for propaganda. As a member of a small group he was fairly well protected from collective influences, customs, and suggestions. He was relatively unaffected by changes in the society at large. He obeyed only if his entire group obeyed. This does not mean that he was freer, but only that he was determined by his local environment and by his restricted group, and very little by broad ideological influences or collective psychic stimuli. The common error was to believe that if the individual were liberated from the smaller organic groups he would be set free. But in actual fact he was exposed to the influence of mass currents, to the influence of the state, and direct integration into mass society. Finally, he became a victim of propaganda. Physically and psychologically uprooted, the individual became much less stable. The stability of the peasantry, for example, is one of the reasons why this group is relatively unaffected by propaganda. Goebbels himself recognized that the peasants could be reached only if their structured milieu was shattered; and the difficulties that Lenin experienced in integrating the Russian peasantry into the pattern of the revolution are well known.

Thus, here is one of the first conditions for the growth and development of modern propaganda: It emerged in western Europe in the nineteenth century and the first half of the twentieth precisely because that was when society was becoming increasingly individualistic and its organic structures were breaking down.

But for propaganda to develop, society must also be a mass society. It cannot be a society that is simply breaking up or dissolving. It cannot be a society about to disappear, which might well be a society in which small groups are breaking up. The society that favors the development of propaganda must be a society maintaining itself but at the same time taking on a new structure, that of the mass society.[2]

The relationship between masses and crowds has been much discussed, and distinctions have been drawn between masses and massification. The first is the gathering of a temporary crowd; the second, the involvement of individuals in a permanent social cycle. Certainly a crowd gathered at a given point is not, properly speaking, a mass. A mass society is a society with considerable population density in which local structures and organizations are weak, currents of opinion are strongly felt, men are grouped into large and influential collectives, the individual is part of these collectives, and a certain psychological unity exists. Mass society, moreover, is characterized by a certain uniformity of material life. Despite differences of environment, training, or situation, the men of a mass society have the same preoccupations, the same interest in technical matters, the same mythical beliefs, the same

[2] Of the innumerable books on the masses, *The Revolt of the Masses*, by José Ortega y Gasset, is still valid despite the criticism of many sociologists.

Elmo Roper's classification of influential groups in the United States is well known: about 90 percent of the population is "politically inert"; they become active only accidentally, when they are set into motion, but they are normally "inactive, inattentive, manipulable, and without critical faculty"—qualities that form the masses. (Roper: "Who Tells the Storytellers?" *Saturday Review*, July 31, 1954.) Throughout we are discussing this mass man, the average man.

prejudices.[3] The individuals making up the mass in the grip of propaganda may seem quite diversified, but they have enough in common for propaganda to act on them directly.

In contemporary society there actually is a close relation between mass and crowd. Because a mass society exists, crowds can gather frequently—that is, the individual constantly moves from one crowd to another, from a street crowd to a factory crowd, or a theater crowd, a subway crowd, a crowd gathered at a meeting. Conversely, the very fact of belonging to crowds turns the individual more and more into a mass man and thus modifies his very being. There is no question that man's psychic being is modified by his belonging to a mass society; this modification takes place even if no propaganda appeal is made to the soul of the crowd or the spirit of the collective. This individual produced by a mass society is more readily available, more credulous, more suggestible, more excitable. Under such conditions propaganda can develop best. Because a mass society existed in western Europe at the end of the nineteenth century and the first half of the twentieth, propaganda became possible *and* necessary.

From mass society emerge the psychological elements most favorable to propaganda: symbols and stereotypes. Of course these also exist in small groups and limited societies, but there they are not of the same kind, number, or degree of abstraction. In a mass society they are more detached from reality, more manipulable, more numerous, more likely to provoke intense but fleeting emotions, and at the same time less significant, less inherent in personal life. The symbols in a primitive society do not permit the free and flexible play of propaganda because they are rigid, stable, and small in number. Their nature is also different: of religious origin at first, they become political (in the broad sense). In mass society, finally, we find the maximum deviation between public opinions and latent private opinions, which are either repressed or progressively eliminated.

Thus the masses in contemporary society have made propaganda possible; in fact propaganda can act only where man's psychology is influenced by the crowd or mass to which he belongs. Besides, as we have already pointed out, the means of

---

[3] A mass society is also a strongly organized society. John Albig makes a profound observation when he says that propaganda is an *inevitable* concomitant of the growth and organization of society.

disseminating propaganda depend on the existence of the masses; in the United States these means are called the mass media of communications with good reason: without the mass to receive propaganda and carry it along, propaganda is impossible.

We must also consider the importance of public opinion in this connection. Public opinion as we presently think of it also needs a mass society. In fact, in the presence of a stimulus or an act there must be exchanges of opinion, actions, and interactions, which are the first steps in the formation of public opinion. There must also be an awareness of existing opinions, of private opinions or implicit public opinions. Finally, there must be a reappraisal of values and attitudes. Only then is there really a crystalized public opinion. It is obvious that in order for this entire process to take place, a very close relationship among a great number of people is necessary. The kind of public opinion we mean, the kind used by propaganda and necessary for it, cannot exist in a community of fifty or one hundred persons, isolated from the outside world (whether it be a monastery or a village of the fifteenth century), or in a society of very low population density in which a man has only very distant contacts with other men. Meeting once a month at the market place, for instance, does not permit the wide dissemination of personal views needed to form public opinion.

Thus, for propaganda to be effective psychologically and sociologically, a combination of demographic phenomena is required. The first is population density, with a high frequency of diversified human contacts, exchanges of opinions and experiences, and with primary importance placed on the feeling of togetherness. The second is urban concentration, which, resulting from the fusion between mass and crowd, gives the mass its psychological and sociological character. Only then can propaganda utilize crowd effects; only then can it profit from the psychological modifications that collective life produces in the individual and without which practically none of the propaganda would "take." Much more, the instruments of propaganda find their principal source of support in the urban concentration.

Buying a newspaper or a radio set or listening to a broadcast is a social act that presumes a mass structure of society, a total subordination to certain imperatives felt only when one is plunged into a mass in which each person places value on the accomplishment of this social act. Even more, to go to the movies or a political meeting presumes a physical proximity and, therefore, the existence of concentrated masses. In fact, a political organizer will not bother to hold his meeting if he knows he can get together only ten or fifteen people; and individuals will not come readily from a great distance. Because regular attendance is essential for attaining propaganda effects through meetings or films, the mass is indispensable. The "majority effect," so essential as a means of propaganda, can be felt only in a mass society; for example, the argument that "all Frenchmen want peace in Algeria" or, on the other hand, "all Frenchmen want to hold on to Algeria" is valid only if "all Frenchmen" represents an immediate and massive reality. Thus the mass society was a primary condition for the emergence of propaganda; once formed, it evoked the power and functions of propaganda.

Although we shall not go into the matter of individual psychology, we must remember, in Stoetzel's excellent words, that "the conditions of life in mass societies tend to multiply individual frustrations. They produce abstract fragmentary relations between people . . . totally devoid of intimacy. . . . One can show how the feeling of insecurity or anxiety develops; trace the contradictions of our environment—the conflicts between socially accepted competition and the preaching of fraternal love, between the constant stimulation of our needs through advertising and our limited finances, between our legal rights and the shackles of reality."

Propaganda responds psychologically to this situation. The fact that propaganda addresses itself to the individual but acts on the mass explains, for example, the unity between the types of propaganda that are apparently diverse—such as propaganda based on the prestige of the leader (of the hero, or even of the expert) and propaganda based on the prestige of the majority. Of course in the exercise of propaganda both types have specific functions. But it is important to emphasize here that these two types are not very different from each other.

The leader or expert who enjoys authority and prestige among the mass is the man who best speaks for that mass. The ordinary man must see himself reflected in his leader. The leader must be a sublimation of the "ordinary man." He must not seem to be of a different quality. The ordinary man must not feel that the leader transcends him. This quality of the average men in the Hero (actor, dictator, sports champion) has been clearly demonstrated in the history of the past thirty years. It is what E. Morin emphasizes in his study of the deification of film stars.

When a man follows the leader, he actually follows the mass, the majority group that the leader so perfectly represents. The leader loses all power when he is separated from his group; no propaganda can emanate from a solitary leader. Moses is dead on the propaganda level; all we have left is a "Johnson" or "De Gaulle," stripped of individual characteristics and clad in the aura of the majority.

Some may raise objections to this analysis, which sees a fundamental requirement for the development of propaganda in the creation of an individualist society *and* a mass society, because only in that combination can the material means and dictatorial will of the state take shape. The first objection is based on the emergence in our society of new local organic groups—for example, political parties and labor unions, which seem to be contrary to the existence of the individualist structure and the mass structure. The answer to this is, first, that such groups are still far from having the solidity, the resistance, the structuring of old organic groups. They have not had time to consolidate themselves. One has only to look at their fragility, their fluctuations, their changes. They are not really groups of resistance against mass influence, though, like a party that exchanges a democratic for a monolithic form, they try to be by taking on authoritarian structures.

Second, such new groups cannot be real obstacles to total propaganda. They can resist *one* particular propaganda, but not the general phenomenon of propaganda, for the development of the groups takes place simultaneously with development of propaganda. These groups develop inside a society propagandized to the extreme; they are themselves *loci* of propaganda; they are instruments of propaganda and are integrated into its techniques. We are no longer in a sociological situation comparable to that of traditional societies in which there was barely any mass propaganda and almost nothing other than local psychological influences. And when propaganda did enter into such societies, it had to fight existing local groups and try to influence and modify them; and these organic groups resisted.

At present we are witnessing the emergence of organic groups in which individuals tend to be integrated. These groups have certain traits of the old organic groups, but their collective life, their intellectual, emotional, and spiritual life is determined by propaganda, and they can no longer maintain themselves without it. They become organic groups in the mass society only if they subject themselves to, and serve as agents of, propaganda. Our society has been completely transformed: when we left the purely individualist stage, which permitted propaganda to develop, we arrived at a society in which primary group structures could still exist, but in which total propaganda was established and the group no longer could be separated from such propaganda. It is curious to see how the few remaining organic groups, such as the family and the church, try at all costs to live by propaganda: families are protected by family associations; churches try to take over the methods of psychological influence. They are now the very negation of the old organic groups. And what is more, the new primary groups (such as political parties or unions) are important relay stations in the flow of total propaganda; they are mobilized and used as instruments and thus offer no fulcrum for individual resistance. On the contrary, through them the entrapped individual is made ready for propaganda.

Another objection comes to mind immediately. Propaganda has developed in societies that were neither individualist nor mass: the Russian society of 1917, present-day China, Indochina, the Arab world. But the point here is precisely that these societies could not and cannot be captured, manipulated, and mobilized by propaganda, except when their traditional structures disintegrate and a new society is developed which is both individualistic and massive. Where this fails to happen, propaganda remains ineffective. Therefore, if the new society does not constitute itself spontaneously, it is sometimes formed by force by authoritarian states, which only then can utilize propaganda. In the Soviet Union, the Caucasus and Azerbaijan were the nursery of agitprop in 1917 because the cosmopolitanism of the region, the great currents of population displacement (Russian and Moslem), the uprootings, the vigor of a nationalist myth, tended to shape mass society. In Soviet Russia, propaganda has progressed exactly in line with the destruction of the old organic groups and the creation of mass society.[4]

---

[4] We know too that the establishment of the Viet-Minh organization in Indochina permitted the structuring of a complete administrative society imposing itself on

We also find this true in Communist China, which attained in three years, through violence, what the Soviet Union took twenty years to attain and what developed naturally in the West in 150 years: the establishment of sociological conditions specific to an environment in which propaganda can be completely effective. It seems that the Chinese government understood perfectly the need to structure a new society. When the French wondered whether the methods of propaganda which had succeeded in Indochina could be applied in Algeria, they faced problems of the same sociological order.[5] We find in the ultra-rapid, forced, and systematic transformation of these societies a dramatic confirmation of our analysis showing that a certain "massification" of society is required for propaganda to be able to develop.

Opinion

We must add to all this the problem of public opinion. We have already said that, on the one hand, propaganda is no longer primarily a matter of opinion, and that, on the other, the existence of a public opinion is connected with the appearance of a mass society.[6] We would like to stress here that opinion formed in primary groups, or small groups, has other characteristics than that which exists in large societies. In small groups, with direct

---

traditional groups. The Lien-Viet, with its independent and centralized hierarchy, artificially provoked a new splitting of the traditional groups of inhabitants, upsetting families, villages, and neighborhoods, and exploding the old forms in order to integrate individuals into new groups. A person is classified according to his age, sex, and occupation. The family group is thus destroyed; children do not belong to the same groups as their parents. Each group thus created is an approximately homogeneous bloc of members with the same needs, the same tastes, the same functions; propaganda can then easily develop and capture individuals forced into these artificial groups. There can be sessions of directed discussion (the themes in the youth groups will be very different from those in the adult groups); sessions of self-criticism (youth can engage in sincere and easy self-criticism when not under parental control). French propaganda in Indochina failed partly because it respected traditional society and its structured small groups.

[5] The attempt of the F.L.N. (*Forces de Libération Nationale*) to imitate the North Vietnamese, coupled with the establishment of a million Arabs in relocation camps by the French authorities, brought about—each in its turn, each by its particular methods—this same sociological transformation. These operations are conducted simultaneously, and in both cases the desire to create a fertile ground for propaganda is not overlooked (far from it).

[6] The conditions under which a group changes its opinion have often been analyzed; we know the problems of ambiguity, opinions based on prejudices, appearances that suddenly collapse, majority effects, and so on. Many limited studies on such local conditions have been made, but their findings have little value by themselves when considered outside the setting of mass society.

contacts between individuals, interpersonal relations are the dominant relations, and the formation of public opinion depends on these direct contacts. Opinion in these is determined by what has properly been called the "preponderant" opinion, which imposes itself automatically on the group as a whole. Interpersonal relations lead to a dominant opinion because, first of all, leadership in such groups is recognized spontaneously. Also, group opinion is called on to regulate concrete situations or common experiences that bring into play the common interests of all the individuals in the group. Moreover, the social level of individuals in such groups is generally the same.

Thus, such primary groups are spontaneously democratic. In fact, opinion is formed directly, for the individuals are directly in contact with the events that demand their participation. Once formed, this opinion is expressed directly and known to everybody. The leaders of the group know what the group opinion is and take it into consideration; they have contributed amply to its formation. But these groups are by no means liberal; minorities within them appear as foreign bodies—for in a relationship such as this, opposition weakens inter-group communication. Sanctions are generally diffuse but energetic. There is no equality; the members accept *leadership,* and of course small groups also recognize instituted authorities (the father of the family, for example). Dominant personalities play a considerable role, and often group opinion will be formed by individuals who are known to all the members of the group, and whose authority is accepted.

Secondary or large societies obviously have a totally different character. In these societies (generally the only ones considered by public opinion studies) individuals do not know and have no direct contact with each other. Moreover, they do not share the direct experience of problems on which they must make decisions. Interpersonal relations do not exist, only over-all relations—those of the individual with the group as a whole. To some extent, the opinion that prevails in such groups will be a majority opinion (which is not to say that public opinion is that of the majority).

In such groups, the formation of public opinion is very complex, and a host of theories exists on the subject. In any event, public opinion has three characteristics. It can shape itself only in a society in which institutionalized channels of information give the people the facts on which they will take a position. Thus, some steps intervene between fact and opinion. The information reaching the people is only indirect, but without it there would be no opinion at all. Moreover, to the extent that we are dealing with information disseminated by intermediaries, opinion does not form itself by simple personal contact. And nowadays, opinion depends to a large extent on such intermediate channels of information.

A second characteristic of public opinion is that it cannot express itself directly, but only through channels. A constituted public opinion is as yet nothing, and does not express itself spontaneously. It will express itself in elections (when electoral opinion and public opinion coincide), through political parties, associations in the newspapers, referenda, and so on. But all that is not enough.

The third characteristic of public opinion is that this opinion is formed by a very large number of people who cannot possibly experience the same fact in the same fashion, who judge it by different standards, speak a different language, and share neither the same culture nor the same social position. Normally, everything separates them. They really should not be able to form a public opinion, and yet they do. This is possible only when all these people are not really apprised of the facts, but only of abstract symbols that give the facts a shape in which they can serve as a base for public opinion. Public opinion forms itself around attitudes and theoretical problems not clearly related to the actual situation. And the symbols most effective in the formation of public opinion are those most remote from reality. Therefore, public opinion *always rests on problems that do not correspond to reality*.

We have pointed out several times before that original small groups are obstacles to propaganda. The opinion structure of these primary groups is opposed to action outside the group (of course, we do not call the group leader's actions propaganda, but this does not mean that the group members are free from propaganda; on the contrary, we have already noted that they are not). Because direct experience, immediate grasp of facts and problems, and personal acquaintance between individuals exist in the small group, propaganda cannot function in such a group. Only in "second-hand" opinion can propaganda play its role; in fact, it cannot fail to play it there. In order for public opinion to form itself in large groups, channels of information and manipulation of symbols must be available. Where public opinion exists, propaganda crystalizes that opinion from the pre-conscious individual state to the conscious public state. Propaganda can function only in secondary groups in which secondary opinion can form itself. But we must remember that we cannot simply juxtapose those two types of groups, because a whole society is also composed of multiple groups. A conflict between primary and secondary opinions will arise. One will dominate the other. Propaganda can exist only in societies in which second-hand opinion definitely dominates primary opinion and the latter is reduced and driven into a minority position; then, when the individual finds himself between the two conflicting types of opinion, he will normally grasp the general, public opinion. This corresponds to what we have said about the mass society.

The Mass Media of Communication

Finally, one more condition is basic for propaganda. We have just stated again that an opinion cannot form itself in entire societies unless mass media of communication exist. This much is evident: without the mass media there can be no modern propaganda. But we must point to a dual factor necessary if the mass media are really to become instruments of propaganda. For they are not such instruments automatically or under just any conditions. They must be subject to centralized control on the one hand, and well diversified with regard to their products on the other. Where film production, the press, and radio transmission are not centrally controlled, no propaganda is possible. As long as a large number of independent news agencies, newsreel producers, and diverse local papers function, no conscious and direct propaganda is possible. This is not because the reader or viewer has real freedom of choice—which he has not, as we shall see later—but because none of the media has enough power to hold the individual constantly and through all channels. Local influences are sufficiently strong to neutralize the great national press, to give just one example. To make the organization of propaganda possible, the media must be concentrated, the number of news agencies reduced, the press brought under single control, and radio and film monopolies established. The effect will be still greater if the various media are concentrated in the same hands.

When a newspaper trust also extends its control over films and radio, propaganda can be directed at the masses and the individual can be caught in the wide net of media.

Only through concentration in a few hands of a large number of media can one attain a true orchestration, a continuity, and an application of scientific methods of influencing individuals. A state monopoly, or a private monopoly, is equally effective. Such a situation is in the making in the United States, France, and Germany—the fact is well known. The number of newspapers decreases while the number of readers increases. Production costs constantly increase and necessitate greater concentration; all statistics converge on that. This concentration itself keeps accelerating, thus making the situation increasingly favorable to propaganda. Of course, one must not conclude from this that the concentration of mass media *inevitably* produces propaganda. Such concentration is merely a prerequisite for it. But that the media be concentrated is not enough; it is also necessary that the individual will listen to them. This seems to be a truism: Why produce a propaganda paper if nobody will buy it?

Buying a paper, going to the movies are unimportant acts in an individual's life; he does them easily. But reception must be equally assured by radio or TV; here we encounter the problem of distributing sets—here the propagandee must take a very positive step: he must buy a set. Only where enough sets are installed can propaganda be effective. Obviously, where not enough TV sets are in use, it makes no sense to conduct propaganda via TV; this happened in 1950 to the TV propaganda of the Voice of America beamed to some Communist countries. But the act of acquiring a set brings up a point that we will discuss at considerable length: the *complicity* of the propagandee. If he is a propagandee, it is because he wants to be, for he is ready to buy a paper, go to the movies, pay for a radio or TV set. Of course, he does not buy these *in order* to be propagandized—his motivations are more complex. But in doing these things he must know that he opens the door to propaganda, that he subjects himself to it. Where he is conscious of this, the attraction of owning a radio is so much greater than the fear of propaganda that he voluntarily agrees to receive propaganda. This is even more true where transmission is by collective receiving sets, as in Communist countries. The hearers gather, even though they know that what they hear is necessarily propaganda. But they cannot escape the attraction of the radio or the hypnotism of TV.

The fact is even more striking with regard to the newspapers, for the reader buys a paper he likes, a paper in which he finds his own ideas and opinions well reflected. This is the only paper he wants, so that one can say he really wants to be propagandized. He wants to submit to this influence and actually exercises his choice in the direction of the propaganda he wishes to receive. If by chance he finds in "his" newspaper an article he dislikes or an opinion that deviates a little from his own, he cancels his subscription. He cannot stand anything that does not run on his rails. This is the very mentality of the propagandee, as we shall see.

Let no one say: "This reader does not submit to propaganda; first he has such and such ideas and opinions, and *then* he buys the paper that corresponds to them." Such an argument is simplistic, removed from reality, and based on liberal idealism. In reality, propaganda is at work here, for what is involved is a progression from vague, diffuse opinion on the part of the reader to rigorous, exciting, active expression of that opinion. A feeling or an impression is transformed into a motive for action. Confused thoughts are crystalized. Myths and the reader's conditioned reflexes are reinforced if he reads *that* paper. All this is characteristic of propaganda. The reader is really subject to propaganda, even though it be propaganda of his choice. Why always fall into the error of seeing in propaganda nothing but a device to *change* opinions? Propaganda is also a means of *reinforcing* opinions, of transforming them into action. The reader himself offers his throat to the knife of the propaganda he chooses.

We have said that no propaganda can exist unless a mass can be reached and set into motion. Yet, the peculiar and remarkable fact is that the mass media really create their own public; the propagandist need no longer beat the drum and lead the parade in order to establish a following. This happens all by itself through the effects of the communication media—they have their own power of attraction and act on individuals in such a fashion as to transform them into a collective, a public, a mass. The buying of a TV set, though an individual act, inserts the individual into the psychological and behavioral structure of the mass. He obeys the collective motivations when he buys it, and through his act opens the doors to propaganda. Where this dual process of concentration of the *sources* of propaganda and wide diffusion of its *recipients* does not take place, no modern propaganda can function in a society.

2. *Objective Conditions of Total Propaganda*

The Need of an Average Standard of Living

Just as there are societies not susceptible to propaganda, there are individuals not susceptible to it. We have just seen, for example, that it takes an individual to read the newspaper and buy a radio or TV set—an individual with a certain standard of living. Modern integration propaganda cannot affect individuals who live on the fringes of our civilization or who have too low a living standard. In capitalist countries, the very poor, who have no radio or TV and rarely go to the movies, cannot be reached by propaganda. Communist countries meet this problem with community receivers and free movies. Thus even the poorest can be reached by propaganda.

But other obstacles intervene. The really poor cannot be subjected to integration propaganda because the immediate concerns of daily life absorb all their capacities and efforts. To be sure, the poor can be pushed into rebellion, into an explosion of violence; they can be subjected to agitation propaganda and excited to the point of theft and murder. But they cannot be trained by propaganda, kept in hand, channeled, and oriented.

More advanced propaganda can influence only a man who is not completely haunted by poverty, a man who can view things from a certain distance and be reasonably unconcerned about his daily bread, and who therefore can take an interest in more general matters and mobilize his actions for purposes other than merely earning a living. It is well known that in Western countries propaganda is particularly effective in the upper segment of the working class and in the middle classes. It faces much greater problems with the proletariat or the peasantry. We shall come back to that.

One must also keep in mind that propaganda must concentrate on the densest mass—it must be organized for the enormous mass of individuals. This great majority is not found among the very rich or the very poor; propaganda therefore is made for those who have attained an average standard of living. In Western countries propaganda addresses itself to the large average mass, which alone represents a real force. But, one might say, in the very poor countries, such as India or the Arab nations, propaganda is addressed to another mass, to the very poor, the *fellahin*. Well, the point is that these poor react only very little and very slowly to any propaganda that is not pure agitation propaganda. The students and merchants react—the poor do not. This explains the weakness of propaganda in India and Egypt. For propaganda to be effective, the propagandee must have a certain store of ideas and a number of conditioned reflexes. These are acquired only with a little affluence, some education, and peace of mind springing from relative security.

Conversely, all propagandists come from the upper middle class, whether Soviet, Nazi, Japanese, or American propagandists. The wealthy and very cultured class provides no propagandists because it is remote from the people and does not understand them well enough to influence them. The lower class does not furnish any because its members rarely have the means of educating themselves (even in the U.S.S.R.); more important, they cannot stand back and look at their class with the perspective needed to devise symbols for it. Thus studies show that most propagandists are recruited from the middle class.

The range of propaganda *influence* is larger and encompasses the lower middle class and the upper working class as well. But by raising people's living standard one does not immunize them against propaganda—on the contrary. Of course, if everybody were to find himself at the upper-middle-class level, present-day propaganda might have less chance of success. But in view of the fact that the ascent to that level is gradual, the rising living standard—in the West, as well as in the East and in Africa—makes the coming generations much more susceptible to propaganda. The latter establishes its influence while working conditions, food, and housing improve, and while at the same time a certain standardization of men, their transformation into what is regarded as normal, typical people, sets in.[7] But whereas the emergence of such

---

[7] This is what Lenin said when he called for a total cultural transformation, with changes in medicine, in the relations between men and women, in the use of alcohol, and so on. This transformation of the entire way of life was linked to agitprop.

a "normal" type used to be automatic and spontaneous, it now becomes more and more a systematic creation, conscious, planned, and intended. The technical aspects of men's work, a clear concept of social relations and national goals, the establishment of a mode of common life—all this leads to the creation of a type of normal man, and conveniently leads all men toward that norm via a multitude of paths.

That is why *adjustment* has become one of the key words of all psychological influence. Whether it is a question of adaptation to working conditions, to consumption, or to milieu, a clear and conscious intent to integrate people into the "normal" pattern prevails everywhere. This is the summit of propaganda action. For example, there is not much difference between Mao's theory of the "mold" and McCarthyism. In both cases the aim is normalcy, in conformance with a certain way of life. For Mao, normalcy is a sort of ideal man, the prototype of the Communist, who must be shaped, and this can be done only by pressing the individual into a mold in which he will assume the desired shape. As this cannot be done overnight, the individual must be pressed again and again into the mold; and Mao says that the individual himself is fully aware that he must submit to the operation. Mao adds that this normalcy does not take shape "except at a certain level of consciousness—that is, at a certain standard of living."[8] We are face to face here with the most total concept of propaganda.

On the other side, and with other formulas, there is McCarthyism. McCarthyism is no accident. It expresses, and at the same time exploits, a deep current in American opinion against all that is "un-American." It deals less with opinions than with a way of life. To find that belonging to a milieu, a group, or a family in which there are Communists is regarded as reprehensible in the United States is surprising, because what matters here is not ideas but a different way of life. This leads to the association of alcoholism and homosexuality with Communism in the literature on un-American activities, and to the rules, promulgated in 1952, which established the "poor security risk" and led to the screening of 7,000 functionaries. No reason for this identification existed other than that the Communist is "abnormal" because he fails to accept the "normal"—that is, the American—way of life. These "abnormal" persons must, of course, be treated as such, relieved of all

[8] See below, Appendix II.

responsibility, and re-educated. Thus American prisoners in the Korean War who appeared to have been contaminated by Communism were hospitalized after their release and given psychiatric and medical treatment in a hospital at Valley Forge. In current American opinion, all efforts to root out what fails to correspond to the American Way of Life and endangers it, are necessarily regarded as good works.

To sum up: The creation of normalcy in our society can take one of two shapes. It can be the result of scientific, psycho-sociological analysis based on statistics—that is, the American type of normalcy. It can also be ideological and doctrinaire—that is, the Communist type. But the results are identical: such normalcy necessarily gives rise to propaganda that can reduce the individual to the pattern most useful to society.

An Average Culture

In addition to a certain living standard, another condition must be met: if man is to be successfully propagandized, he needs at least a minimum of culture. Propaganda cannot succeed where people have no trace of Western culture. We are not speaking here of intelligence; some primitive tribes are surely intelligent, but have an intelligence foreign to our concepts and customs. A base is needed—for example, education; a man who cannot read will escape most propaganda, as will a man who is not interested in reading. People used to think that learning to read evidenced human progress; they still celebrate the decline of illiteracy as a great victory; they condemn countries with a large proportion of illiterates; they think that reading is a road to freedom. All this is debatable, for the important thing is not to be able to read, but to understand what one reads, to reflect on and judge what one reads. Outside of that, reading has no meaning (and even destroys certain automatic qualities of memory and observation). But to talk about critical faculties and discernment is to talk about something far above primary education and to consider a very small minority. The vast majority of people, perhaps 90 percent, know how to read, but do not exercise their intelligence beyond this. They attribute authority and eminent value to the printed word, or, conversely, reject it altogether. As these people do not possess enough knowledge to reflect and discern, they believe—or disbelieve—*in toto* what they read. And as such people, moreover, will select the easiest, not the hardest, reading matter, they are precisely on the level at which the printed word can seize and convince them without opposition. They are perfectly adapted to propaganda.

Let us not say: "If one gave them good things to read . . . if these people received a better education . . ." Such an argument has no validity because things just are not that way. Let us not say, either: "This is only the first stage; soon their education will be better; one must begin somewhere." First of all, it takes a very long time to pass from the first to the second stage; in France, the first stage was reached half a century ago, and we still are very far from attaining the second. There is more, unfortunately. This first stage has placed man at the disposal of propaganda. Before he can pass to the second stage, he will find himself in a universe of propaganda. He will be already formed, adapted, integrated. This is why the development of culture in the U.S.S.R. can take place without danger. One can reach a higher level of culture without ceasing to be a propagandee as long as one was a propagandee *before* acquiring critical faculties, and as long as that culture itself is integrated into a universe of propaganda. Actually, the most obvious result of primary education in the nineteenth and twentieth centuries was to make the individual susceptible to superpropaganda.[9] There is no chance of raising the intellectual level of Western populations sufficiently and rapidly enough to compensate for the progress of propaganda. Propaganda techniques have advanced so much faster than the reasoning capacity of the average man that to close this gap and shape this man intellectually outside the framework of propaganda is almost impossible. In fact, what happens and what we see all around us is the claim that propaganda itself *is* our culture and what the masses ought to learn. Only in and through propaganda have the masses access to political economy, politics, art, or literature. Primary education makes it possible to enter the realm of propaganda, in which people then receive their intellectual and cultural environment.

The uncultured man cannot be reached by propaganda. Experience and research done by the Germans between 1933 and

---

[9] Because he considered the newspaper the principal instrument of propaganda, Lenin insisted on the necessity of teaching reading. It was even more the catchword of the New Economic Policy: the school became the place to prepare students to receive propaganda.

1938 showed that in remote areas, where people hardly knew how to read, propaganda had no effect. The same holds true for the enormous effort in the Communist world to teach people how to read. In Korea, the local script was terribly difficult and complicated; so, in North Korea, the Communists created an entirely new alphabet and a simple script in order to teach all the people how to read. In China, Mao simplified the script in his battle with illiteracy, and in some places in China new alphabets are being created. This would have no particular significance except that the texts used to teach the adult students how to read—and which are the only texts to which they have access—are *exclusively* propaganda texts; they are political tracts, poems to the glory of the Communist regime, extracts of classical Marxism. Among the Tibetans, the Mongols, the Ouighbours, the Manchus, the only texts in the new script are Mao's works. Thus, we see here a wonderful shaping tool: The illiterates are taught to read only the new script; nothing is published in that script except propaganda texts; therefore, the illiterates cannot possibly read—or know—anything else.

Also, one of the most effective propaganda methods in Asia was to establish "teachers" to teach reading and indoctrinate people *at the same time.* The prestige of the intellectual—"marked with God's finger"—allowed political assertions to appear as Truth, while the prestige of the printed word one learned to decipher confirmed the validity of what the teachers said. These facts leave no doubt that the development of primary education is a fundamental condition for the organization of propaganda, even though such a conclusion may run counter to many prejudices, best expressed by Paul Rivet's pointed but completely unrealistic words: "A person who cannot read a newspaper is not free."

This need of a certain cultural level to make people susceptible to propaganda[1] is best understood if one looks at one of propa-

---

[1] We also must consider the fact that in a society in which propaganda—whether direct or indirect, conscious or unconscious—absorbs all the means of communication or education (as in practically all societies in 1960), propaganda forms culture and in a certain sense *is* culture. When film and novel, newspaper and television are instruments either of political propaganda in the restricted sense or in that of human relations (social propaganda), culture is perfectly integrated into propaganda; as a consequence, the more cultivated a man is, the more he is propagandized. Here one can also see the idealist illusion of those who hope that the mass media of communication will create a mass culture. This "culture" is merely a way of destroying a personality.

ganda's most important devices, the manipulation of symbols. The more an individual participates in the society in which he lives, the more he will cling to stereotyped symbols expressing collective notions about the past and the future of his group. The more stereotypes in a culture, the easier it is to form public opinion, and the more an individual participates in that culture, the more susceptible he becomes to the manipulation of these symbols. The number of propaganda campaigns in the West which have first taken hold in *cultured settings* is remarkable. This is not only true for doctrinaire propaganda, which is based on exact facts and acts on the level of the most highly developed people who have a sense of values and know a good deal about political realities, such as, for example, the propaganda on the injustice of capitalism, on economic crises, or on colonialism; it is only normal that the most educated people (intellectuals) are the first to be reached by such propaganda. But this is also true for the crudest kind of propaganda; for example, the campaign on Peace and the campaign on bacteriological warfare were first successful in educated milieus. In France, the intellectuals went along most readily with the bacteriological warfare propaganda. All this runs counter to pat notions that only the public swallows propaganda. Naturally, the educated man does not *believe* in propaganda; he shrugs and is convinced that propaganda has no effect on him. This is, in fact, one of his great weaknesses, and propagandists are well aware that in order to reach someone, one must first convince him that propaganda is ineffectual and not very clever. Because he is convinced of his own superiority, the intellectual is much more vulnerable than anybody else to this maneuver, even though basically a high intelligence, a broad culture, a constant exercise of the critical faculties, and full and objective information are still the best weapons against propaganda. This danger has been recognized in the U.S.S.R., where so much importance is attached to political indoctrination and education, and has frequently been expressed there: too much discussion, too much depth of doctrine risk creating divergent currents and permitting the intellectual to escape social control.

Finally, propaganda can have an effect on the masses who lack any culture. Examples: the Leninist propaganda directed at the Russian peasantry and the Maoist propaganda directed at the Chinese peasantry. But these propaganda methods, are basically the creation of conditioned reflexes on the one hand, and the slow creation of the necessary cultural base on the other. To illustrate the creation of the conditioned reflex: after several months of propaganda in Honan in 1928, children at play would call their opponents "Imperialists."

As noted earlier, poor and uncultured populations are appropriate objects of propaganda of agitation and subversion. The more miserable and ignorant a person is, the more easily will he be plunged into a rebel movement. But to go beyond this, to do a more profound propaganda job on him, one must educate him. This corresponds to the need for "political education." Conversely, an individual of the middle class, of good general culture, will be less susceptible to agitation propaganda but ideal prey of integration propaganda. This has also been observed by Lipset, who holds that ignorance in politics and economics makes the conflicts in these spheres less clear and therefore less intense to the observer, and for this reason the ignorant are less susceptible to propaganda on such questions.

Information

Of course, basic education permits the dissemination not only of propaganda but of information in general. But here we meet with a new condition for propaganda. Contrary to the simplistic differentiation between propaganda and information, we have demonstrated a close relationship between the two. In reality, to distinguish exactly between propaganda and information is impossible. Besides, information is an essential element of propaganda; for propaganda to succeed, it must have reference to political or economic reality. Doctrinal or historical argument is only incidentally effective in propaganda; it has power only in connection with the interpretation of events. It has an effect only when opinion is already aroused, troubled, or oriented in a certain direction by a political or economic event. It grafts itself onto an already existing psychological reality. Such psychological reactions are generally of brief duration, and must be systematically sustained and renewed. To the extent that they will be prolonged and renewed, they will create an "informed opinion."

This informed opinion is indispensable for propaganda. Where we have no informed opinion with regard to political or economic affairs, propaganda cannot exist. For this reason, in most of the older countries, propaganda was localized and restricted to those groups which had direct contact with political life; it was not designed for the masses indifferent to such questions—indifferent because they were uninformed. The masses cannot be interested in political and economic questions or in the great ideological debates based on them, until mass media of communication disseminate information to the public. We know that the most difficult to reach are the peasants, for a variety of reasons already pointed out; but another essential reason is that they are uninformed. Studies of rural milieus have shown that propaganda begins to "bite" among peasants at the exact moment when information is promulgated there, when facts become known and attention to certain questions is aroused. Obviously, if I do not know that war is being waged in Korea, or that North Korea and China are Communist, or that the United States occupies South Korea and that it represents the UN in Korea, any Communist propaganda on alleged American biological warfare means nothing to me. Propaganda means precisely nothing without preliminary information; therefore propaganda to politically ignorant groups can be made only if preceded by extensive, profound, and serious information work.[2] The broader and more objective the information, the more effective subsequent propaganda will be.

Once again, propaganda does not base itself on errors, but on exact facts. It even seems that the more informed public or private opinion is (notice I say "more," not "better"), the more susceptible it is to propaganda. The greater a person's knowledge of political and economic facts, the more sensitive and vulnerable is his judgment. Intellectuals are most easily reached by propaganda, particularly if it employs ambiguity. The reader of a number of newspapers expressing diverse attitudes—just because he is better informed—is more subjected than anyone else to a propaganda that he cannot perceive, even though he claims to retain free choice in the mastery of all this information. Actually, he is being conditioned to absorb all the propaganda that coordinates

---

[2] This is why in the Soviet Union one does not distinguish between the tasks of information and propaganda. The agitator is, above all, a dispenser of information; radio and the press are, above all, media of propaganda. Mr. Palgounov, director of the Tass agency, said in 1956: "Information should be didactic and educative." Not to mention the fact that pure information is an excellent medium of propaganda; bald information without commentary can lead to acceptance of a whole propaganda line.

and explains the facts he believes himself to be mastering. Thus, information not only provides the basis for propaganda but gives propaganda the means to operate; for information actually generates the problems that propaganda exploits and for which it pretends to offer solutions. In fact, no propaganda can work until the moment when a set of facts has become a *problem* in the eyes of those who constitute public opinion.

At the moment such problems begin to confront public opinion, propaganda on the part of a government, a party, or a man can begin to develop fully by magnifying that problem on the one hand and promising solutions for it on the other. But propaganda cannot easily create a political or economic problem out of nothing. There must be some reason in reality. The problem need not actually exist, but there must be a reason why it *might* exist. For example, if the dispensation of daily information leads a man into the labyrinth of economic realities, he will find it difficult to understand these complicated and various facts, and he will therefore conclude that some problems of an economic nature exist. But this takes on an entirely different and much more pronounced aspect when this opinion is in any way connected with personal experience. If he were ignorant of what went on in the nation and in the world, and if his only sources of information were equally uninformed neighbors; in that case propaganda would be impossible, even if that man were actually to suffer personal difficulties as a result of certain political or economic situations. Propaganda had no effect on the populations of the nineteenth century, even when a village was plundered by an army, because in the face of personal experiences people respond spontaneously or by group reflexes, but in any event only to a local and limited situation. They would find it very difficult to generalize the situation, to look upon it as a generally valid phenomenon and to build a specific response to such a generalization—that would demand a considerable amount of voluntary intellectual labor. Thus propaganda becomes possible only when people develop a consciousness of general problems and specific responses to them.

The formation of such responses is precisely what the promulgation of information creates in individuals who have only limited personal contact with social reality. Through information, the individual is placed in a context and learns to understand the reality of his own situation with respect to society as a whole. This will then entice him to social and political action. Take, for example, the problem of the standard of living: The worker who knows nothing about prices and salaries, except from personal experience (or those of his neighbors), may in the event of sharp discontent experience feelings of rebellion, and may eventually rebel against his immediate superiors. And it is well known that such rebellion leads nowhere; that was the great discovery of the nineteenth century. But information will teach this worker that he shares his fate with millions of others, and that among them there can be a community of interest and action. Information allows him also to put his situation into the general economic context and to understand the general situation of management. Finally, information will teach him to evaluate his personal situation. This is what led to the class consciousness of the nineteenth-century workers, a process which—as the socialists rightly maintain—was much more one of information than one of propaganda. At that very moment (when information is absorbed) the spirit of rebellion transforms itself into the spirit of revolution. As a result of information, individuals come to feel that their own personal problems are really invested with the dignity of a general social problem.

From the moment when that sort of information is acquired, propaganda finds the doors open. The elementary form of propaganda in which a few leaders address a few rebels is then replaced by the complex modern propaganda based on mass movements, on knowledge of the great politico-economic realities, and on involvement in certain broad currents fed everywhere by identical information.[3]

Thus information prepares the ground for propaganda. To the extent that a large number of individuals receive the same information, their reactions will be similar. As a result, identical "centers of interest" will be produced and then become the great

---

[3] Moreover, the newer the problems raised, the more vulnerable men will be. The role of information is to introduce individuals to knowledge of new facts and problems. Specialists in opinion research are well aware that the individual is easier to influence by propaganda when he is in new situations, when he is not familiar with possible solutions, when he cannot relate to previous patterns—when, in brief, opinion is "non-structured." The task of information is to put the individual in this situation of non-structured opinion and thus make him more susceptible to influence.

questions of our time made public by press and radio, and group opinions will be formed which will establish contact with each other—one of the essential processes in the formation of public opinion. Moreover, this leads to the formation of common reflexes and common prejudices. Naturally, there are deviationists—individuals who do not share the same responses to the same information, because they already hold other prejudices, because they are "strong personalities," or simply because of habitual contrariness. But their number is much smaller than is generally believed. They are unimportant, and the polarization of attention on certain questions, and on certain aspects of these questions singled out by information, rapidly creates what has been called mass psychology—one of the indispensable conditions for the existence of propaganda.

The Ideologies

Finally, the last condition for the development of propaganda is the prevalence of strong myths and ideologies in a society. At this point a few words are needed on the term *ideology*.

To begin with, we subscribe to Raymond Aron's statement that an ideology is any set of ideas accepted by individuals or peoples, without attention to their origin or value. But one must perhaps add, with Q. Wright, (1) an element of valuation (cherished ideas), (2) an element of actuality (ideas relating to the present), and (3) an element of belief (believed, rather than proved, ideas).

Ideology differs from myth in three important respects: first, the myth is imbedded much more deeply in the soul, sinks its roots farther down, is more permanent, and provides man with a fundamental image of his condition and the world at large. Second, the myth is much less "doctrinaire"; an ideology (which is not a doctrine because it is *believed* and not proved) is first of all a set of ideas, which, even when they are irrational, are still ideas. The myth is more intellectually diffuse; it is part emotionalism, part affective response, part a sacred feeling, and more important. Third, the myth has stronger powers of activation, whereas ideology is more passive (one can believe in an ideology and yet remain on the sidelines). The myth does not leave man passive; it drives him to action. What myth and ideology have in common, however, is that they are collective phenomena and

their persuasive force springs from the power of collective participation.

Thus one can distinguish: the fundamental myths of our society
are the myths of Work, Progress, Happiness; the fundamental
ideologies are Nationalism, Democracy, Socialism. Communism
shares in both elements. It is an ideology in that it is a basic
doctrine, and a myth in that it has an explanation for all questions
and an image of a future world in which all contradictions will
be resolved. Myths have existed in all societies, but there have not
always been ideologies. The nineteenth century was a great
breeding ground of ideology, and propaganda needed an ideological setting to develop.

Ideology in the service of propaganda is very flexible and fluid.
Propaganda in support of the French Revolution, or of United
States life in the twenties, or of Soviet life in the forties, can all be
traced back to the ideology of democracy. These three entirely
different types and concepts of propaganda all refer to the same
ideology. One must not think, for this reason, that ideology
determines a given propaganda merely because it provides the
themes and contents. Ideology serves propaganda as a peg, a
pretext. Propaganda seizes what springs up spontaneously and
gives it a new form, a structure, an effective channel, and can
eventually transform ideology into myth. We shall return later to
the connection between ideology and propaganda.

[III]

THE NECESSITY
FOR PROPAGANDA

A common view of propaganda is that it is the work of a few evil men, seducers of the people, cheats and authoritarian rulers who want to dominate a population; that it is the handmaiden of more or less illegitimate powers. This view always thinks of propaganda as being made voluntarily; it assumes that a man decides "to make propaganda," that a government establishes a Propaganda Ministry, and that things just develop from there on. According to this view, the public is just an object, a passive crowd that one can manipulate, influence, and use. And this notion is held not only by those who think one can manipulate the crowds but also by those who think propaganda is not very effective and can be resisted easily.

In other words, this view distinguishes between an active factor —the propagandist—and a passive factor—the crowd, the mass, man.[1] Seen from that angle, it is easy to understand the moralist's

---

[1] According to this conception, propaganda is a "sinister invention of the military caste," whereas actually it is the expression of modern society as a whole.

hostility to propaganda: man is the innocent victim pushed into evil ways by the propagandist; the propagandee is entirely without blame because he has been fooled and has fallen into a trap. The militant Nazi and Communist are just poor victims who must not be fought but must be psychologically liberated from that trap, readapted to freedom, and shown the truth. In any event, the propagandee is seen in the role of the poor devil who cannot help himself, who has no means of defense against the bird of prey who swoops down on him from the skies. A similar point of view can be found in studies on advertising which regard the buyer as victim and prey. In all this the propagandee is never charged with the slightest responsibility for a phenomenon regarded as originating entirely outside of himself.

This view seems to me completely wrong. A simple fact should lead us at least to question it: nowadays propaganda pervades all aspects of public life. We know that the psychological factor, which includes encirclement, integration into a group, and participation in action, in addition to personal conviction, is decisive. To draw up plans for an organization, a system of work, political methods, and institutions is not enough; the individual must participate in all this from the bottom of his heart, with pleasure and deep satisfaction. If the Common Market is wanted, a unit must be set up to psychologically prepare the people for the Common Market; this is absolutely necessary because the institutions mean nothing by themselves. NATO also needs propaganda for its members. Gasperi's proposal of 1956 to create a Demform that would correspond to the Cominform is extremely significant. Present political warfare is very inadequate; from the economic point of view one may well say that the recession was much more a psychological than a technical or economic development.[2] In order to assure that reforms will have vigor and effectiveness, one must first convince the people that no recession has occurred and that they have nothing to fear. And this is not just Dr. Coué's method of self-imploration, but active participation in an effective recovery.

A specific example: Agricultural "reconstruction" in France is first of all a psychological problem. "Services of Popularization"

---

[2] As early as 1928, Edward Bernays stated: "Propaganda is the modern instrument by which . . . intelligent men can fight for productive ends and help to bring order out of chaos."

are created, which furnish not only technical consultants but primarily psychological agitators, on the pattern of the famous county agents in the United States or the counselors in Scandinavia. Efforts at popularizing and at instilling convictions take place simultaneously. The U.S.S.R. is still much more advanced in the direction of a full-fledged agricultural propaganda, with technically perfect propaganda campaigns at harvest time, hundreds of thousands of propaganda agents roaming through the villages expostulating "motherland" and "production," radio broadcasts and films, and daily publication of harvest results, as in a pennant race. Joining in this campaign are the local papers, the Komsomols, the teamsters, the festivities, dances, folk songs, rewards, decorations, and citations.

The Soviets employ the same methods in factory work, and the formula that best explains the whole effort is: "Full understanding on the part of the workers is the decisive factor in raising productivity." It is necessary to obtain the worker's allegiance to the cause of productivity; he must accept and search for innovations, like his work, support his organization, understand the function of labor. All this is attained by psychological manipulation, by a propaganda conducted with precision over a considerable length of time.

In armies, such techniques are of equal importance. The best example is the new German army; the German soldier must be convinced of the validity of what he defends and patriotism is no longer territorial but ideological. This psychological approach is designed to give the soldiers a *personal* discipline, with a capacity for decision and choice; military techniques are no longer sufficient. All this is pure propaganda, including the notion of the personal decision, for as soon as the individual has been indoctrinated with the "truth", he will act as he is expected to act, from the "spontaneity" of his conscience. This was the principal aim of propaganda in Hitler's army, and the individual German soldier's capacity for personal initiative in 1940 was truly remarkable.

One final example in a different field: In connection with the 1959 census in the U.S.S.R., a gigantic propaganda campaign was unleashed, because both the speed with which such a census can be taken and the accuracy of the results depend on the good will and truthfulness of the citizens. So, in order to obtain speed and accuracy, opinion was mobilized. The entire press and all mass organizations sprang into action in order to envelop the citizens in propaganda, and propagandists roamed the country far and wide to explain to the people what was being planned, to alleviate their prejudices and suspicions with regard to the questions that they would be asked.

These are all examples of entirely different applications of propaganda. But in order for propaganda to be so far-ranging, it must correspond to a need. The State has that need: Propaganda obviously is a necessary instrument for the State and the authorities. But while this fact may dispel the concept of the propagandist as simply an evil-doer, it still leaves the idea of propaganda as an active power vs. passive masses. And we insist that this idea, too, must be dispelled: For propaganda to *succeed*, it must correspond to a need for propaganda on the individual's part. One can lead a horse to water but cannot make him drink; one cannot reach through propaganda those who do not need what it offers. The propagandee is by no means just an innocent victim. He provokes the psychological action of propaganda, and not merely lends himself to it, but even derives satisfaction from it. Without this previous, implicit consent, without this need for propaganda experienced by practically *every* citizen of the technological age, propaganda could not spread. There is not just a wicked propagandist at work who sets up means to ensnare the innocent citizen. Rather, there is a citizen who craves propaganda from the bottom of his being and a propagandist who responds to this craving. Propagandists would not exist without potential propagandees to begin with. To understand that propaganda is not just a deliberate and more or less arbitrary creation by some people in power is therefore essential. It is a strictly sociological phenomenon, in the sense that it has its roots and reasons in the need of the group that will sustain it. We are thus face to face with a dual need: the need on the part of regimes to make propaganda, and the need of the propagandee. These two conditions correspond to and complement each other in the development of propaganda.

1. The State's Necessity

The Dilemma of the Modern State

Propaganda is needed in the exercise of power for the simple reason that the masses have come to participate in political affairs.

Let us not call this democracy; this is only one aspect of it. To begin with, there is the concrete reality of masses. In a sparsely populated country, politics can be made by small groups, separated from each other and from the masses, which will not form a public opinion and are remote from the centers of power. The nearness of the masses to the seats of power is very important. Pericles and Tiberius were well aware of it, as were Louis XIV and Napoleon: they installed themselves in the countryside, far from the crowds, in order to govern in peace outside the reach of the pressure of the masses, which, even without clearly wanting to, affect the conditions of power by their mere proximity. This simple fact explains why politics can no longer be the game of princes and diplomats, and why palace revolutions have been replaced by popular revolutions.

Nowadays the ruler can no longer detach himself from the masses and conduct a more or less secret policy; he no longer has an ivory tower; and everywhere he is confronted with this multiple presence. He cannot escape the mass simply because of the present population density—the mass is everywhere. Moreover, as a result of the modern means of transportation, the government is not only in constant contact with the population of the capital, but also with the entire country. In their relations with the governing powers, there is hardly any difference now between the population of the capital and that of the countryside. This physical proximity is itself a political factor. Moreover, the mass knows its rulers through the press, radio, and TV—the Chief of State is in contact with the people. He can no longer prevent people from knowing a certain number of political facts. This development is not the result of some applied doctrine; it is not because democratic doctrine demands the masses' participation in public power that this relationship between mass and government has developed. It is a simple fact, and the inevitable result of demographic changes. Hence, if the ruler wants to play the game by himself and follow secret policies, he must present a decoy to the masses. He cannot escape the mass; but he can draw between himself and that mass an invisible curtain, a screen, on which the mass will see projected the mirage of some politics, while the real politics are being made behind it.

Except for this subterfuge, the government is in fact under the control of the people—not juridical control, but the kind of control that stems from the simple fact that the people are interested in politics and try to keep up with and understand governmental action, as well as make their opinions known. For, after all, the masses are interested in politics.[3] This, too, is new. Even those who do not read the papers carefully are appalled at the thought of censorship, particularly when they feel that the government wants to hide something or leave them in the dark. Nowadays the masses are accustomed to making political judgments; as the result of the democratic process they are accustomed to be consulted on political alternatives and to receive political information. This may only be a habit, but it is deeply ingrained by now; to try to reverse it would immediately provoke feelings of frustration and cries of injustice. That the masses are interested in politics, whether deeply or superficially, is a fact. Besides, one very simple reason explains this: today, as never before in history, political decisions affect everybody. In the old days, a war affected a small number of soldiers and a negligible piece of territory; today everybody is a soldier, and the entire population and the whole territory of a nation are involved. Therefore, everybody wants to have his say on the subject of war and peace.

Similarly, taxes have increased at least tenfold since the seventeenth century, and those who pay them naturally want some control over their use. The sacrifices demanded by political life keep increasing and affect everybody; therefore everybody wants to participate in this game, which affects him directly. Because the State's decisions will affect *me*, I intend to influence them. As a result, governments can no longer govern without the masses—without their influence, presence, knowledge, and pressure. But how, then, can they govern?

The rule of public opinion is regarded as a simple and natural fact. The government is regarded as the product of this opinion, from which it draws its strength. It expresses public opinion. To quote Napoleon's famous words: "Power is based on opinion. What is a government not supported by opinion? Nothing." Theoretically, democracy is political expression of mass opinion. Most people consider it simple to translate this opinion into action, and

---

[3] Democracy rests on the conviction that the citizen can choose the right man and the right policy. Because this is not exactly the case, the crowd is propagandized in order to make it participate. Under such conditions, how could the mass not be convinced that it is deeply concerned?

consider it legitimate that the government should bend to the popular will. Unfortunately, in reality all this is much less clear and not so simple. More and more we know, for example, that public opinion does not express itself at the polls and is a long way from expressing itself clearly in political trends. We know, too, that public opinion is very unstable, fluctuating, never settled. Furthermore, this opinion is irrational and develops in unforesee-able fashion. It is by no means composed of a majority of rational decisions in the face of political problems, as some simplistic vision would have it. The majority vote is by no means the real public opinion. Its basically irrational character greatly reduces its power to rule in a democracy. Democracy is based on the con-cept that man is rational and capable of seeing clearly what is in his own interest, but the study of public opinion suggests this is a highly doubtful proposition. And the bearer of public opinion is generally a mass man, psychologically speaking, which makes him quite unsuited to properly exercise his right of citizenship.

This leads us to the following consideration: On the one hand, the government can no longer operate outside the pressure of the masses and public opinion; on the other hand, public opinion does not express itself in the democratic form of government. To be sure, the government must know and constantly probe public opinion.[4] The modern State must constantly undertake press and opinion surveys and sound out public opinion in a variety of other ways. But the fundamental question is: Does the State then obey and express and follow that opinion? Our unequivocal answer is that even in a democratic State it does not. Such obeisance by the State to public opinion is impossible—first, because of the very nature of public opinion, and second, because of the nature of modern political activities.

Public opinion is so variable and fluctuating that government could never base a course of action on it; no sooner would govern-ment begin to pursue certain aims favored in an opinion poll, than opinion would turn against it. To the degree that opinion

[4] The Soviet Union, despite its authoritarian character and the absence of opinion surveys, makes just as much effort to keep informed of public opinion—through agitators (who inform the government on the people's state of mind) and through letters to the press. The government does not consult opinion in order to obey it, however, but to know at what level it exists and to determine what propaganda action is needed to win it over. The Party must neither anticipate public opinion nor lag behind it. To determine the State's rhythm of action, it must know the masses' state of mind.

changes are rapid, policy changes would have to be equally rapid; to the extent that opinion is irrational, political action would have to be equally irrational. And as public opinion, ultimately, is always "the opinion of incompetents," political decisions would therefore be surrendered to them.

Aside from the near-impossibility of simply following public opinion, the government has certain functions—particularly those of a technical nature—entirely outside such opinion. With regard to an enterprise that involves billions and lasts for years, it is not a question of following opinion—either at its inception, when opinion has not yet crystalized, or later, when the enterprise has gone too far to turn back. In such matters as French oil policy in the Sahara or electrification in the Soviet Union, public opinion can play no role whatever. The same holds true even where enterprises are being nationalized, regardless of an apparent socialist opinion. In many instances, political decisions must be made to suit new problems emerging precisely from the new political configurations in our age, and such problems do not fit the stereotypes and patterns of established public opinion. Nor can public opinion crystalize overnight—and the government cannot postpone actions and decisions until vague images and myths eventually coalesce into opinion. In the present world of politics, action must at all times be the forerunner of opinion. Even where public opinion is already formed, it can be disastrous to follow it. Recent studies have shown the catastrophic role of public opinion in matters of foreign policy. The masses are incapable of resolving the conflict between morality and State policy, or of conceiving a long-term foreign policy. They push the government toward a disastrous foreign policy, as in Franklin Roosevelt's policy toward the Soviet Union, or Johnson's push-button policy. The greatest danger in connection with foreign policy is that of public opinion manifesting itself in the shape of crisis, in an explosion. Obviously, public opinion knows little about foreign affairs and cares less; torn by contradictory desires, divided on principal questions, it permits the government to conduct whatever foreign policy it deems best. But all at once, for a variety of reasons, opinion converges on one point, temperatures rise, men become excited and assert themselves (for example, on the question of German rearmament). And should this opinion be followed? To the same extent that opinion expresses

itself sporadically, that it wells up in fits and starts, it runs counter
to the necessary continuity of foreign policy and tends to overturn
previous agreements and existing alliances. Because such opinion
is intermittent and fragmentary, the government could not follow
it even if it wanted to.

Ergo: even in a democracy, a government that is honest, serious,
benevolent, and respects the voter *cannot follow* public opinion.
But it *cannot escape* it either. The masses are there; they are
interested in politics. The government cannot act without them.
So, what can it do?

Only one solution is possible: as the government cannot follow
opinion, opinion must follow the government. One must convince
this present, ponderous, impassioned mass that the government's
decisions are legitimate and good and that its foreign policy is
correct. The democratic State, precisely because it believes in the
expression of public opinion and does not gag it, must channel
and shape that opinion if it wants to be realistic and not follow
an ideological dream. The Gordian knot cannot be cut any other
way. Of course, the political parties already have the role of
adjusting public opinion to that of the government. Numerous
studies have shown that political parties often do not agree with
that opinion, that the voters—and even party members—frequently do not know their parties' doctrines, and that people
belong to parties for reasons other than ideological ones. But the
parties channel free-floating opinion into existing formulas, polar-
izing it on opposites that do not necessarily correspond to the
original tenets of such opinion. Because parties are so rigid, because they deal with only a part of any question, and because they
are purely politically motivated, they distort public opinion and
prevent it from forming naturally. But even beyond party influence, which is already propaganda influence, government
action exists in and by itself.

The most benevolent State will inform the people of what it
does.[5] For the government to explain how it acts, why it acts, and
what the problems are, makes sense; but when dispensing such
information, the government cannot remain coldly objective; *it
must plead its case*, inevitably, if only to counteract opposing

---

[5] Is it normal, for example, for the "Plan" in France to be the expression of a
closed technocracy, and for the public never to be really correctly informed
about it?

propaganda.[6] Because information alone is ineffective, its dissemination leads necessarily to propaganda, particularly when the government is obliged to defend its own actions or the life of the nation against private enterprise. The giant corporations and pressure groups, pushing their special interests, are resorting increasingly to psychological manipulation. Must the government permit this without reacting? And just because pure and simple information cannot prevail against modern propaganda techniques, the government, too, must act through propaganda. In France this situation arose in 1954, when the army used films and pamphlets to challenge the government's E.D.C. (European Defense Community) propaganda. But from the moment the soldier can vote, he is subjected to propaganda from outside groups and is himself a member of a pressure group—and what a group! The army itself is potentially a formidable pressure group, and the famous political malaise in France is partly owing to the efforts of successive governments to influence that group by psychological means, and to break it up. How can one deny to the government the right to do what all the other groups do? How can one demand of a modern State that it tolerate an independent group? Pleven's demand of 1954, to the effect that "there must be no propaganda in one direction or the other," is morally most satisfying, but purely theoretical and unrealistic. Moreover, he went on to claim that what had been called propaganda was government-dispensed information, pure and simple. In fact the two realities —information and propaganda—are so little distinct from one another that what the enemy says is nothing but propaganda, whereas what our side says is nothing but information.[7]

But there is more: in a democracy, the citizens must be tied to the decisions of the government. This is the great role propaganda must perform. It must give the people the feeling—which they crave and which satisfies them—"to have wanted what the government is doing, to be responsible for its actions, to be involved in defending them and making them succeed, to be 'with it.' "[8] The

---

[6] This will be examined elsewhere in greater detail.

[7] It is known that in French opinion everything that comes from the State, even what is most honest, will be automatically and without examination called propaganda; so propagandized, rather than free and critical, is the contemporary Frenchman. This is what happened to the speeches by Mendès-France and the communiqués concerning the war in Algeria.

[8] Léo Hamon: *"Le Pouvoir et l'opinion," Le Monde,* April 1959.

writer Léo Hamon is of the opinion that this is the main task of
political parties, unions, and associations. But it is not the whole
answer. More direct and evocative action is needed to tie opinion,
not just to anything, but to acts of political power. The American
writer Bradford Westerfield has said: "In the United States, the
government almost always conducts its foreign policies on its own
initiative, but where the public is interested in a particular question, it can only proceed with the *apparent support* of a substantial majority of the people." Westerfield stresses that at times concessions must be made to the people, but "if the President *really
directs opinion,* and if the public accepts the foreign policy of the
government as a whole, no great concessions will have to be made
to elicit the necessary support."[9] Here we find confirmation that
any modern State, even a democratic one, is burdened with the
task of acting through propaganda.[1] It cannot act otherwise.

But the same analysis must be made from another point of
departure. We have traced the dilemma of the modern State.
Since the eighteenth century, the democratic movement has
pronounced, and eventually impregnated the masses with, the
idea of the legitimacy of power; and after a series of theories on
that legitimacy we have now reached the famous theory of the
sovereignty of the people. Power is regarded as legitimate when
it derives from the sovereignty of the people, rests on the popular
will, expresses and follows this popular will. The validity of this
concept can be debated *ad infinitum* from the theoretical point of
view; one can examine it throughout history and ask if it is what
Rousseau had in mind. In any event, this rather abstract philo-
sophic theory has become a well-developed and irrefutable idea

---

[9] Bradford Westerfield: "Opinion and Parties in American Foreign Policy,"
(A.F.S.P., 1954).
[1] The State can no longer govern without its citizens being directly involved in
its enterprises. Goebbels stated that in 1934 the majority of Germans were for
Hitler. But were they active? Were they happy with this political participation?
Finally, could one hope for continued compliance? To assure such compliance
propaganda is necessary. According to Mégret, "psychological action in a democracy is nothing else than this invisible and discreet servant . . . of the great
functions of the State. . . . It is a way of being, doing, and providing, through
the allegiance of minds, the success of legitimate government actions."
This necessary participation is not necessarily spontaneous. Individuals who claim
to control politics are at the same time very passive. On the one hand, they do not
believe what they are told; on the other, they tend to put their private lives before
everything else and to take refuge in them. The state must compel the individual to
participate (at the most elementary level, it must force him to vote). The principal
role of propaganda, then, would be to fight against opposition and indifference.

in the mind of the average man. For the average Westerner, the will of the people is sacred, and a government that fails to represent that will is an abominable dictatorship. Each time the people speak their minds the government must go along; no other source of legitimacy exists. This is the fundamental image, the collective prejudice which has become a self-evident belief and is no longer merely a doctrine or a rational theory. This belief has spread very rapidly in the past thirty years. We now find the same unshakable and absolute belief in all Communist countries, and begin to see it even in Islamic countries, where it should be rather remote. The contagious force of such a formula seems to be inexhaustible.

Conversely, a government does not feel legitimate and cannot claim to be so unless it rests on this sovereignty of the people, unless it can prove that it expresses the will of the people; otherwise it would be thrown out immediately. Because of this mystical belief in the people's sovereignty, all dictators try to demonstrate that they are the expression of that sovereignty. For a long time the theory of the people's sovereignty was believed to be tied to the concept of democracy. But it should be remembered that when that doctrine was applied for the first time, it led to the emergence of the most stringent dictatorship—that of the Jacobins. Therefore, we can hardly complain when modern dictators talk about the sovereignty of the people.

Such is the force of this belief that no government can exist without satisfying it or giving the appearance of sharing it. From this belief springs the necessity for dictators to have themselves elected by plebiscite. Hitler, Stalin, Tito, Mussolini were all able to claim that they obtained their power from the people. This is true even of a Gomulka or a Rakosi: every plebiscite shows the famous result, which fluctuates between 99.1 and 99.9 percent of the votes. It is obvious to everybody, including those elected, that this is just for the sake of appearance, a "consultation" of the people without any significance—but it is equally obvious that one cannot do without it. And the ceremony must be repeated periodically to demonstrate that the legitimacy is still there, that the people are still in full accord with their representatives. The people lend themselves to all this; after all, it cannot be denied that the voters really vote, and that they vote in the desired way— the results are not faked. There *is* compliance.

Could it be that the people's sovereignty is actually something other than compliance? Might it be hoped that without any prior attempts at influencing the people, a true constitutional form could emerge from the people? Such a supposition is absurd. The only reality is to propose to the people something with which they agree. Up to now we have not seen a single example of people not eventually complying with what was proposed to them. In a plebiscite or referendum the "ayes" always exceed the "nays." We see here once again the instrument used to influence the masses, the propaganda by which the government provides itself with legitimacy through public compliance.

This leads to two further considerations: First, compliance must be obtained, not just with the form of government but with all its important actions. As Drouin has aptly said, "nothing is more irritating to a people than to have the feeling of being directed by Mandarins who let their decisions fall from the height of their power." Thus the need to "inform" the people better. "That the decisions should be wise does not suffice; the reasons for them must be given. For an enterprise . . . to function well, it is best to take it apart in public without concealing its weaknesses, without hiding its cost . . . and to make clear the meaning of the sacrifices demanded of the people."[2] But such information really aims at compliance and participation; it is, in other words, propaganda in the deepest sense. But we have become used to seeing our governments act this way.

In 1957, when the Soviet people were called upon to study and discuss Khrushchev's Theses on Economic Reorganization, we witnessed a truly remarkable operation. The underlying theme of it all was, of course, that everything is being decided by the people. How can the people then *not* be in agreement afterwards? How can they fail to comply completely with what they have decided in the first place? The Theses were submitted to the people first. Naturally, they were then explained in all the Party organizations, in the Komsomols, in the unions, in the local soviets, in the factories, and so on, by agitprop specialists. Then the discussions took place. Next, *Pravda* opened its columns to the public, and numerous citizens sent in comments, expressed their views, suggested amendments. After that, what happened? The entire government program, *without the slightest modifica-*

---

[2] "Sur le Régime de la Vᵉ République," *Le Monde*, April 1959.

tion, was passed by the Supreme Soviet. *Even amendments pre-sented and supported* by individual deputies were *rejected,* and all the more those presented by individual citizens; for they were only individual (minority) opinions, and from the democratic (majority) point of view insignificant. But the people were given the immense satisfaction of having been consulted, of having been given a chance to debate, of having—so it seemed to them—their opinions solicited and weighed.[3] This is the democratic appearance that no authoritarian government can do without.

Beyond that, such practices lead the government to embrace a method which derives logically from the principle of popular democracy, but which could develop only as a result of modern propaganda: the government is now in the habit of acting through the masses as intermediary in two ways. First, it goes to the people more and more frequently for the support of its policies. When a decision seems to meet with resistance or is not fully accepted, propaganda is addressed to the masses to set them in motion; the simple motion of the mass is enough to invest the decisions with validity: it is only an extension of the plebiscite. When the People's Democracy installed itself in Czechoslovakia after a police *coup d'état,* gigantic meetings of the working population were held—well staged, organized, and kindled—to demonstrate that the people were in full agreement. When Fidel Castro wanted to show that his power was based on democratic sentiment, he organized the Day of Justice, during which the whole population was called upon to sit in judgment of the past regime, and to express its sentiments through massive demonstrations. These demonstrations were meant to "legalize" the death sentences handed down by the State courts and thus give a "democratic sanction" to the judgments. In doing this, Castro won the people's profound allegiance by satisfying the need for revenge against the former regime and the thirst for blood. He tied the people to his government by the strongest of bonds: the ritual crime. That Day of Justice (January 21, 1959) was undoubtedly a great propagandistic discovery. If it caused Castro some embarrassment abroad, it certainly was a great success at home. It should be noted

---

[3] Goebbels declared that it was necessary "to expose the acts of government so that the people can recognize by themselves the necessity for the measures taken."

that such provocation of popular action *always* serves to support governmental action. It is in no way spontaneous, and in no way expresses an intrinsic desire of the people: it merely expresses, through a million throats of the crowd, the cry of governmental propaganda.

Second—and this is a subtler process—governmental propaganda *suggests* that public opinion *demand* this or that decision; it provokes the will of a people, who spontaneously would say nothing. But, once evoked, formed, and crystalized on a point, that *will* becomes the *people's will;* and whereas the government really acts on its own, it gives the impression of obeying public opinion—after first having built that public opinion. The point is to make the masses demand of the government what the government has already decided to do. If it follows this procedure, the government can no longer be called authoritarian, because the will of the people demands what is being done. In this fashion, when German public opinion unanimously demanded the liberation of Czechoslovakia, the German government had no choice but to invade that country in obedience to the people. It *yielded* to opinion as soon as opinion—through propaganda—had become strong enough to appear to influence the government. Castro's Day of Justice was cut from the same cloth: it was prepared by an excellent propaganda campaign, and the people who had been aroused with great care then demanded that their government carry out the acts of "justice." Thus the government did not merely obtain agreement for its acts; the people actually demanded from the government incisive punitive measures, and the popular government merely fulfilled that demand, which, of course, had been manufactured by government propaganda. This constant propaganda action, which makes the people demand what was decided beforehand and makes it appear as though the spontaneous, innermost desires of the people were being carried out by a democratic and benevolent government, best characterizes the present-day "Mass-Government" relationship. This system has been put to use in the U.S.S.R. particularly, and in this respect Nikita Khrushchev liberalized nothing—on the contrary. However, the emergence of this particular phenomenon was predictable from the day when the principle of popular sovereignty began to take hold. From that point on, the development of propaganda cannot be regarded as a deviation or an accident.

The State and Its Function

From the government point of view, two additional factors must be kept in mind—the competitive situation in which democracy finds itself in the world and the disintegration of national and civic virtues.

Why a totalitarian regime would want to use propaganda is easily understood. Democratic regimes, if we give them the benefit of the doubt, feel some compunction and revulsion against the use of propaganda. But such democratic regimes are driven into its use because of the external challenges they have to meet. Ever since Hitler, democracy has been subjected to relentless psychological warfare. The question, then, is which regime will prevail, for both types claim to be of universal validity and benefit; this obliges them to act upon each other. As the Communist regime claims to be the harbinger of the people's happiness, it has no choice but to destroy all other regimes in order to supplant them. But for the Western democracies the problem is the same: in their eyes the Communist regime is a horrible dictatorship. Thus one must intervene against one's neighbor, mainly through propaganda and also, so far as the Communists are concerned, through Communist parties in non-Communist countries. This in turn forces the democracies to make *internal* propaganda: if they are to prevail against those Communist parties and against the U.S.S.R., economic progress must be accelerated. In fact, the competition between the two regimes unfolds partly in the economic realm. We all know Khrushchev's economic challenge. This acceleration of the economic development demands an organization, a mobilization of the latent forces in the heart of the democracies, which requires psychological work, special training; and a permanent propaganda campaign on the necessity for increased production. It is one result of the competition between regimes.

But this competition takes place on another level as well: no man in the world can remain unaffected by the competition of the two regimes. Unfortunately, this is the result of global solidarity that some welcome: no people can remain outside the conflict between the Big Two. Democracy feels that it must conquer and hold all the small nations, which otherwise would fall into the Communist orbit. In the pursuit of this objective two means are used in conjunction: the economic weapon and propaganda. In the days of classic imperialism, the economic weapon, supported on occasion by brief military action, was sufficient. Nowadays, the successive failures of the United States prove that the economic weapon is ineffective without propaganda. For example, in 1960 the United States gave three times as much assistance to underdeveloped nations as did the Soviet Union; thanks to propaganda, it is the Soviet Union who is regarded as the great helper and benefactor in whom one can put one's trust. The hearts and minds of the people must be won if economic assistance, which by itself has no effect on opinion, is to succeed. Similarly, propaganda by itself accomplishes nothing; it must be accompanied by spectacular economic acts. Without doubt, the democracies have lost out so far in the contest for the African and Asian peoples only because of the inferiority of their propaganda and their reluctance to use it. Thus, the democracies are now irresistibly pushed toward the use of propaganda to stave off decisive defeat. Psychological warfare has become the daily bread of peace policy. The psychological conquest of entire populations has become necessary, and nobody can escape it. One no longer must decide whether or not to use the propaganda weapon; one has no choice.

Good reasons exist for analyzing this new form of aggression. Military aggression has been replaced by indirect aggression— economic or ideological. Propaganda saps the strength of the regimes that are its victims, depriving them of the support of their own public opinion. Austria and Czechoslovakia had been reduced to impotence by Nazi propaganda before they were invaded; other countries with not a single expansionist aim are constantly subjected to this aggression. They cannot defend themselves except by using the same means of psychological warfare, for no international organization or court of justice can protect them against this form of aggression; psychological action is too protean, too hard to nail down, and cannot be legally adjudicated. Above all, in legally defending against psychological aggression, one must not deny the freedom of opinion and speech guaranteed by the Bill of Rights. The problem thus springs directly from the given situation. Every State must accept the burden of defending itself against propaganda aggression. As soon as *one* country has taken this road, all other countries must eventually follow suit or be destroyed.

A democracy is generally poorly organized for effective psychological warfare. French specialists have said with some justification: "Only the army can engage in psychological warfare, because of its structure." But in the face of the democratic regimes'
need to conduct propaganda, it has also been said that "in a
world of the cold war, domestic political thought *must* become
strategic."[4] Therefore the problem is to resolve the dichotomy between the political and the military and to define and integrate
the army's political function. As a result of the necessity to conduct propaganda, democracy finds itself compelled to change its
structure. But the cold war does not merely demand action against
the external enemy who tries to interfere; it also demands that
things be "kept firmly in hand" at home. The State must psychologically arm, protect, and defend its citizens, all the more when
the ideological structure of a democracy is weak.

Here we face a new problem: in today's world, much more than
in the past, a nation can survive only if its values are secure, its
citizens loyal and unanimous, and if they practice the civic
virtues. But at this time a crisis of basic values and a relaxation
of civic virtues is occurring in a number of Western democracies.
Governments are forced to reconstruct their nations psychologically and ideologically, and this need, in turn, justifies psychological action. In fact, in this connection, hardly anybody objects
to such psychological action. Everybody seems to consider it
necessary and justified "as long as one limits oneself to the moral
education of the soldier and the dissemination of the truth." But
many object to putting pressure on people's minds. Though they
mean well, those who object simply fail to see that the two elements they seek to separate—the telling of the truth and the exercise of pressure on the minds—are, in fact, identical. How can
one rebuild civic virtues—rapidly, in order to reap quick benefits
—without using pressure to change people's points of view?
From the moment when the need of reconstructing a nation
ideologically makes itself felt, methods become inevitable which
are propaganda pure and simple. Of course, the objectives pursued are pure. For example, the French Army says:

> . . . far from engaging in psychological action in order to enslave
> minds, most colonels aim only at securing human liberty. . . .

---

[4] T. Albord, *Le Monde*, 1958.

They understand that one cannot permit a man of free choice to let himself be captured by a doctrine that would reduce him to an object. . . . They know that a possible future war would include an attack against the mind, more precisely against one of the mind's functions: the will. . . . Psychological action in the army aims only at furnishing the men with adequate means for the defense of freedom where it still exists. To this end it is enough to strengthen the will of the resistance if that will to resistance comes under attack. The endangered men must be taught our aims, our mission, and our means of attaining them.[5]

Here psychological action is presented in its most favorable light. We cannot even object to the reasoning: it corresponds to the feelings of most liberals. Here psychological action presents itself as a sort of national education. According to another French writer, psychological action "is designed to shape and develop and sustain the morale, and to immunize the soldiers against enemy psychological attacks." This is intended for wartime, when the first task is to shape an army which "must preserve its proper internal spiritual cohesion." It is described thus:

> . . . a civic and moral education of all people placed under military command, within a context of objective information, opposed to propaganda, designed only to spiritually arm the citizen of a free democracy. . . . The methods employed are those of education and human relations; their principal aim is to engage the cooperation of the individual to whom they are addressed, to explain to him and make him understand the different aspects of problems that confront him.

In other words, the aim is the civic education of the troops. The soldier must learn the civic realities and the values of civilization. This is not just a French problem, incidentally; in Germany we find precisely the same orientation. But it is obvious that the education of the army cannot restrict itself to the troops. Such work becomes infinitely easier if young recruits are already indoctrinated. On the other hand, if the army were alone in maintaining the civic virtues, it would feel isolated. For such work to be effective, it must be done by the entire nation. In this fashion the army will be tempted to become the nation's educator; a psychological action by the State on the entire nation then becomes

---

[5] Colonel Villiers de L'Isle Adam, *Le Monde*, October 1958.

a necessity. The Provisional Proclamation on Psychological Action of 1957 stated that neutralism on the part of the government invited subversion and placed it in a perilous position; that the absence of civic education leads young people to a lack of patriotism, to social egotism, and to nihilism.

This shows the perfectly good intentions, the legitimate concerns, and the serious objectives behind psychological action. But is there not a considerable amount of illusion in the rigorous distinction between psychological action and propaganda, between the enemy's methods and one's own? In fact, one is faced with a mass of individuals who must be formed, involved, given certain nationalistic reflexes; a scale of values must be introduced by which the individual can judge everything. If one had a great deal of time, a vast supply of good educators, stable institutions, and lots of money, and if France were not engaged in war or in international competition, it might be possible to eventually rebuild civic virtues through information and good example. But that is not the case. Action must be fast, with few educators at hand; therefore only one way can be taken: the utilization of the most effective instruments and the proved methods of propaganda. In a battle between propagandas, only propaganda can respond effectively and quickly.

As a result, the effects of one's own propaganda on the personality are exactly the same as those of enemy propaganda (we say on the *personality*, not on some specific opinions). These effects will be analyzed at length later. In any event, one cannot possibly say: we act in order to preserve man's freedom. For propaganda, regardless of origin, destroys man's personality and freedom. If one were merely to say: "The enemy must be defeated, and to this end all means are good," we would not object. That would mean recognizing and accepting the fact that democracy, whether it wants to be or not, *is* engaged in propaganda. But the illusion that one engages in psychological action as a defense, while respecting the values of democracy and human personality, is more pernicious than any cynicism which looks frankly at the true situation.

A thorough study of Information, Education, Human Relations, and Propaganda reveals that in practice no essential differences exist among them. Any politically oriented education which creates certain "special values" is propaganda. And our reference to "special values" leads to yet another consideration. The inclusion of such special values as patriotism in the struggle for civic reconstruction excludes such others as internationalism, anarchism, and pacifism. One assumes that one's national values are given and justified in themselves. And from that one concludes that one faces only the problem of education *because* these national values are the only values. But this is not so. In reality, the affirmation of certain values which one wants to inculcate, and the rejection of others which one wants to eradicate from the minds of the listeners is precisely a propaganda operation.

Thus, by different roads, we keep arriving at the same conclusion: a modern State, even if it be liberal, democratic, and humanist, finds itself objectively and sociologically in a situation in which it must use propaganda as a means of governing. It cannot do otherwise.

2. The Individual's Necessity

If we admit that the government has no choice but to make propaganda, there still remains the image of the aggressive and totalitarian political machine which pounces on the innocent victim—the individual. The individual then appears helpless and crushed by gigantic forces. But I think that propaganda fills a need of modern man, a need that creates in him an unconscious desire for propaganda. He is in the position of needing outside help to be able to face his condition. And that aid is propaganda. Naturally, he does not say: "I want propaganda." On the contrary, in line with preconceived notions, he abhors propaganda and considers himself a "free and mature" person. But in reality he calls for and desires propaganda that will permit him to ward off certain attacks and reduce certain tensions. This leads to the following puzzle: "Propaganda by itself has no power over an individual. It needs certain already existing pillars of support. It creates nothing. And yet, the effectiveness of propaganda is undeniable, even though it seems impossible to define exactly those already existing pillars of support on which it builds." The solution is that these pillars are the individual's need for propaganda. The secret of propaganda success or failure is this: Has it or has it not satisfied the unconscious need of the individual whom it addressed? No propaganda can have an effect unless it is needed, though the need may not be expressed as such but remain unconscious.[6] And if we take into consideration that propaganda exists in all "civilized" countries and accompanies all "progress toward civilization" in underdeveloped countries, this need appears to be practically universal; it is an intrinsic part of the setting in which man finds himself in the technological society.[7] We shall first examine the objective situation of man which generates this need for propaganda, then his psychological situation.

The Objective Situation

We have stressed that the State can no longer govern without the masses, which nowadays are closely involved in politics. But these masses are composed of individuals. From their point of view, the problem is slightly different: they are interested in politics and consider themselves concerned with politics; even if they are not forced to participate actively because they live in a democracy, they embrace politics as soon as somebody wants to take the democratic regime away from them. But this presents them with problems that are way over their heads. They are faced with choices and decisions which demand maturity, knowledge, and a range of information which they do not and cannot have. Elections are limited to the selection of individuals, which reduces the problem of participation to its simplest form. But the individual wishes to participate in other ways than just elections. He wants to be conversant with economic questions. In fact, his government asks him to be. He wants to form an opinion on foreign policy. But in reality he can't. He is caught between his desire and his inability, which he refuses to accept. For no citizen will believe that he is unable to have opinions. Public opinion surveys always reveal that people have opinions even on the most complicated questions, except for a small minority

---

[6] In the Soviet Union it is expressly stated that propaganda results from a dialectical process between the needs of individuals, which the local agitator communicates to the authorities, and the objectives of the Party.

[7] The existence of this universal need is also clearly revealed by circulation of rumors. Why are there rumors? Why do they circulate? They serve the need for explanations in a given situation, and ease emotional tension because man seeks in them answers to what disturbs him. Propaganda responds to the same needs in a much more effective fashion. But spontaneous rumors demonstrate the existence of these needs.

(usually the most informed and those who have reflected most). The majority prefers expressing stupidities to not expressing any opinion: this gives them the feeling of participation. For this they need simple thoughts, elementary explanations, a "key" that will permit them to take a position, and even ready-made opinions. As most people have the desire and at the same time the incapacity to participate, they are ready to accept a propaganda that will permit them to participate, and which hides their incapacity beneath explanations, judgments, and news, enabling them to satisfy their desire without eliminating their incompetence. The more complex, general, and accelerated political and economic phenomena become, the more do individuals feel concerned, the more do they want to be involved. In a certain sense this is democracy's gain, but it also leads to more propaganda. And the individual does not want information, but only value judgments and preconceived positions. Here one must also take into account the individual's laziness, which plays a decisive role in the entire propaganda phenomenon, and the impossibility of transmitting all information fast enough to keep up with developments in the modern world. Besides, the developments are not merely beyond man's intellectual scope; they are also beyond him in volume and intensity; he simply cannot grasp the world's economic and political problems. Faced with such matters, he feels his weakness, his inconsistency, his lack of effectiveness. He realizes that he depends on decisions over which he has no control, and that realization drives him to despair. Man cannot stay in this situation too long. He needs an ideological veil to cover the harsh reality, some consolation, a *raison d'être*, a sense of values. And only propaganda offers him a remedy for a basically intolerable situation.

Besides, modern man is called upon for enormous sacrifices, which probably exceed anything known in the past. First of all, work has assumed an all-pervading role in modern life. Never have men worked so much as in our society. Contrary to what is often said, man works much more nowadays than, for example, in the eighteenth century. Only the working hours have decreased. But the omnipresence of the duties of his work, the obligations and constraints, the actual working conditions, the intensity of work that never ends, make it weigh much more heavily on men today than on men in the past. Every modern man works more than the slave of long ago; standards have been adjusted downward. But whereas the slave worked only because he was forced to, modern man, who believes in his freedom and dignity, needs reasons and justifications to make himself work. Even the children in a modern nation do an amount of work at school which no child was ever asked to do before the beginning of the nineteenth century; there, too, justifications are needed. One cannot make people live forever in the state of assiduous, intense, never-ending labor without giving them good reasons and creating by example a virtue of Work, like that of the bourgeoisie of the nineteenth century, or a myth of liberation through Work, like that of the Nazis or Communists.

Such dedication to work does not happen by itself or spontaneously. Its creation is properly the task of propaganda, which must give the individual psychological and ideological reasons why he needs to be where he is. One cannot get good, steady work out of a man merely by pointing to the need for such work, or even to its monetary rewards. One must give him psychological satisfactions of a higher order; man wants a profound and significant reason for what he does. And as all this is a collective situation, it will be furnished him by collective means. To furnish the collective ideological motivations driving man to action is propaganda's exact task; every time the sum total of labor is to be increased, the increase is accomplished through propaganda. The Soviet Union, with its Five Year Plan, set the example, and the Chinese "leaps forward" are also typical.[8] In France, all increase in production rests on an enormous propaganda campaign. And the citizen really cannot be happy in his work unless he is sustained by such psychological nourishment, by the combination of promises (such as a few years of hard work and a thousand years of happiness) and the value of the motives handed him. The exigencies of work and economic life in the modern world create in man the need for propaganda; in the United States this takes

---

[8] This leads to a comparison of the agitator with the shock worker (*oudarnik*). The agitator, who remains a political force, must at the same time be an exemplary worker; he must introduce new workers into the industrial order, push workers to accomplish the norms. Agitation for "production" was the most important propaganda of the 1930's in the U.S.S.R. The press itself was engaged in this "agitation for production," for very often in its "heroic period" the government had no other means for resolving economic problems than that of propaganda to improve productivity and discipline. But we must not think this was limited to the 1930's. The same movement resumed in 1950 with the reintroduction of Stakhanovism.

the form of Human Relations. American writers have often said that the drive toward efficiency cannot be expected to develop by itself. The man who is subjected to the demands for efficiency will ask: "Efficiency for what?" It is then up to propaganda to give him the answer.

But modern man is not only forced to make sacrifices in his work; he is also saddled by his government with other sacrifices, such as ever-increasing taxes. Every citizen of a modern state pays more taxes than the most heavily taxed people in pre-Napoleonic days. Then the subject was forced to pay, whereas the free citizen of today must pay for reasons of conviction. His conviction will not come about spontaneously, particularly when the taxes are really heavy. The Conviction must therefore be manufactured, ideals must be stimulated in order to give true significance to such a "contribution to the nation"; here, too, propaganda is needed. This is the exact opposite of political freedom.

Let us take the most serious of all sacrifices. The modern citizen is asked to participate in wars such as have never been seen before. All men must prepare for war, and for a dreadful type of war at that—dreadful because of its duration, the immensity of its operations, its tremendous losses, and the atrocity of the means employed. Moreover, participation in war is no longer limited to the duration of the war itself; there is the period of preparation for war, which becomes more and more intense and costly. Then there is the period in which to repair the ravages of war. People really live in a permanent atmosphere of war, and a superhuman war in every respect (the strain of "holding out" for days under bombardment is a much greater strain than a day of traditional battle). Nowadays everybody is affected by war; everybody lives under its threat.

Naturally, it was always necessary to give men ideological and sentimental motivations to get them to lay down their lives. But in our modern form of war the traditional motives—protection of one's family, defense of one's own country, personal hatred for a known enemy—no longer exist. They must be replaced by others. And the more demanded of man, the more powerful must be those motivations. The man of whom such super-sacrifices are demanded finds himself in the middle of an incessant world conflict, pushed to the very limit of his nervous and mental en-

durance, and in a sort of constant preparation for ultimate
sacrifice. He cannot live this way unless sustained by powerful
motivations, which he will not find either inside himself, or
spontaneously. They must be furnished him by society, which
will respond to the need that arises from the individual's actual
situation. Obviously, some simple "information" on the international situation or on the need to defend one's country is insufficient here. Man must be plunged into a mystical atmosphere,
he must be given strong enough impulses as well as good enough
reasons for his sacrifices, and, at the same time, a drug that will
sustain his nerves and his morale. Patriotism must become
"ideological." Only propaganda can put man into a state of
nervous endurance that will permit him to face the tension of
war.[9]

Aside from all these sacrifices, man is not automatically adjusted
to the living conditions imposed on him by modern society.
Psychologists and sociologists are aware of the great problem of
adjusting the normal man to a technological environment—to the
increasing pace, the working hours, the noise, the crowded cities,
the tempo of work, the housing shortage, and so on. Then there is
the difficulty of accepting the never-changing daily routine, the
lack of personal accomplishment, the absence of an apparent
meaning in life, the family insecurity provoked by these living
conditions, the anonymity of the individual in the big cities and
at work. The individual is not equipped to face these disturbing,
paralyzing, traumatic influences. Here again he needs a psychological aid; to endure such a life, he needs to be given motivations
that will restore his equilibrium. One cannot leave modern man
alone in a situation such as this. What can one do?

One can surround him with a network of psychological relations (Human Relations) that will artificially soothe his discom-
forts, reduce his tensions, and place him in some human context.
Or one can have him live in a myth strong enough to offset the
concrete disadvantages, or give them a shade of meaning, a value
that makes them acceptable. To make man's condition acceptable
to him, one must transcend it. This is the function of Soviet and

9 When propaganda is missing, people do not really become involved in war: for
instance, the ridiculous French Government propaganda in 1939, the propaganda
toward Indochina (which went too far), and the propaganda on the Algerian war
(hasty and clumsy as opposed to the remarkably good leftist and F.L.N. propaganda).

Chinese propaganda. In both cases there is psychological manipulation of the individual—an operation that must be classified as propaganda in the broad sense of the word. Such propaganda has a "political" character, if one takes the term *political*, in its broadest sense, as referring to the collective life in a *polis*.

Finally, to understand the need for propaganda that springs from modern man's actual condition, one must remember that one is dealing with an *informed* person. Having analyzed in the preceding chapter how information actually supports propaganda, we must now turn to the manner in which the dispensing of information lays the psychological foundations for a man's becoming a propagandee. If we look at the average man, and not at those few intellectuals whose special business it is to be informed, what do we actually mean when we say this man is informed? It means that, aside from spending eight hours at work and two more commuting, this man reads a newspaper or, more precisely, looks at the headlines and glances at a few stories. He may also listen to news broadcasts, or watch it on TV; and once a week he will look at the photos in a picture magazine. This is the case of the reasonably well informed man, that is, of 98 percent of all people.

What happens next to a man who wishes to be informed and receives a great deal of news each day? First, straight news reporting never gives him anything but factual details; the event of the day is always only a part, for news can never deal with the whole. Theoretically, the reporter could relate these details to other details, put them into context and even provide certain interpretations—but that would no longer be pure information.[1] Besides, this could be done only for the most important events, whereas most news items deal with less important matters. But if you shower the public with the thousands of items that occur in the course of a day or week, the average person, even if he tries hard, will simply retain thousands of items which mean nothing to him. He would need a remarkable memory to tie some event to another that happened three weeks or three months ago. Moreover, the array of categories is bewildering—economics, politics, geography, and so on—and topics and categories change every day. To be sure, certain major stories, such as Indochina

---

[1] I could give a hundred examples of complete distortion of facts by competent and honest journalists, whose interpretative articles appear in serious newspapers.

and Hungary, become the subject of continuous reporting for several weeks or months, but that is not typical. Ordinarily, a follow-up story on a previous news item appears two weeks to a month later. To obtain a rounded picture, one would have to do research, but the average person has neither the desire nor the time for it. As a result, he finds himself in a kind of kaleidoscope in which thousands of unconnected images follow each other rapidly. His attention is continually diverted to new matters, new centers of interest, and is dissipated on a thousand things, which disappear from one day to the next. The world becomes remarkably changeable and uncertain; he feels as though he is at the hub of a merry-go-round, and can find no fixed point or continuity; this is the first effect information has on him. Even with major events, an immense effort is required to get a proper broad view from the thousand little strokes, the variations of color, intensity, and dimension, which his paper gives him. The world thus looks like a *pointilliste* canvas—a thousand details make a thousand points. Moreover, blank spots on the canvas also prevent a coherent view.

Our reader then would have to be able to stand back and get a panoramic view from a distance; but the law of news is that it is a daily affair. Man can never stand back to get a broad view because he immediately receives a new batch of news, which supersedes the old and demands a new point of focus, for which our reader has no time. To the average man who tries to keep informed, a world emerges that is astonishingly incoherent, absurd, and irrational, which changes rapidly and constantly for reasons he cannot understand. And as the most frequent news story is about an accident or a calamity, our reader takes a catastrophic view of the world around him. What he learns from the papers is inevitably the event that disturbs the order of things. He is not told about the ordinary—and uninteresting—course of events, but only of unusual disasters which disturb that course. He does not read about the thousands of trains that every day arrive normally at their destination, but he learns all the details of a train accident.

In the world of politics and economics, the same holds true. The news is only about trouble, danger, and problems. This gives man the notion that he lives in a terrible and frightening era, that he lives amid catastrophes in a world where everything threatens his safety. Man cannot stand this; he cannot live in an absurd and incoherent world (for this he would have to be heroic, and even Camus, who considered this the only honest posture, was not really able to stick to it); nor can he accept the idea that the problems, which sprout all around him, cannot be solved, or that he himself has no value as an individual and is subject to the turn of events. The man who keeps himself informed needs a framework in which all this information can be put in order; he needs explanations and comprehensive answers to general problems; he needs coherence. And he needs an affirmation of his own worth. All this is the immediate effect of information. And the more complicated the problems are, the more simple the explanations must be; the more fragmented the canvas, the simpler the pattern; the more difficult the question, the more all-embracing the solution; the more menacing the reduction of his own worth, the greater the need for boosting his ego. All this propaganda—and only propaganda—can give him. Of course, an outstanding man of vast culture, great intelligence, and exceptional energy can find answers for himself, reconcile himself to the absurd, and plan his own action. But we are not thinking here of the outstanding man (who, naturally, we all imagine ourselves to be), but of the ordinary man.[2]

An analysis of propaganda therefore shows that it succeeds primarily because it corresponds exactly to a need of the masses. Let us remember just two aspects of this: the need for explanations and the need for values, which both spring largely, though not entirely, from the promulgation of news. Effective propaganda needs to give man an all-embracing view of the world, a view rather than a doctrine. Such a view will first of all encompass a general panorama of history, economics, and politics. This panorama itself is the foundation of the power of propaganda because it provides justification for the actions of those who make propaganda; the point is to show that one travels in the direction of history and progress. That panorama allows the individual to give the proper classification to all the news items he receives; to exercise a critical judgment, to sharply accentuate certain facts

---

[2] I know, of course, that it is fashionable today to deny the existence of "superior," "inferior," and "average" men. That argument is generally factitious, and even its proponents usually follow up by analyzing the psycho-sociology of man, describing certain behavior as "*normal*" and using the statistical method.

and suppress others, depending on how well they fit into the framework. This is a necessary protection against being flooded with facts without being able to establish a perspective.

Propaganda must also furnish an explanation for all happenings, a key to understand the whys and the reasons for economic and political developments. News loses its frightening character when it offers information for which the listener already has a ready explanation in his mind, or for which he can easily find one. The great force of propaganda lies in giving modern man all-embracing, simple explanations and massive, doctrinal causes, without which he could not live with the news. Man is doubly reassured by propaganda: first, because it tells him the reasons behind the developments which unfold, and second, because it promises a solution for all the problems that arise, which would otherwise seem insoluble.

Just as information is necessary for awareness, propaganda is necessary to prevent this awareness from being desperate.

The Subjective Situation

Some psychological characteristics of modern man, partly results of his reality situation, also explain his irrepressible need for propaganda. Most studies on propaganda merely examine how the propagandist can use this or that trait or tendency of a man to influence him. But it seems to us that a prior question needs to be examined: Why does a man involuntarily provoke the propaganda operation?

Without going into the theory of the "mass man" or the "organization man," which is unproven and debatable, let us recall some frequently analyzed traits of the man who lives in the Western world and is plunged into its overcrowded population; let us accept as a premise that he is more susceptible to suggestion, more credulous, more easily excited. Above all he is a victim of emptiness—he is a man devoid of meaning. He is very busy, but he is emotionally empty, open to all entreaties and in search of only one thing—something to fill his inner void. To fill this void he goes to the movies—only a very temporary remedy. He seeks some deeper and more fulfilling attraction. He is *available*, and ready to listen to propaganda. He is the lonely man (The Lonely Crowd), and the larger the crowd in which he lives, the more isolated he is. Despite the pleasure he might derive from his solitude, he suffers deeply from it. He feels the most violent need to be re-integrated into a community, to have a setting, to experience ideological and affective communication. That loneliness inside the crowd is perhaps the most terrible ordeal of modern man; that loneliness in which he can share nothing, talk to nobody, and expect nothing from anybody, leads to severe personality disturbances. For it, propaganda, encompassing Human Relations, is an incomparable remedy. It corresponds to the need to share, to be a member of a community, to lose oneself in a group, to embrace a collective ideology that will end loneliness. *Propaganda is the true remedy for loneliness.* It also corresponds to deep and constant needs, more developed today, perhaps, than ever before: the need to believe and obey, to create and hear fables, to communicate in the language of myths. It also responds to man's intellectual sloth and desire for security—intrinsic characteristics of the real man as distinguished from the theoretical man of the Existentialists. All this turns man against information, which cannot satisfy any of these needs, and leads him to crave propaganda, which can satisfy them.

This situation has another aspect. In our society, man is being pushed more and more into passivity. He is thrust into vast organizations which function collectively and in which each man has his own small part to play. But he cannot act on his own; he can act only as the result of somebody else's decision. Man is more and more trained to participate in group movements and to act only on signal and in the way he has been taught. There is training for big and small matters—training for his job, for the driver and the pedestrian, for the consumer, for the movie-goer, for the apartment house dweller, and so on. The consumer gets his signal from the advertiser that the purchase of some product is desirable; the driver learns from the green light that he may proceed. The individual becomes less and less capable of acting by himself; he needs the collective signals which integrate his actions into the complete mechanism. Modern life induces us to wait until we are told to act. Here again propaganda comes to the rescue. To the extent that government can no longer function without the mass (as we have demonstrated above), propaganda is the signal to act, the bridge from the individual's mere *interest* in politics to his political *action*. It serves to overcome collective passivity. It enters into the general current of society, which develops multiple conditioned reflexes, which in turn become signals for man to play his part in the group.

At the same time, the individual feels himself *diminished*. For one thing, he gets the feeling that he is under constant supervision and can never exercise his independent initiative; for another, he thinks he is always being pushed down to a lower level. He is a minor in that he can never act with his full authority. To be sure, we're talking of the average man; obviously a corporation president, high-level administrator, or professional man does not feel diminished, but that fact does not change the general situation. The feeling of being unimportant stems from general working conditions, such as mechanization and regimentation; from housing conditions, with small rooms, noise, and lack of privacy; from family conditions, with loss of authority over children; from submission to an ever-growing number of authorities (no one will ever be able to assess fully the disastrous effect on the human soul of all the bureaus and agencies); in short, from participation in mass society. We know that the individual plunged into the mass experiences a feeling of being reduced and weakened. He loses his human rights and the means to satisfy his ambitions. The multitudes around him oppress him and give him an unhealthy awareness of his own unimportance. He is drowned in the mass, and becomes convinced that he is only a cipher and that he really cannot be considered otherwise in such a large number of individuals. Urban life gives a feeling of weakness and dependence to the individual: he is dependent on everything—public transportation, the tax-collector, the policeman, his employer, the city's public utilities. Separately, these elements would not affect him, but combined they produce this feeling of diminution in modern man.

But man cannot stand being unimportant; he cannot accept the status of a cipher. He needs to assert himself, to see himself as a hero. He needs to feel he is somebody and to be considered as such. He needs to express his authority, the drive for power and domination that is in every man. Under our present conditions, that instinct is completely frustrated. Though some routes of escape exist—the movies give the viewer a chance to experience self-esteem by identification with the hero, for example—that is not enough. Only propaganda provides the individual with a fully satisfactory response to his profound need.

The more his needs increase in the collective society, the more propaganda must give man the feeling that he is a free individual. Propaganda alone can create this feeling, which, in turn, will integrate the individual into collective movements. Thus, it is a powerful boost to his self-esteem. Though a mass instrument, it addresses itself to each individual. It appeals to *me*. It appeals to *my* common sense, *my* desires, and provokes *my* wrath and *my* indignation. It evokes *my* feelings of justice and *my* desire for freedom. It gives *me* violent feelings, which lift *me* out of the daily grind. As soon as I have been politicized by propaganda, I can from my heights look down on daily trifles. My boss, who does not share my convictions, is merely a poor fool, a prey to the illusions of an evil world. I take my revenge upon him by being enlightened; I have understood the situation and know what ought to be done; I hold the key to events and am involved in dangerous and exciting activities. This feeling will be all the stronger when propaganda appeals to my decision and seems to be greatly concerned with my action: "Everything is in the clutches of evil. There is a way out. But only if everybody participates. *You* must participate. If you don't, all will be lost, through your fault." This is the feeling that propaganda must generate. My opinion, which society once scorned, now becomes important and decisive. No longer has it importance only for me, but also for the whole range of political affairs and the entire social body. A voter may well feel that his vote has no importance or value. But propaganda demonstrates that the action in which it involves us is of fundamental importance, and that everything depends on me. It boosts my ego by giving me a strong sense of my responsibility; it leads me to assume a posture of authority among my fellows, makes me take myself seriously by appealing to me in impassioned tones, with total conviction, and gives me the feeling that it's a question of All or Nothing. Thanks to such propaganda, the diminished individual obtains the very satisfaction he needs.

Propaganda in colonial countries plays on this same need of diminished peoples for self-assertion. Africans are even more susceptible to almost any propaganda, because they lived under the guardianship of their colonizers and were reduced to a position of inferiority. But one must not conclude that a feeling of inferiority is to be found only in the oppressed; it is the normal condition of almost every person in a mass society. Also, to the extent that modern man is diminished, he finds himself faced with the almost constant need for repression. Most of his natural tendencies are suppressed by social constraints.

We live in an increasingly organized and ordered society which permits less and less free and spontaneous expression of man's profound drives (which, it must be admitted, would be largely anti-social if completely unleashed). Modern man is tied to a timetable and rarely can act on the spur of the moment; he must pay constant attention to what goes on around him. He cannot make the noise he may want to make; he must obey a growing number of rules of all sorts; he cannot give free reign to his sexual instinct or his inclination to violence. For despite present-day "immorality," of which people complain, contemporary man is much less free in these matters than was the man of the sixteenth and seventeenth century. And in the world of politics, modern man constantly faces obstacles which suppress his tendencies and impulses. But it is impossible to keep the individual in such a situation for long.

The individual who feels himself in conflict with the group, whose personal values are different from those of his milieu, who feels tension toward his society and even toward the group in which he participates—that individual is in a tragic situation *in modern society.* Until recently, such an individual enjoyed a certain freedom, a certain independence, which allowed him to release his tension in external—and quite acceptable—actions. He had a circle of personal activities through which he could express his own values and live out his conflicts. That was the best way of maintaining his equilibrium. But in the technological society, the individual no longer has either the independence or the choice of activities sufficient to release his tensions properly. He is forced to keep them inside himself. Under such conditions the tension becomes extreme and can cause illness. At that very moment propaganda will intervene as the (fake) instrument for reducing these tensions by external action.[3] To seal all outlets and suppress man in all areas is dangerous. Man needs to express

---

[3] It is well known to what extent modern man needs escape. Escape is a general phenomenon of our civilization because man has to battle against far too many contradictions and tensions imposed on him by the conditions of life. He seeks to flee these difficulties, and is encouraged to do so by the contemporary ideology of happiness. Propaganda offers him an extraordinary possibility of escape into action.

his passions and desires; collective social repression can have the same effect as individual repression, which is the concern of psychoanalysts. Either sublimation or release is necessary. On the collective level, the latter is easier than the former, though some of the most oppressed groups were the most easily led to acts of heroism and sacrifice for the benefit of their oppressors. In the need for release we find some spontaneous expression; surely, jazz is a means, for many young people, of releasing repressed impulses, and so are violent displays (James Dean, black leather jackets, the rebellion in Sweden in 1957, and so on.)

But whereas these possibilities of release are very limited, propaganda offers release on a grand scale. For example, propaganda will permit what so far was prohibited, such as hatred, which is a dangerous and destructive feeling and fought by society. But man always has a certain need to hate, just as he hides in his heart the urge to kill. Propaganda offers him an object of hatred, for all propaganda is aimed at an enemy.[4] And the hatred it offers him is not shameful, evil hatred that he must hide, but a legitimate hatred, which he can justly feel. Moreover, propaganda points out enemies that must be slain, transforming crime into a praiseworthy act. Almost every man feels a desire to kill his neighbor, but this is forbidden, and in most cases the individual will refrain from it for fear of the consequences. But propaganda opens the door and allows him to kill the Jews, the bourgeois, the Communists, and so on, and such murder even becomes an achievement. Similarly, in the nineteenth century, when a man felt like cheating on his wife, or divorcing her, he found this was frowned on. So, at the end of that century a propaganda appeared that legitimized adultery and divorce. In such cases the individual attaches himself passionately to the source of such propaganda, which, for him, provides liberation. Where transgression becomes virtue, the lifter of the ban becomes a hero, a demi-god, and we consecrate ourselves to serve him because he has liberated our repressed passions. A good deal of popular allegiance to the republic and of the failure of Catholicism in France at the end of the nineteenth century can be traced to this battle over adultery and divorce.

Propaganda can also provide release through devious channels.

---

[4] Propaganda thus displaces and liberates feelings of aggression by offering specific objects of hatred to the citizen; this generally suffices to channelize passion.

Authoritarian regimes know that people held very firmly in hand need some decompression, some safety valves. The government offers these itself. This role is played by satirical journals attacking the authorities, yet tolerated by the dictator (for example, *Krokodil*),[5] or by a wild holiday set aside for ridiculing the regime, yet paid for by the dictator (for example, the Friday of Sorrows in Guatemala). Clearly, such instruments are controlled by the regime. They serve the function of giving the people the impression that they are free, and of singling out those about to be purged by the government as guilty of all that the people dislike. Thus these instruments of criticism serve to consolidate power and make people cling even more to the regime by providing artificial release of tendencies that the state must keep in check. In such situations, propaganda has an almost therapeutic and compensatory function.

This role is even more prominent in the presence of another phenomenon: anxiety. Anxiety is perhaps the most widespread psychological trait in our society. Many studies indicate that fear is one of the strongest and most prevalent feelings in our society. Of course, man has good reasons to be afraid—of Communist subversion, revolution, Fascism, H-bombs, conflict between East and West, unemployment, sickness. On the one hand, the number of dangers is increasing and, because of the news media, man is more aware of them; on the other, religious beliefs, which allowed man to face fear, have disappeared almost entirely. Man is disarmed in the face of the perils threatening him, and is increasingly alarmed by these perils because he keeps reading about them. For example, the many medical articles on illnesses in the major papers are disastrous because they attract man's attention to the presence of illness: information provokes

[5] Self-criticism in the Soviet Union is well known. It is used to denounce shortcomings and errors of persons and institutions. It is also the means for control of the bureaucracy. But it particularly serves the purpose of relaxing tensions, channelizing aggressive tendencies, and responding to the "poor slob" (*lampiste*) who addresses himself to the government. Thus expressed, criticism ceases to endanger the government and the social order. The bureaucrat becomes the scapegoat and the Party remains above reproach. The same operation is found in the use of letters from readers. It is one of the best propaganda operations: the more criticism of the bureaucrat is permitted, the more the citizen is tied to the government. This practice was greatly expanded by Khrushchev. It is not a matter of liberalization, but of integrating the individual in society and consolidating the power of the State. It is the same method as that of counseling in American Human Relations practices.

fear. This largely explains why the dominant fears in our society are "social" fears, tied to such collective and general phenomena as political situations, much more dominant than such individual fears as those of death or of ghosts. But fear tied to a real threat and of a degree proportionate to that threat is not anxiety. Karen Horney was right in stating that an essential difference between fear and anxiety is that anxiety is a reaction disproportionate to the actual danger or a reaction to an imaginary danger. She was also right in pointing out that anxiety is actually tied to the conditions of our civilization, though the dangers to which a person responds with anxiety may remain hidden from him. The anxiety may be proportionate to the situation, but it still may be experienced for unknown reasons.

With regard to real and conscious threats, a frequent reaction is to expand them with fables. Americans create fables about the Communist peril, just as the Communists create fables about the Fascist peril—and at that moment anxiety sets in. It is tied to rumors, to the fact that the real situation is inassessable, to the diffuse climate of fear, and to the ricocheting of fear from one person to the next.

However that may be, anxiety exists and spreads. It is irrational, and any attempt to calm it with reason or facts must fail. To demonstrate factually in a climate of anxiety that the feared danger is much smaller than it is believed to be, only increases anxiety; the information is used to prove that there is reason for fear. Of course, in psychoanalysis anxiety is often regarded as the source of neurosis. But, as we maintain here that anxiety is a collective phenomenon affecting a very large number of individuals in our society, we do not want to say that all these people are neurotics in the clinical sense. Anxiety provoked by social conflicts or political threats rarely goes so far as to cause neurosis. But such a progression is not impossible; we will simply say that individuals find themselves in a situation in which neurosis is a constant possibility. And neurosis can actually become collective when some event throws a whole group into frenzied anxiety or irrational considerations.

Man also feels himself the prey of the hostile impulses of others, another source of anxiety. Besides, he is plunged into conflicts inherent in our society which place him in conflict with himself, or rather place his experiences in conflict with the social imperatives. Karen Horney has described some of these conflicts, but many more exist. Aside from the conflict between the government's proclaimed respect for our needs and their frustration in reality, between the advertised freedom and the real constraints, peace is worshipped in societies that prepare for war, culture is spread that cannot be absorbed, and so on. The experience of contradiction is certainly one of the prevalent experiences in our society. But man cannot endure contradiction; anxiety results, and man struggles to resolve the contradiction in order to dissolve his anxiety.

Finally, as a result of all the threats and contradictions in contemporary society, man feels *accused, guilty*. He cannot feel that he is right and good as long as he is exposed to contradictions, which place him in conflict with one of his group's imperatives no matter which solution he adopts. But one of man's greatest inner needs is to feel that he is right. This need takes several forms. First, man needs to be right in his own eyes. He must be able to assert that he is right, that he does what he should, that he is worthy of his own respect. Then, man needs to be right in the eyes of those around him, his family, his milieu, his co-workers, his friends, his country. Finally, he feels the need to belong to a group, which he considers right and which he can proclaim as just, noble, and good. But that righteousness is not absolute righteousness, true and authentic justice. What matters is not to *be* just, or to *act* just, or that the group to which one belongs *is* just—but to *seem* just, to find reasons for asserting that one is just, and to have these reasons shared by one's audience.

This corresponds to man's refusal to see reality—his own reality first of all—as it is, for that would be intolerable; it also corresponds to his refusal to acknowledge that he may be wrong. Before himself and others, man is constantly pleading his own case and working to find good reasons for what he does or has done. Of course, the whole process is unconscious.[6]

Such justification corresponds at least partly to what American psychologists call rationalization, *i.e.*, the search for good reasons. But rationalization covers less territory than justification. Rationalization occurs when the individual is prey to the difficulties

---

[6] The individual reconstructs his past to demonstrate that his conduct was right. But this is justification rather than explanation of behavior. Man thus lives in seemingly reasonable fiction.

of social life. The collision with various groups and other individuals provokes tension, conflicts, frustrations, failures, and
anxieties for which man has a low tolerance. He tries to avoid all
this, but cannot. He therefore gives himself excuses and good
reasons for avoiding the disagreeable consequences of such conflicts, or fabricates a conclusion, which explains his failure and
gives it the appearance of success ("sour grapes"); or he justifies
everything by creating a scapegoat, or justifies his conduct by
showing that the other party is to blame (racial prejudice), and
so forth. Clearly, the individual believes the reasons he gives,
all the more so as these reasons are "good" to the extent that they
are shared by a large number of people, if not by everybody.
The individual who justifies himself is always scandalized if told
that the reasons he gives for his conduct are false, that he has
acted for other reasons, and that his explanations are only
embroideries to make his conduct acceptable and to win praise
for it.

This need seems abnormal. On the individual level, it is often
considered pathological, because it shows a dissociation from the
self. But in reality this judgment was discarded because of its
moral implications, the process involved being nothing other than
hypocrisy. It was then concluded that there is nothing pathological in this need—for two reasons. The first is the universality
of the phenomenon. Practically everybody justifies himself all the
time, to himself and to his group, and it is difficult to call a
general attitude pathological. The second is the usefulness of the
process: it is generally accepted nowadays that in his psychic
life man automatically finds what is useful for him and permits
him to exercise "economies." Justification is undeniably useful.
Through justification man not only defends himself against tensions and anxieties, transforming failure into success, but also
asserts his sense of right and wrong, justice and injustice. Often
a man's true beliefs are revealed only through this channel
(justification).

Such hypocrisy has another use: it permits man to cast off some
of his inhibitions without having to assert anti-moral or anti-social
convictions publicly. Whereas inhibited behavior is damaging
to society, an overloud declaration of immoral or asocial convictions is damaging too. Here we encounter the old problem:
Is it better to behave badly and hide it, as in 1900, or to behave

badly and advertise it, as in 1960 (taking into account that the man of 1960 uses different justifications)? The process of justification is thus found everywhere because of its great utility.

On the collective level one can say that most ideologies and political or economic theories are justifications. A study by M. Rubel[7] has shown that Marx's rigid and seemingly uncompromising doctrine was one gigantic intellectual justification for sentimental and spontaneous positions taken by him in his youth.

It is difficult, if not impossible, to accept reality as it is and acknowledge the true reasons for our behavior, or to see clearly the motivations of a group to which we belong. If we practice a profession, we cannot limit ourselves to its financial rewards; we must also invest it with idealistic or moral justification. It becomes our calling, and we will not tolerate its being questioned. Even the most pragmatic, such as the Nazis, try to give their actions moral or social justification: for example, the concern for maintaining the superiority of the Aryan race justified the sadism of the concentration camps. Even the greatest materialists, such as the Communists, try to justify themselves with ideals: for example, humanitarian interests will justify a certain tactic. In the conflict between necessity and moral or religious imperatives, everybody covers himself with the cloak of rationalization to assert that no conflict exists. When a man obeys necessity, he wants to prove that such is not the case and that he really obeys his conscience. On the day when the draft is introduced, everybody discovers he has a fervent love for his country. On the day when Stalin allies himself with Hitler, the Communists discover the excellence of German Socialism. And on the day when the Hungarian Government forces the Christian Church to make peace propaganda, the Church discovers voluntarily that peace is a Christian virtue.

Obviously, the prodigious universality of justification makes it so effective: the man who justifies himself and unconsciously plays this farce not only believes it himself but also has the need for others to believe it. And, in fact, the others do believe it, because they use the same rationalizations and become accomplices of the play in which they are themselves actors. Justification really attains its effectiveness only on the basis of this complicity, which is so all-pervasive that even those who are the victims of justifica-

---

[7] *Karl Marx, Essai de biographie intellectuelle,* 1957.

158)   THE NECESSITY FOR PROPAGANDA

tion go along with it. For example, the racist justifies his prejudice
by saying that the "inferior" group is lazy, anti-social, immoral,
biologically inferior; and in many instances members of the
stigmatized group will accept such judgments and experience a
feeling of inferiority that will justify discrimination in their own
eyes. That is because they, too, use justifications on other levels.

The tremendous diversity of these personal and collective justifications derives from three sources. First, the traditional explanations transmitted to us by the group to which we belong and
instilled in us through school and so forth. For example, the
judgment of the worker by the bourgeoisie, which goes back to
1815 and is carefully transmitted from generation to generation:
"The worker is a lazy brute and a drunk." Or take France's mission
to "spread civilization," used to justify colonialism. Second, there
are the rationalizations which we ourselves fabricate spontaneously. These usually deal with our own conduct rather than with
that of the group.

What interests us most here is the third type of rationalizations,
which are *both* individual and collective, which deal with new
situations and unforeseen necessities, and to which traditional
solutions do not apply. These rationalizations are the fruit of
propaganda. Propaganda attaches itself to man and forces him to
play its game because of his overpowering need to be right and
just. In every situation propaganda hands him the proof that he,
personally, is in the right, that the action demanded of him is just,
even if he has the dark, strong feeling that it is not. Propaganda
appeases his tensions and resolves his conflicts. It offers facile,
ready-made justifications, which are transmitted by society and
easily believed. At the same time, propaganda has the freshness
and novelty which correspond to new situations and give man the
impression of having invented new ideals. It provides man with a
high ideal that permits him to give in to his passions while seeming
to accomplish a great mission. It is precisely when propaganda
furnishes man with these justifications, at once individual and
collective, that propaganda is most effective. We are not talking
here of a simple explanation but of a more profound rationalization, thanks to which man finds himself in full accord with his
group and with society, and fully adjusted to his environment, as
well as purged, at the same time, of his pangs of conscience and
personal uncertainty.

Man, eager for self-justification, throws himself in the direction of a propaganda that justifies him and thus eliminates one of the sources of his anxiety. Propaganda dissolves contradictions and restores to man a unitary world in which the demands are in accord with the facts. It gives man a clear and simple call to action that takes precedence over all else. It permits him to participate in the world around him without being in conflict with it, because the action he has been called upon to perform will surely remove all obstacles from the path of realizing the proclaimed ideal.

Here, propaganda plays a completely idealistic role, by involving a man caught in the world of reality and making him live by anticipation in a world based on principle. From then on man no longer sees contradiction as a threat to himself or as a distortion of his personality: the contradiction, through propaganda, becomes an active source of conquest and combat. He is no longer alone when trying to solve his conflicts, but is plunged into a collective on the march, which is always "at the point" of solving all conflicts and leading man and his world to a satisfying monism. One is always at the point of finishing the war—in Algeria or Vietnam or the Congo, of overtaking the United States, of repelling the Communist threat, of eliminating all frustrations.

Finally, propaganda also eliminates anxieties stemming from irrational and disproportionate fears, for it gives man assurances equivalent to those formerly given him by religion. It offers him a simple and clear explanation of the world in which he lives—to be sure, a false explanation far removed from reality, but one that is obvious and satisfying. It hands him a key with which he can open all doors; there is no more mystery; everything can be explained, thanks to propaganda. It gives him special glasses through which he can look at present-day history and clearly understand what it means. It hands him a guide line with which he can recover the general line running through all incoherent events. Now the world ceases to be hostile and menacing. The propagandee experiences feelings of mastery over and lucidity toward this menacing and chaotic world, all the more because propaganda provides him with a solution for all threats and a posture to assume in the face of them. Crowds go mad when they no longer know what posture to assume toward a threat. Propaganda provides the perfect posture with which to place the adversary at a disadvantage. There is no question here of reassuring the people or of demonstrating the reality of a situation to them; nothing could upset them more. The point is to excite them, to arouse their sense of power, their desire to assert themselves, and to arm them psychologically so that they can feel superior to the threat. And the man who seeks to escape his strangling anxiety by any means will feel miraculously delivered as soon as he can participate in the campaign mounted by propaganda, as soon as he can dive into this liberating activity, which resolves his inner conflicts by making him think that he is helping to solve those of society.

For all these reasons contemporary man needs propaganda; he asks for it; in fact, he almost instigates it. The development of propaganda is no accident. The politician who uses it is not a monster; he fills a social demand. The propagandee is a close accomplice of the propagandist. Only with the propagandee's unconscious complicity can propaganda fulfill its function; and because propaganda satisfies him—even if he protests against propaganda *in abstracto*, or considers himself immune to it—he follows its route.

We have demonstrated that propaganda, far from being an accident, performs an indispensable function in society. One always tries to present propaganda as something accidental, unusual, exceptional, connected with such abnormal conditions as wars. True, in such cases propaganda may become sharper and more crystalized, but the roots of propaganda go much deeper. Propaganda is the inevitable result of the various components of the technological society, and plays so central a role in the life of that society that no economic or political development can take place without the influence of its great power. Human Relations in social relationships, advertising or Human Engineering in the economy, propaganda in the strictest sense in the field of politics —the need for psychological influence to spur allegiance and action is everywhere the decisive factor, which progress demands and which the individual seeks in order to be delivered from his own self.

CHAPTER

[IV]

PSYCHOLOGICAL
EFFECTS OF
PROPAGANDA

Let us begin by examining what psychological effects propaganda operations have on the individual. Aside from the effects that the propagandist seeks to obtain directly—a person's vote, for example—his psychological manipulations evoke certain forces in the unconscious and traumatize the individual in various ways. A person subjected to propaganda does not remain intact or undamaged: not only will his opinions and attitudes be modified, but also his impulses and his mental and emotional structures. Propaganda's effect is more than external; it produces profound changes.

One must also distinguish between different effects produced by different media. Each has its own effects on attitudes or opinions, whether the propagandist purposely provokes them or not. When a man goes to the movies, he receives certain impressions, and his inner life is modified independently of all propaganda. Such psychological effects or changes of opinion, specific to each of the communications media, join those specifically produced by propaganda operations. To analyze where one ends and the other begins is very difficult. If one looks at a propaganda campaign conducted by radio, it is almost impossible to divide its effects into those produced by the campaign and those produced by radio broadcasts in general. Many monographs have been written on the basic effects—independent of propaganda—of the press, radio, and TV, but the effects are also present when those media are used for propaganda. The propagandist cannot separate the general and specific effects. When he launches a radio campaign, he knows that the effects of his campaign and the effects of radio broadcasts in general will be combined. And, as each medium has specific and partial effects, the propagandist will be tempted to combine them because they complement one another. Thus, the propagandist orchestrates.

To study the psychological effects of propaganda, one would therefore have to study the effects of each of the communications media separately, and then the effects of their combination with the specific propaganda techniques. We cannot do this here, but the reader should at all times keep in mind this *complementary* character of propaganda.

Psychological Crystallization

Under the influence of propaganda certain latent drives that are vague, unclear, and often without any particular objective suddenly become powerful, direct, and precise. Propaganda furnishes objectives, organizes the traits of an individual's personality into a system, and freezes them into a mold. For example, prejudices that exist about any event become greatly reinforced and hardened by propaganda; the individual is told that he is *right* in harboring them; he discovers reasons and justifications for a prejudice when it is clearly shared by many and proclaimed openly.[1] Moreover, the stronger the conflicts in a society, the stronger the prejudices, and propaganda that intensifies conflicts simultaneously intensifies prejudices in this very fashion.

Once propaganda begins to utilize and direct an individual's

---

[1] Much more, this hardening of an individual's prejudices permits him to resist facts and the pressure of contrary events.

hatreds, he no longer has any chance to retreat, to reduce his animosities, or to seek reconciliations with his opponents. Moreover, he now has a supply of ready-made judgments where he had only some vague notions before the propaganda set in; and those judgments permit him to face any situation. He will never again have reason to change judgments that he will thereafter consider the one and only truth.

In this fashion, propaganda standardizes current ideas,[2] hardens prevailing stereotypes, and furnishes thought patterns in all areas. Thus it codifies social, political, and moral standards.[3] Of

[2] Propaganda gives the individual the stereotypes he no longer takes the trouble to work out for himself; it furnishes these in the form of labels, slogans, ready-made judgments. It transforms ideas into slogans, and by giving the "Word," convinces the individual that he has an opinion.

[3] Symbols are related to the psychological phenomenon of the stereotype. A stereotype is a seeming value judgment, acquired by belonging to a group, without any intellectual labor, and reproducing itself automatically with each specific stimulation. The stereotype arises from feelings one has for one's own group, or against the "out-group." Man attaches himself passionately to the values represented by his group and rejects the clichés of the out-group. "To share the prejudices of a group is only to demonstrate one's affiliation to this group. Stereotypes correspond to situations which the individual occupies in society, to his groups and his metier." The stereotype, Stoetzel says, is a "genuine category . . . a manner of thinking, of interpreting experience, of behaving"—but founded solely on affective reactions. The stereotype is specific: it relates to a given name or image, which must be precise in order for the stereotype to work. (Jean Stoetzel: *Esquisse d'une théorie des opinions* [Paris: Presses Universitaires de France; 1943], pp. 311 ff.)

The stereotype, which is stable, helps man to avoid thinking, to take a personal position, to form his own opinion. Man reacts constantly, as if by reflex, in the presence of the stimulus evoking the stereotype. This reflex permits him to have a ready-made, though apparently spontaneous, opinion in any situation; in fact, it gives him the sense of a situation; and with regard to an ethical problem the stereotype is the criterion of values. It is usually formed in a limited group, but tends to develop, to extend itself to an entire collective. It is endowed with a force of expansion; moreover, it gradually detaches itself from the primordial images that have aroused it and takes on a life of its own.

In propaganda, existing stereotypes are awakened by symbols. The symbol permits the formation of a favorable response that can be transferred to persons and objects associated with it. To ask a group what it thinks of some sentence written by Victor Hugo, results in the Hugo stereotype; but to ask their opinion of the same sentence without giving the author, evokes no stereotype and elicits a very different opinion.

In a bourgeois milieu the proposition "Communism desires Justice" provokes an unfavorable reaction. But the reaction is favorable among parties that stress justice. Here the stereotype "Justice" wins out; in the former case it is the stereotype "Communism" that is dominant.

If we adopt Lasswell's analysis, we can divide symbols into three categories. There are symbols of *demand*, which express the aspirations of a group seeking to produce events. Then symbols of *identification*, which define the protagonist who acts for us, or the antagonist against whom we act. Finally, symbols of *expectation*, which present facts as immediate or future objectives, but facts that are, in reality, abstracts of themselves and have become simple symbols.

The use of symbols divides the individual conscience against itself. Effective

course, man needs to establish such standards and categories.[4] The difference is that propaganda gives an overwhelming *force* to the process: man can no longer modify his judgments and thought patterns. This force springs, on the one hand, from the character of the media employed, which give the appearance of objectivity to subjective impulses, and, on the other, from everybody's adherence to the same standards and prejudices.[5]

At the same time, these collective beliefs, which the individual assumes to be his own, these scales of values and stereotypes, which play only a small part in the psychological life of a person unaffected by propaganda, become big and important; by the

---

propaganda uses multiple symbols linked in such a way that some evoke known images and appeal to the conscience, whereas others violate the conscience and tend to destroy it or deny it. The symbol is an effective instrument for progressively separating the individual from primitive impulses, from his natural attitudes, and for creating "counter-attitudes" and "counter-behaviors." By this procedure, propaganda succeeds in weakening the individual's conscience and consciousness and in unsettling individual attitudes during a period of transition with a view to furnishing them with a new content. One does not, for example, destroy symbols of authority in order to substitute an attitude of independence; one replaces them with new symbols of authority. But this use of symbols presumes a very advanced propaganda. It is what we find, for example, in Stalinist propaganda.

At a much more elementary stage, all symbols have the purpose of awakening stereotypes, an appropriate function because by their nature they already unite the emotional and the intellectual life.

This function is served by photos and images, which have a special power to evoke the reality and immediacy of the stereotype—itself an image, it is fed by certain other images. The Statue of Liberty, the Arc de Triomphe provoke immediate reactions. The photo carries with it intrinsic qualities of the situation that it represents; it thereby reinforces the stereotype while stimulating it.

Another particularly evocative symbol is the slogan, which contains the demands, the expectations, the hopes of the mass, and at the same time expresses the established values of a group. Slogans determine with considerable precision each type of group toward which an individual is oriented, whether or not he is a member.

Above all, the slogan assures the continuity of the stereotype, which is fixed as a function of the past. But the individual finds himself constantly faced with new situations that the stereotype alone does not permit him to master; the slogan is the connection used by the propagandist to permit the individual to apply his old stereotypes to a new situation. He brushes up and adjusts the ready-made image; at the same time, he integrates the new situation into a classic context, familiar and unconfusing. That is why the slogan flourishes in times of crisis, war, and revolution. It explains also the attraction the slogan has: thanks to it, the individual is not intellectually lost. He clings to it not only because the slogan is easy to understand and to retain, but also because it permits him to "find himself in it." It tends, further, to produce stereotypes in men who did not have them before the crisis situation.

[4] Man works out these simplifications spontaneously in order to avoid effort, error, and difficult choices.

[5] We shall then have what Alfred Sauvy calls an "error by force" or an "effective error" (*erreur force*); although the opinion and judgment are incorrect, they become unimpeachable through the strength of collective belief.

process of crystallization, these images begin to occupy a person's entire consciousness, and to push out other feelings and judgments. All truly personal activity on the part of the individual is diminished, and man finally is filled with nothing but these prejudices and beliefs around which all else revolves. In his personal life, man will eventually judge everything by such crystalized standards. To return to Stoetzel, public opinion within an individual grows as it becomes crystalized through the effects of propaganda while his private opinion decreases.

Another aspect of crystallization pertains to self-justification for which man has great need, as we have seen in the preceding chapter. To the extent that man needs justifications, propaganda provides them. But whereas his ordinary justifications are fragile and may always be open to doubts, those furnished by propaganda are irrefutable and solid. The individual believes them and considers them to be eternal truths. He can throw off all sense of guilt; he loses all feeling for the harm he might do,[6] all sense of responsibility other than the responsibility propaganda instills in him. Thus he becomes perfectly adapted to objective situations and nothing can create a split within him.

Through such a process of intense rationalization, propaganda builds monolithic individuals. It eliminates inner conflicts, tensions, self-criticism, self-doubt. And in this fashion it also builds a one-dimensional being without depth or range of possibilities. Such an individual will have rationalizations not only for past actions, but for the future as well. He marches forward with full assurance of his righteousness. He is formidable in his equilibrium, all the more so because it is very difficult to break his harness of justifications. Experiments made with Nazi prisoners proved this point.

Tensions are always a threat to the individual, who tries everything to escape them because of his instinct of self-preservation. Ordinarily the individual will try to reduce his own tensions in his own way, but in our present society many of these tensions are produced by the general situation, and such tensions are less easily reduced. One might almost say that for collective problems only collective remedies suffice. Here propaganda renders spectacular service: by making man live in a familiar climate of opin-

---

[6] On the contrary, he attributes to the enemy exactly the atrocities that he himself is in the process of committing.

ion and by manipulating his symbols, it reduces tensions. Propaganda eliminates one of the causes of tension by driving man straight into such a climate of opinion. This greatly simplifies his life and gives him stability, much security, and a certain satisfaction.

At the same time, this crystallization closes his mind to all new ideas. The individual now has a set of prejudices and beliefs, as well as objective justifications. His entire personality now revolves around those elements. Every new idea will therefore be troublesome to his entire being. He will defend himself against it because it threatens to destroy his certainties. He thus actually comes to hate everything opposed to what propaganda has made him acquire.[7] Propaganda has created in him a system of opinions and tendencies which may not be subjected to criticism. That system leaves no room for ambiguity or mitigation of feelings; the individual has received irrational certainties from propaganda, and precisely because they are irrational, they seem to him part of his personality. He feels personally attacked when these certainties are attacked. There is a feeling here akin to that of something sacred. And this genuine taboo prevents the individual from entertaining any new ideas that might create ambiguity within him.

Incidentally, this refusal to listen to new ideas usually takes on an ironic aspect: the man who has been successfully subjected to a vigorous propaganda will declare that *all new ideas are propaganda.* To the degree that all his stereotypes, prejudices, and justifications are the fruit of propaganda, man will be ready to consider all other ideas as being propaganda and to assert his distrust in propaganda. One can almost postulate that those who call every idea they do not share "propaganda" are themselves almost completely products of propaganda. Their refusal to examine and question ideas other than their own is characteristic of their condition.

One might go further and say that propaganda tends to give a person a religious personality:[8] his psychological life is organized around an irrational, external, and collective tenet that provides

---

[7] What Sauvy calls the "reactions of defense against the destroyer" (of security, of the myth).

[8] All this is of course confirmed by the religious character that propaganda readily takes on, which tends to create the "sacred" around man and to make him adhere to "sacred" values.

a scale of values, rules of behavior, and a principle of social integration. In a society in the process of secularization, propaganda responds to the religious need, but lends much more vigor and intransigence to the resulting religious personality, in the pejorative sense of that term (as liberals employed it in the nineteenth century): a limited and rigid personality that mechanically applies divine commandments, is incapable of engaging in human dialogue, and will never question values that it has placed above the individual. All this is produced by propaganda, which pretends to have lost none of its humanity, to act for the good of mankind, and to represent the highest type of human being. In this respect, strict orthodoxies always have been the same.

We may now ask: If propaganda modifies psychological life in this fashion, will it not eventually lead to neurosis? Karen Horney[9] deserves the credit for having shown that the neurotic personality is tied to a social structure and a culture (in the American sense of that term), and that certain neuroses share certain essential characteristics springing directly from the problems found in our society. In the face of problems produced by society, propaganda seems a means of remedying personal deficiencies; at the same time it plunges the individual into a neurotic state. This is apparent from the rigid responses of the propagandee, his unimaginative and stereotyped attitude, his sterility with regard to the socio-political process, his inability to adjust to situations other than those created by propaganda, his need for strict opposites—black and white, good and bad—his involvement in unreal conflicts created and blown up by propaganda. To mistake an artificial conflict for a real one is a characteristic of neurosis. So is the tendency of the propagandee to give everything his own narrow interpretation, to deprive facts of their real meaning in order to integrate them into his system and give them an emotional coloration, which the non-neurotic would not attribute to them.

Similarly, the neurotic anxiously seeks the esteem and affection of the largest number of people, just as the propagandee can live only in accord with his comrades, sharing the same reflexes and judgments with those of his group (subjected to the identical propaganda). He does not deviate by one iota, for to remove

---

[9] *The Neurotic Personality of Our Time* (New York: W. W. Norton & Company; 1937), Ch. 1.

himself from the affection of the milieu means profound suffering; and that affection is tied to a particular external behavior and an identical response to propaganda. Naturally, what corresponds to this is the neurotic's hostility toward those who refuse his friendship and those who remain outside his group; the same holds true for the propagandee.

In the neurotic, the extraordinary need for self-justification (which resides in everyone and leads him to insincerity) expresses itself in the projection of hostile motives to the outside world; he feels that destructive impulses do not emanate from him, but from someone or something outside. *He* does not want to fool or exploit others—others want to do that to *him;* and this mechanism is reproduced by propaganda with great precision. He who wants to make war projects this intention onto his enemy; then the projected intention spreads to the propagandee who is then being mobilized and prepared for war, whose hostilities are aroused at the same time as he is made to project his own aggression onto the enemy. As with the neurotic, the "victim-enemy-scapegoat" cycle assumes enormous proportions in the mind of the propagandee, even if we admit that in addition to this process some legitimate reasons always exist for such reactions.

To sum up: When reading Karen Horney's description of the neurotic cycle stemming from the neurotic's environment, one might almost be reading about the cycle typical for the propagandee:

> Anxiety, hostility, reduction of self-respect . . . striving for power . . . reinforcement of hostility and anxiety . . . a tendency to withdraw in the face of competition, accompanied by tendencies to self-depreciation . . . failures and disproportion between capabilities and accomplishments . . . reinforcement of feelings of superiority . . . reinforcement of grandiose ideas . . . increase of sensitivity with an inclination to withdraw . . . increase of hostility and anxiety . . .

These responses of the neurotic are identical with those of the propagandee, even if we take into account that propaganda ultimately eliminates conscious anxiety and tranquilizes the propagandee.

Alienation through Propaganda

To be alienated means to be someone other (*alienus*) than one-self; it also can mean to belong to someone else. In a more profound sense, it means to be deprived of one's self, to be subjected to, or even identified with, someone else. That is definitely the effect of propaganda.[1] Propaganda strips the individual, robs him of part of himself, and makes him live an alien and artificial life, to such an extent that he becomes another person and obeys impulses foreign to him. He obeys someone else.[2]

Once again, to produce this effect, propaganda restricts itself to utilizing, increasing, and reinforcing the individual's inclination to lose himself in something bigger than he is, to dissipate his individuality, to free his ego of all doubt, conflict, and suffering —through fusion with others; to devote himself to a great leader and a great cause. In large groups, man feels united with others, and he therefore tries to free himself of himself by blending with a large group. Indeed, propaganda offers him that possibility in an exceptionally easy and satisfying fashion. But it pushes the individual into the mass until he disappears entirely.

To begin with, what is it that propaganda makes disappear? Everything in the nature of critical and personal judgment. Obviously, propaganda limits the application of thought. It limits the propagandee's field of thought to the extent that it provides him with ready-made (and, moreover, unreal) thoughts and stereotypes. It orients him toward very limited ends and prevents him from using his mind or experimenting on his own. It determines the core from which all his thoughts must derive and draws from the beginning a sort of guideline that permits neither criticism nor imagination. More precisely, his imagination will lead only to small digressions from the fixed line and to only slightly deviant, preliminary responses *within* the framework. In this fashion we see the progressives make some "variations" around the basic propaganda tenets of the Communist party. But the field of such variations is strictly limited.

The acceptance of this line, of such ends and limitations, pre-

---

[1] Consider the role assigned by the Communist Party to propaganda: it must change the very conscience of the Soviet citizen; and we find the same idea in Mao.

[2] But, as we have often recalled, "the persons subjected to propaganda do not consider themselves influenced by it. Each thinks that he himself has found 'the road to truth.'"

supposes the suppression of all critical judgment, which in turn is a result of the crystalization of thoughts and attitudes and the creation of taboos. As Jules Monnerot has accurately said: All individual passion leads to the suppression of all critical judgment with regard to the object of that passion. Beyond that, in the collective passion created by propaganda, critical judgment disappears altogether, for in no way can there ever be collective critical judgment. Man becomes incapable of "separation," of discernment (the word *critical* is derived from the Greek *krino*, separate). The individual can no longer judge for himself because he inescapably relates his thoughts to the entire complex of values and prejudices established by propaganda. With regard to political situations, he is given ready-made value judgments[3] invested with the power of truth by the number of supporters and the word of experts. The individual has no chance to exercise his judgment either on principal questions or on their implication; this leads to the atrophy of a faculty not comfortably exercised under any conditions.

What the individual loses is never easy to revive. Once personal judgment and critical faculties have disappeared or have been atrophied, they will not simply reappear when propaganda has been suppressed. In fact, we are dealing here with one of propaganda's most durable effects: years of intellectual and spiritual education would be needed to restore such faculties. The propagandee, if deprived of one propaganda, will immediately adopt another; this will spare him the agony of finding himself vis-à-vis some event without a ready-made opinion, and obliged to judge it for himself.[4] At the same time, propaganda presents facts, judgments, and values in such confusion and with so many methods that it is literally impossible for the average man to proceed with discernment. He has neither the intellectual capacity nor the sources of information. He is therefore forced either to accept, or reject, everything *in toto*.

We thus reach the same point via different routes: on the one hand, propaganda destroys the critical faculty; on the other, it presents objectives on which that faculty could not be exercised, and thus renders it useless.

[3] Recent events (1962) show, unfortunately, that students and intellectuals integrated in propaganda are no more armed with critical judgment than others are.
[4] This is one of the reasons why the propagandee, as soon as he is separated from his group, disintegrates morally. He needs the collective morale in order to exist.

All this obviously leads to the elimination of personal judgment, which takes place as soon as the individual accepts public opinion as his own. When he expresses public opinion in his words and gestures, he no longer expresses himself, but his society, his group. To be sure, the individual always will express the group, more or less. But in this case he will express it totally and in response to a systematic operation.

Moreover, this impersonal public opinion, when produced by propaganda, is artificial. It corresponds to nothing authentic; yet it is precisely this artificial opinion that the individual absorbs. He is filled with it; he no longer expresses his ideas, but those of his group, and with great fervor at that—it is a propaganda prerequisite that he should assert them with firmness and conviction. He absorbs the collective judgments, the creatures of propaganda; he absorbs them like the nourishment which they have, in fact, become. He expounds them as his own. He takes a vigorous stand, begins to oppose others. He asserts himself at the very moment that he denies his own self without realizing it. When he recites his propaganda lesson and says that he is thinking for himself, when his eyes see nothing and his mouth only produces sounds previously stenciled into his brain, when he says that he is indeed expressing his judgment—then he really demonstrates that he no longer thinks at all, ever, and that he does not exist as a person. When the propagandee tries to assert himself as a living reality, he demonstrates his total alienation most clearly; for he shows that he can no longer even distinguish between himself and society. He is then perfectly integrated, *he* is the social group, there is nothing in him not of the group, there is no opinion in him that is not the group's opinion. He is nothing except what propaganda has taught him. He is merely a channel that ingests the truths of propaganda and dispenses them with the conviction that is the result of his absence as a person. He cannot take a single step back to look at events under such conditions; there can be no distance of any kind between him and propaganda.

This mechanism of alienation generally corresponds either to projection into, and identification with, a hero and leader, or to a fusion with the mass. These two mechanisms are not mutually exclusive: When a Hitler Youth projected himself into his Führer, he entered by that very act into the mass integrated by propaganda. When the young Komsomol surrendered himself to the cult of Stalin's personality, he became, at that very moment, altogether part of the mass. It is important to note that when the propagandee believes to be expressing the highest ideal of personality, he is at the lowest point of alienation. Did we not hear often enough Fascism's claim that it restored Personality to its place of honor? But through one channel or another, the same alienation is produced by any propaganda, for the creation of a hero is just as much the result of propaganda as is the integration of an individual in an activated mass. When propaganda makes the individual participate in a collective movement, it not only makes him share in an artificial activity, but also evokes in him a psychology of participation, a "crowd psychology." This psychic modification, which automatically takes place in the presence of other participants, is systematically produced by propaganda. It is the creation of mass psychology, with man's individual psychology integrated into the crowd.

In this process of alienation, the individual loses control and submits to external impulses; his personal inclinations and tastes give way to participation in the collective. But that collective will always be best idealized, patterned, and represented by the hero. The cult of the hero is the absolutely necessary complement of the massification of society. We see the automatic creation of this cult in connection with champion athletes, movie stars, and even such abstractions as Davy Crockett in the United States and Canada in 1955. This exaltation of the hero proves that one lives in a mass society. The individual who is prevented by circumstances from becoming a real person, who can no longer express himself through personal thought or action, who finds his aspirations frustrated, projects onto the hero all he would wish to be. He lives vicariously and experiences the athletic or amorous or military exploits of the god with whom he lives in spiritual symbiosis. The well-known mechanism of identifying with movie stars is almost impossible to avoid for the member of modern society who comes to admire himself in the person of the hero. There he reveals the powers of which he unconsciously dreams, projects his desires, identifies himself with this success and that adventure. The hero becomes model and father, power and mythical realization of all that the individual cannot be.[5]

---

[5] At the same time the interests of the hero become the personal interests of the propagandee.

Propaganda uses all these mechanisms, but actually does even more to reinforce, stabilize, and spread them. The propagandee is alienated and transposed into the person promoted by propaganda (publicity campaigns for movie stars and propaganda campaigns are almost identical). For this, incidentally, no totalitarian organization is needed—such alienation does not take place merely in the event of a Hitler or a Stalin, but also in that of a Khrushchev, a Clemenceau, a Coolidge, or a Churchill (the myth surrounding Coolidge is very remarkable in this respect).

The propagandee finds himself in a psychological situation composed of the following elements: he lives vicariously, through an intermediary. He feels, thinks, and acts through the hero. He is under the guardianship and protection of his living god; he accepts being a child; he ceases to defend his own interests, for he knows his hero loves him and everything his hero decides is for the propagandee's own good; he thus compensates for the rigor of the sacrifices imposed on him. For this reason every regime that demands a certain amount of heroism must develop this propaganda of projection onto the hero (leader).

In this connection one can really speak of alienation, and of regression to an infantile state caused by propaganda. Young is of the opinion that the propagandee no longer develops intellectually, but becomes arrested in an infantile neurotic pattern; regression sets in when the individual is submerged in mass psychology. This is confirmed by Stoetzel, who says that propaganda destroys all individuality, is capable of creating only a collective personality, and that it is an obstacle to the free development of the personality.

Such extensive alienation is by no means exceptional. The reader may think we have described an extreme, almost pathological case. Unfortunately, he is a common type, even in his acute state. Everywhere we find men who pronounce as highly personal truths what they have read in the papers only an hour before, and whose beliefs are merely the result of a powerful propaganda. Everywhere we find people who have blind confidence in a political party, a general, a movie star, a country, or a cause, and who will not tolerate the slightest challenge to that god. Everywhere we meet people who, because they are filled with the consciousness of Higher Interests they must serve unto death, are no longer capable of making the simplest moral or intellectual distinctions or of engaging in the most elementary reasoning. Yet all this is acquired without effort, experience, reflection, or criticism—by the destructive shock effect of well-made propaganda. We meet this alienated man at every turn, and are possibly already one ourselves.

Aside from the alienation that takes place when the rational individual retreats into the irrational collective, there are other forms of alienation—for example, through the artificial satisfaction of real needs, or the real satisfaction of artificial needs (publicity and advertising).

The first case is the one we have already discussed, in which propaganda develops from the contemporary sociological situation in order to give man artificial satisfaction for real needs. Because man is restless and frustrated, because he understands nothing of the world in which he lives and acts, because he still is asked to make very great sacrifices and efforts—because of all that, propaganda develops.[6] It satisfies man, but with false and illusory satisfactions. It gives him explanations of the World in which he lives, but explanations that are mendacious and irrational. It reassures or excites him, but always at the wrong moment. It makes him tremble with fear of some biological warfare that never did exist, and makes him believe in the peaceful intentions of countries that have no desire for peace. It gives him reasons for the sacrifices demanded of him, but not the real reasons. Thus, in 1914, it called on him to lay down his life for his country, but remained silent on the war's economic causes, for which he certainly would not have fought.

Propaganda satisfies man's need for release and certainty, it eases his tensions and compensates for his frustrations, but with purely artificial means. If, for example, the worker has reasons—given his actual economic situation—to feel frustrated, alienated, or exploited, propaganda, which can really "solve" the worker's problems, as it has already done in the U.S.S.R., alienates him even more by making him oblivious of his frustration and alienation, and by calming and satisfying him. When man is subjected to the abnormal conditions of a big city or a battlefield and has good reason to feel tense, fearful, and out of step, propaganda

---

[6] Goebbels stated expressly that propaganda should reduce frustration, artificially resolve real problems, announce the frustrations to come when one cannot avoid them, and so forth.

that adjusts him to such conditions and resolves his conflicts artificially, without changing his situation in the least, is particularly pernicious. Of course, it seems like a cure. But it is like the cure that would heal the liver of an alcoholic in such a way that he could continue to get drunk without feeling pain in his liver. Propaganda's artificial and unreal answers for modern man's psychological suffering are precisely of that kind: they allow him to continue living abnormally under the conditions in which society places him. Propaganda suppresses the warning signals that his anxieties, maladjustments, rebellions, and demands once supplied.

All this is also at work when propaganda liberates our deepest impulses and tendencies, such as our erotic drives, guilt feelings, and desire for power. But such liberation does not provide true and genuine satisfaction for such drives, any more than it justifies our demands and aggressions by permitting us to feel righteous in spite of them. Man can no more pick the object of his aggression than he can give free reign to his erotic drive. The satisfactions and liberations offered by propaganda are *ersatz*. Their aim is to provide a certain decompression or to use the shock effect of these tremendous forces somewhere else, to use them in support of actions that would otherwise lack impetus. This shows how the propaganda process deprives the individual of his true personality.

Modern man deeply craves friendship, confidence, close personal relationships.[7] But he is plunged into a world of competition, hostility, and anonymity. He needs to meet someone whom he can trust completely, for whom he can feel pure friendship, and to whom he can mean something in return. That is hard to find in his daily life, but apparently confidence in a leader, a hero, a movie star, or a TV personality is much more satisfying. TV, for example, creates feelings of friendship, a new intimacy, and thus fully satisfies those needs. But such satisfactions are purely illusory and fallacious because there is no true friendship of any kind between the TV personality and the viewer who feels that personality to be his friend. Here is a typical mendacious satisfaction of a genuine need. And what TV spontaneously pro-

---

[7] This is what gives value and effectiveness to the technique of propaganda by personal contacts (see above, p. 7).

duces is systematically exploited by propaganda: the "Little Father" is always present.

Another example: In 1958 Khrushchev promised the transition to integrated Communism in the U.S.S.R.; later he declared that it would be realized very soon. Based on this theme was an entire irrational propaganda campaign whose principal argument was that Communism would soon be fully attained because by 1975 the U.S.S.R. would have reached the production level of the United States—which would mean that the United States would then be ready to achieve Communism. Incidentally, the year given by Khrushchev in 1958 for the occurrence of this phenomenon was 1975, but in April 1960, the year he gave was 1980. This campaign was designed to satisfy the needs of the Soviet masses, to regain their confidence and appease their demands. What we see here is a purely theoretical answer, but it satisfies because it is *believed* by the masses and thus made true and real by the mechanism of propaganda.

Let us now look at the other side of the coin. Propaganda creates artificial needs. Just as propaganda creates political problems that would never arise by themselves,[8] but for which public opinion will then demand a solution, it arouses in us an increase of certain desires, prejudices, and needs which were by no means imperative to begin with. They become so only as a result of propaganda, which here plays the same role as advertising. Besides, propaganda is helped by advertising, which gives certain twists and orientations to individual drives, while propaganda extends the effects of advertising by promising psychological relief of tensions in general. Under the impact of propaganda, certain prejudices (racial or economic), certain needs (for equality or success), become all-devouring, destructive passions, occupying the entire range of a person's consciousness, superseding all other aspects of life, and demanding answers.

As a result of propaganda, these superficial tendencies end up by becoming identified with our deepest needs and become confused with what is most personal and profound within us. Precisely in this fashion the genuine need for freedom has been diluted and adulterated into an abominable mixture of liberalism under the impact of various forms of propaganda of the nine-

---

[8] I reserve this study for a subsequent work.

teenth and twentieth centuries. In this psychic confusion, created by propaganda, propaganda alone then imposes order. Just as it is a fact that mass communication media create new needs (for example, the existence of TV creates the need to buy a set and turn it on), it is even more the case when these means are used by propaganda.

And just as propaganda acts to create new needs, it also creates the demand for their solutions. We have shown how propaganda can relieve and resolve tensions. These tensions are purposely provoked by the propagandist, who holds out their remedy at the same time. He is master of both excitation and satisfaction. One may even say that if he has provoked a particular tension, it was in order to lead the individual to accept a particular remedy, to demand some suitable action (suitable from the propagandist's viewpoint), and to submit to a system that will alleviate that tension. He thus places the individual in a universe of artificially created political needs, needs that are artificial even if their roots were once completely genuine.

For example, by creating class-consciousness in the proletariat, propaganda adds a corresponding tension to the worker's misery. Similarly, by creating an equality complex, it adds another tension to all the natural demands of the "have-nots." But propaganda simultaneously offers the means to reduce these tensions. It opens a door to the individual, and we have seen that that is one of the most effective propaganda devices. The only trouble is that all it really offers is a profound alienation: when an individual reacts to these artificially provoked tensions, when he responds to these artificially created stimuli, or when he submits to the manipulations that make him repress certain personal impulses to make room for abstract drives and reduction of these tensions, he is no more himself than he is when he reacts biologically to a tranquilizer. This will appear to be a true remedy, which in fact it is—but for a sickness deliberately provoked to fit the remedy.

As we have frequently noted, these artificial needs assume considerable importance because of their universal nature and the means (the mass media) by which they are propagated. They become more demanding and imperative for the individual than his own private needs and lead him to sacrifice his private satisfactions. In politics as in economics, the development of artificial needs progressively eliminates personal needs and inclinations. Thus, what takes place is truly an expulsion of the individual outside of himself, designed to deliver him to the abstract forces of technically oriented mechanisms.

On this level, too, the more the individual is convinced that he thinks, feels, and acts on his own, the greater the alienation will be. The psychologist Biddle has demonstrated in detail that an individual subjected to propaganda behaves as though his reactions depended on his own decisions. He obeys, he trembles with fear and expands or contracts on command, but nothing in this obedience is passive or automatic; even when yielding to suggestion, he decides "for himself" and thinks himself free—in fact the more he is subjected to propaganda, the freer he thinks he is. He is energetic and chooses his own action. In fact, propaganda, to reduce the tension it has created in the first place, offers him one, two, even three possible courses of action, and the propagandee considers himself a well-organized, fully aware individual when he chooses one of them. Of course, this takes little effort on his part. The propagandee does not need much energy to make his decision, for that decision corresponds with his group, with suggestion, and with the sociological forces. Under the influence of propaganda he always takes the easy way, the path of least resistance, even if it costs him his life. But even while coasting downhill, he claims he is climbing uphill and performing a personal, heroic act. For propaganda has aroused his energy, personality, and sense of responsibility—or rather their verbal images, because the forces themselves were long ago destroyed by propaganda. This duplicity is propaganda's most destructive act. And it leads us to consider next propaganda's effect of psychic dissociation.

The Psychic Dissociation Effect of Propaganda

Philippe de Félice[9] has said that propaganda creates a tendency to manic-depressive (cyclothymic) neurosis. This is obviously an exaggeration, but it is true that propaganda puts the individual through successive periods of exaltation and depression, caused by exposing him to alternate propaganda themes. We have already analyzed the necessity for alternating themes,

---

[9] Foules en délire, extases collectives (Paris: A. Michel; 1947), Ch. 4.

for example, alternating those of terror and of self-assertion. The result is a continuous emotional contrast, which can become very dangerous for individuals exposed to it.[1] Like the shock of contradictory propaganda, this can be one of the causes of psychic dissociation, though it does not have to lead to mental illness, as Félice suggests.

At this point, we shall lay aside the observable dissociations in the propagandee between public opinion and his personal opinion; we have already said that propaganda produces a deep separation between the two.[2] Instead we shall stress the dissociation between thought and action, which seems to us one of the most disturbing facts of our time. Nowadays, man acts without thinking, and in turn his thought can no longer be translated into action. Thinking has become a superfluous exercise, without reference to reality; it is purely internal, without compelling force, more or less a game. It is literature's domain; and I am not referring solely to "intellectual" thought, but to *all* thought, whether it concerns work or politics or family life. In sum, thought and reflection have been rendered thoroughly pointless by the circumstances in which modern man lives and acts. He does not need to think in order to act; his action is determined by the techniques he uses and by the sociological conditions. He acts without really wanting to, without ever reflecting on the meaning of or reason for his actions. This situation is the result of the whole evolution

---

[1] One element we must remember is the overexcitement that propaganda provokes. The propagandee is constantly urged to action and often prevented from accomplishing it. His certainties are absolute; he is constantly overexcited by them; and his ever-renewed aggression toward the symbols of his own culture (as one saw among the French subjected to propaganda against the 1960 Algerian war) leads him rather quickly to disintegration as a result of the extreme discrepancies between this overexcitement and his social milieu.

[2] One aspect of the dissociation which Stolypine has justly emphasized ("Evolution psychologique en U.R.S.S.," *Economie Contemporaine*, 1952) is the division of "consciousness" into three "compartments." *Aligned consciousness*, a term frequently employed in the Stalin regime, refers to the "conscious citizen of the Socialist epoch," who lives in official truth, performs a consistent action, and is completely socialized. This aligned consciousness is a creation of propaganda. But beneath it exists a *premeditated consciousness*, the level at which the citizen personalizes the data of propaganda and persuades himself that the regime is good, the level at which he works out justifications and decisions for behavior which will conform to social demands in such a way as to make him least aware of his bad conscience. Finally, there exists a *secret consciousness*, comprising the refusals, the protestations, the judgments against the regime, combined with a tendency toward cynicism or belief in Christianity. But this secret consciousness is completely repressed, encircled, and constrained, and must struggle against interdictions such as man's spontaneous impulses have never before encountered.

of our society. The schools, the press, and social pragmatism are just as responsible for this as psychotechnics, the modern political structure, and the obsession with productivity. But the two decisive factors are the mechanization of work and propaganda.

The mechanization of work is based entirely on dissociation: those who think, establish the schedules, or set the norms, never act—and those who act must do so according to rules, patterns, and plans imposed on them from outside. Above all, they must not reflect on their actions. They cannot do so anyhow, because of the speed with which they work. The modern ideal appears to be a reduction of action to complete automatism. This is considered to be a great benefit to the worker, who can dream or think of "other things" while working. But this dissociation, which lasts eight hours a day, must necessarily affect all the rest of his behavior.

The other element that plays a decisive role in this connection is propaganda. Remember that propaganda seeks to induce action, adherence, and participation—with as little thought as possible.[3] According to propaganda, it is useless, even harmful for man to think; thinking prevents him from acting with the required righteousness and simplicity. Action must come directly from the depths of the unconscious; it must release tension, become a reflex. This presumes that thought unfolds on an entirely unreal level, that it never engages in political decisions. And this is in fact so. No political thought that is at all coherent or distinct can possibly be applied. What man thinks either is totally without effect or must remain unsaid. This is the basic condition of the political organization of the modern world, and propaganda is the instrument to attain this effect. An example that shows the radical devaluation of thought is the transformation of words in propaganda; there, language, the instrument of the mind, becomes "pure sound," a symbol directly evoking feelings and reflexes. This is one of the most serious dissociations that propaganda causes. There is another: the dissociation between the verbal universe, in which propaganda makes us live, and reality.[4] Propaganda sometimes deliberately separates from man's real world

---

[3] To this is connected, for example, the phenomena of privatization and elasticity of reasoning, as well as the divergence between opinion and action, which we have studied above.
[4] I intend to study this important phenomenon in my next work.

the verbal world that it creates; it then tends to destroy man's conscience.

In connection with the problem of dissociation we must now examine the case of an individual subjected to two intense, opposing propagandas equally close to him. Such a situation can occur in a democracy. It is sometimes said that two competing propagandas cancel each other out; if, however, one regards propaganda not as a debate of ideas or the promulgation of a doctrine, but as psychological manipulation designed to produce action, one understands that these two propagandas, far from canceling each other out because they are contradictory, have a cumulative effect. A boxer, groggy from a left hook, does not return to normal when he is hit with a right hook; he becomes groggier. Now, the modern propagandist likes to speak of his "shock effect." And it is indeed a psychological shock that the individual subjected to propaganda suffers. But a second shock from another angle certainly does not revive him.[5] On the contrary, a second phenomenon is then produced by these contradictory propagandas: the man whose psychological mechanisms have been set in motion to make him take one action is stopped by the second shock, which acts on the same mechanisms to produce another action. The fact that this man will finally vote for anybody at all is not the important point. What counts is that his normal psychological processes are perverted and will continue to be, constantly. To defend himself against that, man automatically reacts in one of two ways.

(a) He takes refuge in inertia,[6] in which case propaganda may provoke his rejection. The conflicting propaganda of opposing parties is essentially what leads to political abstention. But this is not the abstention of the free spirit which asserts itself; it is the result of resignation, the external symptom of a series of inhibitions. Such a man has not decided to abstain; under diverse pressures, subjected to shocks and distortions, he can no longer (even if he wanted to) perform a political act. What is even more

---

[5] The effect of this double shock is so well known that it is utilized as a technique in a single propaganda by the use of either contradictory news or a tranquilizing propaganda designed to appease the public before launching a great shock that will be felt all the more violently: for example, making propaganda for peace before releasing a violent psychological offensive.

[6] In the same way escape—into private life, exoticism, the "ideal"—is explained as a means of fleeing the contradictions of modern life.

serious is that this inhibition not only is political, but also progressively takes over the whole of his being and leads to a general attitude of surrender. As long as political debates were of little importance and election propaganda dealt with water supplies or rural electrification, this escape reflex was not affecting people's entire lives. But propaganda grows in effectiveness as its themes cause more anxiety. Today, when we are concerned with the Rise of Dictators and the Approach of War, the individual cannot avoid feeling himself drawn in. He cannot just shrug his shoulders, but he is rendered passive by propaganda.

The same situation can be found when two contradictory propagandas succeed each other in time. The often-studied skepticism of German youth after 1945, that famous formula *Ohne Mich*, arose from the counter-shock of a propaganda opposed to Nazi propaganda. Similarly, after the Hungarian Revolution of October 1956, youth threw itself into nihilism, into indifference and personal concerns. These examples demonstrate not the ineffectiveness of propaganda, but, on the contrary, its power to profoundly disturb psychic life.

(b) The other defensive reflex is flight into involvement. Political involvement is widespread today because man can no longer bear to remain aloof in an arena of aggressive competition between propagandas. No longer capable of resisting these opposing pulls, which reach the deepest levels of his personality, the individual becomes "involved." He joins a party, to which he then ties himself as totally and deeply as propaganda had intended. From then on his problem will be solved. He escapes the opposing clash of propagandas; now, all that his side says is true and right; all that comes from elsewhere is false and wrong. Thus one propaganda arms him against the other propagandas. This dualism is not entirely contradictory; it can be complementary: To illustrate, in 1959 the *Conseil Français des Mouvements de Jeunesse* observed that youths were distrustful of all political action, but were at the same time inclined to extreme solutions.

Creation of the Need for Propaganda

A final psychological effect of propaganda is the appearance of the need for propaganda. The individual subjected to propaganda can no longer do without it. This is a form of "snowballing": the more propaganda there is, the more the public wants.

The same is true of advertising, which has been said to "feed on its own success." It was believed, for example, that advertising on television would supplant newspaper advertising; but it was found, on the contrary, that television actually increased the total volume of advertising business. The need for a growing volume of propaganda involves two apparently contradictory phenomena: *mithridatization* and *sensibilization.*[7]

Mithridatization. It is known that under the effect of propaganda the individual gradually closes up. Having suffered too many propaganda shocks, he becomes accustomed and insensitive to them. He no longer looks at posters; to him they are just splashes of color. He no longer hears a radio speech; it is nothing but sound, a background noise for his activity. He no longer reads the newspaper, but merely skims distractedly over it. One may therefore be tempted to say: "You see how the excess of propaganda no longer has a hold on this man; he reacts with indifference, he escapes it; he is mithridatized against propaganda."

Nevertheless, this same individual continues to turn on his radio and buy his newspaper. He is mithridatized, yes, but to what? Only to the objective and intellectual content of propaganda. True, he has become indifferent to the theme of propaganda, the idea, the argument—to everything that could form his opinion. He no longer needs to read the newspaper or listen to the speech because he knows their ideological content in advance and that it would change none of his attitudes.

But though it is true that after a certain time the individual becomes indifferent to the propaganda content, that does not mean that he has become insensitive to propaganda, that he turns from it, that he is immune. It means exactly the opposite, for not only does he keep buying his newspaper, but he also continues to follow the trend and obey the rules. He continues to obey the catchwords of propaganda, though he no longer listens to it. His reflexes still function, *i.e.*, he has not become independent through mithridatization. He is deeply imbued with the symbols of propaganda; he is entirely dominated and manipulated. He no longer needs to see and read the poster; the simple splash of color is enough to awaken the desired reflexes in him. In reality, though

[7]*Mithridatization* is a "toxin anti-toxin" process whereby a person is rendered immune to a poison by tolerating gradually increased doses of it. *Sensibilization* is the increase of sensitivity or susceptibility. (Trans.)

he is mithridatized to ideological content, he is sensitized to propaganda itself.

Sensibilization. The more the individual is captured by propaganda, the more sensitive he is—not to its content, but to the impetus it gives him, to the excitement it makes him feel. The smallest excitement, the feeblest stimulus, activates his conditioned reflexes, awakens the myth, and produces the action that the myth demands. Up to this point an enormous amount of manipulation, a substantial dose of cleverly coordinated stimuli was required to achieve this in him. The motivating drives of his psyche had to be reached, the doors of his unconscious had to be forced open, his attitudes and habits had to be broken and new behavior determined. This meant the use of methods and techniques at once subtle and crushing.

But once the individual has been filled with and reshaped by propaganda, action by so many methods is no longer necessary. The smallest dose now suffices. It is enough to "refresh," to give a "booster shot," to repaint, and the individual obeys in striking fashion—like certain drunks who become intoxicated on one glass of wine. The individual no longer offers any resistance to propaganda; moreover, he has ceased to believe in it consciously. He no longer attaches importance to what it says, to its proclaimed objectives, but he acts according to the proper stimuli. Here we find again the dissociation between action and thought of which we spoke earlier. The individual is arrested and crystalized with regard to his thinking. It is in this domain of opinion that mithridatization takes place. But in the domain of action he is actually mobilized. He responds to the changing propaganda inputs; he acts with vigor and certainty, indeed with precipitation. He is a ready activist, but his action is purely irrational. That is the effect of his sensibilization to propaganda.

An individual who has arrived at this point has a constant and irresistible need for propaganda. He cannot bear to have it stop. We can readily understand why this is so when we think of his condition.

(a) He lived in anxiety, and propaganda gave him certainty. Now his anxiety doubles at the very instant when propaganda stops. All the more so because—in this terrible silence that suddenly surrounds him—he, who permitted himself to be led, no longer knows where to go; and all around him he hears the violent clamor of other propagandas seeking to influence him and seduce him, and which increase his confusion.

(b) Propaganda removed him from his subhuman situation and gave him a feeling of self-importance. It permitted him to assert himself and satisfied his need for active participation. When it stops, he finds himself more powerless than before, with a feeling of impotence all the more intense because he had come to believe in the effectiveness of his actions. He is suddenly plunged into apathy and has no personal way of getting out of it. He acquires a conviction of his unworthiness much more violent than he has felt before because for a while he has believed in his worth.

(c) Finally, propaganda gave him justification. The individual needs to have this justification constantly renewed. He needs it in some form at every step, for every action, as a guarantee that he is on the right path. When propaganda ceases, he loses his justification; he no longer has confidence in himself. He feels guilty because under the influence of propaganda he performed deeds that he now dreads or for which he is remorseful. Thus he has even more need for justification. And he plunges into despair when propaganda ceases to provide him with the certainty of his justice and his motives.

When propaganda ceases in a group where it has had powerful effect, what do we see? A social disintegration of the group and a corresponding internal disintegration of the individuals within it. They completely withdraw into themselves and reject all participation in social or political life—through uncertainty, through fear, through discouragement. They begin to feel that everything is useless, that there is no need to have opinions or participate in political life. They are now wholly disinterested in all that was the center of their lives. As far as they are concerned, everything will go on henceforth "without me." The group as such loses its value in the eyes of the individual, and its disintegration follows from this attitude of its members. Egocentricity is the product of the cessation of propaganda—in such fashion that it appears irremediable. Not only egocentric withdrawal, but also genuine nervous or mental troubles—such as schizophrenia, paranoia, and guilt complexes—are sometimes found in those who have been dominated by a propaganda that has ceased. Such individuals must then compensate for the absence of propaganda with psychiatric treatment. These effects could be seen in countries where propaganda suddenly stopped, as in Hitler's Germany in 1945 or in the United States in 1946, to take two very different examples.

The reaction just described corresponds well to the alienation effected by propaganda. Man is diminished; he can no longer live alone, decide for himself, or alone assume the burden of his life; he needs a guardian, a director of conscience, and feels ill when he does not have them.[8] Thus a need for propaganda arises, which education can no longer change. From the moment the individual is caught, he needs his ration of pseudo-intellectual nourishment, of nervous and emotional stimulation, of catchwords, and of social integration. Propaganda must therefore be unceasing.

This leads us back to a question we raised earlier: the durability of propaganda effects. Through the creation of a need for propaganda and the required psychic transformations, propaganda has profound and relatively durable effects. But the specific content of propaganda—the substance that at any given time serves to satisfy this need and to reduce tensions—obviously has only a temporary and momentary effect, and must therefore be refreshed and renewed all the time, particularly as the satisfactions that propaganda gives are always in the immediate present. For this reason propaganda is not very durable.

But this statement must be qualified. We have said that propaganda cannot run counter to an epoch's deep-seated trends and collective presuppositions. But when propaganda acts in the direction and support of these, its effect becomes very durable on both the intellectual and the emotional level. Nowadays propaganda hostile to the State, opposed to "progress," would have no chance whatever of succeeding; but if it supports the State, it will penetrate deeply into man's consciousness. The need for propaganda then tends to make this penetration permanent. The duration, the permanence of propaganda, thus leads to the genuine durability of its effects. When these effects are constantly reproduced and their stimulus is endlessly renewed, they obviously affect the individual in depth. He learns to act and react

---

[8] Sometimes he is even aware of this. Riesman gives the remarkable example of individuals who complain that their psychological services are not active enough, that they have not been manipulated in such a manner as to enjoy the inconveniences in their lives.

in a particular way. (He has not, however, undergone a permanent or total modification of his personality.)

Propaganda is concerned with the most pressing and at the
same time the most elementary actuality. It proposes immediate
action of the most ordinary kind.[9] It thus plunges the individual
into the immediate present, taking from him all mastery of his
life and all sense of the duration or continuity of any action or
thought. Thus the propagandee becomes a man without a past
and without a future, a man who receives from propaganda his
portion of thought and action for the day; his discontinuous
personality must be given continuity from the outside, and this
makes the need for propaganda very strong. When the propagandee ceases to receive his propaganda, he experiences the feeling of being cut off from his own past and of facing a completely
unpredictable future, of being separated from the world he lives
in. Because propaganda has been his only channel for perceiving
the world, he has the feeling of being delivered, tied hand and
foot, to an unknown destiny. Thus, from the moment propaganda
begins, with its machine and its organization, one can no longer
stop it. It can only grow and perfect itself, for its discontinuation
would ask too great a sacrifice of the propagandee, a too thorough
remaking of himself. This is more than he is ready to accept.

The Ambiguity of Psychological Effects

One of the deceptive qualities of an inquiry such as we will
attempt under this heading is the great uncertainty to which we
are ultimately led. For we realize that propaganda can and does
produce contradictory psychological results. This has been made
clear, but should be emphasized here again. We shall therefore
examine four examples of these contradictory effects (aside from
the fact, already studied, that propaganda satisfies certain needs
while arousing others).

Propaganda can simultaneously create some tensions and ease
others. We have shown how it responds to the need of the individual in our society, who lives in an unhealthy state of anxiety;
how it consoles the individual and helps him to solve his conflicts. But it must not be forgotten that it also creates anxiety and

---

[9] Otherwise it is no longer propaganda. It becomes academic, without effect. It is
less a matter of general ideas than of familiarizing the worker with the practical
decisions of the Party.

provokes tensions. Particularly after a propaganda of fear or terror, the listener is left in a state of emotional tension which cannot be resolved by kind words or suggestions. Only action can resolve the conflict into which he was thrown. In the same way, purely critical and negative propaganda seeks to stiffen the individual against his environment; it plays on and stimulates instinctive feelings of aggression and frustration. But even here the effect can be one of two: either the individual will become more aggressive toward the symbols of authority in his group or culture, or he will be crushed by anxiety and reduced to passivity because he cannot stand discord and opposition.

The propagandist must try to find the optimum degree of tension and anxiety. This rule was expressly stated, among others, by Goebbels. Therefore one cannot say that tension is an accidental psychological effect of propaganda. The propagandist knows well what he is doing when he works in this way. As Goebbels indicated, anxiety is a double-edged sword. Too much tension can produce panic, demoralization, disorderly and impulsive action; too little tension does not push people to act; they remain complacent and seek to adapt themselves passively. It is therefore necessary to reinforce anxiety in some cases (for example, concerning the effects of a military defeat), in others, to reduce tensions that become too strong for people to handle by themselves (for example, the fear of air raids).

This ambivalence of propaganda, of creating tension in some cases and reducing it in others, explains itself largely, it seems to us, by the distinction between agitation propaganda and integration propaganda. The first, which aims at rapid, violent action, must arouse feelings of frustration, conflict, and aggression, which lead individuals to action. The latter, which seeks man's conformity with his group (including participation in action), will aim at the reduction of tensions, adjustment to the environment, and acceptance of the symbols of authority. Moreover, the two factors can overlap. For example, a revolutionary political party, such as the Communist or Nazi party, will employ propaganda of tension with respect to things outside the party, propaganda of acceptance with respect to the party itself. This explains the attitude of universal acceptance of all that is said or done in the party, and the opposite attitude of universal challenge and rejection of everything outside it.

Connected with this is the second contradiction by which propaganda creates self-justification and a good conscience, and at the same time guilt feelings and a bad conscience.

We have seen the strength propaganda develops when it furnishes the individual a feeling of security and righteousness. But propaganda also stimulates guilt feelings. In fact, to develop such feelings is its principal objective when it addresses a hostile group. Propaganda seeks to deprive the enemy of confidence in the justice of his own cause, his country, his army, and his group, for the man who feels guilty loses his effectiveness and his desire to fight. To convince a man that those on his side, if not he himself, commit immoral and unjust acts is to bring on the disintegration of the group to which he belongs. This type of propaganda can be made against the government, the army, the country's war aims—even the values defended by an individual's party or his nation. But it can also be made with respect to mere efficiency; to convince the individual of the *inadequacy* of the means employed by his group, or the *uncertainty* of its victory, or the *inability* of its leaders, has the same effect. In addition, propaganda can create a bad conscience in this way, strange as that may seem, probably because of its connection with the primitive belief that God makes good triumph over evil, that the best man wins, that might makes right, that what is not effective is neither true nor just. Of course, the psychological effect sought varies according to the audience propaganda aims at. In any event, propaganda creates a good conscience among its partisans and a bad conscience among its enemies.

The latter effect will be particularly strong in a country or group already beset by doubt. A propaganda of bad conscience succeeded admirably in France in 1939, and even more so at the beginning of 1957 in connection with the Algerian conflict, when it created a general feeling of guilt, sustained by campaigns on torture, colonialism, and the injustice of the French cause. This is characteristically French. This feeling *created* by propaganda (actually partially legitimate) was the essential cause of the victory of the F.L.N., a purely psychological victory, confirming the tenets and conclusions of Mao.

A third contradiction: In certain cases propaganda is an agent of attachment to the group, of cohesion; in other cases it is an agent of disruption and dissolution. It can transform the symbols of a group into absolute truth, inflate faith to the bursting point, lead to a communal state, and induce the individual to completely confuse his personal destiny with that of his group. This often occurs with war propaganda demanding "national unity." But propaganda can also destroy the group, break it up—for example, by stimulating contradictions between feelings of justice and of loyalty, by destroying confidence in the accustomed sources of information, by modifying standards of judgment, by exaggerating each crisis and conflict, or by setting groups against each other.

Moreover, it is possible to provide successive stages for the individual. While he is still a solid member of a group, propaganda can introduce a factor of ambiguity, of doubt, of suspicion. But the individual finds it very difficult to remain long in such a situation. Ambiguity is painful to him, and he seeks to escape it. But he cannot escape it by returning to his previous certainties and total blind allegiance to his former group. This is impossible because the doubt introduced can no longer be assuaged while the individual remains in the original context of values and truths. It is then, by going over to the enemy group, by compliance with what provoked the ambiguity, that man escapes that ambiguity. He then will enter into an absolute allegiance to the truth of the enemy group. His compliance will be all the more radical, his fusion with it all the more irrational, because it is a flight from yesterday's truth and because it will have to protect him against any return to, memory of, or nostalgia for the former allegiance. There is no greater enemy of Christianity or Communism than he who was once an absolute believer.

We shall stress one last type of contradiction. According to circumstances, propaganda creates either politization or what American sociologists call "privatization." First of all, propaganda must lead the individual to participate in political activities and devote himself to political problems. It can be effective only if in man it reveals the *citizen,* and if the citizen has the conviction that his destiny, his truth, and his legitimacy are linked to political activity—even more, that he can fulfill himself only in and through the State, and that the answer to his destiny lies only in politics. At that moment man is a victim perfectly prepared to submit to every propaganda foray.

But the success of propaganda also requires that the individual progressively lose interest in his personal and family affairs. To sacrifice his wife and children to a political decision becomes the ideal of the political hero, and that sacrifice will, of course, be justified as being for the common good, for one's country, or some such symbol. Personal problems then seem paltry, egotistical, mediocre. Propaganda must always fight against "privatization," the feeling that leads man to consider his private affairs as most important and produces skepticism toward the activities of the State, the *Ohne Mich* ideology such as was rife in Germany after 1945, a conviction that all is useless, that to vote means nothing, that "it's not worth-while to die for Danzig." Propaganda has absolutely no effect on those who live in such indifference or skepticism. One of the great differences between propaganda before and after 1940 was that in Western countries the latter had to face skeptical and "privatized" individuals.

A modern State can function only if the citizens give it their support, and that support can be obtained only if privatization is erased, if propaganda succeeds in politizing all questions, in arousing individual passions for political problems, in convincing men that activity in politics is their duty. The churches often participate in campaigns (without understanding that they are propaganda) designed to demonstrate that participation in civic affairs is fundamentally a religious duty.

At the same time, and just as strongly, propaganda is an agent of privatization. It produces this effect sometimes without intending to, sometimes deliberately. This reaction of privatization occurs in the phenomenon of withdrawal and skepticism when two opposing propagandas work on the same group with almost equal force; then the privatization effect is involuntary. But in many cases propaganda deliberately seeks to produce privatization; for example, a propaganda of terror seeks to create a depressing effect on the opponent and leads him to adopt a fatalistic attitude.[1] He must be made to believe that nothing helps, that the opposing party or army is so strong that no resistance is possible. In this connection, the appeal to the value of private life is used; the feeling is aroused that one risks a death which has no meaning—a decisive argument of privatization propaganda. Such arguments are useful for paralyzing an enemy, making him give up the strug-

---

[1] Terrorist action of the O.A.S. in 1962 was of this type.

gle and withdraw into egoism; they are equally valid in political or military conflict.

One aspect of privatization propaganda by the State seems to us even more important: when it creates a situation in which the State has a free hand because the citizenry is totally uninterested in political matters. One of the most remarkable weapons of the authoritarian State is propaganda that neutralizes and paralyzes its opponents (or all of public opinion) by reiterating a simple set of "truths" such as that the exercise of political power is very complex, and must therefore be left to professional politicians; that participation in political controversy is dangerous—so what good does it serve? . . . Why should individuals involve themselves where power is exercised in the name of all and in the public interest? . . . Individuals receive their comfort, well-being, and security from the State—it alone can plan ahead and organize.

Such propaganda is especially easy in an authoritarian system because privatization is a spontaneous reaction of the individual when there is disharmony between him and the leader of the group. The individual protects himself by privatization. His skepticism toward the State is then justified in his own eyes by the actions of the State; but it is propaganda which sustains his attitude of privatization and skepticism, leaving to the government complete freedom to act as it thinks proper.

The "reasonable" appeal of such propaganda will be heeded quite readily because in general man does not like to assume responsibilities. It is enough to remember the sigh of relief that went through all of France in 1852 when the Empire was created, and again in 1958 when a semi-authoritarian State gave Frenchmen the feeling that they would no longer have to make decisions for themselves, that these would now be made for them by others. Thus the State, in various ways—by terror in Hitler's Germany, by "political education" in the Soviet Union—neutralizes the masses, forces them into passivity, throws them back on their private life and personal happiness (actually according them some necessary satisfactions on this level), in order to leave a free hand to those who are in power, to the active, to the militant. This method offers very great advantages for the State.

[V]

THE
SOCIO-POLITICAL
EFFECTS

---

1. Propaganda and Ideology

The Traditional Relationship

A relationship between propaganda and ideology has always existed. The pattern of that relationship became more or less established toward the end of the nineteenth century. I will not give here an original or specific definition of ideology, but will merely say that society rests on certain beliefs and no social group can exist without such beliefs. To the extent that members of a group attribute intellectual validity to these beliefs, one may speak of an ideology. One might also consider a different process by which ideology is formed: ideologies emerge where doctrines are degraded and vulgarized and when an element of belief enters into them. However that may be, it has long been known that some ideologies are compatible with passive behavior, but most of them are active—*i.e.*, they push men into action.

Moreover, to the extent that members of a group believe their ideology to represent the truth, they almost always assume an aggressive posture and try to impose that ideology elsewhere. In such cases ideology becomes bent on conquest.

The drive toward conquest may arise within a society as a conflict between groups (for example, the proletarian ideology vs others within a nation), or it can aim at targets outside, as a nationalist ideology will. The expansion of an ideology can take various forms: it can accompany the expansion of a group and impose itself on collectivities being embraced by the group, as with the republican ideology of 1793 or the Communist ideology of 1945, which accompanied the armies.

Or an ideology such as that of Labor in a bourgeois society may expand by its own momentum on a purely psychological plane. In this case, the ideology assumes a non-imperialist attitude; meanwhile it penetrates the group that represents such an attitude. In this fashion the ideology of Labor helped bring about the bourgeois orientation of all Western society in the nineteenth century.

Finally, an ideology can expand by certain other means, without force and without setting an entire group in motion: at that point we find propaganda. Propaganda appears—spontaneously or in organized fashion—as a means of spreading an ideology beyond the borders of a group or of fortifying it within a group. Evidently, in such cases propaganda is directly inspired by ideology in both form and content. It is equally evident that what counts here is to spread the content of that ideology. Propaganda does not lead a life of its own; it emerges only sporadically—when an ideology tries to expand.

Propaganda organizes itself in conformity with that ideology, so that in the course of history we find very different forms of propaganda, depending on what ideological content was to be promulgated. Also, propaganda is strictly limited to its objective, and its working processes are relatively simple in that it does not try to take possession of the individual or dominate him by devious means, but simply to transmit certain beliefs and ideas. That is the current relationship between ideology and propaganda.

The classic pattern, still in existence in the nineteenth century— and considered valid today by many observers—no longer prevails; the situation has undergone profound changes.

Lenin and Hitler found a world in which the process of ideological expansion was more or less set. But their intervention in this domain would be the same as their intervention in all others. What actually was Lenin's, and thereafter Hitler's, great innovation? It was to understand that the modern world is essentially a world of "means"; that what is most important is to utilize all the means at man's disposal; and that ends and aims have been completely transformed by the profusion of means. The fact that man in the nineteenth century was still searching for ends led him to neglect most of the available means. Lenin's stroke of genius was to see that, in reality, *in our twentieth century,* the ends had come to be secondary to the means or, in many cases, of no importance at all. What mattered was primarily to set all available instruments in motion and to push them to their limits.

Moreover, Lenin was carried along by the conviction that such extreme utilization of all means would, a priori, lead to the establishment of Socialist society. The end thus became a postulate that was easily forgotten. That attitude agreed exactly with the aspirations of the average man and with his firm belief in progress. That is why Lenin designed a strategy and a tactic on the political plane. There as elsewhere he permitted the means to assume first place; but that led him, on one hand, to modify Marx's doctrine, and on the other, to give the doctrine itself a level of importance secondary to action. Tactics and the development of means then became the principal objects even of political science.

With Hitler one finds precisely the same tendency, but with two differences: first of all, a total lack of restraint. Lenin envisaged the application of progressive, limited, adjusted means. Hitler wanted to apply them all, and without delay. Second, the end, the aim, the doctrine, which Lenin merely had demoted to second place, disappeared altogether in Hitler's case—the vague millennium that he promised cannot be regarded as an aim, nor can his anti-Semitism be considered a doctrine. Instead, we pass here to the stage of pure action, action for action's sake.

This completely transformed the relations between ideology and propaganda: ideology was of interest to Lenin and Hitler

only where it could serve an action or some plan or tactic. Where
it could not be used, it did not exist. Or it was used for propaganda. Propaganda then became the major fact; with respect to
it, ideologies became mere epiphenomena. On the other hand,
ideological content came to be of much less importance than had
been thought possible. In most cases, propaganda can change
or modify this content as long as it respects such formal and customary aspects of the ideology as its images and vocabulary.

Hitler modified the National Socialist ideology several times
according to the requirements of propaganda. Thus Hitler and
Lenin established an entirely new relationship between ideology
and propaganda. But one must not think that Hitler's defeat put
an end to that; actually, it has become more widespread. There
is no question that the demonstration was compelling from the
point of view of effectiveness. Moreover, the trend launched by
Lenin and Hitler touched on all prevailing ideologies, all of which
now exist "in connection" with propaganda (*i.e.*, live by propaganda) whether one likes it or not. It is no longer possible to
turn back; only adjustments can be made.

The New Relationship

These new propaganda methods have completely changed the
relationship between propaganda and ideology, and as a result
the role and value of ideologies in the present world have changed.
Propaganda's task is less and less to propagate ideologies; it now
obeys its own laws and becomes autonomous.

Propaganda no longer obeys an ideology.[1] The propagandist is
not, and cannot be, a "believer." Moreover, he cannot believe in
the ideology he must use in his propaganda. He is merely a man
at the service of a party, a State, or some other organization, and
his task is to insure the efficiency of that organization. He no
more needs to share the official ideology than the prefect of a

---

[1] Ideology plays a certain role in propaganda. It can prevent propaganda from
developing when the governmental centers themselves are the seat of an ideology.
We shall see later how democratic ideology accelerates the expansion of propaganda. On the other hand, it has been shown how the belief in certain utopias
(goodwill of the people, harmonization of international interests, and so on) is also
a negative factor here, just as the ideology of democratic elites is less suitable than
that of an aristocracy as the basis for a propaganda plan. Conversely, when the
belief of the elites is progressive, it will lead to a powerful propaganda. Thus
ideology partly determines whether a climate is favorable or unfavorable to the
creation and use of propaganda, but it no longer is the decisive factor.

French department needs to share the political doctrines of the national government. If the propagandist has any political conviction, he must put it aside in order to be able to use some popular mass ideology. He cannot even share that ideology for he must use it as an object and manipulate it without the respect that he would have for it if he believed in it. He quickly acquires contempt for these popular images and beliefs; in his work, he must change the propaganda themes so frequently that he cannot possibly attach himself to any formal, sentimental, political, or other aspect of the ideology. More and more, the propagandist is a technician using a keyboard of material media and psychological techniques; and in the midst of all that, ideology is only one of the incidental and interchangeable cogs. It has often been stated that the propagandist eventually comes to despise doctrines and men (Lasswell, Albig). This must be put into context with the fact, analyzed above, that the organization served by propaganda is not basically interested in disseminating a doctrine, spreading an ideology, or creating an orthodoxy. It seeks, instead, to unite within itself as many individuals as possible, to mobilize them, and to transform them into active militants in the service of an orthopraxy.

Some will object that the great movements that have used propaganda, such as Communism or Nazism, did have a doctrine and did create an ideology. I reply that that was not their principal object: ideology and doctrine were merely accessories used by propaganda to mobilize individuals. The aim was the power of the party or State, supported by the masses. Proceeding from there, the problem is no longer whether or not a political ideology is valid. The propagandist cannot ask himself that question. For him, it is senseless to debate whether the Marxist view of history has more validity than any other, or whether the racist doctrine is true. That is of no importance in the framework of propaganda.

The only problem is that of effectiveness, of utility. The point is not to ask oneself whether some economic or intellectual doctrine is valid, but only whether it can furnish effective catchwords capable of mobilizing the masses *here and now*. Therefore, when faced with an ideology that exists among the masses and commands a certain amount of belief, the propagandist must ask himself two questions: First, is this existing ideology an obstacle to the action to be taken, does it lead the masses to disobey the

State, does it make them passive? (This last question is essential, for example, for propagandists who operate in milieux influenced by Buddhism.) In many cases such an ideology will indeed be an obstacle to blind action, if only to the extent that it sparks some intellectual activity, no matter how feeble, or provides criteria, no matter how insecure, for judgment or action. In this case the propagandist must be careful not to run head-on into a prevailing ideology; all he can do is integrate it into his system, use some parts of it, deflect it, and so on.[2] Second, he must ask himself whether the ideology, such as it is, can be used for his propaganda; whether it has psychologically predisposed an individual to submit to propaganda's impulsions.

In an Arab country colonized by whites, in view of the Islamic ideology that has developed hatred for Christians, a perfect predisposition to nationalist Arab and anti-colonialist propaganda will exist. The propagandist will use that ideology directly, regardless of its content. He can become an ardent protagonist of Islam without believing in the least in its religious doctrine. Similarly, a Communist propagandist can disseminate a nationalist or a democratic ideology because it is useful, effective, and profitable, and because he finds it already formed and part of public opinion, even if he himself is anti-nationalist and anti-democratic. The fact that he reinforces a democratic belief in the public is of no importance: one now knows that such beliefs are no obstacle to the establishment of a dictatorship. By utilizing the democratic ideology that Communism supports, the Communist party obtains the consent of the masses to its action, which then puts the Communist organization in control. Propaganda thus brings about the transition from democratic beliefs to a new form of democracy.

Public opinion is so uncertain and unclear as to the *content* of its ideologies that it follows the one that says the magic words, not realizing the contradictions between the proclamation of a catchword and the action that follows it. Once the "Machine" is

---

[2] This is why one ideology cannot serve as a weapon against another ideology. Propaganda will never proclaim the superiority of an ideology over that of the enemy, for in doing so it would immediately fail. Against an opposing ideology one can only counter with a waiting attitude, an attitude of hope, and with questions as to what the future will bring. By thus asking an ideological adversary concrete questions pertaining to the future, the propagandist follows Marx's method of "progressing from language to life."

in control, there can be no objection to it by those who adhered to the previously prevailing ideology, which is always officially adopted and proclaimed by the new organization in power. People live therefore in the mental confusion that propaganda purposely seeks to create.

In the face of existing, usable ideologies, the propagandist can take one of two paths: he can either stimulate them, or mythologize them. In fact, ideologies lend themselves well to both methods. On the one hand, an ideology can be expressed in a catchword, a slogan. It can be reduced to a simple idea, deeply anchored in the popular consciousness. And public opinion is used to reacting automatically to the expressions of a former, accepted ideology: words such as *Democracy, Country,* and *Social Justice* can now set off the desired reflexes. They have been reduced to stimuli capable of obtaining reflexes in public opinion, which can turn from adoration to hatred without transition. They evoke past actions and aspirations. To be sure, if a formula is to be able to stimulate, it must correspond to existing conditioned reflexes that were forged gradually in the course of history by adherence to an ideology. The propagandist limits himself to what is already present. From there on he can use any ideological content at all, no matter where or when. Differences in application will be determined according to psychological, historical, and economic criteria, to insure the best utilization of ideology in the realm of action. I have said that ideology is a complex system capable of evoking one aspect while leaving out another; the propagandist's ability will consist precisely in making these choices.

On the other hand, the propagandist can proceed by transforming ideology into myth. Some ideologies can indeed serve as a springboard for the creation of myths by the propagandist. Such transformation rarely takes place spontaneously. Generally, ideology is quite vague, has little power to move men to action, and cannot control the individual's entire consciousness. But it furnishes the elements of content and belief. It weds itself to myth by the complicated mixture of ideas and sentiments, by grafting the irrational onto political and economic elements. Ideology differs radically from myth in that it has no basic roots, no relation to humanity's great, primitive myths. I have already said that it would be impossible to create a complete new myth through propaganda. However, the existence of an ideology within a group is the best possible foundation for the elaboration of a myth. In many cases, a precise operation and a more pressing and incisive formulation will suffice. That the message must be formulated for use by the mass media automatically contributes to this: the fact that the widespread belief is now expressed in one third the number of words and shouted through millions of loudspeakers, gives it new force and urgency.

The coloration supplied by psychological techniques, the power of efficiency demonstrated by the integration in an action, the over-all nature attributed to the construction of an intellectual universe in which ideology is the keystone—all that can be accomplished by the propagandist. In such fashion Socialist ideology was transformed into myth by Leninist propaganda, patriotic ideology became national myth, and the ideology of happiness was transformed into myth at the end of the nineteenth century. In this fashion, too, the myth of Progress was constructed from a group of propagandas based on bourgeois ideology.

Finally, the propagandist can use ideology for purposes of justification. I have shown on several occasions that justification is an essential function of propaganda. The existence of a generally accepted ideology is a remarkable instrument for providing a good conscience. When the propagandist refers to collective beliefs, the man whom he induces to act in accord with those beliefs will experience a feeling of almost unshakable self-justification. To act in conformity with collective beliefs provides security and a guarantee that one acts properly. Propaganda reveals this consonance to the individual, renders the collective belief perceptible, conscious, and personal for him. It gives him a good conscience by making him aware of the collectivity of beliefs. Propaganda rationalizes the justification that man discovers in the prevailing ideology, and gives him the power to express himself. This holds true, for example, for the ideology of peace utilized by the Communist party: as soon as this ideology is used, everything, even hatred, is justified by it.

For a long time, man's actions, just as certain of his reactions, have been partially inspired by ideology. The masses may act because of a spontaneous belief, a succinct idea accepted by all, or in pursuit of an objective more or less vaguely outlined by an ideology; democratic ideology sparked such behavior. But the relationship of ideology to propaganda has completely changed this.

In a group in which modern propaganda is being made, man no longer acts in accord with a spontaneous ideology, but only through impulses that come to him from such propaganda. Only the ignorant can still believe that ideas, doctrines, beliefs can make man act without the utilization of psycho-sociological methods. Ideology not used by propaganda is ineffective and not taken seriously. The humanist ideology no longer provokes a response: in the face of modern propaganda, intellectuals have been completely disarmed and can no longer evoke the values of humanism. Torture (of political enemies) is implicitly accepted by public opinion, which expresses its dismay only in words, but not in action. With regard to the war in Algeria, it is well known that the most ardent defenders of P. H. Simon (a young lieutenant who exposed the practice of torture during that war) defended him only verbally and when they could afford to: once they were in combat, plunged into action, such "ideas" were relegated to a secondary level, and the F.L.N. and military propaganda—which, on both sides, accused the enemy of torture and thus legitimized its own actions—took over again. The same is true for Christian ideology, which no longer inspires action: Christians are caught in a psycho-sociological mechanism that conditions them to certain practices, despite their attachment to other ideas. Those ideas remain pure ideology because they are not being taken over by propaganda; and they are not taken over because they are not usable. In this fashion, such an ideology loses its reality and becomes an abstraction. It loses all effectiveness in relation to other ideologies being used by propaganda.

Moreover, in this relationship between ideology and action, we emphasize that nowadays action creates ideology, not vice versa, as the idealists who relate to past situations still would like to believe. Through action one learns to believe in "some truth," and even to formulate it. Today, ideology progressively builds itself around actions sanctioned by propaganda. (For example, in order to justify certain actions in Algeria, an entire, complex ideology was created.) Thus, in various ways—all the result of propaganda—ideology is increasingly losing its importance in the modern world. It is devalued whether propaganda uses it or not; in the latter case because it reveals its ineffectiveness and cannot prevail against the competition; in the former, because when used, it is broken up: some aspects of it are used and others pushed aside.

The same holds true for ideology as for doctrine; when propaganda uses it, it destroys it. The transformation of the Marxist doctrine by propaganda, first Lenin's and then Stalin's, is well known. Works such as those by P. Chambre, de Lefèvre, and Lukacs explain this "evisceration" of doctrine by propaganda very well. All that is believed, known, and accepted is what propaganda has promulgated. It is the same for ideology, which is merely a popular and sentimental derivation of doctrine. One can no longer establish anything at all on genuine ideologies in social groups; one can no longer hope to find in such ideologies a solid point of support for redressing man or society. Ideology has become part of the system of propaganda and depends on it.[3]

2. Effects on the Structure of Public Opinion

I shall not examine the entire problem of the relationship between propaganda and opinion. However, the effects of propaganda on the psychic life of the individual, which I attempted to sketch in the preceding chapter, obviously have collective consequences, mass effects, if only because the mass is composed of individuals and because propaganda designed to act on the mass at the same time changes individuals who are part of that mass. People become influenced and warped; this leads necessarily to modifications in public opinion. But what we consider much more important than mere changes in the *content* of public opinion (for example, whether a favorable opinion of Negroes turns into an unfavorable opinion) is its actual structure.[4]

[3] This can have decisive consequences, for one must not forget that this is the road by which a change in "culture" (in the American sense of the word) can take place, that is, a true change of civilization, which was so far maintained by the stability of ideologies and "chain-thinking."
[4] This coincides with the well-known fact that a relationship exists between the structure of opinion and the size and organization of groups. Propaganda simultaneously modifies the structure of opinion and of the group where such opinion is formed.

Modification of the Constituent Elements of Public Opinion[5]

To begin with, certain factors of change are easy to understand. It has often been said that public opinion forms itself by exchanges of opinion on a controversial question, and shapes itself by the interaction of these different viewpoints. But an examination of the effects of propaganda must radically destroy such a view of the formation of public opinion. On the one hand, as I have already shown, the questions that propaganda takes upon itself cease to be controversial: "truths" are pronounced that do not bear discussion; they are believed or not believed, and that is all. At the same time, interpersonal communications cease. In a propagandized milieu, communications no longer take place in interpersonal patterns, but in patterns set by the propaganda organization. There is action, but no interaction. As I have shown, the propagandee and the non-propagandee cannot discuss: no psychologically acceptable communication or exchange is possible between them. Finally, in large societies in which propaganda is at work, opinion can no longer form itself except via the centralized media of information. "No opinion is of any consequence unless it is first communicated to the masses by the vast media of dissemination and propaganda, and if it is not assimilated on a massive scale." Here we are facing structural changes.

To understand to what extent propaganda can modify the structure of public opinion, it will suffice to look at the "laws" on the formation of public opinion indicated by Leonard W. Doob[6] (who rejects the term "laws"). One can easily see that propaganda plays precisely the role that Doob assigns to public opinion (to reduce frustration, anxiety, and so on), and that propaganda directly creates public opinion by eventually creating conformity and externalizing inner opinions. But I will proceed along another route.

The first effect I will try to analyze is what is vaguely called crystallization of public opinion. Surely Stotzel is right when he

---

[5] On this subject I will not repeat what Jean Stoetzel has already demonstrated (in *Esquisse d'une théorie des opinions* [Paris: Presses Universitaires de France; 1943]), but I am basing my text on his work.
[6] *Public Opinion and Propaganda* (New York: Henry Holt & Company; 1948), Ch. 5.

says, on the basis of American analyses, that the process is not so simple as it seems. Frequently it is said that a few scattered individual opinions suddenly, by a mysterious operation, unite and form public opinion. It is then said that one of the elements in this process is propaganda. Stoetzel has shown that things do not happen that way. Public opinion does not derive from individual opinions: here we are faced with two heterogeneous problems. One cannot speak of a crystallization of individual opinions. Rather, a vague, inconsistent, unformulated, latent opinion, which one might call "raw opinion," is transformed by propaganda through a true process of crystallization into explicit opinion.

What does this imply? From here on we will be in the presence of organized opinion having a certain structure or skeleton. There is no progression at all from a state of private opinion to a state of public opinion, but only from one state of public opinion to another state of that same public opinion.

A changing and versatile opinion becomes fixed, is given strict orientation; propaganda specifies precisely the objectives of that opinion and delineates their exact outlines. In that way, propaganda also affects the individual, reducing his field of thought and angle of vision by the creation of stereotypes.

What were only vague inclinations until the intervention of propaganda, now take the form of ideas. This is all the more remarkable because propaganda, as we have seen, acts much more through emotional shock than through reasoned conviction. It nevertheless produces by that shock an ideological elaboration that gives great precision and stability to the ensuing opinion. But this hardening of the opinion is neither total nor coherent; that is why I speak of a "skeleton."[7] Crystallization takes place at certain points. Propaganda does not produce generalized, undifferentiated ideas, but very specific opinions, which cannot be applied just anywhere. And the degree of effectiveness of a propaganda depends precisely on its choice of crystallization points. If one can harden opinion on a certain key point, one can control an entire sector of opinion from there.

---

[7] This makes even more sense if one keeps in mind that the process of propaganda consists in creating micro-groups, nuclei highly organized and endowed with great strength of conviction. These are precisely destined to crystalize opinion, help it to formulate, and thus to play the role of skeleton. This was Lenin's theory.

This hardening of opinion soon makes it impervious to all contrary reasoning, proof, and fact. MacDougall makes this point: propaganda that plays on opinion influences that opinion without offering proof; latent opinion subjected to such propaganda (if it is well made) will absorb everything, believe everything, without discrimination. This will cause opinion to pass to the stage of crystallization, and from that moment on opinion will no longer accept anything that is different. I already have shown that even a proved fact can do nothing against crystalized opinion.

Such organization of opinion tends always to a certain unification. Opinion will begin to eliminate its own contradictions and establish itself as a function of identical catchwords that will inevitably have a unifying effect. Besides, at that moment, individual opinions also change, for the hardening of public opinion destroys their originality. Details and nuances disappear. The more active the propaganda, the more monolithic and less individualized public opinion will be.

A good example of this process is the formation of class consciousness by Marxist propaganda. After the creation of class consciousness by the promulgation of information (of which I have spoken above) came the transformation of this class consciousness, by propaganda, into a system, a criterion of judgment, a belief, a stereotype. Propaganda led to the elimination of all deviant ideas and finally rendered labor's opinion impenetrable to all that did not conform to the initial pattern. Present-day class consciousness is a typical product of propaganda.

This unifying character leads us to a second propaganda effect on public opinion: by the process of simplification, propaganda makes it take shape more rapidly. Without simplification no public opinion can exist anyway; the more complex problems, judgments, and criteria are, the more diffuse opinion will be. Nuances and gradations prevent public opinion from forming; the more complicated it is, the longer it takes to assume solid shape. But in the case of such diffusion, propaganda intervenes with a force of simplification.

Attitudes are reduced to two: positive and negative. In plain view, propaganda will simply place anyone with more differentiated opinions into one group or the other. For example, a man not altogether favorably inclined toward Communism is simply thrown into the Fascist clique by propaganda even if he tries to think in terms of social justice, and even if he rejects capitalism. Without being an ally of bourgeois imperialism, he becomes one in the eyes of all.

Problems are made simple. Goebbels wrote: "By simplifying the thoughts of the masses and reducing them to primitive patterns, propaganda was able to present the complex process of political and economic life in the simplest terms. . . . We have taken matters previously available only to experts and a small number of specialists, and have carried them into the street and hammered them into the brain of the little man."[8]

Answers to problems are clear-cut, white and black; under such conditions, public opinion forms rapidly, breaks loose, and expresses itself with force. It then carries along on its irresistible course all differentiated and average opinions that have appeared too late for inclusion in the process of crystalizing opinion. We already have seen how, from the psychological point of view, propaganda reinforces and even creates stereotypes and prejudices. But prejudice is not, and cannot be, part of a solely individual psychology; it is the individual in relation to others who has prejudices, and their crystallization leads to a transformation of the structure of public opinion. Of course, prejudices arise spontaneously; but propaganda uses them for the formation of public opinion, which in turn becomes simplified, unreal, rigid, and infantile. Public opinion shaped by propaganda loses all authenticity.

A final propaganda effect we want to trace in this connection is the separation very judiciously demonstrated by Stoetzel between individual and public opinion:

"The distinction between stereotyped opinions and profound attitudes leads us back to the distinction between public and private opinion. Stereotypes are the categories of public opinion. Profound attitudes, on the other hand, exist where people live by the laws of private opinions."

Between the two there is a natural difference, and the two types of opinion can co-exist without interchange or mutual influence.

"We are thus thinking in two ways: as members of a social body and as individuals. In the former case one may say that

---

[8] *Wesen und Gestalt des Nationalsozialismus* (Berlin: Junker und Dünnhaupt; 1935).

we are abandoning ourselves to a thought that is not ours, and there is no reason why diverse opinions of that kind should be coherent or unified in a system (that is the task of propaganda) . . . But we also have our own private views . . ."

The effect of propaganda is to separate the two types of opinion still more. Ordinarily, some interplay between the two sectors continues. But this is being short-circuited, relations are interrupted, when propaganda takes over public opinion. At that moment, public opinion assumes a rigidity and a density that make the expression of individual opinion impossible, and moreover close it in on all sides.

Private opinion clearly becomes devalued where public opinion is organized by propaganda. The more progress we make, the less private opinion can express itself through the mass media; the development of the press and radio has considerably reduced the number of people who can express their ideas and opinions publicly. Far from permitting private opinion to express itself, these media exclusively serve "public" opinion, which is no longer fed by private opinion at all. Individual opinion is without value or importance in a milieu and even in the individual himself as public opinion assumes greater authority and exercises more power.

From there on, private opinion can no longer absorb the various elements of public opinion in order to re-think them and integrate them. Propaganda makes public opinion impossible to be assimilated by the individual; he can only follow impersonally the current into which he is thrown. And the more public opinion becomes massive and expresses itself in a "normal" curve, the more individual opinions become fragmented. On the collective plane, they express themselves in such a dispersed way that their intrinsic uncertainty is revealed. In this fashion, man's psychological process is separated into two unrelated elements.

From Opinion to Action

I have said on several occasions that propaganda aims less at modifying personal opinions than at leading people into action. This is clearly its most striking result: when propaganda intervenes in public opinion, it transforms the public into an acting crowd or, more precisely, into a participating crowd. Often, propaganda translates itself only into "verbal action" (this will be examined later); but what matters is that the crowd pass from the state of being mere spectators filled with opinions to the state of participants.

Even if a movie-goer is "taken" with a film, he remains passive. He has a personal opinion of the picture he sees. He will soon participate in public opinion about it, but that remains external. The spectator at a bullfight is in a somewhat different situation; his participation in the killing ritual is sometimes passive, but sometimes active—when he storms into the ring. Propaganda goes much further and demands an acceptance that is not that of a spectator; it demands his support as a minimum, his active participation as a maximum.[9] Propaganda evidently plays its part where normal, spontaneous development of opinion would not have led to such action but would only have translated itself into private, non-collective attitudes. Only very rarely does opinion by itself lead to action. The great feat of propaganda is to cause the progression from thought to action artificially.

It has often been said that propaganda does not create attitudes but merely uses them. Taking the term in the specific sense of social psychology, I must agree; but the fact is not so simple. It is evident that propaganda itself does not modify attitudes. But when propaganda leads to action, it modifies, first of all, the response that would otherwise be a direct result of the fundamental attitude: the individual expressing his attitude would not act, but under the influence of propaganda he does act. One cannot overlook at this moment a certain warping of his attitudes, which, if often repeated, will change his behavior pattern. Moreover, when the individual is engaged in action that has been set in motion by propaganda, he cannot escape counter-blows, an orientation different from that "preparation for action," which will be an attitude. For this attitude is also determined by the action in which he is engaged, and by the social context. The continuous and automatic action, into which propaganda plunges the individual, undoubtedly also creates attitudes that determine further actions.

How does this progression from opinion to action through the

---

[9] On the subject of passive adherence, a last and remarkable example is contained in a pamphlet by the O.A.S. (February 10, 1962), which states that "we do not ask officers to join our ranks, but merely to show no zeal when applying government directions."

channel of propaganda take place? Doob is one of the few who have tried to describe it.

"Attitudes affect external behavior if their force is so great as to be irreducible except by action. This force, which may be weak or strong in the beginning, accumulates when the individual feels that action is necessary, when he is shown the action in which he might engage, when he thinks such action will be profitable or rewarded. In short, the achievement of a prepared response is only the last of a series of preliminary stages, which, though necessary for the final action to take place, do not guarantee that it will."

Seen in this perspective, action is the result of a certain number of coordinated influences created by propaganda.[1] Propaganda can make the individual feel the urgency, the necessity, of some action, its unique character. And at the same time propaganda shows him what to do. The individual who burns with desire for action but does not know what to do is a common type in our society. He wants to act for the sake of justice, peace, progress, but does not know how. If propaganda can show him this "how," it has won the game; action will surely follow.

The individual also must be convinced of the success of his action, or of the possible reward or satisfaction he will get from it. Man will act when he feels that a certain result needs to be obtained and that the need is urgent. Advertising demonstrates it to him in the commercial domain, propaganda demonstrates it in politics. Finally, man will be helped in this progression to action by example, by similar action all around him. But such similar action would not come to his attention except through the intermediary of propaganda.

This is undoubtedly the true pattern in many aspects. But one element overlooked here is essential in my view:[2] the element of the mass, crowd, or group. Man subjected to propaganda would never act if he were alone. Doob makes an analysis of man by himself, though the mechanisms that he reveals can work only with collective man. An individual can feel the urgency of an

---

[1] One must offer the individual a specific, clear, simple task to be undertaken at a given moment. From the moment propaganda succeeds in personalizing its appeal, the individual who feels concerned is placed in a situation that demands a decision. Mao has achieved this completely with his horizontal propaganda.

[2] This pattern might be completed at several points: for example, the prestige of the person who gives out the information pushes the listener toward action.

action only if it promises to be effective because it is being carried out by many; he cannot engage in action except with others.
This means that if propaganda is to lead to action, it must also
have a collective influence. That influence is composed of two
main factors:

1. Propaganda creates a strong integration of the group, and
at the same time activates the preoccupations of that group. The
mass media provoke an intense participation in the life of a
group and in collective activities; they provide a strong feeling
of community. In our society, the individual communicates with
the group only through the mass media of information. The indispensable psychological contact among members of the group
is produced only by these media. For in the mass society, individuals have a tendency to withdraw from each other more
and more. Their relationship is only artificial; it is only the product
of the information media. Spontaneous relationships change
character when they become organized, systematized, deliberate;
at this point, personal relationships tend to create unanimity, in
the literal sense, and such unanimity always takes on a force of
expansion. When the group acquires a certain uniformity, it
inevitably experiences the need for proceeding to action. At that
moment, the psychological contact, the communication are creating not merely a feeling of communion, but a communal truth.
If such "truth" dealt with eternal verities, it would not push
the group into action. But, at the same time as the mass media
integrate the group, they place it in relation to the present. After
all, the content of press and radio can be nothing but news of the
moment. But this goes much further when the media are purposely used for propaganda. Stoetzel has aptly said that "the
stereotypes of propaganda immediately appear to have the significance of actuality." It is an actuality made aggressive and
fertile, an actuality that is present. A group that is psychologically
unanimous and finds itself face to face with such planned actuality feels concerned to the highest degree. What is this actuality?
It is precisely the world in which the group itself and its fate
are in doubt, and in which the group has the possibility of acting.

When propaganda integrates a group into an actuality, it
necessarily leads it to act in that actuality. The group cannot
remain passive and be content merely to have an opinion regarding that actuality. To understand this mechanism, one must

remember that this group has no other frame of reference by which it could take a different position. In other words, it has only one point of view toward that actuality. The group, therefore, cannot consider it *sub specie aeternitatis*, because its frame of reference is furnished by the very propaganda that unites it in the actuality in the first place. And the group cannot judge its own position; it can only act. At that moment, to participate in any group whatever is to submit to actuality, to become a man without past or future, to have no concern other than action, no belief other than that promulgated by propaganda concerning the present.

2. The other aspect of the progression to action is the great power that propaganda gives to opinion. This opinion is no longer a belief at times unsure of itself, spreading slowly by word of mouth, and difficult for opinion surveys to pinpoint. It is projected outside itself, meets itself and hears itself on the screen and the airwaves invested with power, grandeur, magnificence. Such opinion learns to believe in itself, certain now that it is "truth" because it has seen itself revealed and promulgated on all sides by powerful media. Propaganda reveals such public opinion in need of self-expression.

One can then say without exaggeration that propaganda *replaces* the leader of the group. This is not the banal assertion that propaganda is the instrument of the leader in the group or helps to make a leader. It means that in a group without a leader, but subjected to propaganda, the sociological and psychological effects are the same as if there were a leader. Propaganda is a substitute for him. If we remember the innumerable roles played by the group leader, we can summarize them as Kimball Young does:[3] The leader of a group is the one who first defines a course of action. He is at the same time the man who verbalizes and crystalizes the feelings of the mass. Ultimately, a group subjected to propaganda would not need a leader, but would behave as though it had one. This substitution helps explain the real diminution of the role of local leaders and the abstract character of a national leader. Even in a leadership or *Führerprinzip* system, the chief is never more than a reflection: he is not the real leader of the group. The Gauleiter, like a People's Commissar, is only a surrogate, an administrator. These are not group chiefs. The

[3] *Social Psychology* (New York: F. S. Crofts; 1947), Ch. 10.

only real leader is the one who does not belong to the group—
which is, sociologically speaking, entirely abnormal—but who
substitutes for the true leader by propaganda and exists through
it. Whence comes the possibility of having a chief present when
he is absent. Merely an effigy, integrated into the circuit of
propagandas, suffices. The portraits of Hitler, Stalin, Mao, Roosevelt, play an abstract but sufficient role, for the effects that can
be expected from the leader's presence are obtained instead by
propaganda.

The leader is the one who leads his group to action. This is
the second element of the progression from opinion to direct
action.

3. Propaganda and Grouping

I have selected this rather vague heading because I cannot
undertake a complete study of the propaganda effects on the
aggregate of all groups and societies. For that I would need a
complete theoretical and experimental sociology. Besides, with
regard to the propaganda effect, one must distinguish between
the groups that make it and the groups that are subjected to it.
Often, the two elements are closely related. This study will examine three examples: political parties, the world of labor, and
the churches.

The Partitioning of Groups

All propaganda has to set off its group from all the other
groups. Here we find again the fallacious character of the intellectual communication media (press, radio), which, far from
uniting people and bringing them closer together, divide them
all the more.

When I talked about public opinion, I stressed that everybody
is susceptible to the propaganda of his group. He listens to it
and convinces himself of it. He is satisfied with it. But those
who belong to another milieu ignore it. According to an I.F.O.P.
survey (No. 1, 1954), everybody is satisfied with his own propaganda. Similarly, Lazarsfeld,[4] in his survey of radio broadcasts,

---

[4] "The Effects of Radio on Public Opinion," in *Print, Radio and Film in a Democracy* (Chicago: University of Chicago Press; 1942).

cites the case of programs designed to acquaint the American public with the value of each of the ethnic minority groups in the American population. The point was to demonstrate the contributions each group was making, with the purpose of promoting mutual understanding and tolerance. The survey revealed that each broadcast was listened to by the ethnic group in question (for example, the Irish tuned in the program about the Irish), but rarely by anybody else. In the same way, the Communist press is read by Communist voters, the Protestant press by Protestants.

What happens? Those who read the press of their group and listen to the radio of their group are constantly reinforced in their allegiance. They learn more and more that their group is right, that its actions are justified; thus their beliefs are strengthened. At the same time, such propaganda contains elements of criticism and refutation of other groups, which will never be read or heard by a member of another group. That the Communists attacked Bidault's policies with solid arguments had no effect on Bidault's party, for the supporters of Bidault did not read *L'Humanité*. That the bourgeois paper *Le Figaro* will contain valid criticism of and genuine facts about the dictatorship in the Soviet Union will never reach a Communist. But this criticism of one's neighbor, which is not heard by that neighbor, is known to those inside the group that expresses it. The anti-Communist will be constantly more convinced of the evilness of the Communist, and vice versa. As a result, people ignore each other more and more. They cease altogether to be open to an exchange of reason, arguments, points of view.

This double foray on the part of propaganda, proving the excellence of one's own group and the evilness of the others, produces an increasingly stringent partitioning of our society. This partitioning takes place on different levels—a unionist partitioning, a religious partitioning, a partitioning of political parties or classes; beyond that, a partitioning of nations, and, at the summit, a partitioning of blocs of nations. But this diversity of levels and objectives in no way changes the basic law, according to which *the more propaganda there is, the more partitioning there is.* For propaganda suppresses conversation; the man opposite is no longer an interlocutor but an enemy. And to the extent that he rejects that role, the other becomes an unknown whose words can no longer be understood. Thus, we see before our eyes how a world of closed minds establishes itself, a world in which everybody talks to himself, everybody constantly reviews his own certainty about himself and the wrongs done him by the Others—a world in which nobody listens to anybody else, everybody talks, and nobody listens. And the more one talks, the more one isolates oneself, because the more one accuses others and justifies oneself.

One must not think, incidentally, that such partitioning is in conflict with the formation of public opinion. Although propaganda partitions society, it affects opinion and transcends the groups in which it operates. In the first place, it maintains its effectiveness toward the mass of undecided who do not yet belong to a group. Then, too, it is possible to affect those who belong to a group of a different sort: for example, Communist propaganda that will not affect militant Socialists might affect Protestants; American propaganda that will not affect a Frenchman in his capacity as a Frenchman might influence him with regard to capitalism or the liberal system.

This is particularly important because there is a difference of level between the groups. For example, a nationalist propaganda results in building a barrier against other nations; however, domestically, it respects the isolation of inferior groups, but still affects them by making them join a common collective movement. This is a process comparable to that occurring in the Middle Ages when Christian ideology expanded in the society but in no way affected the aristocracy or the religious orders. A national propaganda is perfectly effective inside a nation and changes public opinion, whereas party propaganda or religious propaganda is effective on another plane—each having the power to modify public opinion on a certain level and to produce a sociological partitioning on another. But only a superior group can affect other groups. That is why, with respect to the two current power blocs—East and West—where neither side is superior, propaganda can only have the effect of increasingly separating them.

A well-organized propaganda will work with all these different elements. This explains the duality of some propagandas, for example, in the U.S.S.R.: on one side, in the papers with large circulation, or on the radio, one finds only ecstatic praise of the regime or vague criticism of it, designed to satisfy the public, but without basis in reality. On the other side, we find extremely violent, specific, and profound criticism in specialized periodicals —for example, in medical journals or magazines on city-planning. If one really wants to know and understand the shortcomings of the Soviet regime, one can find a mine of precise and impartial information in these magazines. How can such duality be tolerated? It can be explained only by partitioning. One must tell the public about the grandeur of the regime and the excellence of the U.S.S.R.; the public must be made to understand this even in the face of contrary personal experience, either to dissociate the individual or to convince him that his personal experience is without importance, without any connection to Soviet reality as a whole. A disappointing personal experience is only an accident without meaning. Such propaganda (directed to the masses), therefore, can only be positive.

Conversely, the violently critical propaganda addressed to technicians in specialized periodicals aims at showing the Party's vigilance, its knowledge of detail, its centralized control, its demand for Communist perfection. It is aimed at the mass of technicians, broken up into groups of specialists. Such propaganda asserts that the regime is excellent, that all services are working very well, except . . . the service in question—medical for the doctors, and so on. How is such duality possible? Precisely by virtue of the partitioning of society, which is to such a large extent propaganda's work. Because one knows that the doctor will not read a magazine on city-planning, and because one knows that the public at large will not read any of the specialized journals, and because one knows that the Ukrainians will not read Georgian newspapers, one can, according to necessity, make contradictory assertions in any and all of them.

Obviously, this procedure further increases separation, for everyone stops speaking the language of the others. No means of communication remains. Different facts are given to different people, the bases of judgment are diverse, the orientations are opposites; there is no longer a meeting point within the confines of the same propaganda, for this propaganda scientifically (not spontaneously, as in the case studied earlier) develops dividing lines, establishes psychological separations between groups, and does all this under a common collective cloak of unreality and verbal fiction.

Effects on Political Parties

What happens when a political party stops acting more or less haphazardly, starts to make systematic propaganda, and instead of trying to win votes at election time, begins to mobilize public opinion in a more permanent fashion? Actually, in the democratic nations, practically no party has tried this. But we can see the emergence of parties grafting themselves onto old ones, or replacing them; and these new parties have such aims, which their predecessors did not have. A transformation is taking place in the political parties of the United States; for about a dozen years now they have been making systematic propaganda. But it is still too early to tell what transformations it may entail in the parties themselves.

Therefore, we will study instead those parties that make propaganda, as distinguished from those that do not, and consider that their structure derives partially from their need to make propaganda.

A party that makes propaganda must, first of all, have the means to express it strongly. It is necessary that the party presents itself as a community in which everybody has a set function, and that its members at the bottom be rigorously organized and strictly obedient. If one wants to reach public opinion constantly, one must proceed with the help of sections and cells; the system of committees, which express themselves weakly, leads only to sporadic and fragmentary action.

In addition, propaganda demands vertical liaison among the party's organizations. This vertical liaison permits both homogeneity of propaganda and speed of application; and we have seen that speed of action or reaction is essential to propaganda. Conversely, in view of the effect of propaganda in creating isolated social and local groups, any horizontal liaison inside the party would be disastrous. Those at the base of the party would not understand why one propaganda is made in one place, another elsewhere. On the contrary, the partitioning by propaganda must correspond to a partitioning within the party, and the only liaison system must be vertical.

More important still is a system of executive cadres. This produces from the beginning a schism between the cadres and the voters or sympathizers, and corresponds precisely to the separation into subjects and objects. Propaganda makes its agent a subject who makes the decisions and uses those systems that must obtain certain results; but the agent looks upon the mass of potential voters or sympathizers as objects. He manipulates them, works on them, tests them, changes them psychologically or politically. They no longer have any personal importance, especially when one realizes that good propaganda must be objective and anonymous, and the masses are considered as merely an instrument for attaining some objective. They are treated as such; this is one of the elements of the profound contempt that those making real propaganda have for all those on the outside, even—and often particularly—for their sympathizers.

Propaganda accentuates this separation between manipulators and sympathizers, even as it tends to personalize power within the party. The inclination of the masses to admire personal power cannot be shunned by good propaganda: it can only be followed and exploited. To disregard it is to throw away an easy and active propaganda element. Propaganda therefore intensifies this inclination by creating the image of a leader and investing it with attributes of omnipresence and omniscience, and by supporting with active evidence what public consciousness only sensed and anticipated. Any party that avoids this personalization of power loses a probably decisive card. We have seen this in the American election of 1952, with Eisenhower.

In most cases this personalized power is closely tied to the organization of propaganda itself. In connection with certain parties, Duverger speaks of a "second power," an obscure power that sometimes dominates the direction of the party. This second power sometimes consists of influential men on a paper whose distribution assures the party's strength. This fact needs to be generalized: In modern parties, the second power is likely to consist of the corps of propagandists. (The same holds true for the State itself.) The propaganda instruments tend to assume a preponderant position, not without occasional serious conflicts, for they are at one and the same time the hub of the entire party and its *raison d'être*.

These are the principal effects of the adoption of modern propaganda on the structure of a political party.

With regard to the relative effects on the interplay of parties in the national fabric, the decisive element is the high cost of propaganda. Propaganda is becoming more and more expensive, partly because of the volume needed, partly because of the instruments required. All parties may stick to traditional and low-level propaganda (posters, newpapers) and go to the government for the more expensive media (radio, TV). Such is the case in France. Under such circumstances, there is a state of equilibrium, but a precarious one. The situation is, in effect, unstable; if one party resorts to propaganda, the whole edifice tumbles.

Our first such hypothesis: A single party takes big propaganda action while the others cannot regroup or put into operation the necessary big apparatus because they lack money, people, organization. From then on, we see such a party rise like a rocket, as Hitler's party did in Germany in 1932, or the Communist parties in France and Italy in 1945. This is clearly a menace to democracy; we are face to face with an overwhelmingly strong party that will capture the government. This party continues to grow stronger as it becomes richer and assumes more solid propaganda foundations. It definitely jeopardizes the democratic system, even if it has no dictatorial ambitions; for the other parties, incapable of regaining the mass of those 75 percent (more or less) undecided, are increasingly unable to use big propaganda. Such a development may, of course, be changed by external influences: this happened when the progress of the Communist parties in France and Italy came to an end after 1948 with a regression of their propaganda, which was by no means attributable to their past mistakes.

A second hypothesis: The opposition parties find a reply to big propaganda. But this can only be through a regrouping of forces, which is hard to attain because internal squabbles are stronger than the need for a common counter-propaganda (as in France between 1949 and 1958), or by an appeal to the government, which may then put communication means and money at the disposal of the party to oppose some totalitarian propaganda. This was the case in Belgium in connection with Rexist counter-propaganda.

The third hypothesis: A party or a bloc of parties almost as powerful as the would-be runaway party starts big propaganda before it is pushed to the wall. This is the case in the United States, and might be in France if the regrouping of the Right should become stabilized. In that situation one would necessarily have, for financial reasons, a democracy reduced to two parties, it being inconceivable that a larger number of parties would have sufficient means to make such propaganda. This would lead to a bipartite structure, not for reasons of doctrine or tradition, but for technical propaganda reasons. This implies the exclusion of new parties in the future. Not only are secondary parties progressively eliminated, but it becomes impossible to organize new political groups with any chance at all of making them heard; in the midst of the concerted power of the forces at work, it becomes increasingly difficult to establish a new program. On the other hand, such a group would need, from the beginning, a great deal of money, many members, and great power. Under such conditions, a new party could only be born as Athena emerging fully grown from Zeus' forehead. A political organism would have had to collect money for a long time in advance, to have bought propaganda instruments, and united its members before it made its appearance as a party capable of resisting the pressures of those who possess the "media."

Not just the mere organization of a new party is becoming increasingly difficult—so is expression of a new political idea or doctrine. Ideas no longer exist except through the media of information. When the latter are in the hands of the existing parties, no truly revolutionary or new doctrine has any chance of expressing itself, *i.e.*, of existing. Yet innovation was one of the principal characteristics of democracy. Now, because nobody wants it any longer, it tends to disappear.

One can say that propaganda almost inevitably leads to a two-party system. Not only would it be very difficult for several parties to be rich enough to support such expensive campaigns of propaganda, but also propaganda tends to schematize public opinion. Where there is propaganda, we find fewer and fewer nuances and refinements of detail or doctrine. Rather, opinions are more incisive; there is only black and white, yes and no. Such a state of public opinion leads directly to a two-party system and the disappearance of a multi-party system.

The effects of propaganda can also be clearly seen in view of what Duverger calls the party with the majority mandate and the party without that mandate. The party with the majority mandate, which ordinarily should command an absolute majority in parliament, is normally the one that has been created by propaganda. Propaganda's principal trumps then slip out of the hands of the other parties. All the latter can do then is to make demagogic propaganda, *i.e.*, a false propaganda that is purely artificial, considering what we have said about the relationship between propaganda and reality. (In other words, the party out of power must pick an artificial issue.)

In that case we find ourselves faced with two completely contradictory propagandas. On one side is a propaganda powerful in media and techniques, but limited in its ends and modes of expression, a propaganda strictly integrated into a given social group, conformist and statist. On the other is a propaganda weak in regard to media and techniques, but excessive in its ends and expressions, a propaganda aimed against the existing order, against the State, against prevailing group standards.

But one must never forget that the party with the majority mandate, which adjusts its propaganda to that mandate and even uses the mandate as a propaganda aim, is nevertheless also the creation of propaganda, which hands it that mandate in a given setting and for a long period of time.

Finally, a last word on the financial problems and their implications: it is improbable that contributions alone would enable a party to pay for the increasingly expensive propaganda media. The parties are therefore forced to look for aid either to capitalists —and thus indenture themselves to a financial oligarchy—or to a government (national or foreign). In the second case, the State comes close to appropriating the instruments. The State then lends them to those who ask for them, which is very democratic, and thus permits secondary parties to live; but this leads to an unstable situation, as I said earlier, and the State is then increasingly forced to exercise censorship over what is being said by means of these instruments. This censorship will be increasingly rigorous as the State itself is forced to make more propaganda.

This leads us to examine the hypothesis of a State that ceases to be neutral in the ideological domain and assumes a doctrine or ideology of its own. At that moment, propaganda by the State is imposed on all parties. To be sure, we are still dealing with propaganda. We have seen in past decades with regard to all "state religions" that power must first be used to shape public opinion, without which they could not operate. Thus, at the beginnings of the Nazi State, or of popular democracies, a certain competition continued between the propaganda of the State and that of the parties out of power. But in such competition the State necessarily emerges victorious; it increasingly denies the use of the mass media of communication to the opposition parties; it works on public opinion until the moment arrives when it can simply suppress opposition parties without fear. But the State can work on public opinion only through the intermediary of a party. This is another effect of propaganda. One could conceive of a State that would suppress *all* parties and live by itself: that was the classic pattern of dictatorship. However, that is no longer possible.

Once public opinion has been aroused and alerted to political problems, it must be taken into consideration. The propaganda mechanism of the State cannot function as an administrative unit; it cannot have reality or efficiency except through the media of the State party. It is impossible to imagine that a modern State could command acceptance without working through a party establishing contact between those who govern and public opinion. The party's fundamental role is to make propaganda for the government, *i.e.*, the propaganda that the government wishes to be made. In one sense, incidentally, we find here the image of a party in its purest state, for ultimately every party is a propaganda machine. But this is much more hidden in other systems in which there still can be nuances and discussions; in dictatorships, the party no longer serves any ideological or political function, no longer expresses social interests, and so on. It is an organ designed to tame and train public opinion, and exists solely because of the State's need. As soon as that need diminishes, the role and prestige of the party also diminish. This happened in Nazi Germany in 1938,[5] and in the Soviet Union after the purges of 1936. But as soon as propaganda again becomes important the party resumes its role.

Propaganda very clearly gives direction to the life of political parties, imposes certain forms and rules on them, sends them down certain paths, and ends up by deciding their life or death until the regime expands to the point at which propaganda and party are totally fused.

---

[5] After the concentration of all powers in the Führer's hands.

In illuminating the role of propaganda from this angle, I was not trying to say that propaganda is the only factor in the evolution of parties; it certainly combines with other elements, of which one can say, however, that they either are of less importance than propaganda, or are tied in with it.

Effects on the World of Labor

We now come face to face with one of the modern world's most crucial problems: the world of labor, *i.e.*, the condition of the worker, created by technological developments, used in the beginning by capitalism and used now by Socialism. Socialism has claimed that the worker's condition was the fruit of capitalism and of the exploitation of workers by finance capital. This does to some extent explain both the depressed condition of the worker and, undoubtedly, the class struggle and certain of its elements. But it is not the major factor. Labor conditions result from the relation between man and machine, and are a consequence of technological developments taken in the broad sense. Urbanization, massification, streamlining, the disappearance of the notion of "work," mechanization, and so on—all these are much more responsible for labor conditions than that the means of production are privately owned. This last fact leads to proletarization according to Marxist theory, but proletarization is only one aspect of the problem. Once Socialism has taken the means of production out of private hands, juridically speaking, the working class, abstractly speaking, is no longer the proletariat; but it remains in the grip of the same concrete problems.

Undoubtedly the problem of poverty can be solved. But nothing indicates that it can be more easily solved under Socialism than under capitalism. Few workers (except farmers) in the United States live in poverty. But one cannot say that the labor problem has been solved even there.

If we look at the situation of labor in Socialist countries we see that the worker still is subordinate to the machine, that he has little personal life, that he is engulfed in the mass, and that he is prey to the problems connected with mechanical work, artificially measured days, boredom, detachment from his work, false culture, ignorance of environment, divorce from nature, artificial life, and so on. But we also see that the problem of profits has not been solved, and that the worker still is not properly paid. The only difference is that the profit is made by the State and not by private individuals.

In addition we see that in Socialist countries most social legislation, though as advanced as in capitalist countries from the point of view of security, family allocations, vacations, and all sorts of financial rewards, has retrogressed with regard to unionism, the right to strike, and work discipline. We see, finally, that the worker in no way participates fundamentally in the life of his factory. In Socialist countries, the works council may make suggestions only with regard to secondary questions; with regard to principal questions, it merely ratifies the decisions of a Five Year Plan.

Furthermore, collective ownership of the means of production is pure fiction. The workers own nothing, and are, with regard to the machines, in the same situation as workers under capitalism. Whether it be the State or the entire collective (which must necessarily be represented by some organization), the proprietor has nothing to do with the workers in the factory. This notion of collective ownership corresponds, on the economic plane, to the old idea of the sovereignty of the people on the political plane. And we know how much harm that idea, that fiction, that abstraction has done to democracy and the power of the people. I cannot pursue this point here, but I can assert that the situation of labor has not really changed as the result of Socialism. *Nevertheless, we must acknowledge that the attitude of the workers is different.*

Except in rare cases, the working class has given its support to the regimes in Communist countries. It is no longer a class in opposition, but is really in accord with the regimes, and the concrete situation seems to be that there no longer is an attitude of rebellion. The workers put their hearts in their work, abandon themselves to their work, no longer wish to engage in slowdowns or strikes. This is so, no matter how much the anti-Communists deny it.

Something undoubtedly has changed with regard to the labor situation in Communist countries, for the workers have not been integrated by force. What has changed, first of all, is the social climate. The worker is no longer excluded from society. The feeling of being excluded from society is felt very strongly by the worker in a capitalist society. He is a pariah, an outsider. The society obeys certain criteria and has certain basic structures, but the worker is not included in them. The problem of private property is only a symbol of that exclusion, which, in turn, produces the proletariat. But in Socialist society, the worker is at the center of a world that is being built. He is in an honored position. The society is ennobled by the working class—this is said constantly, and demonstrated in various cultural, political and economic ways. This climate has changed the worker's reaction. He is now convinced of his importance. He is also convinced that society is not against him but for him; that this society is his achievement, and that he is being granted, or will be granted, the place he deserves because of the importance of his work. He is thus filled with a positive conviction that lets him forget or neglect the external reality of his situation. The worker in the Socialist world no longer looks at this situation in the same way as before; he is now filled with hope.

It is his hope that the coming world will be a just world or, more precisely, a world in which the worker certainly will occupy first place. It is also his conviction and hope that every piece of work, every day of work put in by him has a purpose: to build Socialist society; whereas in capitalist countries work serves only to produce a wage and profits only the capitalist. There the worker experiences frustration; under Socialism, he experiences a feeling of fulfillment.

The changes that have taken place in labor's situation are not actual changes, but only those of a different perspective, conception of life, conviction, and hope. This is indeed Socialism's only genuine innovation, but the transformation is effective; the workers work more and better, put more heart in their work, and accept strict discipline with conviction.[6]

This reminds me of what M. G. Friedmann has said on the importance of the psychological factor in working conditions and productivity. He believes that the psychological necessities can be satisfied only by the Socialist perspective. Only in Socialism can the worker, rid of his complexes and resentments, attain the psychological freedom that permits him to dedicate himself to his work.

---

[6] In 1960, at a conference in Moscow, Leonid Ilyichev, chief of agitprop, stated that ideological education must aim at increasing productivity, the norms of the workers, and personal sacrifices. I have already said that the principal function of propaganda in the U.S.S.R. is to help fulfill the Five-Year Plan, to speed up work, *i.e.*, to increase the worker's effort.

But nothing indicates that this is the only solution. Even the facts of Public Relations in the United States tend to show that psychological means not only change the general climate considerably, but also change the inner persuasion of each worker and integrate him more into his enterprise. But this alteration has not yet reached full bloom, and we must wait to see whether a profound transformation of the working class by Public Relations is possible.

This long detour leads us to say that the labor problem results to some extent from the factual situation and to some extent from psychological factors. If we want to be honest, we must admit that for the factual situation no solution is available in any of the social, political, or economic theories. Of course, one can make the worker happy and give him security; a mixture of palliatives, already known and partly utilized, can modify the *consequences* of his situation, but not really the situation itself. One must recognize, without trying to make a mystery out of the working class, that no solution exists for its concrete problems.

There is, however, a psychological solution. The modification that was attained by Socialist psychology can be attained by other means, other forms of integration, other convictions, other hopes.[7] From the moment one knows that, *unfortunately,* Socialism has only psychological answers, one is forced to state that what is involved here is a simple matter of propaganda. The working class, fooled by the bourgeoisie, is fooled by Communism in other ways. And just as Communism has taught bourgeois governments the use of propaganda on the political plane, it is now teaching them to use it on the social plane and on the problems of labor. Nowadays, we see complete disregard for the problem of labor and a screen put around whatever problems cannot be solved. As in all propaganda, the point is to make man endure, with the help of psychological narcotics, what he could not endure naturally, or to give him, artificially, reasons to continue his work and to do it well. This is a task of propaganda, and there is no doubt that if it is done well, it will make possible the integration of the working class and make it accept its condition happily. In one way or another, propaganda is called upon

---

[7] According to the cynical formula reported by Vance Packard: "Make them work and like it."

to "solve" the labor problem, to the extent that the problem becomes a political factor and can be treated as such in the mechanism of the modern world.

Only those who do not know the capabilities of modern propaganda can doubt the possibility of such a solution. Of course, to make such integration propaganda of the labor class successful, several conditions must obtain. First of all, the material conditions of labor must improve. I have constantly stressed the link between propaganda and true reforms. But that does not suffice in the least. On the contrary the improvement of material conditions of the worker can become a springboard for better revolutionary agitation, as history shows. A certain development of *technical* education and information is needed: the more the worker becomes a technician, the more he becomes a conformist. At the same time, if he is provided with a broader base of information, he will become more susceptible to propaganda, according to the mechanism analyzed earlier.

Finally, some unity of psychological action is needed. As long as the worker is enclosed in such organizations as parties or unions, which subject him to a propaganda opposed to his integration in the society, the partitioning, which we discussed earlier, takes place. One of the most important factors in this connection is that in Socialist countries the unions have become organizations in harmony with the society and make the same propaganda. The same holds true in the United States; the unions, though they defend their members, are also organs of the society and in no way question the American Way of Life. Consequently, the propaganda made by the unions is important for the integration of the workers. But such propaganda, by itself, transforms the unions.

Like the political parties, the unions have felt the need to make propaganda. One may say that, on the one hand, most of the propaganda effects already studied with regard to political parties also obtain for unions. But there are other, particular effects here, which derive from the fact that unions are by nature organs of combat, of defense, which represent more or less—but undeniably—foreign elements in a society. Whether the society is capitalist or not, a union has its own battle to fight; this is inherent in the structure and rationale of unions.

But from the moment that the union wants to engage in propaganda, it runs head-on into the necessity of using the mass media of communication.

Of course, union propaganda has a character of its own: it is much more "human," costs less, uses the devotion of union members, their close human contact, and so on. But it cannot help using the great media of modern propaganda, particularly the newspaper and the poster, as the problem no longer is merely one of getting people to attend meetings, but one of promulgating policy positions and of setting up a true labor mentality. This presumes a certain intellectual agility that the labor militants do not possess.

From the moment the union begins to use newspapers and posters, it runs into money problems. And the more propaganda tries to reach individuals, the more it must use the important media—and the more expensive it will be. The financial problems do not recede when the union becomes larger; the expenses for propaganda grow more rapidly than revenues (except in the United States). This leads the union either to acquire its own instruments of propaganda, or to seek financial assistance of a more or less dubious and constraining nature.[8]

When the union hits upon a successful propaganda, it reaches public opinion. It wins this opinion over to the cause of labor, alerts it to problems of social injustice, and mobilizes people pro or con. Whether one wants it or not, this is the basic objective of propaganda. This mobilized public opinion will then translate the propaganda effect in one of two ways. First of all, union membership will grow: propaganda obviously leads to increase in the number of members. But here we see a well-known mass effect: the more the union grows, the less revolutionary, the less active, the less militant it becomes. Mass lends more weight to its demands, but those demands become less decisive and radical. The mass union becomes peaceful and bureaucratic; its

[8] One can give the example of the American unions, which are the most powerful in the world and which have become progressively modified by the very propaganda that helped them attain their power. There are a few union publications with editions of several hundred thousand copies. They also use film and TV. Over two hundred transmissions from unions are broadcast each day in the United States. In Chicago, a radio station belongs to a union. Here, the considerable expenses are paid by contributions. But this rests on an accord between the unions and the employers: the employers have agreed to employ only union labor (it is obligatory) and to collect these contributions by deducting them from the employees' wages. This means that all this enormous propaganda cannot endanger the economic powers in the United States.

moves become less and less spontaneous; a gap opens between its members and its general staff. That is the first result of alerting public opinion through propaganda.

The second result derives from the fact that sooner or later the government will be affected by this development. It will then tend to legitimize and legalize such labor action in some way; this is also an effect of propaganda. But when the government legalizes a union, a relationship arises between union and government, which is not one of conflict. Its legalization leads the union to adapt itself, more or less, to its lawful status and to conduct its social struggle on the legal plane. What matters then is to obtain new legal concessions from the State. But that is a long way from the original objectives of a union.

Thus propaganda leads a union to become a "have" rather than a "have-not" organization, to present itself as a constituent member of society, to play the social game. This is true integration into society, and as a result the union is no longer in opposition: its opposition is purely apparent and fictitious. Whether, from then on, it becomes part of capitalist society, as in the United States, or of Socialist society, as in the U.S.S.R., matters not in the least; the results are identical. The union cannot win public opinion without adapting itself to it, without accepting the essential premises of the society in which it seeks a public, an audience, and supporters. Here we find again the conforming effect that I have already analyzed, and which derives from propaganda.

Effects on the Churches

Obviously, church members are caught in the net of propaganda and react pretty much like everyone else. As a result, an almost complete dissociation takes place between their Christianity and their behavior. Their Christianity remains a spiritual and purely internal thing. But their behavior is dictated by various appurtenances, and particularly by propaganda. Of course, a certain gap has always existed between "ideals" and "action." But today this gap has become total, general, and deliberate. This widening of the gap, particularly its systematic widening, is the fruit of propaganda in the political or economic domain, and of advertising in the private domain.

Because Christians are flooded with various propagandas, they absolutely cannot see what they might do that would be effective and at the same time be an expression of their Christianity. There-fore, with different motivations and often with scruples, they limit themselves to one or another course presented to them by propa-ganda. They too take the panorama of the various propagandas for living political reality, and do not see where they can insert their Christianity in that fictitious panorama. Thus, like all the others, they are stumped, and this fact removes all weight from their belief.

At the same time, because of its psychological effects, propa-ganda makes the propagation of Christianity increasingly diffi-cult. The psychological structures built by propaganda are not propitious to Christian beliefs. This also applies on the social plane. For propaganda faces the church with the following dilemma:

Either not to make propaganda—but then, while the churches slowly and carefully win a man to Christianity, the mass media quickly mobilize the masses, and churchmen gain the impression of being "out of step," on the fringes of history, and without power to change a thing.

Or to make propaganda—this dilemma is surely one of the most cruel with which the churches are faced at present. For it seems that people manipulated by propaganda become increas-ingly impervious to spiritual realities, less and less suited for the autonomy of a Christian life.

We are seeing a considerable religious transformation, by which the religious element, through the means of the myth, is being absorbed little by little by propaganda and becoming one of its categories. But we must ask ourselves what happens if the church gives in and resorts to propaganda.

I already have stressed the total character of propaganda. Chris-tians often claim they can separate material devices from propa-ganda techniques—*i.e.*, break the system. For example, they think they can use press and radio without using the psychological principles or techniques that these media demand. Or that they can use these media without having to appeal to conditioned reflexes, myths, and so on. Or that they can use them from time to time, with care and discretion.

The only answer one can give to these timid souls is that such restraint would lead to a total lack of effectiveness. If a church wants to use propaganda in order to be effective, just as all the others, it must use the entire system with all its resources; it cannot pick what it likes, for such distinctions would destroy the very effectiveness for which the church would make propaganda in the first place. Propaganda is a total system that one must accept or reject in its entirety.

If the church accepts it, two important consequences follow. First of all, Christianity disseminated by such means is not Christianity. We have already seen the effect of propaganda on ideology. In fact, what happens as soon as the church avails itself of propaganda is a reduction of Christianity to the level of all other ideologies or secular religions.

This can be seen happening throughout history. Every time a church tried to act through the propaganda devices accepted by an epoch, the truth and authenticity of Christianity were debased. This happened in the fourth, ninth, and seventeenth centuries (of course, this does not mean that no more Christians were left as a result).

In such moments (when acting through propaganda), Christianity ceases to be an overwhelming power and spiritual adventure and becomes institutionalized in all its expressions and compromised in all its actions. It serves everybody as an ideology with the greatest of ease, and tends to be a hoax. In such times, there appear innumerable sweetenings and adaptations, which denature Christianity by adjusting it to the milieu.

Thus reduced to nothing more than an ideology, Christianity will be treated as such by the propagandist. And in the modern world we can repeat in connection with this particular ideology what we have already said on the subject of ideologies in general. What happens is that the church will be able to move the masses and convert thousands of people to its ideology. But this ideology will no longer be Christianity. It will be just another doctrine, though it will still contain (sometimes, but not always) some of the original principles and the Christian vocabulary.

The other consequence affects the church itself. When it uses propaganda, the church succeeds, just as all other organizations. It reaches the masses, influences collective opinions, leads sociological movements, and even makes many people accept what seems to be Christianity. But in doing that the church becomes a false church. It acquires power and influence that are of this world, and through them integrates itself into this world.

From the moment the church exposes itself to the conflict between sociological determinants and a contrary inspiration that comes from God and is directed toward God—from the moment the church uses propaganda and uses it successfully, it becomes, unremittingly, a purely sociological organization. It loses the spiritual part, for it now transmits only a false Christianity; it subordinates the essence of its being to sociological determination; it submits to the laws of efficiency in order to become a power in the world, and, in fact, it succeeds: it does become such a power. At that moment it has chosen power above truth.

When the church uses propaganda, it always tries to justify itself in two ways: It says, first of all, that it puts these efficient media in the service of Jesus Christ. But if one reflects for a moment, one realizes that this means nothing. What is in the service of Jesus Christ receives its character and effectiveness from Jesus Christ. The media that possess in themselves all their effectiveness and contain in themselves their own presuppositions and ends, cannot be put in the service of Jesus Christ. They obey their own rules, and this cannot be changed in the slightest, either by the content of their transmissions or by theological reasoning, despite what simplistic reasoning can make some people believe. In fact, a statement by the church that it is placing the media at the service of Christ, is not a logical or ethical explanation, but a pious formula without content.

One tries to escape from this trap by saying that one cannot see why the church should be prevented from using such an instrument of dissemination or power, so long as it does not put its confidence in such instruments; for one recalls from the Bible that confidence in anything other than God is condemned. But here it is enough to ask oneself: if one really does not believe in these instruments and really does not put one's confidence in them, why use them? If one uses them, one has confidence in their value and effectiveness; to deny this is hypocrisy. Of course, in connection with all this, we are thinking of real propaganda, not of some limited use of press or radio to transmit a Mass or service.

At the end of this brief analysis we can conclude that propaganda is one of the most powerful factors of de-Christianization in the world through the psychological modifications that it effects, through the ideological morass with which it has flooded the consciousness of the masses, through the reduction of Christianity to the level of an ideology, through the never-ending temptation held out to the church—all this is the creation of a mental universe foreign to Christianity. And this de-Christianization through the effects of one instrument—propaganda—is much greater than through all the anti-Christian doctrines.

4. Propaganda and Democracy

Democracy's Need of Propaganda

On one fact there can be no debate: the need of democracy, in its present situation, to "make propaganda."[9] We must understand, besides, that private propaganda, even more than governmental propaganda, is importantly linked to democracy. Historically, from the moment a democratic regime establishes itself, propaganda establishes itself alongside it under various forms. This is inevitable, as democracy depends on public opinion and competition between political parties. In order to come to power, parties make propaganda to gain voters.

Let us remember that the advent of the masses through the development of the democracies has provoked the use of propaganda, and that this is precisely one of the arguments of defense of the democratic State—that it appeals to the people, who are mobilized by propaganda; that it defends itself against private interests or anti-democratic parties. It is a remarkable fact worthy of attention that modern propaganda should have begun in the democratic States. During World War I we saw the combined use of the mass media for the first time; the application of publicity and advertising methods to political affairs, the search for the

---

[9] Perceptive authors agree that without propaganda a democratic State is disarmed at home (vis-à-vis the parties) and abroad, the latter as a result of the famous "challenge" that sets the democracies and the totalitarian States against each other. But one must not overlook the many setbacks that democracy has suffered for lack of propaganda. Maurice Mégret shows (in *L'Action psychologique* [Paris: A. Fayard; 1959]) that the crisis in which the French Army found itself from 1950 on was in large part caused by an absence of psychological action on the part of the government, and he demonstrates that the famous Plan was less than a great success for the same reasons. Finally, we must remember that if the democratic State is denied the right to make propaganda, such propaganda appears in the form of Public Relations at the expense of the State, and is all the more dangerous because camouflaged.

most effective psychological methods. But in those days German propaganda was mediocre: the French, English, and American democracies launched big propaganda. Similarly, the Leninist movement, undeniably democratic at the start, developed and perfected all propaganda methods. Contrary to some belief, the authoritarian regimes were not the first to resort to this type of action, though they eventually employed it beyond all limits. This statement should make us think about the relationship between democracy and propaganda.

For it is evident that a conflict exists between the principles of democracy—particularly its concept of the individual—and the processes of propaganda. The notion of rational man, capable of thinking and living according to reason, of controlling his passions and living according to scientific patterns, of choosing freely between good and evil—all this seems opposed to the secret influences, the mobilizations of myths, the swift appeals to the irrational, so characteristic of propaganda.

But this development within the democratic framework can be understood clearly if we look at it not from the level of principles but from that of actual situations. If, so far, we have concluded that inside a democracy propaganda is normal and indispensable, even intrinsic in the regime, that there are one or more propagandas at work, nothing seems to make propaganda obligatory in *external* relations. There the situation is entirely different. There the democratic State will want to present itself as the carrier of its entire public opinion, and the democratic nation will want to present itself as a coherent whole. But that creates some difficulty because such desire does not correspond to a true and exact picture of democracy. Moreover, this implies an endemic, permanent state of war. But, whereas it is easy to show that permanent wars established themselves at the same time as democratic regimes, it is even easier to demonstrate that these regimes express a strong desire for peace and do not systematically prepare for war. By this I mean that the economic and sociological conditions of the democracies possibly provoke general conflicts, but that the regime, such as it is, is not organically tied to war. It is led there, *volens nolens*. And it adjusts poorly to the situation of the Cold War, which is essentially psychological.

Another circumstance imprisons democracy in the ways of propaganda: the persistence of some traits of the democratic

ideology. The conviction of the invincible force of truth is tied
to the notion of progress and is a part of this ideology. Democracies have been fed on the notion that truth may be hidden for
a while but will triumph in the end, that truth in itself carries
an explosive force, a power of fermentation that will necessarily
lead to the end of lies and the shining apparition of the true.
This truth was the implicit core of the democratic doctrine.

One must stress, furthermore, that this was in itself a truth of
an ideological kind that ended by making history because it imposed itself on history. This attitude contained the seeds of, but
was at the same time (and still is) the exact opposite of, the
current Marxist attitude that history is truth. Proof through history
is nowadays regarded as *the* proof. He in whose favor history
decides, was right. But what is "to be right" when one speaks
of history? It is to win, to survive, *i.e.*, to be the strongest. This
would mean that the strongest and most efficient, nowadays, is the
possessor of the truth. Truth thus has no content of its own,
but exists only as history produces it; truth receives reality through
history.

One can easily see the relationship between the two attitudes
and how one can pass easily from one to the other: for if truth
possesses an invincible power that makes it triumph through
itself alone, it becomes logical—by a simple but dangerous step
—that triumph is truth. But—and this is frightening—the consequences of the two attitudes are radically different.

To think that democracy must triumph because it is the truth
leads man to be democratic and to believe that when the democratic regime is opposed to regimes of oppression, its superiority
will be clear at first sight to the infallible judgment of man and
history. The choice is thus certain. What amazement is displayed
again and again by democrats, particularly Anglo-Saxon democrats, when they see that a man selects something else, and that
history is indecisive. In such cases they decide to use information.
"Because democratic reality was not known, people have made a
bad choice," they say, and even there we find the same conviction
of the power of truth. But it is not borne out by facts. We will
not establish a general law here, to be sure, but we will say that
it is not a general law that truth triumphs automatically, though
it may in certain periods of history or with respect to certain
verities. We cannot generalize here at all. History shows that plain

truth can be so thoroughly snuffed out that it disappears, and that in certain periods the lie is all-powerful.

Even when truth triumphs, does it triumph through itself (because it is truth)? After all, the eternal verities defended by Antigone would, in the eyes of history, have yielded to Creon even if Sophocles had not exited.

But in our time, the conviction of democracy and its claim to inform people collide with the fact that propaganda follows an entirely. different mechanism, performs a function entirely different from that of information, and that nowadays facts do not assume reality in the people's eyes unless they are established by propaganda. Propaganda, in fact, creates truth in the sense that it creates in men subject to propaganda all the signs and indications of true believers.

For modern man, propaganda is really creating truth. This means that truth is powerless without propaganda. And in view of the challenge the democracies face, it is of supreme importance that they abandon their confidence in truth as such and assimilate themselves to the methods of propaganda. Unless they do so, considering the present tendencies of civilization, the democratic nations will lose the war conducted in this area.

Democratic Propaganda

Convinced of the necessity for using the means of propaganda, students of that question have found themselves facing the following problem. Totalitarian States have used propaganda to the limit, domestically in order to create conformity, manipulate public opinion, and adjust it to the decisions of the government; externally to conduct the Cold War, undermine the public opinion of nations considered enemies, and turn them into willing victims. But if these instruments were used principally by authoritarian States, and if democracies, whose structure seemed made for their use, did not use them, can they now be used by democracies? By that I mean that the propaganda of the authoritarian State has certain special traits, which seem inseparable from that State. Must democratic propaganda have other traits? Is it possible to make democratic propaganda?

Let us quickly dismiss the idea that a simple difference of content would mean a difference in character. "From the moment that propaganda is used to promulgate democratic ideas, it is good; if it is bad it is only because of its authoritarian content." Such a position is terribly idealistic and neglects the principal condition of the modern world: the primacy of means over ends. But one may say—and this is a matter worthy of reflection— that democracy itself is not a good "propaganda object." Practically all propaganda efforts to promulgate democracy have failed. In fact, one would have to modify the entire concept of democracy considerably to make it a good propaganda object, which at present it is not.

Also, in passing, I will mention the following thought: "From the moment that democracy uses this instrument (propaganda), propaganda becomes democratic." This thought is not often expressed quite so simply and aggressively, but it is an implicit notion found in most American writers. Nothing can touch democracy: on the contrary, it impresses its character on everything it touches. This prejudice is important for understanding the American democratic mythology and the tentative adoption of this principle by other popular democracies.

Such positions are so superficial and so remote from the actual situation that they do not need to be discussed. Besides, they usually come from journalists or commentators, and not from men who have seriously studied the problem of propaganda and its effects. Even the majority of the latter, however, retain the conviction that one *can* set up a propaganda system that expresses the democratic character and does *not* alter the working of democracy. That is the double demand that one must make of propaganda in a democratic regime.

It is argued that the first condition would be met by the absence of a monopoly (in a democracy) of the means of propaganda, and by the free interplay of various propagandas. True, compared with the State monopoly and the unity of propaganda in totalitarian States, one finds a great diversity of press and radio in democratic countries. But this fact must not be stressed too much: although there is no State or legal monopoly, there is, nevertheless, indeed a private monopoly. Even where there are many newspaper publishers, concentration as a result of "newspaper chains" is well established, and the monopolization of news agencies, of distribution and so on, is well known. In the field of radio or of motion pictures the same situation prevails: obviously not everybody can own propaganda media. In the United States, most radio and motion picture corporations are very large. The others are secondary and unable to compete, and centralization still goes on. The trend everywhere is in the direction of a very few, very powerful companies controlling all the propaganda media. Are they still private? In any event, as we have already seen, the State must make *its* propaganda, if only under the aspect of disseminating news.

Assuming that information is an indispensable element of democracy, it is necessary that the information promulgated by the State be credible. Without credibility, it will fail. But what happens when a powerful private propaganda organization denies facts and falsifies information? Who can tell where truth lies? On whom can the citizen rely to judge the debate? It is on this level that the dialogue really takes place. The problem then is whether the State will support a private competitor who controls media equal or superior to its own but makes different propaganda. It may even be entirely legitimate for the State to suppress or annex such a competitor.

Some will say: "Freedom of expression is democracy; to prevent propaganda is to violate democracy." Certainly, but it must be remembered that the freedom of expression of one or two powerful companies that do not express the thoughts of the individual or small groups, but of capitalist interests or an entire public, does not exactly correspond to what was called freedom of expression a century ago. One must remember, further, that the freedom of expression of one who makes a speech to a limited audience is not the same as that of the speaker who has all the radio sets in the country at his disposal, all the more as the science of propaganda gives to these instruments a shock effect that the non-initiated cannot equal.

I refer in this connection to the excellent study by Rivero,[1] who demonstrates the immense difference between the nineteenth and twentieth centuries in this respect:

> In the nineteenth century, the problem of opinion formation through the expression of thought was essentially a problem of contacts between the State and the *individual*, and a problem of *acquisition of a freedom*. But today, thanks to the mass media, the individual finds himself outside the battle . . . the debate is

---

[1] "Technique de formation de l'opinion publique," in *L'Opinion Publique* (1957).

between the State and powerful groups. . . . Freedom to express
ideas is no longer at stake in this debate. . . . What we have is
mastery and domination by the State or by some powerful groups
over the whole of the technical media of opinion formation . . .
the individual has no access to them . . . he is no longer a participant in this battle for the free expression of ideas: he is the stake.
What matters for him is which voice he will be permitted to hear
and which words will have the power to obsess him. . . .

It is in the light of this perfect analysis that one must ask
oneself what freedom of expression still means in a democracy.
But even if the State held all the instruments of propaganda
(and this becomes increasingly probable for political, economic,
and financial reasons—particularly so far as TV[2] is concerned),
what characterizes democracy is that it permits the expression
of different propagandas. This is true. But it is impossible to
permit the expression of all opinion. Immoral and aberrant
opinions are justifiably subject to censorship. Purely personal
opinions and, even more, certain political tendencies are necessarily excluded. "No freedom for the enemies of freedom" is
the watchword then. Thus the democracies create for themselves
a problem of limitation and degree. Who then will exclude certain propaganda instruments? For the Fascist, the Communists
are the enemies of truth. For the Communists, the enemies of
freedom are the bourgeois, the Fascists, the cosmopolitans. And
for the democracy? Obviously all enemies of democracy.

Matters are even more serious. In time of war, everybody agrees
that news must be limited and controlled, and that all propaganda
not in the national interest must be prohibited. From that fact
grows a unified propaganda. The problem that now arises is
this: We have talked of the Cold War. But it seems that the
democracies have not yet learned that the Cold War is no longer
an exceptional state, a state analogous to hot war (which is
transitory), but is becoming a permanent and endemic state.

There are many reasons for that. I will name only one: propaganda itself.

Propaganda directed to territories outside one's borders is a
weapon of war. This does not depend on the will of those who
use it or on a doctrine, but is a result of the medium itself.

---

[2] In France. (Trans.)

Propaganda has such an ability to effect psychological transformations and such an impact on the very core of man that it inevitably has military force when used by a government and directed to the outside. There is no "simple" use of propaganda; a propaganda conflict is hardly less serious than an armed conflict. It is inevitable, therefore, that in cold war the same attitude exists as in the case of hot war: one feels the need to unify propaganda. Here democracies are caught in a vicious circle from which they seem unable to escape.

The other principal aspect of democratic propaganda is that it is subject to certain values. It is not unfettered but fettered;[3] it is an instrument not of passion but of reason.[4] Therefore, democratic propaganda must be essentially truthful. It must speak only the truth and base itself only on facts. This can be observed in American propaganda: it is undeniable that American information and propaganda are truthful. But that does not seem to me characteristic of democracy. The formula with which Americans explain their attitude is: "The truth pays." That is, propaganda based on truth is more effective than any other. Besides, Hitler's famous statement on the lie is not a typical trait of propaganda. There is an unmistakable evolution here: lies and falsifications are used less and less. We have already said that. The use of precise facts is becoming increasingly common.

Conversely, the use of nuances and a certain suppleness reveals an attitude peculiar to democracy. At bottom there is a certain respect for the human being, unconscious perhaps, and becoming steadily weaker, but nevertheless still there; even the most Machiavellian of democrats respects the conscience of his listener and does not treat him with haste or contempt. The tradition of respecting the individual has not yet been eliminated, and this leads to all sorts of consequences. First, it limits propaganda. The democratic State uses propaganda only if driven by circumstances—for example, traditionally, after wars. But whereas private and domestic propaganda is persistent in its effects, governmental and external propaganda evaporate easily. Besides,

---

[3] Propaganda as such is limited in the democracies by law, by the separation of powers, and so on.

[4] See, for example, "Trends in Twentieth-Century Propaganda," by Ernst Kris and Nathan Leites, who contrast the appeal to the super-ego and to the irrational by authoritarian propaganda with democratic propaganda, which is directed at the ego.

such propaganda is not total, does not seek to envelop all of human life, to control every form of behavior, to attach itself ultimately to one's person. A third trait of democratic propaganda is that it looks at both sides of the coin. The democratic attitude is frequently close to that of a university: there is no absolute truth, and it is acknowledged that the opponent has some good faith, some justice, some reason on his side. It is a question of nuances. There is no strict rule—except in time of war— about Good on one side and Bad on the other.

Finally, the democratic propagandist or democratic State will often have a bad conscience about using propaganda. The old democratic conscience still gets in the way and burdens him; he has the vague feeling that he is engaged in something illegitimate. Thus, for the propagandist in a democracy to throw himself fully into his task it is necessary that he believe—*i.e.*, that he formulate his own convictions when he makes propaganda.

Lasswell has named still another difference between democratic and totalitarian propaganda, pertaining to the technique of propaganda itself, and distinguishing between "contrasted incitement" and "positive incitement." The first consists of a stimulus unleashed by the experimenter or the authorities in order to produce in the masses an effect in which those in power do not participate. This, according to Lasswell, is the customary method of despotism. Conversely, the positive incitement, symbolizing the extended brotherly hand, is a stimulus that springs from what the powers that be really feel, in which they want to make the masses participate. It is a communal action. This analysis is roughly accurate.

All this represents the situation in which democracies find themselves in the face of propaganda, and indicates the differences between democratic and authoritarian propaganda methods. But I must now render a very serious judgment on such activity (democratic propaganda): all that I have described adds up to ineffectual propaganda. Precisely to the extent that the propagandist retains his respect for the individual, he denies himself the very penetration that is the ultimate aim of all propaganda: that of provoking action without prior thought. By respecting nuances, he neglects the major law of propaganda: every assertion must be trenchant and total. To the extent that he remains partial, he fails to use the mystique. But that mystique is indispensable for well-made propaganda. To the extent that a democratic propagandist has a bad conscience, he cannot do good work; nor can he when he believes in his own propaganda. As concerns Lasswell's distinction, the technique of propaganda demands one form or the other, depending on circumstances. In any event, propaganda always creates a schism between the government and the mass, that same schism I have described in the book *The Technological Society*, and that is provoked by all the techniques, whose practitioners constitute a sort of aristocracy of technicians and who modify the structures of the State.

According to Lasswell's analysis, propaganda based on contrasted incitation expresses a despotism. I would rather say that it expresses an aristocracy. But the famous "massive democracy" corresponds to that, *is* that. Ultimately, even if one tries to maintain confidence and communion between the government and the governed, all propaganda ends up as a means by which the prevailing powers manipulate the masses.

The true propagandist must be as cold, lucid, and rigorous as a surgeon. There are subjects and objects. A propagandist who believes in what he says and lets himself become a victim of his own game will have the same weakness as a surgeon who operates on a loved one or a judge who presides at a trial of a member of his own family. To use the instrument of propaganda nowadays, one must have a scientific approach—the lack of which was the weakness that became apparent in Nazi propaganda in its last few years: clearly, after 1943, one could see from its content that Goebbels had begun to believe it himself.

Thus, some of democracy's fundamental aspects paralyze the conduct of propaganda. There is, therefore, no "democratic" propaganda. Propaganda made by the democracies is ineffective, paralyzed, mediocre. We can say the same when there is a diversity of propagandas: when various propagandas are permitted to express themselves they become ineffective with respect to their immediate objective. This ineffectiveness with regard to the citizens of a democracy needs more analysis. Let us merely emphasize here that our propaganda is outclassed by that of totalitarian States. This means that ours does not do its job. But in view of the challenge we face, it is imperative that ours be effective. One must therefore abandon the traits that are characteristic of democracy but paralyzing for propaganda: the combination of effective propaganda and respect for the individual seems impossible.

There is a last element, which I shall mention briefly. Jacques Driencourt has demonstrated that propaganda is totalitarian in its essence, not because it is the handmaiden of the totalitarian State, but because it has a tendency to absorb everything. This finding is the best part of his work.[5] It means that when one takes that route, one cannot stop halfway: one must use all instruments and all methods that make propaganda effective. One must expect—and developments over the past dozen years show it—that the democracies will abandon their precautions and their nuances and throw themselves wholeheartedly into effective propaganda action. But such action will no longer have a special democratic character.

We must now examine the effects that the making of propaganda has on democracy. To measure that, we must distinguish between external and domestic propaganda. We must not retain the illusion that propaganda is merely a neutral instrument that one can use without being affected. It is comparable to radium, and what happens to the radiologists is well known.

Effects of International Propaganda

In the domain of external politics and the propaganda that is directed toward the outside, there is practically no more private propaganda or any diversity of propagandas. Even parties indentured to a foreign government, and thus making propaganda different from that of their own national government, direct their propaganda to the interior. But what character does this unique form of propaganda (directed to the outside) take, and what repercussions has it on a democracy that conducts it? Can it be that it really exists in the domain of information?

We have abundant proof nowadays that straight information addressed to a foreign country is entirely useless.[6] Where the problem is to overcome national antipathies (which exist even between friendly nations), allegiance to a different government, to a different psychological and historical world, and finally to

---

5 *La Propagande, nouvelle force politique* (Paris: A. Colin; 1950).
6 We are talking here primarily of propaganda directed at the Communist countries.

an opposite propaganda, it is fruitless to expect anything from straight information: the bare fact (the truth) can accomplish nothing against such barriers. Facts are not believed. Other than in exceptional cases (military occupation and so on), people believe their own government over a foreign government. The latter's facts are not believed. In fact, propaganda can penetrate the consciousness of the masses of a foreign country only through the myth. It cannot operate with simple arguments pro and con. It does not address itself to already existing feelings, but must create an image to act as a motive force. This image must have an emotional character that leads to the allegiance of the entire being, without thought. That is, it must be a myth.

But then democracy takes a path that needs watching. First of all, it begins to play a game that drives man from the conscious and rational into the arms of irrational and "obscure forces"; but we already know that in this game the believer is not the master, and that forces thus unleashed are rarely brought under control again. To put it differently: mythical democratic propaganda in no way prepares its listeners for democracy, but strengthens their totalitarian tendencies, providing at best a different direction for those tendencies. We will have to come back to this. But above all we must ask ourselves what myth the democracies should use. From experience we have seen that the democracies have used the myths of Peace, of Freedom, of Justice, and so on.

All that has now been used, and is all the more unacceptable because everybody uses these words. But the myth used by propaganda must be specific: the myth of Blood and Soil was remarkable. What specific myths are left for democracy? Either subjects that cannot possibly form the content of a myth, such as well-being or the right to vote, or democracy itself.

Contrary to what one may think, the myth of democracy is far from exhausted and can still furnish good propaganda material. The fact that Communist authoritarian regimes also have chosen democracy as the springboard of propaganda tends to prove its propagandistic value. And to the extent that democracy is presented, constructed, and organized as a myth, it can be a good subject of propaganda. Propaganda appeals to belief: it rebuilds the drive toward the lost paradise and uses man's fundamental fear. Only from this aspect does democratic propaganda have some chance of penetration into non-democratic foreign countries. But one must then consider the consequences.

The first consequence is that any operation that transforms democracy into a myth transforms the democratic ideal. Democracy was not meant to be a myth. The question arose early—in 1791 in France. And we know what, shortly after, Jacobinism made of French democracy. We must understand this: Jacobinism saved the country. It claimed to have saved the Republic, but it is clear that it only saved the Jacobin regime by destroying all that was democratic. We cannot analyze here at length the influence of the myth on the abolition of democracy during 1793–5. Let us merely say that democracy cannot be an object of faith, of belief: it is expression of opinions. There is a fundamental difference between regimes based on opinion and regimes based on belief.

To make a myth of democracy is to present the opposite of democracy. One must clearly realize that the use of ancient myths and the creation of new ones is a regression toward primitive mentality, regardless of material progress. The evocation of mystical feelings is a rejection of democratic feelings. Considerable problems arise in the United States because of such diverse myths as, for example, the Ku Klux Klan, the American Legion, or Father Divine. These are anti-democratic, but they are localized, only partial, and private. The matter becomes infinitely more serious when the myth becomes public, generalized, and official, when what is an anti-mystique becomes a mystique.

Of course, we have said that such democratic propaganda is created for external use. People already subjected to totalitarian propaganda can be reached only by the myth, and even that does not change their behavior or mentality; it simply enters into the existing mold and creates new beliefs there. But looking at things this way implies two consequences.

First, we accept the fact that such external democratic propaganda should be a *weapon*, that we are dealing here with psychological warfare, and that we adjust ourselves to the enemy's train of thought; and that, proceding from there, the people that we subject to our propaganda are not those whom we want to see become democratic but whom we want to defeat. If we actually work on such a nation with the help of the myth, we confirm it in a state of mind, in a behavior, and in a concept of life that is anti-democratic: we do not prepare it to become a democratic nation, for on the one hand we reinforce or continue the methods of its own authoritarian government; and on the other, we cannot give the people, by such means, the desire to adhere to something else in another way. We are simply asking for the same *kind* of acceptance of something else, of another form of government. Is this sufficient to make people switch allegiance? That is the democratic propaganda problem in Germany and Japan.

In the second place, such methods imply that we consider democracy an abstraction; for if we think that to cast different ideas in the mold of propaganda is sufficient to change the nature of propaganda, we make a mere theory or idea of democracy. Propaganda, whatever its content, tends to create a particular psychology and a determined behavior. Superficially there can be differences, but they are illusory. To say, for example, that Fascist propaganda, whose subject was the State, and Nazi propaganda, whose subject was the race, were different from each other because of their difference in content, is to become a victim of unreal and academic distinctions. But "the democratic idea" when promulgated by means that lead to non-democratic behavior only hardens the totalitarian man in his mold.

This does not take into account that this democratic veneer and the myth of democracy as a propaganda subject are very fragile. It is, in fact, one of propaganda's essential laws that its objects always adjust themselves to its forms. In this, as in so many other domains of the modern world, the means impose their own laws. To put it differently: the objects of propaganda tend to become totalitarian because propaganda itself is totalitarian. This is exactly what I said when I spoke of the necessity to turn democracy into a myth.

Thus, such propaganda can be effective as a weapon of war, but we must realize when using it that we simultaneously destroy the possibility of building true democracy.

I have said that such propaganda was for external use, that the myth was directed to the outside. But it is not certain that one can impose such a limitation. When a government builds up the democratic image in this fashion, it cannot isolate the external and internal domains from each other. Therefore the people of the country making such propaganda must also become convinced of the excellence of this image. They must not merely know it, but also follow it. This, incidentally, sets a limit to the degree to which propaganda can lie; a democratic government cannot present to the outside world a radically inexact and mendacious picture of its policies, as can a totalitarian government.

But one must qualify this thought in two ways: on the one hand a democratic nation is itself more or less in the grip of propaganda and goes along with the idealistic image of its government because of national pride; on the other, even authoritarian governments are aware that in propaganda the truth pays, as I have said: this explains the final form of propaganda adopted by Goebbels in 1944.

From there on, the myth created for external use becomes known at home and has repercussions there; even if one does not try to influence people by making propaganda abroad, they will react indirectly. Therefore, the repercussions on a democratic population of the myth developed by its government for external use must be analyzed; these repercussions will lead primarily to the establishment of unanimity.

This is a primary and very simple consequence. A myth (an image evoking belief) can stand no dilution, no half-measures, no contradictions. One believes it or does not. The democratic myth must display this same form, incisive and coherent; it is of the same nature as other myths. In order for the myth to be effective abroad, it must not be contradicted at home. No other voice must arise at home that would reach the foreign propaganda target and destroy the myth.

Can anyone believe that it was possible to make effective propaganda, for example, toward Algeria, when it was immediately contradicted at home? How could the Algerians—or any other foreigners—take seriously a promise made by General de Gaulle in the name of France when the press immediately declared that one part of France was in disagreement with it?[7]

This will lead to the elimination of any opposition that would show that the people are not unanimously behind the democracy embodied by the government. Such opposition can completely destroy all effectiveness of democratic propaganda. Besides, such propaganda is made by a government supported by a majority. The minority, though also democratic, will tend to be against

7 This non-coherence, leading to the ineffectuality of the myth, was the cause—among many others—of years of unsuccessful negotiations.

such propaganda merely because it comes from the government (we saw this in France after 1945). From there on, though in accord with the idea of democracy, this minority will show itself hostile to the democratic myth. Then the government, if it wants its propaganda to be effective, will be forced to reduce the possibility of the minority's expressing itself—*i.e.*, to interfere with one of democracy's essential characteristics; we are already used to this from wartime, as with censorship. Here we are face to face with the fact discussed above: propaganda is by itself a state of war; it demands the exclusion of opposite trends and minorities—not total and official perhaps, but at least partial and indirect exclusion.

If we pursue this train of thought, another factor emerges: for the myth to have real weight, it must rest on popular belief. To put it differently: one cannot simply project a myth to the outside even by the powerful modern material means; such an image will have no force unless it is already believed. The myth is contagious because beliefs are contagious. It is indispensable, therefore, that democratic people also believe the democratic myth. Conversely, it is not useful that the government itself should follow suit; but the government must be sure that its propaganda abroad is identical with its propaganda at home, and understand that its foreign propaganda will be strong only if it is believed at home. (The United States understood this perfectly between 1942 and 1945.) And the more the myth will appear to be the expression of belief of the entire nation, the more effective it will be. It thus presumes unanimity.

We have seen how all propaganda develops the cult of personality. This is particularly true in a democracy. There one exalts the individual, who refuses to be anonymous, rejects the "mass," and eschews mechanization. He wants a human regime where men are human beings. He needs a government whose leaders are human beings. And propaganda must show them to him as such. It must create these personalities. To be sure, the object at this level is not idolatry, but idolatry cannot fail to follow if the propaganda is done well. Whether such idolatry is given to a man in uniform bursting with decorations, or a man in work shirt and cap, or a man wearing a business suit and soft hat makes no difference; those are simple adaptations of propaganda to the feelings of the masses. The democratic masses will reject the uniform, but idolize the soft hat if it is well presented. There can be no propaganda without a personality, a political chief. Clemenceau, Daladier, De Gaulle, Churchill, Roosevelt, MacArthur are obvious examples. And even more, Khrushchev, who, after having denounced the cult of personality, slipped into the same role, differently, but with the same ease and obeying the same necessity. The nation's unanimity is necessary. This unanimity is embodied in one personality, in whom everyone finds himself, in whom everyone hopes and projects himself, and for whom everything is possible and permissible.

This need for unanimity is accepted by some of those who have studied the problem of propaganda in democracy. It has been claimed that this unanimity indicates the transition from an old form of democracy to a new one: "massive and progressive democracy." In other words, a democracy of allegiance; a system in which all will share the same conviction. This would not be a centrifugal conviction, *i.e.*, one expressing itself in diverse forms and admitting the possibility of extreme divergences. It would be a centripetal conviction with which everything would be measured by the same yardstick; democracy would express itself in a single voice, going further than just forms—all the way to rites and liturgies. It would, on the other hand, be a democracy of participation in which the citizen would be wholly engaged; his complete life, his movements would be integrated into a given social system. And one of the authors gives as an example the Nuremberg Party Congress! What a strange example of democracy.

It is true that only such a unanimous and unitary society can produce propaganda that can be effectively carried beyond the borders. But we must ask ourselves whether such a society is still democratic. What is this democracy that no longer includes minorities and opposition? As long as democracy is merely the interplay of parties, there can be opposition; but when we hear of a massive democracy, with grandiose ceremonies in which the people participate at the prompting of the State, that signifies, first of all, a confusion between the government and the State, and indicates further that anyone who does not participate is not merely in opposition, but excludes himself from the national community expressing itself in this participation. It is a truly extraordinary transformation of the democratic structure, because there can no longer be any respect for the minority opposition to the State—an opposition that, lacking the means of propaganda —or at least any means that can compete with those of the State— can no longer make its voice heard.

The minority is heard even less because the effects of the myth, inflated by propaganda, are always the same and always antidemocratic. Anyone who participates in such a socio-political body and is imbued with the truth of the myth, necessarily becomes sectarian. Repeated so many times, being driven in so many different forms into the propagandee's subconscious, this truth, transmitted by propaganda, becomes for every participant an absolute truth, which cannot be discussed without lies and distortion. Democratic peoples are not exempt from what is vaguely called "psychoses." But such propaganda, if it is effective, predisposes people to—or even causes—these psychoses.

If the people do not believe in the myth, it cannot serve to combat totalitarian propaganda; but if the people do believe in it, they are victims of these myths, which, though democratic on the surface, have all the traits of all other myths, particularly the impossibility, in the eyes of believers, of being questioned. But this tends to eliminate all opposing truth, which is immediately called "error." Once democracy becomes the object of propaganda, it also becomes as totalitarian, authoritarian, and exclusive as dictatorship.

The enthusiasm and exaltation of a people who cling to a myth necessarily lead to intransigeance and sectarianism. The myth of democracy arose, for example, during the period of the Convention; there we had forms of massive democracy, with great ceremonics and efforts at unanimity. But was that still democracy? Are there not also changes in the mores of the United States when everything is called un-American that is not strict conformism? This term, *un-American*, so imprecise for the French, is in the United States precise to the extent that it is a result of the belief in the myth. To provoke such belief and launch a people on the road to such exaltation, without which propaganda cannot exist, really means to give a people feelings and reflexes incompatible with life in a democracy.

This is really the ultimate problem: democracy is not just a certain form of political organization or simply an ideology—it is, first of all, a certain view of life and a form of behavior. If democracy were only a form of political organization, there would be no problem; propaganda could adjust to it. This is the institutional argument: propaganda is democratic because there is no unitary State centralized by propaganda. If, then, we were merely in the presence of an ideology, there still would be no problem: propaganda can transmit any ideology (subject to the qualifications made above) and, therefore, also the democratic ideology, for example. But if democracy is a way of life, composed of tolerance, respect, degree, choice, diversity, and so on, all propaganda that acts on behavior and feelings and transforms them in depth turns man into someone who can no longer support democracy because he no longer follows democratic behavior.

Yet propaganda cannot "create" democratic behavior by the promulgation of a myth—which is the only way of making propaganda on the outside, but which modifies the behavior of the people at home. We shall find the same problem in examining certain effects of domestic propaganda.

Effects of Internal Propaganda

I have tried to show elsewhere that propaganda has also become a necessity for the internal life of a democracy. Nowadays the State is forced to define an official truth. This is a change of extreme seriousness. Even when the State is not motivated to do this for reasons of action or prestige, it is led to it when fulfilling its function of disseminating information.

We have seen how the growth of information inevitably leads to the need for propaganda. This is truer in a democratic system than in any other.

The public will accept news if it is arranged in a comprehensible system, and if it does not speak only to the intelligence but to the "heart." This means, precisely, that the public wants propaganda, and if the State does not wish to leave it to a party, which will then provide explanations for everything (*i.e.,* the truth), it must itself make propaganda. Thus, the democratic State, even if it does not want to, becomes a propagandist State because of the need to dispense information. This entails a profound constitutional and ideological transformation. It is, in effect, a State that must proclaim an official, general, and explicit truth. The State can then no longer be objective or liberal, but is forced to bring to the overinformed people a *corpus in-*

telligentiae. It can no longer tolerate competition, because a State that assumes this function no longer has the right to err; if it did, it would become the laughing stock of the citizenry, and its information would lose its effect, together with its propaganda. For the information it dispenses is believed only to the extent that its propaganda is believed.

This State-proclaimed truth must be all-embracing: the facts, which are the subjects of information, are becoming more and more complex, are covering larger segments of life; thus the system into which they are arranged must cover all of life. This system must become a complete answer to all questions occurring in the citizens' conscience. It must, therefore, be general and all-valid: it cannot be a philosophy or a metaphysical system—for such systems appeal to the intelligence of a minority. To describe the system, we must go back to an ancient primitive notion: the etiological myth. In fact, a propaganda that corresponds to the body of information in a democratic State, and aims at alleviating the troubles of its citizens, must offer them an etiological myth.

This would not be necessary if the citizens were to work only three or four hours a day and devote four hours daily to personal reflection and cultural pursuits, if all citizens had a similar cultural level, if the society were in a state of equilibrium and not under the shadow of tomorrow's menace, and if the moral education of the citizens enabled them to master their passions and their egotism. But as these four conditions are not fulfilled, and as the volume of information grows very rapidly, we are forced to seek explanations *hic et nunc*, and publicly parade them in accordance with popular demand.

But the creation of the etiological myth leads to an obligation on the part of democracy to become religious. It can no longer be secular but must create its religion. Besides, the creation of a religion is one of the indispensable elements of effective propaganda. The content of this religion is of little importance; what matters is to satisfy the religious feelings of the masses; these feelings are used to integrate the masses into the national collective. We must not delude ourselves: when one speaks to us of "massive democracy" and "democratic participation," these are only veiled terms that mean "religion." Participation and unanimity have always been characteristics of religious societies, and only of religious societies. Thus we return by another route to the problem of intolerance and the suppression of minorities.[8]

On the other hand, democracy is more and more conceived as a simple external political structure, rather than as a complete concept of society, of behavior of man. This concept, this Way of Life, is tied to political democracy. Certain qualities on the part of the citizens are needed if democracy is to exist. It is easy to see that democracy wants to preserve this treasure that is its reason for, and its way of, existing. The government must maintain this Way of Life, without which democracy would no longer be possible. It thus becomes understandable and consistent that American prisoners, repatriated from Korea, were put in quarantine and subjected to mental and psychological treatment to detoxicate them of Communism. They had to be given an American brainwashing, corresponding to the Chinese brainwashing, to make them fit to live once again according to the American Way of Life.

But what is left of a man after that? We understand that democracy wants to control the mental and psychological state of the people who serve it, according to the notion of the Security Risk. Public servants cannot be permitted criminal or immoral conduct, alcoholism, dope-addiction, or the like; they would be so far removed from the virtues a democratic citizen must exhibit that this exercise of control and the massive education by propaganda for a life congruous with democracy are easy to understand. The civic virtues created by the mass media will guarantee the maintenance of democracy. But what remains of liberty?

I want to touch upon one other fact: I have tried to show, in my book *The Technological Society*, that modern technical instruments have their own weight and by themselves change

---

[8] Let us recall another effect of such propaganda on democracy: an aristocratic category of men arises which has no common bond with democracy. The propagandist is a technician and a member of an aristocracy of technicians that establishes itself above the institutions of a democracy and acts outside its norms. Besides, the employment of propaganda leads the propagandist to cynicism, disbelief in values, non-submission to the law of numbers, doubts on the value of opinions, and contempt for the propagandee and the elected representatives: he knows how public opinion is fashioned. The propagandist cannot subject himself to popular judgment and democracy. Finally, the propagandist is privy to all State secrets and acts at the same time to shape opinions: he really has a position of fundamental direction. The combination of these three elements makes the propagandist an aristocrat. It cannot be otherwise. Every democracy that launches propaganda creates in and by such propaganda its own enemy, an aristocracy that may destroy it.

political structures. Here I will ask only one question: What will be the effect on democracy of the use of TV for propaganda?

One can see the first effects: TV brings us close to direct democracy. Congressmen and cabinet members become known; their faces and utterances come to be recognized; they are brought closer to the voter. TV permits political contact to extend beyond election campaigns and informs the voters directly on a daily basis. More than that, TV could become a means of control over public servants: In his capacity as TV viewer, the voter could verify what use his representatives make of the mandate with which he has entrusted them. Certain experiments conducted in the United States showed that when sessions of Congress were televised, they were much more dignified, serious, and efficient; knowing that they were being observed, the congressmen took greater pains to fulfill their function. But one must not hope for too much in this respect:[9] there is little chance that governing bodies will accept this control. In reality, statesmen fully understand how to use it for *their* propaganda, and that is all. In fact, TV probably helped Eisenhower to win over Stevenson, the Conservatives to win over Labour.[1] The problem is first one of money, second of technical skill. But the use of TV as a democratic propaganda instrument entails the risk of a profound modification of democracy's "style."

What can democracy use for TV propaganda? Democracy is not well adapted to that. So far, the technical instruments are in accord with democratic activities: democracy speaks, and its entire being is expressed in words (this is not meant ironically; I believe that speech, in the most powerful and rhetorical sense, is one of the highest expressions of man). The instruments of propaganda, particularly press and radio, are made for words.

Conversely, democratic propaganda made by motion pictures is weak. Democracy is not a visual form of government. The ceremony of the Flame under the Arc de Triomphe—one of the most

[9] John Albig states correctly that this "personification" by TV corrodes and inhibits personal, analytical reflection, standardizes personal images, and transmits a "false reality": a televised session of Congress or the Cabinet is not a *true* session, *cannot* be a true session. In such a televised session, "the public sees the responsible government in action, but only as a political show performed by humanized stars who play a role." This seems an excellent description.
[1] This has been challenged by Angus Campbell (in "Television and the Election"). Campbell, on the other hand, gives important indications of TV's decisive influence on elections.

successful pictures—has little propaganda impact even though it is spectacular. Actually, when democracy wants to use the film for propaganda, it can think of nothing but military parades, which cannot be presented too often. Propaganda needs both repetition and diversity. So far, democracy's inability to use motion pictures for its propaganda has not seemed serious, the films being a secondary arm. But it seems that TV is destined to become a principal arm, for it can totally mobilize the individual without demanding the slightest effort from him. TV reaches him at home, like radio, in his own setting, his private life. It asks no decision, no a priori participation, no move from him (such as going to a meeting). But it holds him completely and leaves him no possibility of engaging in other activities (whereas radio leaves a good part of the individual unoccupied). Moreover, TV has the shock effect of the picture, which is much greater than that of sound.

But in order to use this remarkable arm, one must have something to show. A government official giving a speech is not a spectacle. Democracies have nothing to show that can compare with what is available to a dictatorship. If they do not want to be left behind in this domain, which would be extremely dangerous, they must find propaganda spectacles to televise. But nothing is better than massive ceremonies, popular marches—the Hitler youth and the Komsomols—or an entire population enthusiastically assembled to build new ships or a new university (as in Yugoslavia). The exigencies of TV will lead democracy to engage in such hardly democratic demonstrations.

We are now reaching the most important problem. Earlier, I examined the psychological transformations that the individual undergoes when subjected to an intense and continuous propaganda. We have also seen that the existence of two contradictory propagandas is no solution at all, as it in no way leads to a "democratic" situation: the individual is not independent in the presence of two combatants between whom he must choose. He is not a spectator comparing two posters, or a supreme arbiter when he decides in favor of the more honest and convincing one. To look at things this way is childish idealism. The individual is seized, manipulated, attacked from every side; the combatants of two propaganda systems do not fight each other, but try to capture *him*. As a result, the individual suffers the most profound psychological influences and distortions. Man modified in this fashion demands simple solutions, catchwords, certainties, continuity, commitment, a clear and simple division of the world into Good and Evil, efficiency, and unity of thought. He cannot bear ambiguity. He cannot bear that the opponent should in any way whatever represent what is right or good. An additional effect of contradictory propagandas is that the individual will escape either into passivity or into total and unthinking support of one of the two sides.

It is striking to see how this current, which is the point of departure of totalitarian parties, is beginning to take hold in the United States. These two different reactions—passivity or total commitment—are completely antidemocratic. But they are the consequence of some democratic types of propaganda. Here is the hub of the problem. Propaganda ruins not only democratic ideas but also democratic behavior—the foundation of democracy, the very quality without which it cannot exist.

The question is not to reject propaganda in the name of freedom of public opinion—which, as we well know, is never virginal —or in the name of freedom of individual opinion, which is formed of everything and nothing—but to reject it in the name of a very profound reality: the *possibility* of choice and differentiation, which is the fundamental characteristic of the individual in the democratic society.

Whatever the doctrine promulgated by propaganda, its psychosociological results are the same. To be sure, some doctrines are more coherent subject matter for propaganda than others, and lead to a more efficient and insistent propaganda; other doctrines —republican and democratic—are rather paralyzing and less suitable. But the only result is the progressive weakening of the doctrine by propaganda.

Conversely, what gives propaganda its destructive character is not the singleness of some propagated doctrine; it is the instrument of propaganda itself. Although it acts differently, according to whether it promulgates a closed system or a diversity of opinions, it has profound and destructive effects.

What am I saying then? That propaganda can promulgate a democratic doctrine? Absolutely. That it can be used by a government elected by majority vote? Absolutely. But this gives us no guarantee that we still are dealing with democracy. With the help of propaganda, one can disseminate democratic ideas as a *credo* and within the framework of a myth. With propaganda one can lead citizens to the voting booth, where they seemingly elect their representatives. But if democracy corresponds to a certain type of human being, to a certain individual behavior, then propaganda destroys the point of departure of the life of a democracy, destroys its very foundations. It creates a man who is suited to a totalitarian society, who is not at ease except when integrated in the mass, who rejects critical judgments, choices, and differentiations because he clings to clear certainties. He is a man assimilated into uniform groups and wants it that way.

With the help of propaganda one can do almost anything, but certainly not create the behavior of a free man or, to a lesser degree, a democratic man. A man who lives in a democratic society and who is subjected to propaganda is being drained of the democratic content itself—of the style of democratic life, understanding of others, respect for minorities, re-examination of his own opinions, absence of dogmatism. The means employed to spread democratic ideas make the citizen, psychologically, a totalitarian man. The only difference between him and a Nazi is that he is a "totalitarian man with democratic convictions," but those convictions do not change his behavior in the least. Such contradiction is in no way felt by the individual for whom democracy has become a myth and a set of democratic imperatives, merely stimuli that activate conditioned reflexes. The word *democracy*, having become a simple incitation, no longer has anything to do with democratic behavior. And the citizen can repeat indefinitely "the sacred formulas of democracy" while acting like a storm trooper.

All democracy that is maintained or propagated through propaganda eventually scores this success, which is its own negation with regard to the individual and the truth.

But can things really be that way?

I said above that, generally, those who tend to deny propaganda's efficacy unconsciously hold a concept of the inalienable value of the individual. Those who accept its efficacy hold a materialistic concept. So far as I am concerned, I would much prefer to be able to assert that man is invulnerable, that few dangers exist for him in present-day society, that propaganda can do nothing to him. Unfortunately, the experiences of the last half century are not encouraging in this respect. Moreover, it seems to me that the belief in propaganda's harmlessness and the spreading of this belief are ultimately detrimental to man. For man then is reassured in the face of attacks, he believes in his invulnerability and in the ineffectiveness of the attack, and his will to resist is greatly diminished. Why lose one's time and waste one's efforts defending oneself against propaganda if propaganda is merely child's play and empty talk by ridiculous tyrants? Why exert one's mind, one's personality, one's strength of character if the tigers are paper tigers, if the methods are so absurd and obvious that even the biggest fool can manage to escape them? Why make discerning choices if propaganda, using only what is already there and leading me along roads I would have traveled without it, can in no way modify my actions? If the propagandee takes that attitude, he is in the most favorable position to obey without knowing it, to drift into the routine of propaganda while claiming to be supremely superior.

The only truly serious attitude—serious because the danger of man's destruction by propaganda is serious, serious because no other attitude is truly responsible and serious—is to show people the extreme effectiveness of the weapon used against them, to rouse them to defend themselves by making them aware of their frailty and their vulnerability, instead of soothing them with the worst illusion, that of a security that neither man's nature nor the techniques of propaganda permit him to possess. It is merely convenient to realize that the side of freedom and truth for man has not yet lost, but that it may well lose—and that in this game, propaganda is undoubtedly the most formidable power, acting in only one direction (toward the destruction of truth and freedom), no matter what the good intentions or the good will may be of those who manipulate it.

APPENDIX

[I]

EFFECTIVENESS
OF PROPAGANDA

———————————————————

———————————————————

Approaching the problem of gauging propaganda results, we must carefully distinguish between effectiveness and involuntary effects. On the one hand, the propagandist aims at certain objectives: he wants to modify the content of an opinion, change majority views, or destroy the morale of an enemy. With regard to such aims we can speak of effectiveness: either the propagandist attains his objective or he does not. This is what people usually study under the subject heading "Propaganda Effects." But this is a misconception. For other effects are much deeper and more important, even though not willed. I have tried to analyze these in chapters IV and V.

In this appendix I will limit myself to examining direct effectiveness.

1. Difficulties of Measuring Effectiveness

As soon as we pose the problem of effectiveness, we approach the question of effects and the measurement of such effects (in this annex, I will take the word in its ordinary sense, as it is generally used by students of propaganda—*i.e.*, as *desired* effects sought by the propagandist). Can the propagandist change an opinion or can't he? This is what some people try to measure (because, in line with contemporary scientific prejudices, only what can be expressed in figures is certain).

Difficulty of the Subject

Let us begin by stating that propaganda sets itself a great diversity of objectives, and that it is often difficult to distinguish among them. The propagandist may seek to sustain the morale of his troops, to reinforce their courage, to excite them, to get them to sacrifice their lives. The existence of other propagandas and the difficulty of measurement will combine here to make it impossible to know and register the point of departure—*i.e.*, the degree of enthusiasm, and so on, before and after the propaganda operation. It must be particularly stressed that, aside from the difficulty of finding reliable testing methods, the individuals in question were not untouched by propaganda in general before a particular operation was launched. For instance, mobilized troops already have been propagandized to some extent. We cannot find a "zero" point from which to begin, not only because none of us has remained immune to propaganda, but also because supporters of a cause have become supporters through propaganda. From there on, mere modifications in consequence of a propaganda campaign are of little significance.

A propagandist might also aim at neutralizing an enemy by destroying his morale. But to measure the effectiveness of such propaganda would require measuring the *difference* between two propagandas, for the enemy also is subjected to positive propaganda by his own side. And it is *never* possible to evaluate the effects of two propagandas at the same time. No nation or organization can undertake such an analysis at the time of the propaganda operation. There can only be retrospective inquiries, and we shall see later how insignificant they are.

The propagandist can aim at some external, formal, and temporary adherence, as in an election campaign by trying to get undecided voters to vote for a certain candidate. At this point we generally encounter the traditional argument that because two or three conflicting propagandas cancel each other out, the voter is free to make his own choice. In the event of a referendum, there are as many arguments for as against advanced everywhere; therefore, it is maintained, no opinions are changed. This is only partially correct, and one cannot reach decisive conclusions as to propaganda effectiveness in general by noting the success or failure of an election campaign. The shift of some votes is never significant. In fact, one cannot really talk about propaganda in connection with an election campaign. A campaign is the simplest, most imperfect form of modern propaganda; the objective is insufficient, the methods are incomplete, the duration is brief, pre-propaganda is absent, and the campaign propagandist never has all the media at his disposal. Thus, the one case in which the measurement of effects is comparatively easy (shift of votes) is also by far the least significant.

The propagandist may also aim at many other objectives, such as the destruction of micro-groups, labor unions, associations, and other groups; he may seek some determined action (strike, boycott, pogrom) from a group more or less directly under his influence; he may seek to influence some public opinion, aiming not at immediate actions, but only at changing a climate or evoking an atmosphere of sympathy or antipathy; he may, finally, if he is a commercial propagandist, simply try to get people to buy some product.

I have pointed out the extreme diversity of possible objectives in order to show that propaganda's effectiveness cannot be measured on the basis of results obtained in one of these domains. If I look at propaganda made within a large group and find that it has failed to push the group toward some proposed action (a strike, for example), I will be tempted to conclude that it was ineffective. But if I find that this same propaganda campaign has broken up some of an adversary's micro-groups, or has created some strong resentment and restrained aggressiveness on the part of a group of militants, I must conclude that from this point of view propaganda *has* succeeded and can serve as basis for future action. If I see that few votes were won and that the undecided were not reached by the campaign, I will tend to regard it as a failure. But the same propaganda may have galvanized the militant group, reinforced the party, given it a chance to experiment with new methods, or led to the solidarity of certain micro-groups—equally important results. Therefore, given the diversity of effects sought by the propagandist, one can draw absolutely no conclusions about the effectiveness of his propaganda with regard to any of his objectives.

Moreover, even if one could isolate one from among the many and prove that the propagandist aimed only at that particular one (for example, to obtain votes in a referendum), it is absolutely impossible to transfer such findings to other domains of propaganda. To do so would be to be hasty and to misunderstand basic differences. It has been well recognized, for example, that certain advertising methods are ineffective in political propaganda. Getting a man to adhere to a political movement and getting him to buy a car are not the same problem. Nor is it the same problem to get people to vote a certain way or to promote heroism in combat. It has also been clearly demonstrated that propaganda directed toward other countries cannot be the same as propaganda made at home. The techniques of exercising influence will be different, as will the methods of measuring effectiveness.[1]

Aside from the complexity of the problem itself, the extreme difficulty of defining the facts themselves must also be taken into account. Even on the simplest level, most easily translated into figures, one cannot determine with any degree of accuracy how many people are being reached by a propaganda campaign. We know of the efforts made by some American services after 1944 to determine how many German soldiers had read American leaflets. But the number remained completely uncertain. We also know Lasswell's effort to determine how many persons were reached by Communist propaganda in Chicago: despite his use of a very complicated method, the results are completely unreliable.[2] This also is true for Rossi's figures regarding Communist propaganda in France. But if we do not even know how many people are subjected to propaganda (on the simplest level, by counting a single medium—leaflets, or meetings, or the circulation figures of a newspaper), we certainly cannot estimate

---

[1] It should be added that it is impossible to measure the effectiveness of "black" propaganda, propaganda through unconventional channels, or rumors. Also, to measure propaganda, it would be necessary to demand criteria of obvious effectiveness; Daniel Lerner has tried this without much success. Finally, a direct correlation would have to be established between the effects and the means, which is practically impossible.

[2] Harold D. Lasswell and Dorothy Blumenstock: *World Revolutionary Propaganda* (New York: Alfred A. Knopf; 1939), Ch. 11.

the quantitative effect of propaganda because we cannot learn the percentage of people reached as compared with the total population, or the percentage of people affected as compared with the total number reached. Therefore, we can have no solid basis for evaluation.

When we leave this most elementary sphere of attempts at evaluation, we encounter even greater difficulties. The question becomes complicated from four points of view: first of all, propaganda tends to affect people in depth, and not just with respect to certain circumscribed actions. How, then, can we measure an entire situation, particularly if the effects are latent?

A second difficulty is the delay—not always of the same duration—between the moment when the propagandist acts and the one when certain effects begin to show. Doob maintains that we see here a "period of indetermination." Obviously, the propagandist's task is to reduce this period of indetermination as much as possible. But he cannot eliminate it. And the student of propaganda effects must take it into account. He must answer this question: "At what point can one say that propaganda has failed?"—*i.e.*, at what point has opinion emerged from the period of indetermination to take a direction different from that suggested by propaganda? This question is hard to answer.

A third problem concerns the "payoff." Propaganda becomes increasingly expensive. Therefore the question inevitably arises: do the results justify the costs? Are the returns worth the game? Do constantly rising costs produce increased results? What is the optimal level? These three questions concerning the returns of propaganda efforts demand an answer, but we are far from being able to answer them.[3]

The fourth difficulty derives from the propagandist's need to predict effects. Effects must be gauged beforehand because propaganda must be directed and adjusted if maximum results are to be obtained. But we are barely able to see *past* effects, about which nothing can be done any longer. This is all the more serious because propaganda consists of holding the masses in hand in order to steer them in various directions; when we find

---

[3] The question of returns is also asked in the U.S.S.R., but under a different aspect: the cost of propaganda there is established in terms of the contribution that the propaganda media can make to the effective administration of the country by the Party. As a result, the problem of money is of less importance.

on the basis of *past* effects that some propaganda is *failing*, that means that it has *already failed;* that the masses, failing to respond, have escaped it. And propaganda can no longer recapture them. This happened with Communist propaganda in France between 1949 and 1952; the masses ceased to obey, and the Party's self-criticism came too late. The same holds true for the Psychological Action in Algeria; its failure became apparent only in 1960.

The difficulty of evaluating propaganda effects is increased by the social interactions in which propaganda unfolds. Doob has taken devilish pleasure in enumerating them. His definition of these interactions: all propagandists are influenced by the public opinion they seek to influence. Interest provokes propaganda, but propaganda provokes an interest. Propaganda provokes habitual responses, which are reinforced or modified by the simple fact of being evoked by propaganda. The individual perceives only that propaganda that his personality lets him perceive, but his personality is changed by that propaganda.

The propagandist is influenced by public opinion and by preceding propaganda action. Propaganda is influenced by the propagandist, by public opinion, and by the perception an individual has of that propaganda. But the perception itself is influenced by propaganda, public opinion, and the personality of the man who perceives it. Such interactions, which make it impossible to isolate a single propaganda effect in its pure state, can easily be multiplied.

Continuing in the same direction, we must understand that it is impossible to dissociate propaganda effects from other factors, as I pointed out in chapter I. We cannot name every factor working upon an individual. It would be wrong even to attempt this, for propaganda is not an isolated phenomenon with clearly delineated boundaries; it is completely integrated and immersed in a social entity. It is related to the general sociological structure, and to try to dissociate it and reduce it to its pure state would be to strip it of its true nature.

Let us consider a final difficulty: it is practically impossible to study propaganda effects exactly where they are made, in the society in which they develop. The sociologist or psychologist absolutely cannot work in the living, contemporary environment of an intense propaganda, because this environment is much too polarized and activated for an analysis to be possible. Just as it is not possible to make public opinion surveys or complicated psychological observations during a battle, so one cannot make them in this kind of psychological war, which *all* propaganda is. It was completely impossible to research propaganda effectiveness in Fascist and Nazi societies: Such research would have been suspect, and the results could not have been published. Such efforts would have collided not only with the resistance of the authorities, but also with that of the interested parties, who either would not be affected by the propaganda and therefore hostile to the regime, without daring to say so in the course of a sociological investigation, or would be partisans of the regime. This is the situation in all countries where true propaganda is being made, such as China, the U.S.S.R., Algeria, and so on. The researcher is therefore forced to limit himself to an analysis in real-life situations in which there is no real propaganda or only limited or sporadic propaganda in connection with an election campaign, a referendum, or a minority party trying to gain members. One could still try to measure effects a posteriori, but such measurement is necessarily inexact.[4] Finally, one can conduct tests, and this will be discussed next in detail.

Inadequacy of Methods

In the face of total propaganda, it is clear that tests are useless; the reality can never be duplicated. You cannot stop a man in the heat of a meeting to ask him what he thinks. You cannot measure with any precision the effects of a film because you cannot dissociate it from current newspaper articles and radio broadcasts on the same subject. Finally, in a country steeped in propaganda, you cannot take a key group of supporters and measure the effects on other groups of their bearing witness to the cause: both groups already are shaped by earlier propaganda, and the difference between the two means nothing. Considering propaganda as it really is in its totality, tests are impossible.[5]

---

[4] For example, as long as one cannot interrogate Nazis in Germany, one will interrogate prisoners.

[5] In "Le Dynamisme des groupes," *Revue d'Action Populaire* (1958), Badin stresses very convincingly the problem of "psychic continuity": the use of experimental groups assumes "ahistoric" groups, without a past and without context. From the reactions of such groups can one really draw conclusions that apply to real groups that have a past and are tied to the whole range of institutions in their society?

The problem itself defies definition. Also, the methods used to analyze the effects generally are inadequate. One method has been used frequently by American researchers: its object being to determine whether some propaganda instrument could change the opinions or prejudices of a group. Students were divided into two or three groups, with one of them designated a control group untouched by propaganda. The nature of their opinion on some specific question, such as that of race, was then established. Then the groups to be influenced were subjected to carefully prepared psychological manipulations via pamphlets, films, conferences, and so on. After the period of propaganda, an evaluation of opinion changes by ordinary methods was attempted, with the control group as basis of comparison. The evaluation of opinion took place twice—once immediately after the manipulations, once after some time, in order to establish the persistence of the modifications. These experiments have been described by many American writers. Generally, the conclusion has been that such propaganda had very little effect, that patterns and stereotypes were little changed, and that group opinion remained unchanged. Moreover, the slim results that were obtained disappeared rapidly.

I claim that such results mean nothing because the method is totally inadequate. Its shortcomings are numerous. First, the question under experimentation is the experimenter's choice—it is not a burning, explosive question of immediate concern. I have demonstrated, however, that propaganda can only work in the face of profound *immediacy*. Second, such propaganda efforts always employ very modest means (some pamphlets, one or two films), have no real orchestration, and are of short and inadequate duration. Evidently, we cannot expect to eradicate a race prejudice after a few days or weeks of propaganda, no matter how well made. Moreover, such experiments take place in a vacuum, in that the individuals subjected to them are cut off from their normal milieu. The normal conditions under which propaganda works are in no way reproduced. Such propaganda takes place in no sociological context. Then, there is no crowd effect, no psychological tension, no interaction of individuals caught in a mass and exciting each other—the experiment is shared by only a few, in a laboratory atmosphere. These conditions are the very opposite of propaganda. There is no participation in a general action, in a general line, in party activities. There is no tie to any organization. There is no call for action, nor any chance of engaging in any—but those are essential elements of propaganda. Finally, these laboratory experiments mean nothing because they do not reproduce the true milieu of real propaganda or its methods. They are at best attempts at partial influence, and it is completely useless to draw conclusions from them about the efficacy of real propaganda. To believe otherwise reveals considerable ignorance of the phenomenon.

On the other hand, attempts at analyzing public opinion have been made. Here the researcher at least deals with real situations. A whole collection of devices has been used for such research, which, however, has been carried out in diffuse and fragmentary fashion. In this way researchers in the United States have analyzed votes by groups, localities, classes; have systematically analyzed the mail received by a newspaper after a particularly significant article; have made surveys in theaters and movie houses in connection with propaganda films, particularly war films. In the last-named instances, various expressions of approval and disapproval were scientifically collected. They have even tried to measure noises in theaters by using special equipment (noise meters, applause meters), but this turned out to be a failure because the spectators soon realized what was going on and modified their reactions. In principle, it is necessary that the analyst be completely hidden and neutral. Finally, certain words and the significance attributed to them before and after a propaganda campaign were analyzed. Of course, such analysis must be carried out in extremely diversified milieux and places. The use of "key words" is in fact very revealing with respect to unconscious absorption of propaganda.

In such surveys the public must be unaware of the research being done. However, when the method of "participants" is used, the subjects of the experiment know they are under observation. The participating observer must live in a given group, which should be localized and as unaware of him as possible; and he must be progressively assimilated into the group. He learns to know it inside out and becomes integrated into it. His primary task is to observe daily events as an anthropologist observes primitive peoples, and these facts bearing on behavior allow the researcher to classify successive effects of various forms of propaganda. This will yield a complete pattern of individual

attitudes and of changes in these attitudes within the social structure. This is probably the best and most precise method. From
the limited results it produces, certain conclusions are warranted.
But a major obstacle stands in the way: trained teams of observers
are needed—real social scientists, not partisans of a propaganda.
These people must be well paid for a long time for (apparently) doing nothing. In reality, only the State can employ this
method.

Finally, there is a much easier and faster method, such as surveys by Roper or Gallup. This method can be employed frequently
and yields reasonably sure, fast results. But it presumes genuine
education on the part of the public. The public must not only
understand the meaning of these services and lend itself to them,
but it must also be without fear. For this reason, the usefulness
of surveys to establish propaganda effects is limited; it cannot
be used in a totalitarian system because the connection between
the propaganda-makers and the police is well known in such
regimes and because the public cannot respond properly to the
questions asked. Similarly, surveys cannot gauge the effects of
terror propaganda because the public will be intimidated. Finally,
surveys cannot be used on minorities that feel oppressed: prole-
tarians, Negroes, other racial or religious minorities. Nevertheless,
surveys can evaluate what François Bourricaud calls the elasticity
of propaganda, which is a sure indication of its effectiveness.

Vast propaganda sectors, therefore, cannot be measured with
the help of surveys. Moreover, surveys give much better results
in connection with "instantaneous" propaganda—*i.e.*, during periods of intense propaganda (elections) or crisis. They reveal
much less regarding sociological propaganda, propaganda promulgating a myth, or in periods of calm. In fact, surveys must ask
precise questions, offer limited choices, and refer to some localized
common experience.

Surveys are helpless in periods of calm and with regard to
propaganda's broader aims: at best they can discern certain tendencies or establish whether some word is "more" or "less" on the
public's mind. But they cannot penetrate the myth whose hold
on it the public does not recognize. There, psychoanalytic surveys would be needed, but such research can be conducted only
on individuals.

Even from another point of view, such opinion surveys, designed to reveal propaganda influences, are very uncertain in their results. They rest on two presuppositions that I consider very debatable. The first is that propaganda's principal aim is to *modify* public opinion, to replace some current of opinion, to manipulate individual opinions. But that certainly is not accurate. There can be profound propaganda effects that do not manifest themselves outwardly by changes of public opinion on one subject or another. The second presupposition is that surveys reveal the composition of public opinion, and that such composition is the only thing that counts. But in reality another equally important element needs to be studied: the intensity of opinion. That intensity cannot be established by opinion analysis, despite all weighted indices, the multiplicity of questions, the cross-questions, and so on. It must be remembered that two groups of the same size in a society may be entirely different with regard to the intensity of their opinions and the degree of their integration in society. For example, in 1948, to say that there were 25 percent Communists and 25 percent anti-Communists in France (to take the simplest possible example) means nothing. For on one side, there are militants who are ready to throw themselves headlong into action and to sacrifice themselves, and—what is even more important—are well-organized; whereas on the other, there are unorganized people who have no intention of emerging from their passive individual state. And it must be understood that propaganda operates increasingly on the qualitative level, in the domain of intensities.

Any propaganda that had not changed a single vote, but had pushed a revolutionary group to white heat or diminished the conviction and devotion of another group, would have success without an opinion analysis being able to register it. Conversely, such analysis might register opinion changes—for example, among the undecided—which appear in the wake of a "one-shot" propaganda, but which ultimately surprise the propagandist by failing to last.

Finally, I must raise a last question. Opinion surveys concern themselves with public opinion and must address themselves to the entire group whose opinion is to be analyzed. For this reason, surveys operate with representative samples. Yet, an aggressive propaganda will not necessarily address itself to all of public opinion. It will take into its sights only a particular sub-group, fraction, or tendency. Because propaganda has precise objectives, it does not concern just anybody. To analyze whether such selective propaganda is effective, it would be necessary to analyze only the target group or the particular tendency that was to be modified. But, generally, it will not be known which sector will be attacked by the propagandist, and when it is known, it will be too late. For all these reasons, public opinion survey methods are not really adequate to measure the effectiveness of propaganda.

Analyses of individual cases are being made concerning individuals who have been subjected to propaganda. In the wake of World War II, American and British psychologists and sociologists undertook a large job: they made studies of German soldiers who surrendered in 1945 in an attempt to determine whether American propaganda, aimed at persuading them to surrender, had been effective (Shils and Janowitz, Dicks, Gurfein and Janowitz on German PWs); studies of German civilians in 1946, to determine whether they had been affected by Nazi propaganda (Padover); studies of captured elite troops in the United States and Canada in 1945 (Hicks); studies of refugees from the U.S.S.R., to determine the effects of Soviet propaganda (Inkeles). A series of investigations in the American army, undertaken in 1942-3, to determine whether American soldiers were conscious of "war aims" must be included in these research projects. Most of these investigations had negative results—*i.e.*, they showed that propaganda had had no decisive effect. But I feel that *all* these studies suffered from inadequate methods.

First of all, concerning Germans interrogated by the British and Americans—what credibility can be accorded to statements by men who are prisoners, vanquished, accused, who have gone through tremendous ordeals and who are in the presence of their masters, their victors, their eventual judges? To think that these men spoke the truth simply because they were promised anonymity or impunity is childish. Precisely because they had lived under Nazism, and even more because they had accepted it, they could not give the least credence to such guarantees—the Nazi regime had used the same stratagems to uncover and eliminate its enemies. These prisoners necessarily lived in a universe of combat, of lies, of commitment, whereas the researchers placed themselves—and wanted to place the prisoners—in a liberal, unconstrained, frank universe: this misunderstanding vitiated all the findings of these investigations. Without being paradoxical, one might even say that the more these investigations showed that the prisoners had not been affected by propaganda, the more they really proved that the men were still living the lives of propagandees.

On the other hand, how can one believe in the sincerity of responses concerning a man's Nazis convictions in Germany after 1945, when Nazism had been outlawed and Nazis were being eliminated from the German administration? With regard to prisoners, how can one fail to see that for a PW of one or two years, no longer subjected to propaganda, his position vitiates all conclusions one can possibly draw from such inquiries?[6] Because only 15 percent express Nazi convictions, 10 percent express feelings favorable to Nazism, 50 percent are indifferent, and 25 percent are hostile, to assume that a mass of individuals subjected for ten years to Hitler's propaganda retained their critical capacity vis-à-vis the regime is to draw conclusions that are entirely uncertain, despite the enormous labor undertaken.

The most serious fault of all these investigations seems to be the following: they preserve the old notion that the effect of propaganda manifests itself in clear, conscious opinions and that the propagandee will respond in a specific way according to the propagandist's slogans. But this is less and less true. One must understand that just as there is dissociation between private and public opinion, there is dissociation between opinion and action. Propaganda works in that direction. It is not because some individual holds clearly defined Nazi or Communist *convictions* that he will *behave* for the benefit of the Nazi or Communist regime. On the contrary. It is increasingly understood that those who have clear, conscious convictions are potential heretics who discuss action in the light of doctrine. Conversely, because a man cannot clearly express his war aims does not mean he will comport himself less well on the battlefield if he is properly indoctrinated with propaganda—or fail to exterminate Jews just because he is

---

[6] Some of these authors are aware of the shortcomings of this method: for example, Gurfein says that German prisoners were not familiar with the methods of surveys, were inhibited by their long subjection in Germany, and so on. Nevertheless, these authors still use these methods and draw conclusions from their findings.

not an articulate racist,[7] or fail to be a devoted militant because he cannot formulate the dogma of the class struggle. What matters to the propagandist is to have a good soldier, a devoted militant, a pogromist. Thus, to declare that 50 percent of German PW's were indifferent to Nazism because of their negative response to trick questions is to bypass the problem. What is important to know is *what they did*. Did they participate in Jew hunts and the destruction of ghettos, in executions of civilians, bombardments of cities, torpedoing of hospital ships, and so on? If they did these things, they did so because they had a motivation far stronger than their opinions, one that will not be revealed by a questionnaire of this sort.

Similarly, to conclude that propaganda had little effect on the German soldiers and left them on a private, individualized level merely because they were much more interested in the fate of their families than in anything else seems to me to have little relation to reality. When the average militant is captured, is out of action and protected against propaganda, he will obviously return to his personal problems. This does not mean that he was not under the influence of propaganda when he was plunged into action. On the contrary—as I have shown, the cessation of propaganda leads the propagandee into "privatization."

With regard to the inquiries of American soldiers, they suffered from the same faults. To conclude that there is a contrast between war propaganda and individual opinion because less than 20 percent can name the officially promulgated war aims, less than 10 percent know the basic points of the Atlantic Charter, and more than 50 percent define their war aims in purely personal terms—is to think very negligently. For the aim of propaganda obviously was to obtain the most courageous and efficient soldiers, and not necessarily those inspired by a moral ideal.

---

[7] A good example of such opposites is the following: In connection with the trial of a Jewish defendant (Boricki), many judiciary chroniclers wrote anti-Semitic reports, as revealed by Mrs. Hesse (*Evidences*, 1959). But *none* of these writers was a *racist*. On the contrary, they were anti-Nazis, and they strongly protested their friendship for the Jews. Still, their reports were what they were. While writing them and trying to explain the actions of the defendant by his origins, the writers actually adhered to the stereotypes, images, and prejudices of anti-Semitic propaganda, which had remained fully unconscious, but still determined their actions, though on the conscious level they were absolutely not anti-Semites. And when they became aware of what they had done, they insisted they had never meant to say that.

Propaganda played on the most elementary drives to make a man engage wholeheartedly in combat. In that, it was effective— even if it could not express itself in ideological "war aims." Or it restricted itself to the formulation and dissemination of war aims. Then it was a childish form of propaganda that could not move anybody, and one must not be surprised if individuals formulated their own war aims differently. Moreover, attention must also be paid to the effect in depth that occurs when these war aims (liberty, war against barbarism, etc.) are absorbed. This effect can be very active but will not necessarily be expressed by the propagandee *in the same terms* as by the newspapers. Differences between propagandistic formulas and their repetition by the propagandee do not mean that he fails to act.

It must be concluded that this entire research method cannot measure propaganda effectiveness.

Finally, a word on efforts to measure tangible effects: shifting of votes, increased sales in the wake of an advertising campaign, joining a party as a result of a membership drive. This is all very limited. Political parties always make such efforts to evaluate their actions. They try to interpret all indications and to accord propaganda the part that it played. A very good example of this form of analysis has been furnished by Sergei Tchakhotin[8] after studying the 1932 election results in Germany; in that study the effects of Social Democratic propaganda in Hesse emerge very clearly. Then there are the research studies by American political parties to explain the 1952 elections, and particularly the shift of Catholic votes away from the Democrats. This was apparently the result of a variety of propaganda efforts; propaganda on un-American activities, nationalist propaganda, military and even religious propaganda (hopes of seeing an American pope). Eisenhower tied the struggle against Communism to religious nationalism (religion is the counterweight to tyranny). This apparently greatly influenced Catholics.

Finally, the Communist party, after having made propaganda in some district or village, evaluates the results by the number of petitions, collections, signatures, and so on. But no real significance can be attributed to such research operations. The criticism of Tchakhotin's analysis is well known, as is the attribu-

---

[8] *The Rape of the Masses* (New York: Alliance Book Co.; 1940).

tion of entirely other causes than Social Democratic propaganda to the election defeat in Hesse. Nothing certain emerges from such analyses.

Other attempts at measuring effects are being tried by commercial firms in regard to advertising. The object is different, but the methods are related. Commercial firms are interested in immediate results in order to learn whether it is advantageous to advertise, whether advertising produces "side" benefits, when they should advertise (before or after launching a new product), at what time of the year, how far to go, how not to overshoot the mark. At best, all this can emerge only from analyses of past effects.

But we must also ask *who* is reached by advertising. There are thousands of ways of looking for this—loss leaders, free samples, questionnaires, and so on. But they all disregard the influence on the unconscious, the most important part. This education of reflexes and instilling of habits is propaganda's true effect, and cannot be gauged by direct inquiry, but only by the massive participation it evokes. What counts is to assess the total effect of advertising. In the commercial world it will be measured in money; the cost of advertising is compared with the returns. Generally, advertising costs are between 5 percent and 20 percent of the sales price. If they exceed 20 percent, one may doubt that the returns justify the added expense, but there are exceptions when such costly campaigns are accompanied by a great improvement in the quality of the product—for example, advertising doubled the sales of the French cigarette *Gitanes* in one year (1938). The problem of return is central in commercial affairs.

The State does not always have to count propaganda costs and limit them.[9] In fact, the aim frequently exceeds simple questions of money. If the object is to gain 10 percent more votes in order to marshal unanimity behind some economic program, stimulate energies, eliminate an opponent's psychological resistance, influence foreign public opinion—all this can be well measured, and the importance of the démarche is such that money is spent without being counted. In other situations, the State fre-

---

[9] It is easy to see the disproportion between the enormous sums expended and the returns in the cases of Nazi Germany, the U.S.S.R., and also the Americans during the war (the effects of the three billion leaflets showered on the German army between June 1944 and March 1945 were obviously not in proportion to the effort made).

quently cannot even try to measure the propaganda returns; for example, in wartime, propaganda directed to an enemy cannot be measured by its repercussions (feed-back). In any event, if the psychological shock succeeds, it must remain hidden, for otherwise the propagandees would immediately be arrested by their own police and all propaganda effect would stop. Besides, if a government knows that some foreign propaganda is effective, it will make appropriate counter-propaganda.

To sum up this analysis of the inadequacy of the various methods designed to evaluate the effectiveness of propaganda, let us add the following observations:

1. Most sociologists and politicians consider the mathematical method the most exact and efficient. But this method seems to me not just debatable, but wrong. The mathematical methods (statistics, etc.) can be applied only within very narrow limits, and to problems that generally have had to be taken out of context. Most sociological phenomena defy this method. The desire to reduce a situation to precise figures presumes a threefold prior operation:

a. The removal of the fact to be quantified from its psychological, religious, sentimental, historic contexts and its removal from the individual's *Weltanschauung* as a whole.

b. The reduction of the phenomenon to its simplest state, by elimination of all complexities and subsidiary aspects— which may actually be the most important.

c. Consideration of the external phenomena only, though they may be merely extensions of more important, different factors. But quantification must restrict itself to external aspects, behavior, visible attitudes, and so on.

This would be barely acceptable if it were admitted that the results are rather thin and relatively insignificant. But because they are expressed in figures, and because we have a maniacal faith in the exactness of mathematics, it is claimed that such methods produce the truth itself, and that the rest is literature. But it is precisely the rest that is most important, so long as we do not have a total "robot" image of man. It is the rest that is important, so long as we do not discount man altogether, as do the Kinsey Report and others. What is particularly serious in this connection is that the socio-psychologists, who use such mathematical methods, are quick to claim that what cannot be reached by their methods does not exist. But I have tried to show that such methods are inadequate for the problems studied here, and I must add that the results attained and the figures arrived at never go beyond what is already obvious and merely common sense. To prove with figures, after long statistical inquiries, that women are more receptive to emotional propaganda than men is hardly an astounding revelation. Common sense also tells us that man has a certain psychic stability that cannot be altered radically by propaganda; figures, charts, and ratios add little to that.

2. My second observation is that these so-called scientific methods are extremely partial. *All* analyses of effectiveness with regard to propaganda that I have seen reveal an unconscious bias. To give just one example: Most American studies on the relative effectiveness of Nazi and American propaganda conclude that Nazi propaganda did not have a profound effect on the Germans, that Nazi propaganda in no way whatever reached American opinion, but that American propaganda had certain tactical effects on German soldiers, inducing them to surrender in 1945. But Goebbels also had some rather thorough, systematic studies made that invalidate the first two claims. With regard to the third, even the American specialists themselves are in disagreement (Shils and Warburg).

The psychologists and sociologists who have held that propaganda had little effect *all* share certain views based on the choice of values. They are humanists who believe in the resolute character of human nature, the permanence of personality, the irrational but stable foundations of psychic life, and who (unconsciously) refuse to admit that men can be entirely mastered, dominated, conditioned. Or they are convinced democrats who believe in the democratic presupposition that the citizen must be able to retain autonomy of will and judgment because without it elections would mean nothing, elected representatives would represent nothing, and there could no longer be talk of the sovereignty of the people.

It is completely acceptable to have such a view of man, but it is a metaphysical view. It is perfectly acceptable that a man should remain an optimist and idealist, and for that reason declare that propaganda is not very formidable and make it an act of faith that man will always come out on top. But people should not claim to have reached such conclusions by scientific analysis, statistics, and sociological experiments.[1]

3. Propaganda's effectiveness—or the absence thereof—cannot be established by such methods. It can be done only by observation of general phenomena, by the best possible use of our general knowledge of man and his socio-political environment, by a mixture of judgments of approximation, and by the best possible use of the clearest of reasons. This cannot lead to figures or to strict certainties, but it yields certain probabilities and, above all, precludes the massive errors into which the exact methods lead us.

2. Ineffectiveness of Propaganda

In the following we will look at four problems connected with propaganda's ineffectiveness.

On the basis of general considerations about the psychic life of the individual, many psychologists, particularly the Americans, reach the conclusion that propaganda is ineffective. I will select two out of many examples. The first concerns the stability of stereotypes. Most observers (Young, Krech and Crutchfield, Mac-Dougall) think it practically impossible to change stereotypes by psychological manipulation. I agree quite readily, without investigating whether these stereotypes are spontaneous or produced by propaganda. It should be added that these stereotypes are equally impervious to personal experience and hard facts, and that if propaganda cannot budge them, information can budge them even less. But it cannot be denied that certain stereotypes are the result of propaganda. They acquire the same stability and force as the others. For example, the stereotypes of the Communist ideal, proletarian Messianism, and the identification of the U.S.S.R. with peace and revolution (propaganda had little trouble associating these two contradictory terms) produced

---

[1] Let us also remember that the American socio-psychologists are not unanimous in their estimates of effectiveness. In general, one can see the full success of all forms of propaganda of justification: the individual always firmly believes in whatever justifies him. I would also like to suggest a relatively simple experiment: study Lenin's propaganda principles and apply them to the actions of the Soviet leaders. The results that they seek by propaganda almost always emerge very clearly and are generally obtained.

by propaganda, have easily withstood the impact of such shocking facts as the Nazi-Soviet Pact, the deportations from the Baltic
countries and the Ukraine (1944–5), and the Hungarian massacre
(1956). Actually, such massive facts do shake opinion for a brief
time and momentarily efface stereotypes, but after a few weeks
the fact is relegated to the past. It becomes engulfed in explica-
tions, its obvious significance disappears, and the old stereotype,
completely unchanged, resumes its place and vigor. For example,
Sartre's personal evolution lasted from October 1956 to January
1957. How can one, then, conclude from the existence of stereotypes that propaganda is ineffective?

On the other hand, the non-relation between opinion and action
needs to be considered here once again. For example, in a recent
struggle over public schools, I found the following: Some of my
friends mouthed the stereotypes of support for public schools—
unity of youth, independence of the faculty, intellectual quality,
and so on. They expressed their views very clearly—but sent their
own children to private schools. This is not unusual. But I have
shown that propaganda is principally interested in shaping action
and behavior, and with little thought. For this reason, propaganda's comparative inability to modify stereotypes does not permit the conclusion that it is ineffective so long as it is able to
obtain, beyond opinions, irrational acts; nevertheless, I will admit
this relative inability. The same holds true for my second example:
pre-existing attitudes.

The question of attitudes is now considered fundamental. It can
be defined in different ways:

Krueger states that an attitude is "a residue of experience that
conditions and controls activity. A mental organization that predisposes an individual to a certain type of activity vis-à-vis people
or situations is installed."

Young says that "attitude is a form of unconscious habit that
expresses profound tendencies in a drive toward action."[2]

Krech and Crutchfield consider attitude "a durable organization
of the emotive, perceptive and cognitive motivations related to
one aspect of the world."

These definitions suffice to show that on the basis of such con-

[2] We have shown how, from that point on, the individual "selects" this or that
information and rejects this or that stimulus, or how the individual escapes all
attacks on his presuppositions.

siderations attitude is a personal factor leading to action. Of course, man's personality does not consist of one attitude, but of a complex of integrated and interrelated attitudes. The way in which an individual reacts to a stimulus depends on the entire pattern of his attitudes. Whether the stimulus is a private or public event makes no difference; nor does it make any difference whether the stimulus is accidental or the result of a plan. Consequently, a person in the grip of propaganda will react according to his pre-existing attitudes and to the degree that these attitudes lead him to react. Therefore propaganda must base itself on existing tendencies to have the greatest effect. If it goes against ingrained attitudes, it cannot have any effect.[3] MacDougall says, for example, that Baptist propaganda does not reach conscious Catholics and that Western propaganda does not reach convinced Communists. Still, there are defections: some Catholics do become Baptists and vice versa. The temptation then will be to say that their previous attitudes were only superficial. But that is not serious reasoning. It is like the argument of predestination that will say of a Christian who has committed a trespass: this proves that he did not have proper faith to begin with.

Doob goes further: "Any response to the stimulus of propaganda depends entirely on the past experiences of the individual. Propaganda limits itself to evoking a response he has already learned. This response was already part of his personality. . . . The propagandist must follow the current of public opinion." In Doob's view, if one were to examine whether propaganda has had an effect, one would have to individually examine those who have obeyed propaganda, in order to see whether they already had attitudes pushing them toward action in a given direction. Doob is sure they had.

This view has been criticized with good arguments by Miotto, who reasons as follows:

1. How could Goebbels's propaganda keep the Germans in line

---

[3] Many experiences on which these statements are based are very debatable. For example, Cartwright claims that the enormous propaganda in the United States, between 1941 and 1945, to buy Defense Bonds did not change attitudes. In fact, the reasons given by purchasers remained the same for four years despite the diversity of those reasons: individual motivations did not change. Actually, this proves that people need simple reasons for their acts. The propaganda reasons were too complicated. If a man has a clear reason for doing something, why should he adopt other complicated and vapid reasons for doing the same thing?

and fighting to the last minute against all evidence and feelings of fear and their desire for peace?

2. How, on the other hand, can one explain the famous "undecided" in elections and on all political questions? The undecided do not make their decisions in consonance with pre-existing tendencies, but according to where they are being pushed by propaganda.

3. The importance of pre-existing attitudes may be valid in peacetime when the crowds are not subjected to psychic tensions and social groups are stable. Propaganda must adapt itself to their habits in such times. But inside a society in a state of disintegration, with considerable class changes and high nervous tension, propaganda need not move in traditional patterns; it can interfere brutally and carry the decision beyond all accustomed considerations.

4. Finally, how can one explain the violent twists and turns of propaganda, as, for example, in the case of the Communists or the Nazis? Attitudes have not the time to follow suit, and yet, in most cases, the people follow. It cannot be said that they do this through obedience. In following propaganda, the people believe it.

Let us add here a thought by Stoetzel. He has evolved a theory that a person can have two opinions on the same subject—his private opinion, which he keeps carefully to himself or expresses only to a very small number of persons, and his "public" opinion, which he shares with his group. Propaganda uses this coexistence of two opinions. By doing so, it can "make an individual take an action completely different from the action that would be sparked by his private opinion." But the expression of public opinion is not necessarily based on pre-existing elements. It springs much more frequently from circumstances, external currents, and so on.

Finally, two remarks: Obviously, a pre-existing attitude exists in the face of *one* propaganda act. If one makes *one* speech, or publishes *one* article, the response to it will obviously be conditioned by people's prior positions. But that is not propaganda. Does anyone believe that pre-established attitudes will resist a real propaganda that surrounds the individual without pause from morning to night, from childhood to old age, in all that he reads, sees, hears, without giving him respite, a moment to pause, think, catch his breath?

Under such conditions, pre-existing attitudes will fade quickly.

They cannot resist the psychological bombardment of a real propaganda campaign.

Even if one thinks that such a description applies only to propaganda in totalitarian countries, we must remember what we have said about sociological propaganda in other countries.

Thus, this theory (that propaganda is dependent on pre-existing attitudes) does not mean much. On that basis, no psychological explanation of propaganda is possible.

All that needs to be preserved of this theory is that propaganda must always use existing tendencies, as I have already said. But pre-existing attitudes are only a temporary factor of secondary importance, which needs to be considered only at the *inception* of a propaganda campaign.

Some have claimed to find proof of the ineffectiveness of propaganda elsewhere. Propaganda, they say, generally leads to indifference. When an individual in a democracy is placed between two propagandas, there is no reason for him to decide Yes or No, and the propagandas cancel each other out. The example most frequently given is an election campaign. With regard to totalitarian countries, where the individual is assailed by excessively heavy propaganda, it is said that he knows that he is being lied to and no longer listens, escaping into political absent-mindedness. He closes up and can no longer be reached. Examples of this are said to be the attitudes of the Soviet people vis-à-vis Stalinist propaganda, or Hungarian opinion; according to a 1958 survey: "The majority of the respondents were favorable toward Kadar" (obviously!), but it was also noted that "Hungarians are primarily interested in their personal and local problems, and very little interested in political and international problems." This, it is claimed, shows propaganda's ineffectiveness.

In the same direction, the observations of Lazarsfeld: In the United States, the FCC demands that every private radio and TV station devote some hours to civic programs. But, says Lazarsfeld, the results are not very encouraging; the listeners and viewers turn off their sets—"the difficulty is not to make the horse drink, but to lead it to the water. . . . It even has happened that out of sheer contrariness the listener reinforced the prejudices and opinions he was asked to surrender." This well-known effect is called *boomerang*, and incidentally it often is cited in support of claims of the ineffectiveness of propaganda.

But these examples are not very convincing. We have studied the phenomenon of indifference in the case of unilateral propaganda in totalitarian countries and have found that it is not a failure but a success of propaganda. With regard to the alleged ineffectiveness of two contradictory election propagandas, I will limit myself to three remarks, complementary to what has already been said on this subject:

1. Those who assert this independence on the part of the listener faced with opposing publicity campaigns are always intellectuals, who look at the phenomenon from a distance; moreover, they are always men who already have a fixed opinion and refuse to let themselves be influenced.

2. It must be remembered how difficult it is to gauge the effectiveness and intensity of a propaganda. Can we really speak of two equal propagandas? It is hard to believe. Incidentally, this does not mean that the more intense and better made propaganda will win *automatically* and *in short order*. Even election propaganda can have long-term effects if it is made systematically. In France, between 1921 and 1936, the Communist party made progress mainly as a result of election propaganda, and the same was true for the Nazi party during 1929–33. It is, therefore, almost impossible to claim that just because there are two propagandas, they cancel each other out. This common sense objection is entirely superficial. Let us add that, in any case, he who fails to make propaganda will be defeated immediately. This at least shows that propaganda is needed.

3. Let us return to the example of the American public's not being interested in civic programs on the radio. But are such programs propaganda? We know that propaganda's first requisite is to be heard, to excite individuals and make them look or listen. It must, therefore, be assumed, at the very least, that the techniques employed are not the best. Let us look at the subject of the broadcasts: the opening of a new hospital, with a full description of its services; the opening of a new public library, with speeches on the value of reading matter; conferences on alcoholism, friendship between peoples . . . It was not necessary to make a survey here; simply by looking at the list I could have told Mr. Lazarsfeld that 75 percent of the listeners would turn off the program. Here we have information that may be perfectly honest but is ineffective. This is, as demonstrated elsewhere, an

example of the great weakness on the part of information vis-à-vis propaganda. The latter, not claiming to be educational, hurls people into burning actuality, appeals to everything that excites them. Then they do not turn off the program. The health bar that sells fruit juice is evidently less attractive than the bar that sells liquor.

Marxism, too, readily takes a critical attitude with regard to the effectiveness of propaganda. I will offer only one example. Mao Tse-tung, in his report on the internal differences between Communist countries, made in February 1951 (published in June 1957), declared that one cannot force a people to renounce idealism or to believe in Marxism. Propaganda, he said, can "force" people to become Marxist, but is ineffective in that case. Mao added that "one must use democratic methods such as public discussion, criticism, persuasion, appropriate education." That sounds like a program of Human and Public Relations. But one must remember that the aim is, nevertheless, fixed and precise: the people must become Marxist. Mao rejects only certain methods of psychological pressure and the most elementary forms of propaganda. But what is "appropriate education?" It is to teach children a Marxist catechism, to give them a Marxist conception of the world in history and science. What is public discussion and criticism? Who will conduct the sessions if not a leader who knows where they should lead and who will imperceptibly lead his speakers to that point in the course of the discussion. What is persuasion other than one of propaganda's most current forms? Mao describes only the more modern and personalized forms of propaganda. With regard to the democracies, we know from the experience of group dynamics how false is the assertion that propaganda is ineffective (see Whyte, Sorokin, etc.). To put it differently, all that matters is what one means by propaganda. Besides, even if it were impossible for propaganda to get people to believe in Marxism, propaganda was very successful in China in making the people act in accord with the government's wishes. The "great leaps forward" and the communes are admirable examples of propaganda's efficiency.

To support the thesis of propaganda's ineffectiveness, many refer to great historic examples. For example, American sociologists were forced to acknowledge that American propaganda failed when it tried to make the Germans resist their government in 1943-5. In particular, the German civilian population continued to resist despite bombings and food shortages. Industrial production remained at a surprisingly high level despite far-reaching destruction; morale did not disintegrate in any way (see Warburg). Propaganda specialists thought that morale would break down after the Normandy invasion, but the will to fight persisted. And all this despite strong psychological action. Ergo—propaganda was not effective.

But one should perhaps look at the other side of the problem and examine what caused the high German morale, what produced the resistance that led a people to fight until the very end of its material means for at least a year, without hope, when twenty-eight years earlier *the same people* gave in while its army was in less danger than in 1944. There can be no doubt that it was the result of Nazi education—in other words, propaganda, propaganda that exalted sacrifice, war, military values, faith in the Führer, the common weal, the superiority and invincibility of the German race. Such propaganda had begun fifteen years earlier, *i.e.*, had had time to take effect. American propaganda that began to penetrate only in 1943 could not stem the tide; it had no time. The general morale, resting on propaganda—and not the survival of cadres and groups, as Shils's microscopic analysis would have it—led to the German resistance;[4] for at least four months before the end of the war, communications were cut off, the police and the party exercised pressures only very sporadically, the ad-

---

[4] This is the conclusion of Gurfein and Janowitz, who showed, for example, that from June 1944 to April 1945 more than 60 percent of German soldiers still retained their faith in Hitler, and that in February 1945, 40 percent believed that Germany could still win the war. These authors concluded that it was useless to attack the German soldier on ideological grounds because he was protected by virtue of being a propagandee. But, in contrast, there is the explosive study by Shils, which attempts to show that German propaganda had little effect, and that he found such values as honor, fatherland, and so on existed where small groups, and particularly military groups, had succeeded in surviving. To the extent that an individual is satisfied with his small group, he cannot be attacked, and his resistance to outside force will not spring from propaganda. This interpretation (Shils's) conflicts in my view with basic considerations. With regard to small groups, why were there such great differences, some groups dissolving without apparent reason, and so on? There is a basic problem here: the morale of the group. And that morale, precisely, is the result of propaganda. If a newly turned anti-Nazi is judged by his fellows, a transposition of the importance of slogans takes place on the personal level: ideological unity and "morale" then constitute the unifying force of the primary group. If, conversely, we see an individual's morale collapse quickly when he is separated from his group, that is (except for other obvious reasons) because propaganda is a mass phenomenon, so that the isolated individual *ipso facto* ceases to be a propagandee. Thus Shils is right, but stops halfway. Propaganda is present in a combat group.

ministration no longer functioned. If the people, and not just the combat groups studied by Shils, resisted, it was not because they were surrounded by official pressure, but because they had been propagandized in depth. And that also rendered them immune to American propaganda.

A second and classic example: Hungary. From the moment of the Hungarian Revolution in 1956, it was said that Communist propaganda had failed: even though this propaganda had been going on for ten years, the people had retained their critical sense and had not been convinced. That was the standard argument. The Western bourgeoisie was delighted to welcome those anti-Communists, valiant fighters for the Free World. How great was the astonishment and the general covering up when it was discovered that these revolutionaries were almost all Communists, or at least Socialists. And the Hungarian refugees of 1945, almost all adherents of Horthy's regime, refused to have anything to do with the new arrivals, on the ground that they represented the extreme left. This is another propaganda success. Within ten years a population with a large majority of moderate rightists, an important moderate leftist group, and a small Communist minority (8 percent) was turned into an almost entirely Communist nation. I say "almost entirely," because the opponents of the regime who fled were also Communists who, even when beyond the reach of the police State, continued to say so though they knew that Communists were not popular in the countries to which they had gone. They had not revolted against a form of government or against Communism, but against a man, against excessive restrictions, against the presence of the Russians. This means that not just anything can be attained through propaganda and that only surface propaganda, tactical propaganda, had failed, whereas fundamental propaganda had succeeded. But it obviously is much more important to show that propaganda succeeded in transforming a nation into Communists than to show that it could not make them accept certain food restrictions.

Another example of the ineffectiveness of propaganda is Algeria.[5] It is true that psychological action directed at the Arabs generally fails. Very few fellaghas were persuaded by propaganda to lay down their arms and come over to the French side. The few cases in which this occurred do not seem to have been the result

---

[5] This was written in 1959, and is included unchanged.

of propaganda. Among "neutral" Arab populations, no great successes can be registered either, nor does pro-French sentiment seem to have increased. On the contrary. Therefore, it is said, propaganda was ineffective. But here one must make distinctions.

Let us say first that propaganda was quite effective with regard to the French groups. Young soldiers, often hostile to the war in Algeria in the beginning, changed their attitude after a few months there. This was not the exclusive result of psychological action, but it played its part and was related to other things, such as man's inclusion in groups, his participation in a state of mind—all things that I have shown to be closely related to propaganda. With respect to French civilians, propaganda was equally effective, and the events of May 13 cannot be explained without the careful psychological preparations that took place for the events of that day. The failure of propaganda toward the Arabs—aside from the fact that propaganda toward such groups is most difficult—must be attributed mainly to its extreme mediocrity and the shortcomings of its methods. Some meetings, usually conducted by young people without experience, a few pamphlets (some of which were well done), some phonograph records—who can expect to convince anybody of anything by such means? The failure of propaganda must also be attributed to the complete absence of both a usable ideology and subjects that could cause excitement or enthusiasm: nothing had been marshaled against the nationalist passion. There was no effective stimulus on any level. How can one claim to judge propaganda under such conditions? What happened in the camps can hardly be mentioned.[6] All that can be concluded from this failure is that propaganda cannot be improvised or made in just any fashion.[7]

---

[6] See "brainwashing," Appendix II.

[7] Here are some other well-known examples of failure of propaganda: Goebbels's propaganda of 1929 against the Young Plan; the 1945 mayorality elections in Boston; the 1948 Presidential elections in the United States; the psychological preparation for the Suez campaign (1956); the European Defense Community in France. But these failures were almost all the result of faulty judgment concerning the territory where propaganda was to be applied, or of the overwhelming power of an opponent.

3. Effectiveness of Propaganda

It is impossible, in my view, to establish precise measurements of the effectiveness or ineffectiveness of propaganda. In honesty, one can judge it only in conjunction with very broad facts and very general ideas. I shall give here some criteria of judgment, often very banal and simplistic, which permit the conclusion that propaganda is indeed effective.

First, some very general reasons deserve to be considered. The first is that today all politicians and all big businessmen agree that psychological action, propaganda, advertising, human relations, and public relations are indispensable and definitely produce results. Could one say that these men obey a new fashion, are victims of an illusion, or have not really thought about it? In view of the deliberate attempt on the part of some socio-psychologists to demonstrate that political men err when they "believe" in the effectiveness of propaganda, one might ask who is the real victim of illusions here. If we think of men motivated entirely by the desire for efficacy, like Lenin, or of businessmen entirely motivated by the desire for higher profits, it would be hard to admit that such people, who are very realistic, allow themselves to be taken in by illusions in this domain.

A second argument on the same order is the following: All those who have lived in a strongly propagandized environment and have been subjected to the effects of propaganda (while trying to remain unaffected), all those who have seen propaganda in massive action, are agreed that propaganda is effective. Those who deny it live in countries that are still liberal and not subjected to intense propaganda. Today hardly any Germans, Russians, or Algerians question the effectiveness of propaganda. Only those who see it from afar, who are not directly subjected to it, who do not witness opinion-changes caused by propaganda, who confound the brushfire of a McCarthy with the propaganda of a Goebbels, express doubts. Moreover—and this is characteristic—they do it to the same degree that they fail to see the true propaganda practiced on them. This explains why many American socio-psychologists deny the effectiveness of propaganda, but admit that of Public Relations and Human Relations: for these are precisely the form propaganda takes in the United States.

There, it is the only truly developed, systematized, and long-lasting form of propaganda.

We must now turn to some very general and broad facts that are open to various interpretations. First: How can the following developments be explained without an admission that opinion and behavior changes took place as a result of the use of mass media?

1. The attainment of consciousness on the part of the labor class between 1848 and 1917. Marx is perfectly right when he says that the actual condition of the proletariat is nothing unless the proletariat is aware of that condition; that such awareness is simultaneously the creator of the labor class and the revolutionary will, and that it cannot occur spontaneously or individually. It is the fruit of what the workers are told by certain intellectuals, the result of an "education"—in reality, of a propaganda. Propaganda, sometimes uncertain and searching for a way but effective in the long run, has led the working class to where it is now, and has done so by closely mixing action, education, mass meetings, and "propaganda" in the strict sense of the term, according to the formula that I have indicated as typical for propaganda in the broad sense.

2. The spread of the Socialist mentality in France between 1900 and 1950: How did this famous shift to the left come about? Why did the number of Socialist and, later, Communist votes increase constantly? Why were the Socialist reforms of the State and the economy effected without revolution? Who would question today the nationalization of certain enterprises, social security, paid vacations, and so on? A distinction must be made between those who vote Socialist and those—whose number is far greater—who are so imbued with Socialism that they no longer even recognize as Socialist what were considered to be purely Socialist demands fifty years ago. Here again we see a slow penetration by propaganda.

3. The revolutions of 1917 and 1933 are the results of propaganda, in the very words of those who made them. Lenin and Trotsky, Hitler and Goebbels said time and again that the success of their revolutions was the result of propaganda, which made the masses become adherents of a minority.

4. The spread of Communism and the Communization of the populations in the people's democracies and China are also the result of propaganda. Those populations are progressively trans-

formed into Communists by enlisting them in a psychological mass movement, by systematic education, and by involving them in certain actions designed for psychological ends. The problem of truth or of doctrinal persuasion is of no importance in the process.

5. The explosions of nationalism in the Cameroons, Algeria, Indochina, and so on cannot be explained except as results of propaganda. Their people were without historical or racial coherence, a common State, or a national existence. On the other hand, nationalism was a specific phenomenon of the Europe of the nineteenth century, contrary to the thesis that nationalism is a necessary historic "stage" between feudalism and socialism, a purely Marxist assertion not borne out by history. In reality, the colonial peoples saw in nationalism the image, the grandeur, the effectiveness of their victors, and adopted its form and passion to become victors in their turn—which is completely normal. But this reasoning on the part of some intellectuals had no reality, no force, no efficacy until that nationalist passion inflamed hearts, until there was the systematic *creation* of a national exaltation with regard to a nation that did not exist. This was done through propaganda.

I could cite other instances. In all, these facts are of infinitely greater importance in judging the effectiveness of propaganda than any analyses of a voting pattern or of the effects of a pamphlet. To be sure, for all these examples documentation is needed. For some of them, such documentation exists; in connection with others, research is being done. I cannot trace every element here. But I will say that my assertions are not gratuitous or lightly made. One qualification is essential to prevent misunderstanding: I do not mean to say that these developments were the result of *one* propaganda *only,* and even less of propaganda in the narrow sense of psychological manipulation of symbols. Of course, the Revolution of 1917 or the emergence of Algerian nationalism was a confluence of many factors. There were preexisting conditions, an evolution of events, a spontaneous evolution of opinions, the growth of some organizations and the decline of others, economic phenomena, and so on.

But these facts by themselves are incapable of producing such massive human movements as the labor movement of the Nazi revolution. What is *decisive* is the propaganda factor, which sets these developments into motion, coordinates them, makes people conscious of them. Obviously, propaganda does not exist by itself. But without it, nothing would happen. It really starts the engine. And once the movement is underway, propaganda keeps it going, directs it, and ensures its success. From a different point of view one can also see the importance of this fact if one realizes that no enterprise now is possible anywhere without psychological preparation, conditioning, persuasion, and so on. Every event in our society supposes the allegiance or approval of all, and such participation in mind or action can be obtained only by propaganda. The fact that it is utilized in so many different fields shows that our society is in the process of becoming a total society, *e.g.*, a society in which no single act can be a matter of indifference; every act and feeling assumes a political character; no act is purely personal. Not to participate in Hitler's *Winterhilfe* (winter collection for the poor), not to participate in the national enthusiasm in some new African State, not to take an interest in the problem of school systems in France in 1959, is no longer an individual act but a breaking of ties with community; and the community cannot function today unless its citizens are sufficiently integrated so that every reform, no matter what kind, is carried out by all, and assumes a political character. From there on, propaganda is necessary. At the same time, one must assert that the mechanism works this way and generally achieves its aim because propaganda is effective.

Is it necessary to remind the reader here of the phenomenon of advertising? I have said that one cannot draw general conclusions from its workings, but it seems impossible nowadays to deny that it is effective in its own sphere; I need not reiterate the examples found in all the books—about cigars smoked by gangsters in films or about cigarette-manufacturers who thought they had conquered the market, stopped advertising, and soon lost their sales. But I must give at least three indications. Even the careful reader, alert to exaggerations, must take seriously facts and examples given by Vance Packard, which testify to the public's enormous sensitivity to advertising. Second, every month new products appear for which there is no prior need, but which take their place in the market without much resistance. That is exclusively the result of propaganda. New needs are created from the day a new product appears. After a few months of getting used to a product, its absence will be felt because an effective need will have been created. But the need was created exclusively by advertising. If the product were presented without advertising, nobody would buy it. Third, the reappearance and rapid spread of advertising in the U.S.S.R. After the Communists had considered advertising to be a capitalist phenomenon, a non-productive expenditure, and so on, and after having abolished it as useless in a Socialist country, they have brought it back during the past ten years. It goes hand in hand with belief in production. We may be certain that when production will have increased further and produced new and more refined products, advertising will show an upsurge similar to that in the United States. Does this not show that advertising is really effective?

Let us now examine another field in which propaganda is effective: in private life, and in matters that seem entirely outside its field, but, nevertheless, show the individual's extraordinary sensitivity to propaganda.

Can it be said that propaganda affects an individual taken separately? If we accept Stoetzel's division between the rather superficial public opinions of an individual and the profound attitudes that remain with him, we might conclude that propaganda works on the former and not on the latter. This is the generally prevailing—and reassuring—view. The individual would be reached by propaganda only to the extent that he participates in public opinion (or to the extent that he is "massified"), and then only in the upper levels of his individual psychology, and only collectively at that. In this way, psychological effects would not transcend the effects of public opinion and would have no effect on the core of personality. Seeking mass effects, propaganda would determine only collective behavior, and that would show why propaganda has so little effect on private conduct.

Typical examples are propaganda against alcoholism or for a higher birth rate. Such propaganda, it is said, does not work because it deals with private matters. The stereotypes of health or national power, publicly accepted by everybody, should lead inevitably to respect for temperance and for large families, but they have not reduced alcoholism or increased the size of families. Ergo: propaganda, even if it succeeds in sparking specific collective actions, is incapable of affecting personality.

This is a facile analysis, but it does not seem to correspond to facts. First of all, it is not correct to say that in France the respect for temperance and large families is general; among the working class and the bourgeoisie, the general judgment that a large family is madness and gentle intoxication agreeable is at least as strong as that respect. What might be called the mentality of the *Canard Enchaîné* is surely that of the majority in this connection. And the stereotype of the bon vivant who enjoys his wine, plays around, and is not concerned with having children is certainly more powerful than the stereotype of the water-drinking family man.

But the anti-alcoholic propaganda posters in the Paris subways are slowly beginning to reach the individual. There are no actual figures as yet, but the protests by producers of wine and alcohol, addressed to the French Parliament, are a significant indication. To cause such excitement, effects on liquor consumption must have been felt. The same is true for propaganda in favor of a higher birth rate. One can no longer doubt that propaganda has had a profound effect on births. What really is curious is that there has been a considerable increase in births without a similar change in surface public opinion in favor of large families. It seems hardly debatable today that in Nazi Germany, in Fascist Italy, and in France since 1941, the increase in births resulted from propaganda.

In the same way that propaganda can work for a higher birth rate it can (contrary to what I myself believed until recently) also work for a lower one. The surprising experience in Japan is significant. It is well known that a country begins, spontaneously, to produce more children after a defeat. Japan, already very prolific before, was no exception to this rule: beginning in 1945 its birth rate increased rapidly. But it was quickly realized that this would lead to disaster. As a result, propaganda for a lower birth rate was launched in 1945. To be sure, in accord with what I have said many times, the campaign did not have an immediate effect. But propaganda conducted solidly for four years managed to show results in 1950. From 34.3 per thousand in 1947, the rate dropped to 29 in 1950, to 20 in 1954, and to 17.2 in 1957, a decline of 50 percent in ten years, which had never been seen before. Japan now has one of the world's lowest birth rates.[8] A striking

---

[8] "Outlook of Studies," in *Population Problems in Japan*, IV, 1959. It is true that since 1959 the birth rate has been increasing again.

aspect of this development is that birth control spreads faster in rural areas than in the cities.

A final example: since 1950 at least, there has been concern in France that there were too many students in the Arts and in Law, too few in Science and in Technology. But there was no change until it was decided that "a propaganda action should be undertaken with the parents, to direct their children toward the deficient areas" (November 1951). From that moment on, a change took place, even though the propaganda was not particularly coherent, insistent, or continuous. The propaganda launched in 1952 began to take hold in 1956: from 1956 until 1959 a shift of 25 percent of students in the desired direction took place.

It follows that even in his personal conduct the individual is very sensitive to propaganda in some domains. I think this leads to the conclusion that the same is true of political behavior. In fact, where the purchase of a product is concerned, the individual can rely on personal experience as to his needs, the value of the product, and so on. He can make comparisons before shopping; all this is on the level of his direct experience, a simple process.[9] Now, if he can be influenced in this domain (though only up to a point—he will not again buy products that turn out to be inferior), he can be influenced all the more on the level of economics or politics outside his range of personal experience, never simple, and always hard to compare. Similarly, where his private conduct is concerned—to have children or not, or what to make them study—the individual generally knows what he wants and obeys motivations that are truly personal and concern him closely. So, if he can be influenced even there, will he not be susceptible to being influenced on much more remote and exciting questions that concern him less directly?

Finally, to demonstrate further the extreme susceptibility of the individual, we must look at *rumors* and *fashion*—two closely linked phenomena. Every rumor that circulates has a certain effect. It is an amazing fact that rumors whose origins are not known have a small audience *in the beginning*, a large audience after some time. The farther away the source and the greater the

---

[9] But behavior has been effectively changed on this level. For example, a 32 percent increase in the consumption of slaughtered beef after a well-conducted campaign has been recorded. Similar success has been achieved in connection with fruit juices and cod-liver oil.

number of individuals who have passed it on, the more the objective fact loses importance and the more the rumor is believed by the multitudes who adhere to it. An individual does not remain unaffected by a rumor that is spontaneously circulated in his milieu by a growing number of persons. Obviously, he pays no attention to it unless he is already personally interested. In fact, no rumor can circulate if the individual is not concerned. He may be concerned, or feel he is, simply on the basis of the judgment —or what he thinks is the judgment—of his milieu. This is where we find fashion. But it may be objected that the decisive element is a commercial mechanism: a fashion is launched by the producers, and advertising plays the biggest role (in the form of an organized rumor launched by propagandists). This is true in the majority of cases, even in the case of such absurd fashions as the Yo-Yo, the Hula Hoop, or Davy Crockett. But it is not always that way: sometimes an absurd fashion spreads without advertising, from only one point of departure, such as in the astonishing case of the Scoubidou. Beginning with an article in a children's magazine, and without any commercial interest being involved, France was submerged within a month by Scoubidous made by children and adults. Evidently, we are face to face with the phenomenon of imitation, pure and simple, but to the extent that this imitation is caused by an article that reaches only a limited number of children, it is an example of the individual's extreme susceptibility, his capacity to be influenced and propagandized. Even if he defies it, even if he stiffens in the presence of true propaganda, he still is extremely vulnerable. These reflections and statements, selected arbitrarily from various fields and based on different methods, lead us to conclude that the effectiveness of propaganda is indeed great and decisive.

4. The Limits of Propaganda

Propaganda, though effective, obviously does not have unlimited powers. It would be erroneous to conclude that anything at all can be obtained from people by propaganda. I have already pointed out some limitations. Certain psychological or sociological conditions must pre-exist for the mechanism to work. For example, the needs to be satisfied by propaganda must be kept in mind.

Obviously, no psychic changes or reversals of opinion can be produced suddenly. I have also said that well-established opinion should not be attacked head on. However, propaganda consists first of all of a stocktaking of existing limitations. Outside those limits it is obviously ineffective. But it would be absurd to deny the efficiency of automobiles as a means of transportation merely because they cannot travel on open fields or on the beach. At the same time, the limits of propaganda's field of action are very large.[1]

In an attempt to trace these limits, we might first remember four elements already examined:

1. Pre-existing attitudes. In the beginning, propaganda cannot move except within the framework of these attitudes, which it can modify only very slowly.

2. The general trends and sociological factors of the society in which it acts. The first limitation is relative and can be overcome, but this second is an absolute limit. Propaganda cannot reverse fundamental trends in a society. For example, in the United States no propaganda that would be against a democracy (formally) and in favor of a monarchy would be able to "take." Nor could any propaganda against Socialism be successful in the U.S.S.R., nor any propaganda, anywhere in the world, against technology, progress, happiness, and so on.

3. A third limitation is the necessity for consonance with the facts. A basic fact is always necessary. Propaganda can never be a propaganda of ideas, but must pronounce judgment on certain facts (whether these judgments are accurate or not). Propaganda cannot prevail against facts that are too massive and definite: Goebbels changed his propaganda after Stalingrad because it was impossible to transform that debacle into a victory. His propaganda of success was followed by his propaganda of heroism.[2]

4. A last limit that abridges the capabilities of all propaganda is time, from two points of view. To have any effect, the psycho-

---

[1] It is not a question of propaganda in a panicky group in the grip of excessive terror or in a milieu that flees into fiction to protect and justify itself. Similarly, it makes no sense to insist that propaganda is limited by the structure of the mass media. Finally, in a totally adverse sociological situation, propaganda can do nothing. All this constitutes evidence.

[2] After Hess's escape, Goebbels said: "There are situations against which the best propagandist in the world cannot fight."

logical action must be lasting and continuous. But time imposes a limitation because of the weak durability of the direct effects. In German public opinion, the Nazi doctrine is now disappearing. All propaganda evaporates progressively when it ceases. One therefore cannot hope to create a final current of opinion or a type of man. But here again this limit is growing less restricting: the longer a propaganda has been made, the more durable its effects. The more profound, total, and technically superior it has been, the more it will have changed man. The propagandist's work is never done. After forty years of remakable propaganda in the U.S.S.R., much remains to be done to capture man completely. Points that were believed to be won and no longer in need of propaganda treatment, must be taken up again and given a different treatment.[3] I shall now turn to two new elements.

One limitation upon the effectiveness of propaganda has not yet become clear: foreign countries. The conditions for the development and effectiveness of propaganda analyzed here were mainly concerned with *internal* propaganda, inside a large group, society, or nation. Propaganda is most effective, most dangerous, and least noticed inside a group. Propaganda addressed to the outside is inevitably ineffective to a large extent:[4] there is the propagandist's psychological ignorance of the attitudes, centers of interest, and presuppositions of his target, and the spontaneous suspicion on the part of the target of all that comes from the outside. There is the difficulty of establishing continuity, the impossibility of being in real "communication," the inevitable delay with regard to immediate events, the impossibility of all the mass media, of making "pre-propaganda," of using obsessive propaganda, and so on. Even when a country is occupied by a foreign power, the latter cannot really make effective propaganda (for example, German propaganda toward the occupied countries during World War II). A poster or an article that evokes a response in one country may fail to do so in a neighboring one.[5] Only very elementary operations are possible, very much prey to

---

[3] Let us remember the violent attacks of 1960–1 against poorly made propaganda. Much of the propaganda was considered boring and dogmatic; it had to change to an action method to stimulate higher productivity; it must cease being abstract and relate to facts.

[4] This is how most of the failures of German propaganda were regarded in neutral and occupied countries.

[5] From which it follows that one cannot export propaganda.

unforeseeable circumstances—and that really is not modern propaganda. What is remarkable is that such propaganda is actually evoking the greatest interest, and that it should represent the form by which the effectiveness of propaganda as such is being judged. Psychological warfare is of passionate interest to people, though it is the least convincing type of propaganda. I have already discussed this.

Too often propaganda has been judged by its effects on a stranger or an enemy. From its effects on the German army, Americans have concluded that propaganda is not effective (moreover, with variations of evaluations). I, in turn, am astonished that even one soldier should have surrendered as the result of a leaflet. Similarly, propaganda toward the Socialist countries has only very limited value or effect (even if it is heard, which is not certain, so many receiving sets being official). It is giving such propaganda undeserved honor to attribute to it the revolts in East Berlin and Hungary. It is more likely that, once the revolts had broken out, the rebels remembered and took seriously the formulas of that propaganda, and that when those were not followed by action, the rebels felt they had been deceived and rejected the West doubly: this is the famous boomerang effect, which undeniably occurs. At the most, such propaganda can create a certain ambiguity in the thoughts and feelings of the foreigner; it can disturb certain ideas and judgments, show up certain claims of domestic propaganda as false, and create a certain amount of bad conscience. All that is not negligible, but must not be exaggerated or considered as typical with regard to the effects of propaganda. Spear[6] has analyzed perfectly the weakness of propaganda addressed to the outside. He even considered such questions as: who, in an opposed nation, is really the enemy? Should one aim at the military elite as much as at the political elite? Who, in such a nation, is a potential or actual ally? Who exercises the real power? What can and should be modified by propaganda—the ideological bases, political structures, social institutions?

None of these questions can be given a precise answer, for to answer them we would need psychological investigations that cannot be carried out in a foreign country, even less in an enemy

[6] In Daniel Lerner (ed.): *Propaganda in War and Crisis* (New York: George W. Stewart; 1951).

country. One can be guided only by general ideas and estimates. And one must not think that it is easier to operate with propaganda in a democratic country than in a dictatorship. Obviously, in the former case, the injection of propaganda from the outside is easy, but on the one hand, it may be more readily felt as propaganda (because the domestic governmental propaganda is less evident, less well recognized) and is therefore mistrusted; on the other hand, it responds much less to a need. In a totalitarian country, most people, before they are fully integrated, want to hear what is forbidden, the other line, which, incidentally, is the only support foreign propaganda has. But in a democracy, this need is much less felt, so that even though the reasons are less obvious, it is as difficult to conduct external propaganda against a democracy as against a dictatorship. These limitations on the effectiveness of "foreign" propaganda also apply when foreigners live in a territory controlled by the propagandist. This held true for the Arabs and the Kabyles in Algeria. There, French propaganda was addressed to a people who remained foreigners.

We are really facing here the greatest obstacle to psychological action: it can be fully effective only in the hands of nationals addressing themselves to their fellow citizens. This is undoubtedly the secret of the great force and effectiveness of Communist propaganda. The homeland of socialism does not make its propaganda directly to other peoples. That propaganda is made by the Communist parties, which are national parties, and which, consequently, are within easy elbow-rubbing distance of those to be seduced. Subjects and methods may then vary greatly from country to country. This does not mean contradiction between various Communist parties, but only a certain freedom of action on the level of propaganda, which must be adapted to every nation. Every time a unification of propaganda dogmas was attempted (for example in 1949–50), effectiveness was reduced. Thus, even though coming from the outside and doing the work of the U.S.S.R., Communist propaganda nevertheless is a national propaganda playing on inclinations and using facts known directly and understood.

A last limitation must be considered. Despite all technique, in the final analysis, a certain inability to foresee the response that the individual is called upon to give remains. As the result of a stimulus, a personality may react with various responses, opinions, or actions. The number of possible responses differs from person to person. Obviously, an esthete's reaction to a poster will differ from a worker's. The response really depends on the entire social context of an individual, on his milieu, his education, his family, his profession. In this domain of immediate and localized response, the theory of *pre-existing* attitudes applies most clearly. It has been proved, for example, that in the case of a film, those who approached it with the most favorable attitude were most influenced by it. (U.S. Army Information Service, 1944.) Also, people will be more influenced by the propaganda of their own group, more prone to give it the expected response.

To know exactly what response to expect from a given individual, a complete psychological analysis would be necessary. One factor that profoundly modifies responses is culture. A high culture is favorable to propaganda because it makes man more able to understand facts, become interested in problems, form judgments, and learn new attitudes. But this capability is decisive only if the propaganda is really serious. Conversely, culture makes the propagandist's work harder, for it will lead to a wider variety of responses to a stimulus, responses that will often be contradictory: the propagandist is then not certain of his effect. Culture makes men see several solutions, discuss them, feel uncertain of their own convictions, and for those reasons, either not act at all, or make an unexpected response. Conversely, the man without culture learns responses more slowly and is less easily incited or provoked into giving a response; but when the incitation is felt, such a man will not have a great variety of responses, least of all contradictory ones. The propagandist's work will be different in this case: a weak incitation to begin with, reinforced by a second argument, and excluding a plurality of responses when he speaks to a cultured milieu; but a violent incitation, without secondary argumentation, in the face of an uncultured public.

It must be remembered, however, that culture is only one of the elements that determine the response. The problem for the propagandist is to obtain, from among all the responses of which a person is capable, the one directly related to the political objective of his propaganda. This will be the "related response," *i.e.*, the specific, expected response, in harmony with both the proposed aim and the instrumental process that was put into motion. This "related" response can never be obtained automatically if one works on a free public opinion: too many factors are put into motion to make it possible to predict the results. The situation is different if there has been pre-propaganda. But aside from that case, propaganda can fail when the power of the stimulus is too weak, if the stimulus runs counter to existing opinions, or if the power of other responses is stronger than that of the desired one. The choice of the stimulus, its reach, its power, with relation to the propagandee's sociological and psychological milieu, are the propagandist's work that will make certain responses more or less likely.

On the other hand, the propagandist can facilitate the response, either by auxiliary responses, or by developing prior responses, called "pre-active responses" by Doob. An auxiliary response is one evoked with certainty by viewing or hearing something; it may not relate directly to the pursued aim, but will facilitate the hoped-for response. All advertising is based on such auxiliary responses. A well-done ad evokes a favorable over-all response, makes one stop in his tracks to examine it; there is an esthetic response that may be followed by the desired response. Those are auxiliary responses to the one hoped for: the purchase of the advertised product.

Similarly, the presentation of certain merchandise by a pretty young girl provokes an esthetic or erotic response, or one of sublimation or identification—auxiliary responses to the main decision expected from the viewer. There is no direct connection between the auxiliary response and the "related" response. The latter does not necessarily follow the former, which merely facilitates it. The auxiliary response may arouse attention, create a favorable climate, erase some other unfavorable feeling, increase the force of a subsequent stimulus, but it will not lead directly to acceptance or to action. It may, however, make the individual more receptive to an unexpected response from the propagandist.

The propagandist must look for other means to induce action. In a certain sense, one can say that "propaganda is a form of communication demanding the learning of new responses. These responses cannot be 'learned' except after the perception of a propaganda stimulus, and after the evocation of individualized responses related to the objective of propaganda" (Doob). In fact, the desired response can take place only *after* a spontaneous response. Learned responses are attitudes and predispose people to certain actions. Learned responses that become integrated in the sum total of an individual's responses must be taken into account. If these responses were learned through propaganda, they may be called, as by Doob, "pre-action responses"; this indicates their proximity to, and their distance from, action. Propaganda can, in fact, modify opinions and obtain responses that will remain without external manifestation for a certain period of time. That is the passive participation discussed earlier.

A man may be in agreement with the propagandist and yet not act as the propagandist would have him. In certain cases, the propagandist will be satisfied with such agreement without external manifestation: the paralysis provoked by a propaganda of terror completely achieves the aims of the propagandist. But most often—for example, in connection with election propaganda —the individual must be led from this "pre-action" response to action.

The propagandist will, therefore, try to give to this pre-action response the greatest possible power of involvement. The individual who learns a certain response and becomes capable of it, feels, as a result of this response, the need to go past it, to pass over to action, which then appears as a consequence of the "pre-action" response established by propaganda. Such a response will have power if it represents a central drive in the personality. It will be stronger if it is more recent and if reinforced by auxiliary responses.

All this allows us to understand the response sought by the propagandist. But this response is never certain whether a vote or allegiance to a party is concerned. To the extent that such response, even if learned, even if supported by all auxiliary responses, even if based on every possible calculation, must be the result of a determined, specific propaganda campaign, it remains unforeseeable. It is all the more so if the propagandist addresses himself to specific persons (trying to anticipate how a *particular* person will react to a *particular* propaganda), and if a definite act is to be obtained. Only *after* a campaign can it be seen whether the response was favorable or not. But such a situation is unacceptable to the propagandist. Because he is a technician, he cannot simply accept this uncertainty, which a sociologist would be satisfied to have emphasized. The propagandist seeks more certain and automatic responses.

To begin with, he will give up anticipating how the *individual* will react. He will think of the *group* and be satisfied with a generally favorable result—for example, with 80 percent of the responses obtained. On the other hand, he will also make less of an effort to elicit a specific response toward a localized action than to obtain a general attitude that, in turn, will create local responses.

Therefore, the propagandist's effort will aim at the elimination of individualizing factors. The expected response must be less and less conditioned by natural elements (milieu, education, and so on) and more and more by the "pre-education" provided in depth by propaganda. At the moment when the attitudes learned by propaganda begin to prevail over the "natural" attitudes that are man's second nature, they become collective, and the propagandist who has taught them can then calculate more easily what a given stimulus will elicit from them.

APPENDIX

[II]

MAO TSE-TUNG'S PROPAGANDA[1]

Mao rigorously applied the principles of Leninist propaganda, adapting them to his own circumstances. He did no more than that, but he did it with remarkable precision and perfect comprehension of the given facts. From the point of view of propaganda, the situation had three essential aspects: the complete absence of mass media (no newspapers and practically no posters), the vast number of people to be reached, and the revolutionary character of the war he led. Because of that situation, the two principles of his propaganda had to be education and organization.

By "education" is not meant here merely intellectual instruction or the promulgation of information. Information—directed and manipulated, moreover, on the Leninist pattern—was, to-

---

[1] On Mao's propaganda, see Mao Tse-tung: *Selected Works* (New York: International Publishers; 1954–6), Vols. I, III; Roderick MacFarquhar (ed.): *The Hundred Flowers Campaign and the Chinese Intellectuals* (New York: Frederick A. Praeger; 1960); and Tibor Mende: *China and Her Shadow* (New York: Coward-McCann; 1962).

gether with instruction, incorporated into an education whose aim
was to modify the whole human being by giving him a totally new
view of the world and awakening in him a range of feelings, reactions, thoughts, and attitudes entirely different from those to
which he was accustomed.[2]

By "organization" is meant that every individual must be put
into a network comprising many organizations that surround him
on all sides and control him on all levels. But the aim is not to
stifle the individual through organization; it is to make him an
active member of that organization.

These principles underwent modifications according to changing circumstances. Obviously, the period of war must be distinguished from the period of consolidation.

1. The War: From 1926 to 1949

Education

In conquered and more or less controlled territories, the task
was to spread the principal revolutionary theses of Marxism
via slogans, through explanations of the "Three Principles of the
People," and by meetings at which the wealthy and the exploiters
were to be denounced. Political education was aimed less at
agitation and rebellion and more at slow and deep infusion of
certain economic notions based on the widespread desire for land
distribution. Meetings, marches, banners, and posters were used
for the dissemination of these slogans. Explanations always took
place in naturally structured groups, such as the Peasant Union.
Political education clearly was pushed much harder in the principal
propaganda organization: the army. With the help of a permanent
Marxist education, an attempt was made to raise the political
level of party and army members. This was accompanied by the
struggle against putschism, individualism, egalitarianism, and so
on.

The object was, therefore, not so much immediate rebellion as
"political mobilization," in the course of which propaganda had

---

[2] Although Mao always gave first place to education, propaganda in the first period
received equally intense attention. The aim was to elicit hatreds, to spur national
and patriotic feelings, to play on the prestige of the soldier and on the fear of
reprisals. Here we see the traditional traits of propaganda.

to set into motion the masses, who would *themselves* realize the catchwords and promises of propaganda. This may well be an original idea conceived by Mao: he who formulates a slogan not being the one to fulfill the promise it contains. The slogan will mobilize the people, who will then have to do the work to attain the objective contained in the formula that excited them in the first place. In non-controlled territories, this type of work was much less intense. On the one hand, attempts were made to reach enemy troops through prisoners. Captured enemy soldiers were subjected to intensive propaganda, new political formation, complete transformation of their view of the world (this process later became brainwashing); then they were released. This liberation was in itself a propaganda act designed to show the Communist's generosity toward their opponents, but beyond that, the released soldiers were meant to exhibit their new attitudes in the midst of the old army.

On the other hand, the revolutionary struggle led Mao temporarily to occupy zones that were later abandoned—and frequently —with much infiltration and a great flow of people back and forth. Here the purpose was to leave an ideologically formed population behind when the revolutionary army had to withdraw. In the face of an enemy without any ideological weapon, this permitted Mao little by little to contaminate the enemy army when it occupied these territories. To be sure, these zones could not be left too long without propaganda; infiltration and partial occupation had to take place to renew and strengthen "political education." At that stage, political education consisted in taking the prevailing misery, the widespread oppression, and the spontaneous reactions against it as points of departure for providing coherent explanations, for designating enemies who could serve to catalyze existing hatreds, for sketching out the myth of liberation, and for showing the means of that liberation (cooperation of the people and adherence to Communism), with all these elements united into a solid whole.

Organization

The propagandized people had to be inserted into a system. During the period of battle, Mao's organization contained three elements. First, "Peasant Unions" designed to organize the peasants of a region, to disseminate slogans, and to explain them

in discussion groups. These unions, with their very large membership and their—at first glance—very liberal orientation, were
under the official direction of the Party. Mao could say with
justification: "Would it have been possible, even if we had set
up tens of thousands of schools for political education, to educate
all the men and women even in the remotest villages in so short
a time?" These Peasant Unions were neither combat nor action
organizations, but large groupings to serve the purposes of psychological organization and polarization.

The second element was the famous parallel hierarchy. Side by
side with the official administration (still the administration of
the enemy government in the battle areas), a clandestine, revolutionary, and complete administration was being built. This ad-
minstration had its own finances, its own police—and very precise
propaganda functions. The point was, Mao said, "to mobilize the
masses by resorting to organization work."

Actually, this administration transformed general ideas and
new views, acquired as a result of political education, into action:
rations, supplies, wages, and so on. Social and economic transformation had to take place on the inside and secretly until it
could be superimposed on prior organization, and the participation of the individuals on all levels was needed to strengthen the
conviction that this transformation was not imposed from outside
and above. "The methods of mobilizing the masses must not be
bureaucratic," Mao said. The parallel hierarchy was called upon
to "make propaganda in every instance" in order to create a sense
of participation in the common work, with Mao knowing full
well that as soon as this feeling of participation was acquired, all
action would provide its own justification and would involve the
individuals more deeply. Mao often insisted that the creation of
the parallel hierarchy could serve no purpose without this propaganda designed to lead people to act "spontaneously."

Finally, the third propaganda organization was the army: "The
Chinese Red Army is an armed organization fulfilling the political
tasks of the revolution . . . it has important tasks to fulfill:
propaganda among the masses, organization of the masses, and so
on. . . . The Red Army does not make war for war's sake: *this
war is a war for propaganda in the midst of the masses.*" The
first task was to shape the soldiers of that Red Army, to teach
them why they had to fight, and then to turn them into propa-

gandists and carriers of these ideas. They had to live symbiotically with the civilians in order to conquer the people ideologically and progressively assimilate them.

Such propaganda methods are subtle and numerous. They cover the whole gamut from terror to indoctrination, from parades to involvement in action. But it can take place only in the case of a strictly popular army. This emerges from the famous and oft-repeated formula: "The army must function among the people like a fish in water." This implies, of course, that such an army must be recruited from the population, express it, find support in it, share its interests, never act as it would in a conquered country, serve the public—and that its struggle have positive meaning for the people. If these prior conditions are not fulfilled, no propaganda instrument can be made out of the army (this accounts for the failure of the attempt to adopt Mao's methods in Algeria). The Red Army is a propaganda apparatus because it is formed on the basis of ideology and because its presence mobilizes the people: they have no choice but to participate and to become involved.

2. Since 1949

After victory, the propaganda principles remained unchanged, but were applied differently. On February 27, 1957, in his report to the Supreme Conference of the State, Mao said: "One cannot force a people to renounce idealism or force a people to believe in Marxism. To settle ideological problems, one must act through the democratic methods of discussion, criticism, persuasion, and appropriate education." But we must remember the—incidentally quite remarkable—method of the "Hundred Flowers." As in Nazi Germany in 1943,[3] there was a period of apparent liberalism when expressions of all sort of criticism, deviationism, idealistic and religious inclinations, and so on, were tolerated, authorized, even encouraged. Then, after all opponents had spoken, the wave of repression hit them: arrests, jail sentences, and, above all, political re-education took place. The purpose of the "Hundred Flowers Campaign" was to make opponents come

---

[3] A liberalization of the regime's press at the end of 1934 was designed to make opponents reveal themselves.

out in the open so they could be arrested and eliminated. The subsequent "rectification" campaign could not, in Mao's words, be "gentle as a breeze or a summer rain for the enemies of the people."

Even a propaganda centered on education cannot do without terror. In order to arrive at full compliance with propaganda, the 7 percent "incorrigible" individualists must be eliminated. The objective of Mao's propaganda is a double one: to integrate individuals into the new body politic as deeply as possible, and, at the same time, to detach them from the old groups, such as the family or traditional village organizations. These groups must be disintegrated, always through action from within. For this there must be maximum conformity on the part of the individual.[4] According to men like R. Guillain and Tibor Mende, this enterprise was successful. Mende has written: "Rendered perfectly malleable by ten years of pounding, the prototypes, mass-produced by the party, are now replacing the categories imposed earlier by Confucian scholars." On the other hand, the task is to make the individual work beyond his strength for economic development. All these "leaps forward" rest exclusively on propaganda. Propaganda may take the form of excitation, mass demonstrations (China must overtake the United States, and hatred for capitalists is aroused), or emulation *à la Piatiletka,* but it is mainly in the form of education and persuasion in the economic domain. When orientations change, methods change as well.

Education

There have been three innovations.

1. The traditional processes of propaganda are on the increase: everybody is being taught to read, newspapers and brochures are placed at everyone's disposal, and so on. At the same time, child education is completely integrated into propaganda: from the nursery on, little children are conditioned so as to make their subconscious receptive to the verities of Socialism. This takes place on all levels of instruction.

2. The expansion of the discussion system. In his 1957 report, Mao said: "We have developed in 1942 the slogan 'Unity—

---

[4] This conformity is ideological and total. Mao could well say that "not to have the correct ideological point of view is like having no soul."

Criticism–Unity,' to define this democratic method of resolving conflicts through criticism and subsequent efforts to arrive at a new unity on a new basis." Mao reminded his listeners that the first successes of this method go back to 1927. He stated that the method of persuasion could be used only on workers. Others must be forced: "Benevolence for the people, dictatorship for the enemies of the people." There is a genuine propaganda effort for those who can be integrated; the others are eliminated. It follows that "discussion–criticism–unity" is a method that operates only within a limited circle, on the basis of common presuppositions and without questioning the common interests. On this subject, Tibor Mende reported the answer of a director of a steel foundry in Anshan, concerning organization of work and establishment of norms: "We arrive at decisions after long discussions. Opposition? We rely only on persuasion. There is no chance that someone might resist the decision that is taken after the discussion, when everybody has been persuaded that the road taken is the right one." And how can one tell that this road is really the right one? "White is not black. We know where the truth lies. There is only one truth, and with patience it can be explained." This complements Mao's method perfectly.

But let us remember the democratic method: a man knows the absolute truth. He poses problems for which there are solutions. He encourages objections (in a limited circle). The discussion that follows does not have as its aim the common search for truth or a plan based on the opinions of all, which will take shape gradually. The aim of the discussion is to use the opposition and to drain the opponents of their energy and their convictions. Its aim is to "work over" every member of the group until, fully and of his own free will, he adheres to a proposition declared to be the absolute truth by the leader.

3. The other new aspect in education is the theory of the mold, also described in the 1957 report. The point is to press man in a mold, placing him there periodically, to "re-mold" him systematically. Whatever his convictions or inclinations may be, even if he is a convinced Communist. Mao said: "When one builds a Socialist society, every person must be placed in the mold, the exploiters as well as the workers. Who says that the working class does not need this? Naturally, molding the exploiter and the worker are two different operations. . . . We ourselves are being

placed in the mold every year. . . . I have gone through a remolding of my own thoughts . . . and I must continue."

There is, on the one hand, a mold of the perfect Socialist man which appears as the absolute ideal. There is, on the other hand, a method to press people again and again into this mold, to give them this shape conforming to the ideal. This is no longer the spontaneous formation of the new man as a result of changes in the social structure, as with Karl Marx. Nor is it the voluntary formation of a new man who must be built, but whose eventual entity is not known, as under Lenin. For Mao, the idea of the mold implies the idea of a recognizable ideal prototype to which every man must be tailored. This interpretation by Mao is confirmed by his concern for laying down criteria of action, dogmatic definitions as to what a man should be, and, among others, his six criteria of Good. "Acts can be judged good by these six criteria: if they serve to unite the people rather than divide them, if they are favorable to the building of Socialism, if they consolidate the people's democratic dictatorship, if they consolidate democratic centralism, if they reinforce the direction of the Communist party, if they are favorable to international Socialist solidarity." These criteria of *Good* reflect Mao's concern with furnishing simple means of judgment for Socialists and clearly defining what kind of man is to be shaped by the mold. Party members must also go through the mold. But this assumes that there is a man or a group making the diagnosis, and placing people in the mold. In any event, it is above all a psychological and ideological operation. But the aim is perfect conformity of the individual to the Marxist doctrine and the new structure of society. And the adaptation will be slow, progressive, and systematic as a result of successive remoldings.

Encirclement

I have already covered this important point in my discussion of horizontal propaganda. Let us only remember that the army no longer has a favored role as a propaganda instrument.

3. Brainwashing[5]

This term has become famous, though it is only a secondary aspect of Chinese propaganda. To be sure, brainwashing has nothing to do with the type of magic described in *L'Express*, in 1957, under that title. The aim of brainwashing is to retrieve enemies and transform rather than eliminate them—either to make them exponents of Marxism and then send them back home, or to turn them into edifying examples. The process, to the extent that it can be recognized, has three principal aspects:

1. The individual is cut off from everything, from his former social milieu, from news and information. This can be done only if he is placed in a prison cell or a camp. The individual is totally uprooted. The absence of news places this man, who has been used to receiving information, in a vacuum, which is hard to endure after a certain time. Complementary methods are added to this: a certain privation of food and sleep to weaken his psychological resistance, to make him more susceptible to influences (though there is no intention of exhausting him), frequent isolation and solitude, which cause a certain anxiety, increased by the uncertainty of his fate and the lack of a definite sentence or punishment; also frequently incarceration in windowless cells with only electric light, with irregular hours for meals, sleep, interrogations, and so on, in order to destroy even his sense of time. The principal aim of these psychological methods is to destroy a man's habitual patterns, space, hours, milieu, and so on. A man must be deprived of his accustomed supports. Finally, this man lives in a situation of inferiority and humiliation, aimed not at destroying him but at reconstructing him.

2. A man placed in the above circumstances is subjected to a bombardment of slogans by radio or by fellow-prisoners, who, though prisoners themselves, shower him with reproaches and slogans because they already are on the road to their own re-

---

[5] See A. M. Meerloo: *The Rape of the Mind: The Psychology of Thought Control, Menticide, and Brainwashing* (New York: World Publishing Company; 1956); Eleutherius Winance: *The Communist Persuasion: A Personal Experience of Brainwashing*, trans. Emeric A. Lawrence, O.S.B. (New York: P. J. Kenedy & Sons; 1959); and Robert Jay Lifton: *Thought Reform and the Psychology of Totalism: A Study of Brainwashing in China* (New York: W. W. Norton & Company; 1961).

construction. There is an endless repetition of formulas, explanations, and simple stimuli. Of course, in the beginning all this
merely evokes the subject's scorn and disbelief. After some time,
however, erosion takes place; whether the subject likes it or not,
he ends up knowing by heart certain formulas of the catechism
repeated to him a thousand times; he ends up inhabited by
these slogans, which still carry no conviction; he does not yield
to some advertising slogan, for example, just because he knows
it. But it must not be forgotten that the prisoner hears nothing
else, and that the incessant repetition of these slogans also
prevents any personal reflection or meditation. The noise of the
slogan is present all the time. The result is an involuntary penetration and a certain intellectual weakening, added to the impossibility of leading a private intellectual life.

3. The third element of brainwashing, closely tied to the two
others, is group discussion according to the "democratic method."
Obviously, the leader must be an agile man, intellectually superior, able to answer all questions and objections. But clearly
the aim of such discussions is not that of free groups. The first
objective will be to create an ambiguity in the mind of the
prisoner with regard to his ideas and convictions, an uncertainty,
a doubt (after all, could this be true?) on questions of fact—
for example, on information that the leader (the only source of
information) will provide, and at the same time a feeling of guilt
based on ideas of morality in the individual himself. (I belonged
to a group, a class, a people that has done much harm, great
wrongs to humanity. This kind of thinking will attach itself
quite easily to a Christian conscience, for example.) The creation
of a guilt feeling obviously leads to the desire to get rid of it,
to cleanse, purify, and redeem oneself.

When it appears that ambiguity of conviction and guilt feelings
are well established in the group, a new stage can be reached:
explanations. These explanations are furnished on two levels. One
set deals with the personal situation of the prisoner, his guilt,
his humiliation, his imprisonment: he is shown the legitimacy
of all that, its logic, its validity, so as to eliminate his resentment
toward his jailer. The jailer, on the other hand, reveals his goodwill and his good intentions toward the prisoner. The other set
of explanations concerns the general problems of the world and the
political situation. History and the universe are depicted with

the help of very clever dialectics. An entire *Weltanschauung* is unfolded progressively, not dogmatically and with great speeches, but adjusted bit by bit to the personal experience of the prisoner, and with individual explanations given him. Gradually, his traditional—Christian, bourgeois, liberal, or feudal—view of the universe is removed and replaced by a different view. At the same time, the slogans previously learned by heart now fall into place. From then on, elementary formulas, repeated a thousand times, are alternated with explanatory discussions in depth unceasingly. Then there is a final stage: "The Road to Redemption." Once entered into the new *Weltanschauung*, and even more convinced of his guilt, "the individual is eager to deliver himself, to purify himself." He then accepts the rules of belonging, and the actions proposed to him. He thus justifies himself both in his own eyes and in the eyes of others.

This is approximately the technique of brainwashing. It must be noted that because it is slow and uses complex methods and highly qualified personnel, it can be practiced only on a very small number of individuals, who are hand-picked and special persons. Moreover, its effects are not very durable except when the prisoner, once liberated, enters a society with the same *Weltanschauung* as the one imposed on him. If he does not, what was built up will eventually wear off. In any case, this technique is only of incidental importance in Mao's system.[6]

---

[6] This type of brainwashing was practiced in the Algerian internment camps after 1957. In January 1958 an official notice dealing with the French Psychological Action was published in the camps, simply confirming what we have said earlier. Some details deserve to be remembered:

(a) The classification of individuals into "incorrigible," "soft," "retrievable."

(b) The notion that, according to the Chinese, brainwashing took between six months and two years, depending on the level of the prisoner. But in Algeria less time was needed (which undoubtedly accounted for the French failures).

(c) The division into three stages: (1) disintegration of the individual, (2) creation of a collective conscience, plus reindoctrination, (3) self-criticism and full engagement in the new line.

(d) The creation of collective self-discipline, with sanctions applied by the inmates themselves.

(e) The system of semi-weekly "waves": waves of discipline, waves of gaiety, waves of work, study, and so on. This created a collective current.

(f) The mechanism of liberation: "The people have the right to pardon criminals"; the collectivity of the camp in a general meeting, with discussion, criticism, and self-criticism on the part of those to be liberated who had become members of the New French Algeria.

All this failed almost entirely because there was no really usable ideology, and particularly because there were no sufficiently well organized cadres.

BIBLIOGRAPHY

Albig, John William: *Modern Public Opinion.* New York: McGraw-Hill Book Company; 1956.

Allport, Gordon W.: "The Basic Psychology of Rumor." In Katz *et al.*

———— and Leo Postman: *The Psychology of Rumor.* New York: Henry Holt & Company; 1947.

Aroneanu, Eugène: *La définition de l'aggression: exposé objectif.* Paris: Editions Internationales; 1958.

Barthes, Roland: *Mythologies.* Pt. II. Paris: Editions du Seuil; 1957.

Bartlett, Fred Charles: "The Aims of Political Propaganda." In Katz *et al.*

————: *Political Propaganda.* Cambridge, Eng.: Cambridge University Press; 1940.

Baschwitz, Kurt: *Du und die Masse, Studien zu einer exacten Massenpsychologie.* 2nd ed. Leiden: E. J. Brill; 1951.

Bernays, Edward L.: *The Engineering of Consent.* Norman, Okla.: University of Oklahoma Press; 1955.

————: *Propaganda.* New York: H. Liveright; 1928.

Bogardus, Emory Stephen: *The Making of Public Opinion.* New York: Association Press; 1951.

Bourricaud, François: *Esquisse d'une théorie de l'autorité.* Paris: Plon; 1961.

Bruner, Jerome S.: "The Dimension of Propaganda." In Katz *et al.*

Bryce, James: "The Nature of Opinion." In Katz *et al.*

Campbell, Angus: "Television and the Election." In Katz *et al.*

Cantril, Hadley. *Gauging Public Opinion.* Princeton: Princeton University Press; 1944

Publisher's Note: This bibliography is somewhat less extensive than the bibliography in the original French edition since it includes only those works which are readily available in American libraries.

———— and Gordon W. Allport: *The Psychology of Radio*. New York: Harper & Brothers; 1935.

Cartwright, Dorwin: "Principles of Mass Persuasion." In Katz *et al.*

Citoyen français, Le. Special issue of *Problèmes* (1958).

Cooper, Eunice, and Marie Jahoda: "The Evasion of Propaganda." In Katz *et al.*

Davidson, P.: *Propaganda and the American Revolution*. Chapel Hill, N.C.: University of North Carolina Press; 1941.

de Plas, Bernard: *La Publicité*. Paris: H. Verdier; 1947.

Dicks, Henry V.: "German Personality Traits and Nazi Ideology." In Lerner (ed.).

Domenach, Jean-Marie: *Les Dessous psychologiques de l'homme de la rue*. C.E.G.O.S.; 1956.

————: *La Propagande politique*. Paris: Presses Universitaires de France; 1949.

Doob, Leonard W.: "Goebbels' Principles of Propaganda." In Katz *et al.*

————: *Public Opinion and Propaganda*. New York: Henry Holt & Company; 1948.

————: *Propaganda: Its Psychology and Technique*. New York: Henry Holt & Company; 1935.

Driencourt, Jacques: *La Propagande, nouvelle force politique*. Paris: A. Colin; 1950.

Dupouy, Bernard: *La Propagande dans la guerre d'Algérie* (1956–1958). Algiers: Maison des Livres; 1958.

Einsiedel, Heinrich: *Tagebuch der Versuchung*. Berlin: Pontes Verlag; 1950.

Eldersveld, Samuel J.: "Personal Contact or Mass Propaganda." In Katz *et al.*

Ellul, Jacques: "Propagande et évangélisation." *Revue de l'Evangélisation* (1959).

————: "La Crise de l'opinion et la propagande." *Foi et Vie* (1958).

————: "Les Mythes modernes." *Diogène* (1958).

————: "Information et propagande." *Diogène* (1957).

————: "Les Présuppositions sociologiques collectives." *Evangelische Theologie* (1957).

————: *La Technique ou l'enjeu du siècle*. Paris: A. Colin; 1954. [Translated as *The Technological Society*. New York: Alfred A. Knopf; 1964.]

————: "La Propagande." *Bulletin de l'I.F.O.P.* (1954).

————: *Les Techniques de propagande*. Cours polycopié; 1951.

Farrago, Ladislas: "British Propaganda." *United Nations World* (1948).

Félice, Philippe de: *Foules en délire, extases collectives*. Paris: A. Michel; 1947.

Goebbels, Joseph: *Der Angriff, Aufsätze aus der Kampfzeit*. Munich: F. Eher; 1942.

————: *Wesen und Gestalt des Nationalsozialismus.* Berlin: Junker und Dünnhaupt; 1935.

Gramsci, Antonio: *Gli intelletualli e l'organizzazione della cultura.* Turin: G. Einaudi; 1949.

Grosser, Alfred: *Hitler, la presse et la naissance de la dictature.* Paris: A. Colin; 1959.

Guerre révolutionnaire, La. Special issue of *Revue Militaire d'Information* (1957).

Gurfein, Murray I., and Morris Janowitz: "Trends in Wehrmacht Moral." In Lerner (ed.).

Hadamovsky, Eugen: *Propaganda und die nationale Macht, die Organisation der öffentlichen Meinung für die nationale Politik.* Oldenburg: G. Stalling; 1933.

Hagemann, Walter: *Publizistik im Dritten Reich: Ein Beitrag zur Methodik der Massenführung.* Hamburg: Hansischer Gildenverlag; 1948.

Hartley, Eugene L.: *Fundamentals of Social Psychology.* New York: Alfred A. Knopf; 1952.

Harvey, Ian: *The Technique of Persuasion.* Grey Walls, Eng.: Falcon Press; 1951.

Horney, Karen: *The Neurotic Personality of Our Time.* New York: W. W. Norton & Company; 1937.

Hovland, Carl I., and Walter Weiss: "Influence of Source Credibility on Communication Effectiveness." In Katz *et al.*

————, Arthur A. Lumsdaine, and Fred D. Sheffield: "Experiments on Mass Communications." *Studies in Social Psychology in World War II.* Princeton: Princeton University Press; 1944.

Hummel, William, and Keith Huntress: *The Analysis of Propaganda.* New York: William Sloane Associates; 1949.

Hyman, Herbert H., and Paul B. Sheatsly: "Some Reasons Why Information Campaigns Fail." In Katz *et al.*

Inkeles, Alex: *Public Opinion in Soviet Russia.* Cambridge, Mass.: Harvard University Press; 1958.

Institute International de Presse: *Les Pressions du pourvoir sur la presse,* 1955.

Irion, Frederick C.: *Public Opinion and Propaganda.* New York: Thomas Y. Crowell; 1950.

Janis, Irving L., and Seymour Feshbach: "Effects of Fear-arousing Communications on Reaction to a Subsequent New Event." In Katz *et al.*

Katz, Daniel, Dorwin Cartwright, Samuel J. Eldersveld, and Alfred McClung Lee: *Public Opinion and Propaganda.* New York: Dryden Press; 1954.

Kohn-Bramstedt, Ernst: *Dictatorship and Political Police.* Oxford: Routledge; 1945.

Krech, David, and Richard S. Crutchfield: *Theories and Problems of Social Psychology.* New York: McGraw-Hill Book Company; 1948, 1962.

Kris, Ernst, and Nathan Leites: "Trends in Twentieth-Century Propaganda." In Lerner (ed.).

——, Hans Speier, *et al.*: *German Radio Propaganda*. Studies of the Institute of World Affairs. New York: Oxford University Press; 1944.

Lange, Max Gustav: *Totalitare Erziehung, das Erziehungssystem der Sowjetzone Deutschlands*. Frankfurt am Main: Verlag der Frankfurter Hefte; 1954.

LaPiere, Richard Tracy: *A Theory of Social Control*. New York: McGraw-Hill Book Company; 1954.

Lasswell, Harold D.: *Psychopathology and Politics*. New York: Viking Press; 1960.

——: "Rôle des Idéologies." *Rapport AISP* (1952).

——: "Political and Psychological Warfare." In Lerner (ed.).

——: "The Strategy of Soviet Propaganda." In Lerner (ed.).

——: "Propaganda and Mass Insecurity." *Psychiatry* (1950).

—— and Dorothy Blumenstock: *World Revolutionary Propaganda*. New York: Alfred A. Knopf; 1939.

Lazarsfeld, Paul F., Bernard Berelson, and Hazel Gaudet: *The People's Choice*. New York: Columbia University Press; 1948, 1960.

—— and Robert K. Merton: *Studies in Radio and Film Propaganda*. Transactions of the New York Academy of Sciences, Series II, 6, 1943.

Lee, Alfred McClung: *How to Understand Propaganda*. New York: Rinehart; 1952.

Lenin, V. I.: *Selected Works*. Moscow: Peoples Publishing House; 1954.

Lerner, Daniel (ed.): *Propaganda in War and Crisis*. New York: George W. Stewart; 1951.

——: "Effective Propaganda, Conditions and Evaluation." in Lerner (ed.).

Lewin, Kurt: *Resolving Social Conflicts: Selected Papers on Group Dynamics*. New York: Harper & Brothers; 1948.

Lipset, S. M.: "Opinion Formation in a Crisis Situation." In Katz *et al.*

MacDougall C.: *Understanding Public Opinion*. New York: The Macmillan Company; 1952.

MacFarquhar, Roderick (ed.): *The Hundred Flowers Campaign and the Chinese Intellectuals*. New York: Frederick A. Praeger; 1960.

Maier, Norman R. F.: *Principles of Human Relations*. New York: John Wiley & Sons; 1952.

Mao Tse-tung: *Selected Works*. New York: International Publishers; 1954–6. Vols. I, III.

Maucorps, Paul: *Psychologie des mouvements sociaux*. Paris: Presses Universitaires de France; 1950.

Mégret, Maurice: *L'Action psychologique*. Paris: A. Fayard; 1959.

Merton, Robert K.: *Mass Persuasion: The Social Psychology of a War Bond Drive*. New York: Harper & Brothers; 1946.

Miotto, Antonio: "Folla e propaganda." *Psicologia e vita contemporanea* (1952).

————: *Psicologia della propaganda*. Florence: Editrice Universitaria; 1953.

Monnerot, Jules: *La Guerre en question*. Pt. I. Paris: Gallimard; 1952.

————: *Sociology and Psychology of Communism*. Boston: Beacon Press; 1953.

Morin, Edgar: *The Stars*. New York: Grove Press; 1960.

Munson, Edward L.: *The Management of Men: Handbook on Systematic Development of Morale and Control of Human Behavior*. New York: Henry Holt & Company; 1921.

Ogle, Marbury B.: *Public Opinion and Political Dynamics*. Boston: Houghton Mifflin Company; 1950.

Opinion Publique, L'. Ouvrage collectif (1957).

Packard, Vance O.: *The Hidden Persuaders*. New York: David McKay Company; 1957.

Pearlin, Leonard I., and Morris Rosenberg: "Propaganda Techniques in Institutional Advertising." In Katz *et al.*

Pohle, Heinz: *Der Rundfunk als Instrument der Politik, von 1923 bis 1938*. Hamburg: Hans-Bredow Institut; 1955.

Pol, Quentin: *La Propagande politique, une technique nouvelle*. Paris: Plon; 1943.

Polonski, Jacques: *La Presse, la propagande et l'opinion publique sous l'occupation*. Paris: Plon; 1943.

Pritchett, Charles Herman: *The Tennessee Valley Authority: A Study in Public Administration*. Chapel Hill, N.C.: University of North Carolina Press; 1943.

Propaganda Techniques of German Fascism. New York: Institute of Propaganda Analysis; 1938.

Rauschning, Hermann: *The Revolution of Nihilism: Warning to the West*. New York: Alliance Book Co.; 1939.

Reiwald, P.: *De l'Esprit des masses: traité de psychologie collective*. Pts. II, V. Neuchâtel: Delachaux et Niestlé; 1949–50.

Riesman, David: *The Lonely Crowd*. New Haven: Yale University Press; 1950.

Riess, Curt: *Joseph Goebbels: A Biography*. New York: Doubleday & Company; 1948.

Robin, Armand: *La Fausse parole*. Paris: Editions de Minuit; 1953.

————: "Expertise de la fausee parole." Series of articles in *Combat* (1949).

Sauvy, Alfred: *La Nature sociale*. Paris: Presses Universitaires de France; 1957.

————: *L'Opinion publique*. Paris: Presses Universitaires de France; 1956.

Schramm, Wilbur L.: *Communication in Modern Society*. Urbana, Ill.: University of Illinois Press; 1948.

Shils, Edward A., and Morris Janowitz: "Cohesion and Disintegration in the Wehrmacht." In Lerner (ed.).

Siepmann, Charles A.: *Radio, T.V., and Society.* New York: Oxford University Press; 1950.

Six, Franz A.: *Die politische Propaganda der N.S.D.A.P. im Kampf um die Macht.* Heidelberg: Winter; 1936.

Sladen, Frank J.: *Psychiatry and the War.* Pts. III, IV. Springfield, Ill.: Charles C Thomas; 1943.

Smith, Bruce L.: "Propaganda Analysis and the Science of Democracy." *Public Opinion Quarterly,* V (1941).

Speier, Hans: "Morale and Propaganda." In Lerner (ed.).

———— and Margaret Otis: "German Radio Propaganda." In Lerner (ed.).

Stoetzel, Jean: *Equisse d'une théorie des opinions.* Paris: Presses Universitaires de France; 1943.

Tarde, Gabriel de: *L'Opinion et la foule.* Paris: Alcan; 1901.

Taylor, Edmond: *The Strategy of Terror.* Boston: Houghton Mifflin Company; 1940.

Tchakhotin, Serge: *The Rape of the Masses.* New York: Alliance Book Co.; 1940.

Traxler, Arthur E.: *Techniques of Guidance.* New York: Harper & Brothers; 1945.

Truman, David B.: *Governmental Process: Political Interests and Public Opinion.* New York: Alfred A. Knopf; 1951.

Waldrop, Frank C., and Joseph Boskin: *Television: A Struggle for Power.* New York: William Morrow & Co.; 1938.

Whyte, William H.: *The Organization Man.* New York: Simon and Schuster; 1956.

Young, Kimball: *Social Psychology.* New York: F. S. Crofts; 1947.

Index

action-reflex, obtained by propaganda, 28–9, 30

advertising, 40, 63, 68, 69, 84, 119, 160, 174, 176, 209, 274, 290–1; and motivational research, 27 *n.*; veracity in, 53–4; ineffectiveness of, in political propaganda, 262; based on auxiliary responses, 300

Africa, propaganda in, 42, 54, 74, 134, 150

agitation propaganda, 20, 32 *n.*, 70–4, 76, 77, 78, 79, 105, 112, 188

Albig, John, xi *n.*, 3 *n.*, 94 *n.*, 197, 253 *n.*

Albord, T., 135 *n.*

Algeria, 13 *n.*, 23 *n.*, 29 *n.*, 43 *n.*, 57, 61, 76, 79, 86, 89, 99, 127 *n.*, 143 *n.*, 189, 201, 246, 264, 265, 285, 286, 298; and failure of French attempts at brainwashing, 313 *n.*

Algérie française (film), 85, 86

alienation, through propaganda, 169–78

aligned consciousness, in Soviet Union, 179 *n.*

American Legion, 244

anti-Semitism, 195, 272 *n.*

anxiety, in modern society, 153, 154, 155, 188

army, civic education of, in Western democracies, 135–6

Aron, Raymond, 116

Asia, propaganda in, 42, 110, 134

Athenian democracy, 14, 89

Austria, 134

auxiliary response, 300

Azerbaijan, 98

Bartlett, F. C., x *n.*

behaviorism, 36, 39

Belgium, 218

Bernays, Edward L., 71, 119 *n.*

Bidault, Georges, 213

birth rate, increased by propaganda, 292

black (covert) propaganda, 15, 16 and *n.*, 59 *n.*, 262 *n.*

Blumenstock, Dorothy, 262 *n.*

boomerang effect, 34 *n.*, 38 *n.*, 281, 297

Bourricaud, François, 268

brainwashing, 305, 311–13

Bruner, Jerome S., 12 *n.*

Buddhism, 198

Bulganin, Nikolai, 12

Byzantium, 49

cadres, executive, within political party, 216–17

"campaign," propaganda, 12

Campbell, Angus, 253 *n.*

Camus, Albert, 146

Canada, 172

capitalism, 222, 223, 224

Cartwright, Dorwin, 279 *n.*

Castro, Fidel, 58, 72, 78, 131, 132

Catholicism, failure of, in France, 152

Caucasus, 98

censorship, 16 *n.*, 123, 220

centralized state, 41

Chambre, P., 202

China, Communist, 61, 63, 71–2, 78, 89, 98, 99, 110, 141, 265, 283, 288; *see also* Mao Tse-tung

Chinese Red Army, 306–7

Christianity, 63, 201, 228–32

class consciousness, 37, 115, 177, 205

Cold War, 89, 135, 233, 235, 238, 239

Common Market, 119

Communes, medieval, 14

communication, mass media of, 102–5, 162

Communism, 163 *n.*, 169 *n.*, 176, 197, 198, 205, 225, 243, 262, 288; as ideology and myth, 117, 194; *see also* China, Communist; Khrushchev, Nikita; Lenin, Nikolai; Mao Tse-tung; Soviet Union; Stalin, Josef

Communist parties, propaganda by, as national parties, 298

Communists, 29, 30, 34 *n.*, 35, 45, 82, 133, 154, 157, 188, 213, 273, 280, 282

conditioned reflex, 5, 36, 80, 112; created by propaganda, 31, 32

confessions, in great show trials, 14
Congo, 74, 77, 85
Conseil Français des Mouvements de Jeunesse, 182
Constant, Benjamin, 63
Coolidge, Calvin, 173
covert (black) propaganda, 15, 16 and n., 59 n., 262 n.
Crutchfield, Richard S., 63 n., 65, 277, 278
crystallization, psychological, 162–8
cultural transformation, Lenin's call for, 106 n.
culture: individual psychology shaped by, 34 n.; average, as prerequisite for propaganda, 108–12; responses to propaganda modified by, 299
Czechoslovakia, 131, 132, 134

Dean, James, 152
de Gaulle, Charles, 246, 248
demand, symbols of, 163 n.
democracy: propaganda by, 16, 235–42, 253, 254, 255, 256; as fundamental ideology, 117; and public opinion, 123 and n., 124, 126, 127, 128 n., 129, 131, 139–40; subjected to psychological warfare, 133, 134, 235; propaganda weapon forced upon, 133, 134, 135, 137, 138, 232–5 passim, 250; opposing propagandas in, 181; obligation to become religious, 251
depth psychology, 36, 89
Dewey, John, 5
Dicks, Henry V., 270
diplomacy, and propaganda, 13
direct propaganda, 15
dissociation effect of propaganda, 178–182
Doob, Leonard W., xii, 12 n., 63 n., 203, 209, 263, 264, 279; quoted, 209, 279, 300, 301
Driencourt, Jacques, x–xi, 242

East Berlin, revolt in, 297
Egypt: and United Arab Republic, 23 and n.; weakness of propaganda in, 106
Eisenhower, Dwight D., 217, 253, 273
election campaign, ineffectiveness of propaganda during, 19, 261
elite, formation of organic groups of, 91
escape, as need of modern man, 151 n., 181 n.
European Defense Community, 127, 286 n.
existentialism, 148
expectation, symbols of, 163 n.
Express, L', 11, 311

factuality, problem of, 53–7
falsehood, as instrument of propaganda, 53, 60 and n., 61
family, as obstacle to horizontal propaganda, 82
Fascism, 172, 205, 245, 265
fashion, susceptibility to, 293, 294
fear, in modern society, 153, 154
federalism, 41
Félice, Philippe de, 178, 179
Figaro, Le, 213
Forces de Libération Nationale (F.L.N.), 21, 58, 61, 72, 79, 99 n., 143 n., 189, 201
France, 51, 63, 89, 109, 111, 126 n., 127 and n., 137, 141, 189, 192, 218, 246, 247, 290; Jeanson network in, 13 n.; trend toward socialization in, 42, 288; American propaganda ineffective in, 70; agricultural "reconstruction" in, 119; failure of Catholicism in, 152; Communist party in, 218, 269, 282; regrouping of Right in, 219; Communist propaganda in, 262, 264; anti-alcohol propaganda in, 292; increased birth rate in, 292; propaganda in, for increase in number of science and technology students, 293; Scoubidous in, 294
French Psychological Action, 313 n.
French Revolution, 117
Freud, Sigmund, 5
Friedmann, M. G., 224
Fundamentals of Social Psychology, 12 n.

Gallup, George, 268
Germany, 136, 245, 273; at time of Weimar Republic, 51; Nazi, 51, 186, 192, 218, 279, 292, 307 (*see also* Goebbels, Josef; Hitler, Adolf; Nazis); new army in, 120
Goebbels, Josef, 13 n., 16n., 18 n., 20 n., 25 n., 32 n., 36 n., 41 n., 43 n., 53 and n., 54 n., 55 n., 56, 57 n., 60 n., 93, 128 n., 174 n., 188, 241, 246, 276, 279, 286 n., 288, 295; quoted, x n., 25 n., 26 n., 36 n., 43 n., 131 n., 206, 295 n.
government, propaganda by, 127, 128, 130, 131, 132; *see also* State
group dynamics, 80, 81
grouping, and propaganda, 212–32
groups, partitioning of, 212–16
Guatemala, Friday of Sorrows in, 153
Guillain, R., 308
guilt feelings, stimulated by propaganda, 189
Gurfein, Murray I., 270, 271 n., 284 n.

Haltung, distinguished from *Stimmung*, 25 *n.*

Hamon, Léo, 127 *n.*, 128

Hartley, Eugene L., 12 *n.*

hatred, role in propaganda, 73, 74, 76, 77, 152, 163, 200

hedonism, 39 *n.*

Herald Tribune, New York, 70

hero, cult of, 172 and *n.*, 173

history, as fundamental myth, 40

Hitler, Adolf, 5, 12 *n.*, 17 *n.*, 18 *n.*, 52 and *n.*, 53, 57, 60 and *n.*, 61, 62, 71, 78, 85, 89, 128 *n.*, 133, 195, 196, 239, 284 *n.*, 288, 290

Hitler Youth, 171, 254

Ho Chi Minh, 72

horizontal propaganda, 80–4, 209 *n.*, 310

Horney, Karen, 154, 155, 167; quoted, 168

Hovland, Carl I., 44 *n.*

Human Engineering, 160

Human Relations, 143, 148, 160, 283; in United States, 141–2, 153 *n.*, 287

humanism, 201

Humanité, L', 213

"Hundred Flowers" campaign, Mao's, 307–8

Hungarian Revolution (1956), 22, 182, 285, 297

identification, symbols of, 163 *n.*

ideology, 116–17; and propaganda, 36, 193–202; definition of, 116

Ilyichev, Leonid, 224 *n.*

incitement, direct and indirect, 16–17, 240

India, 54, 56, 106

individual: propaganda addressed to, as part of mass, 6–9, 105–6, 150; need of, for propaganda, 37 and *n.*, 121, 138–53, 158–60; and collective center of interest, 49, 50, 51; diminished by participation in mass society, 149, 151; need of, for repression, 151

individualist society, 90, 91, 92, 93, 97

Indochina, 56, 89, 98 and *n.*, 99 and *n.*, 143 *n.*, 144, 289

information: distinguished from propaganda, 84; personal judgment eliminated by surfeit of, 87; propaganda related to, 112–16, 144–7, 250

Inkeles, Alex, 60 *n.*, 270

innuendo, technique of, 56–7

Institute for Propaganda Analysis, xi, 12 *n.*

integration propaganda, 29, 70, 74–9, 81, 84, 105, 112, 188, 210

Iraq, 23

Irion, Frederick C., 53

Islam, 198

Italy: Fascist, 51, 292; Communist party in, 218

Jacobinism, 244

Janowitz, Morris, 9 *n.*, 270, 284 *n.*

Japan, 245; propaganda for lower birth rate in, 292

Jeanson network, in France, 13 *n.*

Johnson, Lyndon B., 125

Khrushchev, Nikita, 12, 41 *n.*, 45 and *n.*, 46, 48, 55, 56, 59, 62, 132, 133, 153 *n.*, 176, 248; and Theses on Economic Reorganization, 130

Kinsey Report, 275

Komsomols, 120, 130, 171, 254

Korean War, 34 *n.*, 108, 252

Krech, David, 63 *n.*, 65, 277, 278

Kris, Ernst, 85 *n.*, 90 *n.*, 239 *n.*

Krokodil, 153

Kronstadt Rebellion, 78

Krueger, quoted, 278

Ku Klux Klan, 244

labor: ideology of, 194; propaganda effects on, 222–8 *passim*

language, as "pure sound" in propaganda, 180

Lasswell, Harold D., x *n.*, xi, 16, 80, 163 *n.*, 197, 240, 241, 262 and *n.*

Lazarsfeld, Paul F., 212, 281, 282

leadership, and group opinion, 100

Leites, Nathan, 85 *n.*, 90 *n.*, 239 *n.*

Lenin, Nikolai, 12 *n.*, 13, 29 *n.*, 32 *n.*, 53 and *n.*, 60 *n.*, 62, 71, 78, 93, 106 *n.*, 109 *n.*, 195, 196, 204 *n.*, 287, 288, 310; and Doctrine of the State, 13

Lerner, Daniel, xii *n.*, 262 *n.*, 297 *n.*

liberal democracy, suppressed by propaganda, 26

lie, as instrument of propaganda, 53, 60 and *n.*, 61

Lien-Viet, 99 *n.*

Lifton, Robert Jay, 311 *n.*

Lipset, S. M., 112

literacy, as prerequisite for propaganda, 110

literature, and propaganda, 14

"lonely crowd," 8–9, 147, 148

Louis XIV, 122

Lumumba, Patrice, 74, 77, 85

McCarthyism, 68, 107

MacDougall, C., 65, 205, 277, 279

Macht Propaganda, 21

Malenkov, Georgi, 55

Mao Dun, quoted, 14

Mao Tse-tung, 13 and *n.*, 21, 25 *n.*,
  26 *n.*, 29 *n.*, 32 *n.*, 33 *n.*, 53 *n.*, 72,
  78, 79, 82, 83, 84, 85, 89, 110, 169 *n.*,
  209, 283; and theory of "mold," 72 *n.*,
  79, 107, 209–10; propaganda of, 303–
  313; "political education" by, 304–5;
  and brainwashing, 305, 311–13; Peasant Unions organized by, 305–6;
  Chinese Red Army organized by,
  306–7; "Hundred Flowers" campaign
  by, 307–8; "discussion-criticism-
  unity" method of, 308–9; and "criteria of Good," 310; *see also* China,
  Communist
Marshall Plan, 69–70
Marx, Karl, 37, 157, 195, 198 *n.*, 288,
  310
Marxism, 110, 283, 289, 304, 307, 311
mass media of communication, 102–5,
  162
mass society, 90, 91, 92, 93, 94 and *n.*,
  95, 96, 97, 98, 99, 210; individual
  diminished by, 149, 151; cult of hero
  in, 172, 173
masses: propaganda addressed to, 6–9;
  participation of, in political affairs,
  121–7, 130, 132, 139
materialism, 39 and *n.*
Meerloo, A. M., 311 *n.*
Mégret, Maurice, xiii *n.*, xiv *n.*, 29 *n.*,
  59 *n.*, 128 *n.*, 232 *n.*
Mende, Tibor, 303 *n.*, 308, 309
Mendès-France, Pierre, 56, 127 *n.*
micro-sociology, 75 *n.*
middle class, propagandists recruited
  from, 106
Ministry of Propaganda, in modern
  state, 20, 118
Miotto, Antonio, xii, 18, 279
mithridatization, 183–4
mobilization of individuals, as objective
  of propaganda, 25 *n.*, 30 and *n.*
"mold," Mao's theory of, 72 *n.*, 79, 107,
  309–10
Monde, Le, 23 *n.*, 43 *n.*, 127 *n.*, 130 *n.*,
  135 *n.*, 136 *n.*; quoted, 48
Monnerot, Jules, 170
Morin, E., 97
Moscow trials (1936), 14
Motion Picture Association, 67
motion pictures, utilized by propaganda,
  10, 64, 103, 105, 254
motivational research, 27 *n.*
Munich, success of propaganda operation at, 58
Mussolini, Benito, 44, 129
myth, 36, 40, 116, 117, 243, 244, 245,
  246, 247, 249; utilized and created
  by propaganda, 11, 31–2, 38, 40, 41,
  42, 199–200

Napoleon, 13, 52 *n.*, 122, 123
Nasser, Gamal Abdel, 23, 58
National Association of Manufacturers,
  66
nationalism: aroused by propaganda,
  38, 41, 289; as fundamental ideology,
  117
NATO, 119
Nazis, 16, 29, 30, 57 *n.*, 71, 157, 188,
  196, 197, 221, 241, 245, 265 and *n.*,
  270, 271, 272, 276, 280, 282, 284;
  in pact with Soviet Union, 278
needs, met and utilized by propaganda,
  37 and *n.*, 121, 138–53, 158–60
Negro problem, in United States, 42
neurosis, 167–8, 178
New Economic Policy, in Soviet Union,
  109 *n.*
newspapers, 10, 102, 103, 104, 109 *n.*
North Korea, 110
North Vietnam, 78
Nuremberg trials, 14

O.A.S., 191 *n.*, 208 *n.*
Observateur, L', 11
Ogle, Marbury B., 65–6; quoted, xi
Ohne Mich ideology, 182, 191
operational terms, 46
opinion, public, *see* public opinion
Organization Man, The, 84
Ortega y Gasset, José, 93 *n.*
orthopraxy, 25–32
overt (white) propaganda, 15, 16 and
  n.

Packard, Vance, 225 *n.*, 290
paranoia, 185
participation, obtained by propaganda,
  26 *n.*, 26–7, 30
parties, political, *see* political parties
partitioning of groups, 212–16
Pavlov, Ivan, 5
peace, propaganda for, 45–6
Pearlin, Leonard I., 75
Pericles, 122
Pleven, René, 127
political education, in Communist sense,
  32 *n.*, 33 *n.*, 78, 83, 192, 304–5
political parties, 126, 128, 232, 273;
  propaganda made by, 216–22
political propaganda, 62, 80, 262
politics, as present-day focus of interest,
  49, 50
population density, 122; required for
  effective propaganda, 95
poster, utilized by propaganda, 10
Pravda, 14, 130
pre-active response, to propaganda, 300,
  301

prejudice, and propaganda, 33, 35, 38, 162, 164, 166, 206

premeditated consciousness, in Soviet Union, 179 n.

pre-propaganda, 15, 22, 30–1, 32 and n., 296, 300

press, utilized by propaganda, 10, 102, 103, 104, 109 n.

privatization, 180 n., 190, 191, 192, 272

progress, belief in, 39, 40, 41, 43, 186, 200

proletariat, 222, 288

propaganda: based on psychology, 4, 5, 6, 33–8 *passim;* scientific basis of, 4–6, 241; American, 5, 32, 60, 61, 63–5, 69–70, 85 (*see also* United States); Stalinist, 5, 60, 61, 62, 164 n., 202, 281 (*see also* Soviet Union; Stalin, Josef); Hitlerian, 5, 60 and n., 61, 62, 245 (*see also* Hitler, Adolf; Nazis); addressed to individual as part of mass, 6–9, 105–6, 150; external characteristics of, 6–32; total, 9–17, 97, 105–17, 242; myths utilized and created by, 11, 31–2, 38, 40, 41, 42, 199–200; of self-criticism, 11–12, 153 n.; Soviet, 11–12, 13 and n., 14, 16 n., 22 and n., 26 n., 29 n., 32 and n., 43 n., 52–3, 60, 61, 75 and n., 78, 84, 98, 111, 113 n., 120, 139 n., 214–15, 277, 278; and diplomacy, 13; and literature, 14; direct, 15; overt, 15, 16 and n.; covert, 15, 16 and n., 59 n., 262 n.; sociological, 15, 62–72, 81; democratic, 16, 235–42, 253, 254, 255, 256; continuity and duration of, 17–20; changeability of, 18 and n.; of agitation, 20, 32 n., 71–4, 76, 77, 78, 79, 105, 112, 188; psychological and physical action as inseparable elements of, 20–1; organization of, 20–4, 28–9, 29 n.; human-relations technique of, 24; and orthopraxy, 25–32; nature of relationship to public opinion, 26, 171, 202–12; participation obtained by, 26 n., 26–7, 30; action-reflex obtained by, 28–9, 30; of integration, 29, 70, 74–9, 81, 84, 105, 112, 188, 210; internal characteristics of, 33–61; and boomerang effect, 34 n., 38 n., 281, 297; stereotypes, prejudices, and established opinions utilized by, 35–6, 37, 38, 162, 163 and n., 164, 166, 206, 277, 278; and ideology, 36, 193–202; human needs met and utilized by, 37 and n., 121, 138–53, 158–60; sociological presuppositions utilized by, 38, 39, 40, 41; related to technology, 40, 49, 64; of timeliness, 43–8; for peace, 45–6; related to superficial aspects of events, 47; and the Undecided, 48–52, 54, 280; based on collective center of interest, 49, 50, 51, 52; religious, 49, 279; and truth, 52–61; falsehood as instrument of, 53, 60 and n., 61; silence as technique in, 56; innuendo as technique in, 56–7; intentions and interpretations in, 57–61; Leninist, 60 and n., 62, 89, 111, 200, 202, 232, 277 n., 303 (*see also* Lenin, Nikolai; Soviet Union); definition of, 61; present-day Chinese, 61, 63, 71–2, 80, 81, 111 (*see also* China, Communist; Mao Tse-tung); categories of, 61–87; Khrushchev's, 62 (*see also* Khrushchev, Nikita; Soviet Union); political, 62, 80, 262; vertical, 79–80, 82; horizontal, 80–4, 209 n., 310; distinguished from information, 84; rational and irrational, 84–7; sociological conditions for existence of, 90–105; combination of demographic phenomena required for, 95; as means of reinforcing opinions, 104; and need of average standard of living, 105–8; average culture required for, 108–12; related to information, 112–116, 144–7, 250; necessity for, 118–60, 182–7 *passim;* by government, 127, 128, 130, 131, 132; as necessary weapon for democracy, 133, 134, 135, 137, 138, 232–5 *passim,* 250; personality and freedom destroyed by, 137, 171, 178; required to provide motivations for sacrifices, 142–3, 174, 177; as remedy for loneliness, 148; psychological effects of, 161–92; complementary character of, 162; religious personality conferred by, 166–7; critical judgment suppressed by, 169–171, 173; alienation through, 169–78; artificial needs created by, 176, 177; psychic dissociation effect of, 178–182; thought devalued by, 179, 180; overexcitement provoked by, 179 n.; transformation of words in, 180; shock effect of, 181 and n., 204, 237; mithridatization against, 183–4; sensibilization to, 184–7; ambiguity of psychological effects of, 187–92; guilt feelings stimulated by, 189; war, 190, 274 n., 275; privatization utilized by, 191, 192; socio-political effects of, 193–257 *passim;* "skeleton" role in, 204 and n.; translated into "verbal action," 207; and grouping, 212–32; made by political parties,

propaganda (*continued*)
216–22; effects on labor, 222–8 *passim;* effects on churches, 228–32; effects of international, 242–50; effects of internal, 250–7; need for serious attitude toward, to defend against, 257; difficulties of measuring effectiveness of, 250–77, 287; elasticity of, 268; inadequacy of mathematical methods for measurement of, 275–7; problems connected with ineffectiveness of, 277–86; violent turns in, 280; effectiveness of, 287–294; limits of, 294–302; internal, as most effective, 296–8; by Communist parties, reason for effectiveness of, 298; "related response" to, 299–300; "pre-active response" to, 300, 301; Mao Tse-tung's, 303–13 (*see also* China, Communist)

psychoanalysis, 152, 154

psychological action, by Western democracies, 135–7

psychological crystallization, 162–8

psychology, 89; propaganda based on, 4, 5, 6, 33–8 *passim;* behavioristic, 36, 89; depth, 36, 89; of instincts, 36; and effects of propaganda, 161–192; *see also* individual

public opinion, 36 n., 68, 89, 95, 99–102, 114, 165, 198, 199; nature of relationship to propaganda, 26, 171, 202–12; in modern state, 123–8, 130, 132, 139–40, 221; attempts at analysis of, in United States, 267; limited usefulness of surveys of, 267–70

Public Relations, 283; in United States, 225, 287

racial prejudice, propaganda ineffective against, 33

radio, 212–13; utilized by propaganda, 7, 8, 10, 11, 103, 104, 105, 162

Rank, J. Arthur, quoted, 67

rationalization, 155–6, 157, 158

Rauschning, Hermann, 60

Reader's Digest, 64, 70

reflex, conditioned, *see* conditioned reflex

Reformation, 14

Reichstag fire, 14

"related response," to propaganda, 299–300

religious propaganda, 49, 279

Renaissance, 14

repetition, principle of, 17 n., 18

response: related, 299–300; auxiliary, 300; pre-active, 300, 301

Review of the German Democratic Republic, 85

Revolt of the Masses, The, 93 n.

Revue d'Action Populaire, 265 n.

Reisman, David, 186

Riess, Curt, 12 n., 59 n.

Rivero, quoted, 237–8

Rivet, Paul, 110

Roman Empire, 51

Roman Republic, 14

Rommel, Erwin, 57 n.

Roosevelt, Franklin D., 125, 248

Roper, Elmo, 93 n., 268

Rosenberg, Morris, 75

Rousseau, Jean-Jacques, 128

Rubel, M., 157

rumor, susceptibility to, 293–4

Russian Revolution, 89

Sartre, Jean-Paul, 278

Sauvy, Alfred, 53 n., 56 n., 59 n., 77, 164 n., 166 n.

schizophrenia, 185

science, as fundamental myth, 40

secret consciousness, in Soviet Union, 179 n.

selection, technique of, 56 and n.

self-criticism, propaganda of, 11–12, 153 n.

sensibilization, 184–7

Shils, Edward A., 9 n., 270, 276, 284 and n., 285

shock effect, of propaganda, 181 and n., 204, 237

Simon, P. H., 201

"skeleton" role, in propaganda, 204 and n.

slogans: as evocative symbols, 164 n.; Mao's, 304, 305, 306, 308–9, 311, 312

Socialism, 222, 223, 224, 225, 226, 288; as fundamental ideology, 117; *see also* Communism

society: individualist, 90, 91, 92, 93, 97; mass, *see* mass society

sociological propaganda, 15, 62–71, 81

sociology, 89; propaganda based on, 4, 5, 6; and collective presuppositions in modern world, 38, 39, 40, 41

Sophocles, 235

Soviet Union, 132, 134, 221, 265, 295, 296; propaganda of, 11–12, 13 and n., 14, 16 n., 22 and n., 26 n., 29 n., 32 and n., 43 n., 52–3, 60, 61, 75 and n., 78, 84, 98, 111, 113 n., 120, 139 n., 214–15, 277, 278; orthodox Church in, 13 n.; reflex utilized by, 32; Khrushchev's claims for agricultural production of (1957), 59–60; pose

Soviet Union (*continued*)
of, as defender of democracy, 60;
Piatiletka campaign in, 72; Kronstadt
Rebellion in, 78; culture of, integrated into universe of propaganda,
109; public opinion in, 124 n., 125,
130–1; Five Year Plans of, 141,
224 n.; agitators and shock workers
in, 141 n.; self-criticism in, 153 n.;
compartments of consciousness in,
179 n.; cost of propaganda in, 263 n.;
in pact with Nazis, 278; reappearance
of advertising in, 291; *see also* Communism; Khrushchev, Nikita; Lenin,
Nikolai; Stalin, Josef
Speier, Hans, 59 n.
Stakhanovism, 141 n.
Stalin, Josef, 5, 46, 62, 129, 172, 179 n.
State: centralized, 41; propaganda
necessary for, 121; and public
opinion, 123–8, 130, 132, 139–40,
221; function of, 133–8; and privatization, 191, 192; and political
parties, 220, 221; propaganda costs
not always counted by, 274–5; *see
also* government
statistics, 54, 275
stereotypes, utilized by propaganda,
34, 35, 36, 37, 163 and n., 164, 166,
206, 277, 278
Stevenson, Adlai E., 253
Stimmung, distinguished from *Haltung*,
25 n.
Stoetzel, Jean, 173, 203 and n., 204,
280, 291; quoted, 96, 163 n., 165,
206, 210
structure of expectation, of propaganda,
37 n.
Suez propaganda operation, 58
surveys, limited usefulness of, 267–70
Sweden, 152
symbols, related to stereotypes, 163 n.,
164 n.
Syria, 22, 23 n.

Taft-Hartley law, 66
taxation, 123, 142
Tchakhotin, Serge, xiv n., 273
Technological Society, The, 241, 252
technology: propaganda related to, 40,
49, 64; modern man obsessed by, 49, 50
television, 8, 175–6, 238; utilized by
propaganda, 103, 104, 105, 253, 254
Tiberius, 122
timeliness, propaganda of, 43–8
Tito, Marshal, 129
torture, of political enemies, 201
total propaganda, 9–17, 97, 105–17,
242; objective conditions of, 105–17

Trotsky, Leon, 288
truth, and propaganda, 52–61

unconscious, the, reached by propaganda,, 27
Undecided, the, and propaganda, 48–
52, 54, 280
unionism, 223, 226–8
United Arab Republic, 23
United Nations, 23 n.
United States, 89, 120, 186, 219, 236,
244, 247, 255, 273, 279 n., 286 n.,
295; myth utilized by, 32; tests in, of
experimental propaganda, 36, 37;
Negro problem in, 42; factuality in
propaganda manuals of, 53; pose of,
as defender of liberty, 60; conformity in, 68, 249; "agitators" in,
69; propaganda of integration in,
75–6; mass media of communication
in, 95; underdeveloped nations aided
by, 134; Human Relations in, 141–2,
153 n., 287; cult of hero in, 172;
transformation in political parties of,
216; Public Relations in, 225, 287;
unions in, 226, 227 and n., 228;
attempts at analysis of public opinion
in, 267
United States Army Information Service,
299

"verbal action," 207
vertical propaganda, 79–80, 82
Viet-Minh, 98 n.
Villiers de L'Isle Adam, Colonel,
quoted, 135–6
Voice of America, 22, 103

war propaganda, 190, 274 n., 275
Weiss, Walter, 44 n.
Westerfield, Bradford, 128 and n.
white (overt) propaganda, 15, 16 and n.
Whyte, William H., 84, 283
Winance, Eleutherius, 311 n.
Winterhilfe, Hitler's, 290
work: role in modern life, 140–2;
mechanization of, 180
World War I, 89, 232
World War II, 89; and inquiries into
"war aims" of American soldiers,
270, 272; studies of German soldiers
in wake of, 270–2, 276, 284 and n.;
and failure of German propaganda in
occupied countries, 296 and n.
Wright, Q., 116

Young, Kimball, 173, 211, 277, 278
Yugoslavia, 254

Jacques Ellul was born in Bordeaux in 1912. A Graduate in Jurisprudence in 1936, he thereafter taught in French universities until he was discharged by the Vichy regime. He then joined and fought in the Resistance. After France's liberation, while attached to the city government of Bordeaux, he was named Professor at the law school there. In 1947, he was appointed to a chair in law and social history at the Institut d'Etudes Politiques. His increasing reputation as a significant social and political philosopher was first established in the United States by the publication here of *The Technological Society* (1964), *Propaganda* (1965), and *The Political Illusion* (1967).